A Shadow
at the
Gate

A Shadow
at the
Gate

By
Don Bloch

NORTH STAR PRESS OF ST. CLOUD, INC.
St. Cloud, Minnesota

ISBN: 978-0-87839-785-3

First edition: March 1, 2015

Printed in the United States of America

Published by:
North Star Press of St. Cloud, Inc.
P.O. Box 451
St. Cloud, MN 56302

www.northstarpress.com

Introduction

IT IS A MISTAKE to take this book seriously. It is written from memory, and my life has been a hurricane of confusion. I was always trying to figure out what was going on—and failing. It started with my parents. They taught me to judge people according to their actions and their professions. But as I grew up, I found my parents greatly overrated some professions and greatly underrated others. I lost a good deal of respect for many of the professions my parents esteemed and gained a good deal for many they did not. Among the losers were politicians, professors, reporters, and priests. Among the gainers were bootleggers, hoboes, snitches, and whores. This book is about how these things came to be.

Young men hunger for adventure. Sometimes they volunteer, and sometimes it is forced upon them. Thirst for adventure drives young men to ignore danger and go with happy, childlike bliss into the unknown hazards of travel, love, and war. They volunteer for foolishness just to see where it leads. For a while I studied to be a priest, for a while I was an Air Force pilot, and finally I made a career with the Drug Enforcement Administration. That was a fine career for me, because I had a great lust for travel. With DEA credentials, my fellow agents and I traveled all over the United States and into many foreign countries. We carried guns and rounded up outlaws. We spent enormous amounts of federal tax money on "The Great War on Drugs." We got paid to eat the world's best food, drink the finest whiskey, and sleep in the best hotels in dozens of cities, islands, and countries, where tourists paid thousands to do the same. I wish to thank the taxpayers of the United States of America for their generosity. I would love to tell you all that the millions—no, billions—I helped squander on the anti-drug campaigns during those years did at least some good. But that would not be true. When I left, we were worse off than when I got there. I also feel obligated to thank the foreign countries where my cohorts and I worked; they did not throw us out at gunpoint, as they should have.

Some of the things done in airplanes in this book are illegal, some dangerous, some both. They are set down only as history, not as recommendations.

This story is *gans und gar die Varheit* (the honest to goodness truth), as I saw it. But I know from doing criminal investigations that eye witnesses are often the worst witnesses. And there is a saying: "who writes history, makes history." If you are in this book and don't like the way it is written down, don't complain to me—write your own book. Or take solace in the fact that memories are fallible, or in this from Mark Twain: "The very ink with which all history is written is merely fluid prejudice." One cannot avoid recording from one's own point of view.

Some of the conversations I have here are from my logs, and those are accurate; others are made up from memory and, although they are accurate as to the meaning, they are not (unless some miracle has occurred) as to the words. It is likely some names are misspelled, and some may be wrong. This is not intentional.

This much I have learned; this much I know: Life is full of contradiction and is rife with irony. The greatest of these is this: what a man wants most and what he looks for all his life he already has, but does not know it. The restlessness, longing, and wanting of my life came from man's normal need to be free and at peace. Everyone wants this—rich man and poor man. Monks seek it in their monasteries, drunks in their drink, movie stars in their fame. But no amount of devotion, or drink, or fame can bring this to you, until you realize you already have it at the core of your being.

"Enter by the narrow gate; for the wide gate and the broad way lead to destruction . . ."
    –Matthew 7:13

Part I

Little did my mother think
The day she cradled me
What lands I had to travel through
What death I had to see.

−from an old folk song

Chapter One

I WOKE UP. The light was on. My older brothers had already gone outside. There was frost on the wall where I had been breathing. I took my shirt and pants and tucked them under the blanket next to me to warm them. I pulled the blanket up over my nose to help warm the clothes. Outside, I could hear the wind roar in the oak trees by the house. In a few minutes I sat up and pulled on my shirt. I put on my pants standing on the bed, because I did not want to stand with bare feet on the icy floor. I ran downstairs and stood on the furnace grate, where I pulled on socks and shoes. They were nice and warm. Dad had been up early and stoked the furnace.

"Why are you up so early?" Mom asked. She was coming out of the bedroom, pinning back her hair.

"I want to go outside."

"It's snowing and blowing out there," she said. "You'll catch cold."

"How come Leroy can go?"

"He's older than you. Come, you help me get the stove going."

I followed her into the kitchen. A small, bare light bulb on a wire over the table made pale twilight in the room. She opened the little door on the front of the stove next to the oven. She stirred the ashes to make them fall through the grating and put several small pieces of wood on the grating.

"Get me the kerosene pail," she said.

I went to the lean-to off the kitchen where we kept firewood. There was an old, smoke-blackened pot with a broken handle that had kerosene in it. In the pot were a dozen corncobs standing up, soaking in the kerosene. I brought the pot to Mom. She took a cob and poked it into the stove between the pieces of kindling. She scratched a match on the stove top and touched it to the cob. The flame came up immediately. She piled more kindling, and added a larger piece of oak, leaving the stove door open to increase the draft until the fire got a good start. Then she shut the door and slid the bottom draft control to half-closed and glanced up to check the damper on the stove pipe.

Mom took the coffee pot to the sink and, using a dipper, poured water into it from the drinking pail. She set the pot on the stove and threw in a handful of coffee. She took the hot-water kettle to the sink. This she filled from the cistern pump. It was the first pumping of the day so she had to prime the pump to make it work by pouring the last water from the kettle into the top of the pump. After a few gurgling, gasping strokes, the water came. She set the full kettle on the stove by the coffee pot. The fire was now making a soft rumble in the stove, and every chink was flickering with flame.

I loved to watch Mom work. She went from one thing to another with swift assurance. There was smoothness and a rhythm, like she knew exactly the next step before she finished the last. A solid, safe feeling surrounded her. She went to the door that led upstairs and, opening it, yelled, "Time to get up!"

That was for my sister Leona, who was to watch me and my younger siblings so we wouldn't set the house on fire while Mom went out to help with the milking. Mom got her big coat and her wool cap from the nail behind the door. She buckled on her boots.

"You behave now," she said, pointing a mitten at me. As she went out, a gust of wind swirled snow from the porch onto the rag-rug by the door.

Leona came down. "Why do you have to get up so early?" she said.

"I want to go to the barn."

"Listen to the wind. It's a blizzard out there. Go look. You can hardly find the barn."

I went to the window. It was covered with frost.

"I can't see out," I said.

"Well, melt some off," she said in a hopeless tone.

She came over and, holding her hand on the window, melted a spot so I could look out. The wind was driving snow fiercely across the yard. The sky was clear and the moon was out, but I could only see it occasionally through sheets of blowing snow. The path where Mom had walked was already erased. I held my hand on the window to make the spot bigger. Our dog, Sport, was at his bowl gnawing at the frozen bits he had left from last night. The wind rippled his yellow hair as he worked, but he was unaware of the weather.

Leona went to the stove and lifted a lid. She poked at the wood and sent up a spray of sparks. She laid in another piece of oak and replaced the lid.

"Why don't you help out Mom and fill the wood box?" she said.

I went to the lean-to and began bringing in armloads of wood and dropping them into the box by the stove. If I stacked carefully I could lay in enough wood to last Mom for several days. I kept going back to the shed for more wood until the box was full, which took a long time because the box was big and I was not. I put an armful by the stove so it would be handy for Mom.

Several times I tripped on my shoelaces. I had a busted string. I pulled open the junk drawer to find a substitute. I rummaged around and picked out shoelaces from among stubs of broken pencils, bits of erasers, wrinkled band-aids, safety pins, hair pins, a kid's tooth, a flashlight, a broken pocket knife, green pennies, and a book for pasting in Green Stamps. Most of the laces were too dirty or too frayed or too knotted, but I finally found one that was kind of brown like mine and with only one knot. I maneuvered this around in my shoe, stringing it various ways until I had two ends that could be tied into a loop. I had missed a few holes but it was holding fine, so I didn't try again.

Leona was back upstairs now, helping the others get dressed. I went to the window to look for pictures in the frost, and to watch for Mom returning from milking. Mom's dark figure appeared through the swirling snow. She was already halfway up from the barn before I saw her. She walked unevenly with small steps, struggling to stay on the path. She was leaning forward, her head turned downwind, one hand by her face for protection, her scarf flying to the side with her breath. I was glad to see her, because she would start breakfast as soon as she came in. I could hear thumping upstairs as my sisters got up.

"Will you make bacon?" I asked Mom as she hung up her clothes.

"No, I already told Dad blood sausage."

She washed her hands and dried them on a dishtowel as she walked to the cupboard. She got out her big cast iron pan. I didn't like blood sausage much, but I didn't say anything. At least it wasn't liver sausage, which I didn't like at all. I stood at the end of the stove and watched her stoke the fire. She ladled blood sausage from one of her canning jars into the pan. The white fat slowly turned to clear liquid as it melted. Soon the black mixture was sizzling and the aroma of breakfast rose in the air.

Mom began taking the breakfast dishes down and stacking them on the cupboard. My sister Loretta came down from upstairs, and Mom said, "Okay, sleepyhead, you can start setting the table, and you," she nodded at me, "can help. Wash your hands first."

"There's hardly any soap left," I complained.

Mom sighed. She came over to the sink and unwrapped a bar of new soap. She wet one side and took the sliver of old soap and pressed it hard against the new bar, smoothing down the edges with her fingers so the dirty old sliver was pasted firmly to the fragrant new one.

"There, are you happy now?"

Actually, I was. I liked being the first one to use a new bar of soap, even if it had the old bar pasted on one side. I just used the new side. Mom's lye soap was on the sink, too, but that was for really dirty hands like my brothers, Lawrence and Gilbert, always had after chores.

I knew that setting the table was girls' work. I wanted to tell Mom I had already worked hard at man's work and stacked all that wood in the wood box, but that might be bragging. So I took the silverware Loretta handed me and began to put a knife and fork by each plate as she set them on the table. My younger brother came into the kitchen dragging his blanket. He stood in the middle of the room, watching Mom intently. Leona brought my little sister in by the hand.

"She says she's not feeling good," she told Mom.

Mom lay down her spoon and knelt in front of my little sister and smiled. My sister smiled back. Mom pushed back a strand of hair and held the back of her hand against her forehead.

"You'll be fine," Mom said, nodding. My sister nodded, too.

The phone rang, a long ring, then a short. That was our ring. Mom hurried across the room. "You kids stay out of my way. Leona, stir that sausage and cut the bread. Loretta, get the jelly and butter on the table."

She lifted the receiver and yelled into the mouthpiece. "Hello," she rattled the receiver-hook up and down. "Hello? Hello. Oh, Hi."

I went to the window and scraped frost with my fingernail.

"Papa's coming!" I yelled.

Mom covered the mouthpiece and shushed me.

There was thunder on the porch as dad stomped the snow from his boots. He came in, the door squealing on its frosty hinges. Leaning against the door with one hand, he unbuckled his overshoes.

Mom walked back to the stove and began breaking eggs into a big pan of smoking butter.

"That was Gurty," she said. "There's no catechism today."

Dad grunted. "I still have to get the cream to town."

He hung his coat and cap on a peg among all the other clothes. He went to the sink and pumped water from the cistern into the enamel washbowl. Mom brought the steaming kettle from the stove and poured hot water into the bowl until Dad said it was enough.

The aroma of the frying eggs and sausage mixed with the smell of wood smoke made the kitchen warm and cozy. My older brother LeRoy came in from the barn with a syrup can full of cream.

"Hey, close that door!" Leona said, as she closed it herself. "Were you born in a barn?"

Mom took the can from LeRoy and looked at his boots.

"Next time stomp your boots off on the porch before you come in."

Mom turned to the stove and began flipping eggs. Dad went behind the table and, with one knee on the long bench, took a key from the shelf and wound the clock. Mom brought the sizzling pan of eggs to the table just as my two older brothers stomped in. The heavy smell of barn began to overpower the kitchen aromas as my brothers hung up their coats and washed up. They dried their partially washed hands on the roller towel by the sink and added to the dirty smudges they had put there last night.

Dad said, "You boys hurry up. You have to shovel through those drifts on the driveway right after breakfast. The snow plow just went through. I have to get to town before the roads drift shut again. There's no catechism today."

"Oooweeh!" my brother Gilbert yelped in celebration. Dad gave him a dark look.

"A little more catechism would do you good," he said, and Gilbert tried to make himself smaller.

We all sat down to the breakfast table. Mom brought the pan of greasy sausage and set it in the middle of the table on pot holders. Gilbert watched the smoking pan, rubbing his hands together and grinning broadly. He loved blood sausage. He reached for the spoon.

"Wait 'til we pray," Leona said, slapping at his hand and missing.

Dad sat at the head of the table scowling, one hand raised to his forehead—the signal for quiet. The table fell silent, and Dad began the long prayers before meals: "*In Namen des Vaters, und des Sohnes und des Heiligen Geistes . . .*"

Chapter Two

THE SAUK RIVER begins its journey to the Mississippi at Lake Osakis in the western hill country of Minnesota. It curls and twists for a hundred miles through hardwood forests and through wide stretches of prairie until it meets with the Mississippi near St. Cloud. On that journey it runs through Stearns County. There it passes through Sauk Lake and a great maze of lakes near Richmond. It pours over a dam at Cold Spring, and finally empties itself into the Father of Waters at the place called Sauk Rapids, named for the turbulent waters eternally churning there as they roll by the city.

The Sauk drains water from some of the best farmland in America. A piece of that farmland, in the center of Stearns County between Albany and Freeport, belonged to my father. It was a small homestead of 160 acres of very fertile soil. No matter how deep we set the plow, the earth that rolled off the share was a rich, black loam in which anything could be grown in abundance.

Minnesota has sections of prairie, hardwood forest, oak savannah, and evergreen forest. My father's farm had samples of all four. The farmhouse stood in the middle on a hill. To the south and west was a great, flat stretch of prairie, which served as fields for grain, corn, and alfalfa. To the east was pasture of oak savannah where cows and horses grazed, and where they drowsed in the shade of scattered oaks on hot summer days. To the north great hardwood trees gave shade and acorns to the pigs that roamed below. On the northwest side stood a grand grove of black spruce whose fragrant spires reached a majestic seventy feet into the heavens and sheltered the yard from winter winds.

I was born in the farmhouse, in the middle of that farm, in the middle of Stearns County, in the middle of Minnesota, in the middle of a great family. My father's first wife bore him seven children before she died of complications of childbirth and asthma. Then he married my mother, who bore him another eleven children. There were eight boys and ten girls. I was number twelve in the family, the seventh son of my father.

The house was an old log cabin that had been fixed with siding outside and plaster inside so it looked like a regular little white house except that the walls were tremendously thick. A large kitchen had been added on the south side. It had a huge dining table and a large wood-burning cook stove. In one corner by a rusty water pump was a chipped-enamel cast iron sink, where my sisters did the dishes and where my older brothers and I washed off the dirt when we came in from doing chores.

That house was a leaky, drafty old structure. The northwest winds that swept across the fields on winter nights drove the cold through the siding and the chinks in the logs so the plaster inside was cold as ice. On those nights the windows were covered with thick frost with fantastic designs, and Mom would say Jack Frost had been there painting pictures. The framing around the windows leaked, and little jets of wind moved the curtains. But it was a wonderful home, because Mom was there. Many times when I was outside on cold evenings I looked back at the house with the warm glow of light through the frosty windows and a column of wood smoke rising from the kitchen chimney, and I felt warm and wonderful. I knew it was cozy in there, that Mom was cooking supper, and that all was well.

It was Flag Day, the summer of 1942, when I first saw light. World War II was at full boil. The Japanese had bombed Pearl Harbor only a few months before. The British began striking back at Germany that year, and the battle of Midway was just over. But the event getting the most headlines that June morning was the building of the "Great Alaska Highway." The U.S. Army was building a road through 1,500 miles of forest and mountains, through Yukon muskeg and permafrost, and through an endless swarm of mosquitoes and gnats. That road was to hook the United States to the Territory of Alaska. I was, of course, unaware of this. I only mention it because twenty-three years later I would use that road. I traveled its entire length in summer of 1965, when I was having one of the best times of my life.

I was not a precocious baby; however, before I was a month old, I had already renounced Satan and all his works and all his pomps. I didn't know what pomps were, but I renounced them anyway. In fact, I didn't know what renouncing was any more than a turnip. It was all done for me by proxy with my godparents—mom's sister, Aunt Teresa, and Dad's cousin, Henry—standing in. Nor do I know if Theresa or Henry knew what they were doing. They were simply answering the priest's questions. He was following the normal baptismal rites of the Roman Catholic Church as practiced at the local Church of the Seven Dolors at Albany, Minnesota:

"Do you renounce Satan?"

"I do renounce him."

"And all his works?"

"I do renounce them."

"And all his pomps?"

"I do renounce them."

I was only three when the Second World War ended. I still did not know what was going on. Except for the death of my Uncle Ben in the European theater (mom's oldest brother), the war had little effect on our immediate family. My father was too old to go to war and my oldest brothers were too young. Jobs on the farm were the same in war as in peace. The women did the housework, the men did the field work.

I was lucky to grow up where I did. I was in a big family and on a dairy farm. From early morning to late night I always had something to do. Little brothers and sisters to play with. Big brothers and sisters to take care of us. Our farm had horses, cows, chickens, pigs, dogs, cats, and all kinds of wild animals. Skunks, raccoons, and chicken hawks watched our yard for chances to steal. A cow was always giving birth or a sow having piglets. Hens laid eggs. Horses with clinking harness pulled wagons or sleds. We had two big, black horses: a mare named Pearl and a gelding named Prince. They were tame as kittens, so we could stand right by their legs and pet them. It was fun to watch grown-ups chase cows, slop hogs, sharpen axes, and put up hay. There was a constant parade of machinery as Dad and older brothers did the work of planting and harvesting. The best time of all was the fall, when the great machines of the harvest went into action. Then we got to watch the grain binder, the enormous threshing machine, the corn binder, the silo filler, and the great thundering corn shredder.

And we were lucky to have Mom. She was constantly washing, cleaning, and cooking. She recharged the kitchen table with an everlasting parade of steaming pancakes, hams, soups and stews, and puddings and pies. A huge tub of mashed potatoes and a bowl of thick onion gravy always anchored the middle of the table. She made dumplings from potatoes and floated them in steaming lakes of meat sauce. Platters of corn on the cob, creamed peas, fried carrots, buttered beets, stewed tomatoes, and baked apples appeared according to the season. Mom had a great talent for turning leftovers into feasts. She put unrecognizable mushes of milk and potatoes into cast iron pans, shut them in the oven for an hour, and pulled out rich, golden-skinned casseroles that warmed us to our toes on a cold winter's eve. She gave her entire life to her family; in fact, to two families. She treated the children of my father's first wife as her own.

Chicken Cordon Bleu and coq au vin were unheard of in Mom's kitchen. I have eaten fancy dishes like that all over the world, but they are an anemic excuse for food when compared to Mom's chicken and dressing with mashed potatoes and chicken gravy. Mom baked bread every Saturday. When city people came to visit our farm they said Mom's bread was a marvel and they would buy some from her to take home. But we were so used to eating her bread, we thought the town bread was better. We called that stuff "boughten bread." We liked it especially in summer when Mom made mashed strawberries and cream to put on top.

Mom's hands were magic. She could sew a shirt or jacket as well as any tailor. She repaired our clothes instead of buying new. I often wore overalls with knee patches sewed upon knee patches. I wore the clothes my older brothers had outgrown. I could see the magic hands especially when Mom was milking. She could milk a cow faster than any human. She easily milked five cows in less time than it took me to do three, even after I was experienced in the art. Not only that, she usually had the heaviest milkers. Dad always made sure Mom got the gentlest cows, and those were the ones with the biggest bags, and the ones who gave the most milk.

My dad was a tireless farmer with an iron will and an unwavering belief that hard manual labor was good for the soul. He believed intensely and often paraphrased Genesis 3:19 by saying, "It is by your sweat that you get to eat, until you go back to the ground where you came from." He believed life was hard and serious. He allowed himself no luxuries except one five-cent cigar on Sunday afternoons. When Dad was around, we worked. There was no horsing around, no playing games, no boisterous laughing. He spent his days out in the barns and fields of his farm. He made his living by the soil and he had a deep suspicion of anyone who made a living another way.

The only "playing" dad took part in was cards and fishing. And even those were not real recreation for him. Fishing was not about rest and relaxation, but about the serious task of getting food for the family. And he treated card playing like a business. In winter when the snow and the cold stopped the work in the fields, the farmers got together in the evenings and played Solo, a card game they brought over from Germany. On those evenings, as we kids lay in bed before falling asleep, we could smell cigar smoke coming from downstairs and could hear the low rumble of men's talk and the snapping of cards, and then an occasional bang on the table as someone trumped someone else's ace. Dad played and seemed to have fun, but he kept track of his winnings and suffered over his losses.

Dad was the boss. He made all the major decisions and controlled the money in the family. We did not argue with dad. He was right even when he was wrong. He got to interact with neighbors much more than Mom did. He went into Albany almost every day to deliver the cream and to do the grocery shopping from the list Mom gave him. Mom did not drive, so she was tied to the house and had little social life. Dad always wore his newest bib overalls to town, and a hat—felt in winter, straw in summer. He would get the latest news from other farmers in Albany at the creamery, where he dropped off cream and picked up butter, or at Jesh's Hatchery, where he sold eggs.

We kids never got to go to town except on Saturdays for catechism or when we needed a shoe or a tooth fixed. Dad always repaired worn-out soles of shoes, but when there was a hole in the top that needed sewing, we went to Pundsack, the shoemaker in Albany. Pundsack had a little shop in part of his house. It was a wondrous place for a kid to visit. It had mammoth sewing machines and mysterious tools, and smelled wonderfully of leather and oil. To fix a tooth we had to go to Dr. Hockert, but his place was a house of horrors. That doctor used to drill holes in our teeth without giving us Novocain. I still squirm in my chair when I think of it.

Mom could always tell from looking at our dirty socks when there was a hole in the sole of our shoes. Then she would tell us to take that shoe to Dad. He would take the shoe and turn it over in his hands, shaking his head and clucking his tongue. He took the shoe to his tool shop and nailed on a "new" sole, which was a clumsy piece of rubber cut out of an old tire. I remember as he sat over his shoe last with tacks in his mouth and, as he tapped with his hammer, he would say with the unoccupied part of his lips, "I don't understand how anyone can wear out a pair of shoes so fast," and I felt bad that Dad had to go through all that trouble. I wished I had a pair of shoes that would never wear out.

Dad played at shoemaker, and he played at veterinarian. He showed us how to treat farm animals for various afflictions. By the time I was ten, I knew how to treat a constipated calf by forcing down Epsom salt in water. I knew exactly how baby animals came about. I had seen the whole process in detail—from the male insemination, to the female growing fat, to the agonies of the birth. I knew how to help along at each stage if things were not going as established by the Creator.

The cows were bred in winter. They were timed to "get fresh" (give birth) in late autumn. The cows "dried off" (gave no milk) for a few weeks before birthing. That way the job of milking was greatly reduced when the harvest work was under way. In winter, if Dad or Lawrence noticed a cow in heat, we let the big bull out of his pen and into the yard with the cows. In a few minutes he figured out which was his target, and immediately set about doing his business. One winter we had a rather small bull. He was still very young and green for the job. His predecessor had gone mad and had to be shipped early. This little bull always looked confused when we let him out of his pen. It took him a long time to do his investigation of the herd, and then, if the target cow was big, he had a devil of a time with it. His hind legs left the ground when he made his final assault. Sometimes he fell off the cow, and she was left standing looking over her shoulder and wondering what the fool was up to now. One day the little bull made an entire backward summersault when he fell. After that hash job, dad had us build a ramp for him. When a cow was in heat we backed her up to the ramp and brought out the little bull. He went up on the ramp, checked her out to make sure he wasn't wasting his time, and then he mounted and pretended he was just a regular big bull. He had no more trouble after that. The bull and Dad were both happy.

I saw the birth of many calves. It was a messy, bloody thing for a little kid to watch, but it was worth it, because I could not help believing in miracles when I saw a birth. This feeble, wet, little thing lying on the straw behind the cow, all of a minute old, would rise on trembling legs, and blinking around at its new world, would totter to the side of the cow and start bumping her udder for milk.

Most births are routine, with the calf sliding into the world as easy as sledding down a hill. Normally the cow is lying down to have the calf. The time is near when she has a bloody mucus discharge. She has her head up, looking around nervously, uncomfortable, and showing white in her eyes. In a little while, she begins groaning and straining, and the calf's forefeet show. There is a thin, silvery, membranous sack all around the calf. The leading front hoof punches a hole in that sack, and then the sack is stripped off as the calf comes out. When the calf is out, the cow gets up and starts nuzzling and licking the little thing and making happy little rumblings in her throat.

But sometimes there is trouble. If the feet are wrong or if they fail to break the sack or if the head is bent back, the calf can suffocate. If the calf is backwards, the cow will not be able to drive it out. All these things can be set right if you know how, if you are big enough and strong enough, and if you have a long enough arm. Several times I saw my father with his arm inside a cow, blood and slime dribbling on his overalls, his face contorted, teeth clenched, eyes like slits, trying to rectify what nature had screwed up. The process is repulsive and disgusting, but ever so satisfying when that little calf makes it out alive and staggers to its feet.

We helped deliveries with twine, rope, and sometimes wire stretcher. One August afternoon when dad and I were cutting grain, he saw a cow was down. She lay in the pasture next to the fence and was trying to give birth to an enormous calf. After trying everything else to help her, he cut the fence and had me bring the tractor. He pulled long strands of binder twine from the roll in the binder's twine box and tied them to the feet of the calf. He braided them into a rope and we dragged that calf out with the tractor. Calf and cow both lived, though it was hard on the cow. It was several days before she could rise and come home from the pasture. Every few hours while she was down, Dad made us roll her on her other side to keep the circulation going. Dad knew his way around cows.

He also knew his way around pigs. One night in the late fall when the frost was already on the grass and the bed felt extra snug against the cold, I woke up to find I had to go. This was bad planning. "Going" during the night meant leaving a warm bed and visiting a cold outhouse. I got the flashlight from the junk drawer, but the batteries were low and the light so feeble I left it there. It was well into the middle of a night with only a sliver of a moon. Outside the darkness seemed to magnify the farm noises so that the grunt of a pig or the clomp of a hoof gave me goosebumps and made me stop and hold my breath to listen. My sister Dorothy had been reading *Treasure Island* to me, and images of the hunched blind man tapping around in the darkness and of Billy Bones with a bloody cutlass were fresh in my brain. I was making my way back from the outhouse when my heart jumped into my throat. A black, lumbering figure was coming toward me in the darkness, a feeble lantern swinging by its side. I was frozen in my tracks, my throat dry, my heart pounding. I made up my mind to hail the phantom with a confidant, vigorous voice, but nothing came out. I was thinking I should find a stick to use as a club, but the figure was upon me: it was Dad, the steam of his breath fogging in the lamplight as he held it up to see who I was.

"Go call Lawrence," he said. "Tell him to come to the pig barn right away. And hurry up."

I started immediately, but then he stopped me.

"Wait," he said. "You should be old enough to do this. You can hold a lantern, can't you?"

"Ye-yes," I said with considerable doubt about coming up to the standards of lantern-holding set by my parent.

But this was an honor of inexpressible proportions. I was to do the work of my big brother, Lawrence, who was Dad's right hand man. I followed Dad, watching how he held the lantern. I resolved to be the best lantern-holder who had ever held up a light. We went to the milk house and he dipped water out of the holding tank with a milk bucket. We headed for the pig barn. One of the sows was down. She had been struggling for hours in the throes of birthing, but had produced nothing. We got into the pen with that enormous pig. She made a few warning sounds that made me shrink back against the wall, but Dad yelled at me to hold the light closer. Since I feared Dad more than the sow, I moved in. I could tell she was in distress. She was breathing fast and shallow. Her mouth was half open, and her big teeth gleamed a dirty yellow in the lamplight. The pleasant smell of the kerosene lamp was overpowered by the unpleasant smell of pig. Dad got down on all fours at her back end. I stood opened-mouthed as he began to explore the bloody vaginal opening with his fingers. Suddenly she started up on her forelegs with a ferocious bark that blew me back against the partition. Dad jumped back, too, and froze, but the sow seemed too weak to get up. She made ugly popping noises with her teeth. We held still. She looked very tired, and she lay back down. To my great relief, Dad lifted me outside the pen and told me to hold the lantern over the partition.

I held the lantern low over the straw. The flame sputtered and Dad's shadow jumped up and down as he knelt behind her. He petted her a little and said nice things to her in German. He wet his hand in the water and began slowly reaching inside the sow again. It was not pleasant to see Dad stick his hand in there with all that blood and mucous and whatever. But he didn't seem to mind it a bit, and kept stirring around in there. He kept repositioning himself on the straw to get a better angle. Nothing gives you perspective on life like seeing your father on all fours in a pigsty with an arm up the rear of a smelly old hog. In a little while he gave a grunt of approval. He pulled, and out came a piglet that lay lifeless in the bloody straw.

"Too late for that one," he said grimly.

He went in again. This time he came out immediately with another lifeless thing, much smaller than the first one. The little thing looked dead to me, but Dad squeezed and stretched him and molded him like clay. The little creature began to wiggle. It gave a cough, and Dad set him by the sow's teats. The little fellow began pulling on a teat immediately, and it made Dad smile. Having that little one at her udder seemed to awaken the old sow. She began to drive hard, and piglets came out one after another. It was easy now. Dad said nothing, but I knew the trouble was over. Dad took the piglets as the sow pushed them out and put them by her udder, where they began to draw milk. She had eleven little ones—all squeaking, pushing, and shoving to get at a nipple. Dad moved them around so that, with the final arrangement, everybody had his own teat. Sucking sounds filled the air. The sow gave regular little grunts of contentment. That sow turned from fierce monster to tender mother. She raised that whole litter without squashing any by lying on them or crippling any by stepping on them, like the clumsy mothers did.

Dad washed his hands in the cold water, wiped them on the partition and then on his overalls. He took the lantern from me and we walked to the house. "You get to bed," he said. He never said "Thank you," or "Everything's fine now," or "Good job." But I knew.

Dad was not always successful at playing vet. The worst thing I ever saw was when a cow drove out her uterus. One morning when we came into the barn, there it was: a huge bloody thing hanging behind a young heifer. She had given birth during the night and kept pushing until she had delivered her entire uterus. It looked like half her insides were hanging down behind her—a huge slimy thing you had to see to believe.

Dad said we would have to push it all back in there. We washed it and picked off the tiny bits of straw and manure. Then Dad, Lawrence, and Leroy began putting it back, pushing, grunting, sweating, and the cow danced nervously from side to side clanging her stanchion. I patted her head to calm her but it did no good. She tried again and again to drive that stuff back out, but they kept pushing it in. Once it was all back inside her, she calmed down and stood still. Dad had us build up a platform with boards so that the cow's hind end was higher in the air. This would keep it from coming out again.

We finished milking. Everything was fine. We ate breakfast. We returned to the barn. Oh, God, there it was again! The whole thing was back out. Dad stared. He squeezed his eyes shut and took a deep breath. Without a word he turned and walked to the house. He hated to call a vet. He hated to spend the money.

The Albany vet was a man named Tomsche. He breezed in with bottles and hoses and needles, and with a rubber suit that looked like he meant business. He laughed and doubled over, slapping his knee, when Dad told him about our morning's work. But he did tell Dad it was a nice try and that we should leave the platform in place for a few days.

When Tomsche approached the cow, she regarded him nervously. He was a stranger and she strained forward against the stanchion to get away from him. He basically did exactly as we had, except he injected the cow with a local anesthetic like Novocain, and bingo, she lost interest in the whole operation. She stood calmly and pulled at her hay. Tomsche washed the uterus with an antiseptic solution. Pushing it back in was a lot easier now because the cow didn't drive anymore. Occasionally she looked around to see what the clowns were doing back there. Tomsche inserted some antibiotics and then—he sewed it shut! Yes, he sutured that vaginal opening so for days the cow had to pee through the stitching. But it worked. The cow was fine, she never did that again, and she became a good milker.

Chapter Three

WHEN I WAS REALLY LITTLE, we all spoke German around the home. All the neighbors spoke German, as well as the businessmen in Albany. I did not know Dad was fluent in English until I was about five years old. A lady walked into our yard one summer day, wearing a yellow dress, matching hat, and matching necklace and high heels. She patted my head and smiled and spoke to me in English. I just frowned at her. My younger sister and brother were with me and they stared at her like she was a circus act. We had never seen a lady dressed up like this except in church on Sundays. She kept talking and smiling until, having decided I was dim-witted, she bent down, her face close to mine.

"Paaapaa, Paaapaa?" she said.

I pointed to the barn, but seeing Dad was already coming, I shifted my finger to him. She spoke to Dad in English and to my amazement, he answered in English. Dad went with her and changed a tire on her car, which was parked up the hill on the highway near our mailbox.

When I started school I had a hard time learning English, so Mom made a rule that we could speak only English at the dinner table. It was a good rule. My younger siblings did not have the language problem when they went to school. I learned English quickly after that, but for a while I mispronounced words because the adults pronounced them with a German accent.

"I tink dats right," I would say with absolute confidence. And I misunderstood words. For a long time I thought the words "have" and "half" were the same. I thought that "feed floor," upon which we fed the pigs, was "feet floor." That seemed perfectly logical, because our pigs walked on it with their feet. There were only a few kids at school who made fun of that German accent. Most of them talked the same way, and most had parents and other close relatives who did.

We survived on very little money. The only cash intake of the farm came from selling cream, eggs, pigs, and occasionally a bull or a worn-out cow. We had a cream separator, a centrifuge, to spin the cream out of the milk. The skim milk was fed to the hogs, and the cream sold at the creamery in town. We had about 200 chickens. We ate their eggs, we ate their meat, and we sold the surplus in town. Every six months we sold a batch of hogs. Farmers got very little for their products at the time. When Dad sold a dozen eggs, he was lucky to get twenty cents. If you figured in the cost of chicken feed and labor, there was nothing left. When hog prices were good, Dad might get thirty dollars for a two-hundred-pound pig, but he had to pay the trucker's fee to haul it to the stockyard in South St. Paul, and he had to pay the stockyard a commission for processing. There was little money left to buy flour, salt, and sugar. But things were cheaper in those days. In Albany we could buy a pound of bacon or hamburger for fifty cents, a gallon of milk for eighty cents, and a loaf of bread for little more than a dime. A brand new Ford could be bought for less than two thousand dollars.

We lived well. We ate like kings, getting our meat from the farm animals and our vegetables from Mom's garden. My parents economized in every way. Dad bought sugar in fifty-pound sacks and flour in one hundred-pound sacks. Mom made dresses from flour sacks. She kept a huge garden and wasted nothing. We either ate the produce fresh or she canned it for winter. We had a big smokehouse stuffed every fall with sausage and ham. If Mom wanted fresh pork, chicken, or beef, we went out and butchered an animal. We had no freezer, so Dad took the excess meat to town and stored it in a rented freezer-locker. When he went to the creamery with the cream, he stopped at the locker to get meat for the next day or two.

I learned from watching the work of my parents. From my father I inherited a sense of pride in the performance of manual labor, and a determination to get a job done no matter how hard it was. From my mom I got a strong sense of duty. I know I have some of my father's iron will, and if there is any sensitivity or gentleness in me, it comes from Mom.

THE PEOPLE OF CENTRAL Stearns County were deeply religious, but they were also deeply German. Many of them were sad their children were learning English and were forgetting the language of the old country. They knew the end of the German language was the end of their German culture, and many thought it was also the end of their religion.

We walked to school. It was only about a mile across the fields, but in spring, when the frost was leaving the ground, it got so muddy we had to go around the fields on the gravel road. This made it three times as far. When we took the long way, we passed by Gene Garding's farm. But when we took the short way, we went right through his yard and through his fences. If he saw us, he would sometimes engage us in conversation. One day he asked me if we prayed at home. This was none of his business, but I didn't know that. So I said we did. He asked in what language. This was none of his business either, but I didn't know that. I said we did our meal prayers in German. He seemed to approve. Then I said Mom had us do our morning and evening prayers in English, so we would learn the language better. This did not sit well. He said I should inform Mom that God spoke German, and that it was a waste of time to pray in English.

I didn't like Gene. He was a dirty, unshaven old bachelor and always smelled like old rags and stale cigarette smoke. He let rats run around on his farm. His kitchen floor was as dirty as our back stoop where we cleaned our boots. I never told Mom about God speaking only German. I figured she knew better than a grumpy old bachelor who didn't know enough to paint his barn. However, for a while after that, in the evening after we had said our prayers in English, and I was in my bed, I would try to say some of the important parts again in German, just in case.

My parents were Catholic. They never—never—missed church on Sunday or on feast days. Except for the milking and the feeding of the animals, Dad allowed no work on Sundays. Even when hay lay in the field and rain threatening, if it was Sunday, Dad sat in his rocking chair with a cigar and read the *Albany Enterprise* and the *St. Cloud Times*. God worked for six days to create the universe, and rested on the seventh. Farmers were not creating universes, but the Church decreed they must do likewise. It was a great scandal to see a neighbor working in his field on a Sunday and even greater if he did not go to Mass. He was committing a mortal sin. If you skipped out on Sunday Mass and then died, you went straight to hell—do not pass go, do not collect $200—Hell! And Catholic feast days (called Holy Days of Obligation) were the same. Parishioners were under the same obligation as Sundays.

If you thought you might have committed a mortal sin, you went to confession. The safest way was to go "regularly." In our family that was every three weeks. You went into church and spent a few minutes preparing a list of sins to confess, and figuring how to tenderize them as much as possible so as not to shock the confessor. Then you stood in line in front of the confessional and waited your turn. There were two lines, one for the left stall and one for the right. You counted the people and chose the shortest line. Then you listened carefully to the mumblings inside the confessional to see if you could make out what sins were being discussed. This was usually a failure, but if someone was in there a long time, you assumed they were getting scolded for some really bad sins and couldn't wait to see who it was that would finally draw aside the curtain and make a red-faced exit.

Going to church would not have been such a burden had it not been for the turmoil of preparation. Most boys on a Sunday morning had only a mother to check their ears, neck, fingernails, and elbows for such things as dirt, grime, ticks, oil, schmutz, and other stains that could only be detected by female eyes. I had not only Mom but a cadre of big sisters, who all considered it a sacred duty to shine any parts of me that stuck out of my clothes. I had to pass half a dozen ear-pulling, neck-twisting inspections every Sunday morning. I had to have a part in my hair as straight as a ruler. I got the most scrutiny because of my birthmark. On my right elbow, I had a sinister little brown mark that looked just like a stain of oil or grease. My sisters entertained themselves every few Sunday mornings by passing me and a hard scrub brush from one to another until my elbow was raw.

"It's not dirt," I would whine, "It's a birthmark. It won't come off."

"Birthmark my foot. We'll see about that! "

The more they scrubbed the mark, the more it resembled dirt, because it shined up the skin around it and made it stand out. Eventually I was passed to Mom, who would administer the final brushing and declare that yes, indeed, it did appear to be a birthmark, but anyway we'd have to live with it, or we'd be late for Mass.

They all had bad memories, and a month or two later they would repeat the whole ceremony and find again that it was a birthmark. It was great in winter when a long sleeve covered the mark, but that also allowed them time to forget it again, and they renewed the assault in spring. The birthmark has faded over the years, but I am sure that even today, if one of my older sisters detects that mark on my elbow they wish I would wash once in a while.

On Sunday mornings my sisters would get into arguments about religion, like whether brushing teeth broke the Eucharistic fast, or whether genuflecting had to be done on the right knee, and if it was done accidentally on the left knee, did it count or did you have to do it over? Sometimes Mom would settle the arguments by impatiently declaring, "Oh, go ahead and brush, just don't eat the toothpaste," or "Yes, it has to be the right knee, but one genuflection is enough."

The big tube radio in the corner was tuned to WCCO in Minneapolis, which carried a Sunday morning program out of Renfro Valley, Kentucky. A church bell chimed while a choir sang a song that began, "I was born in Renfro Valley," and ended with "We'll be back in Renfro Valley as in days of long ago." They often sang about a little brown church in the wildwood, and Dad would listen while he straightened his tie and checked his billfold for collection money and his pockets for the car keys.

When everyone was ready we piled into Dad's 1939 Chevrolet, Dad at the wheel, Mom with the baby in her lap to his right, and one little sister in the middle. In the back were six or seven of the rest of us, with elbows, knees, and heads bumping and causing minor fights, which Mom attempted in vain to stop, but which kept going until one word from Dad caused a thunderous silence in the car, and everyone was completely content to ride with an elbow in the ribs.

If my older sister Dorothy was along, she would take a survey of the younger kids, asking, "Do you have your nickel?" She would make sure we all had something to put in the collection box. And I would dig into my pocket to check and would elbow LeRoy in the process, and that would begin another round of discontent. If you didn't have a nickel Dorothy would get out her purse, hold it over the head of little sister in the front where there was some room to rummage, and would take out a nickel and give it to you. Or Mom would hand the baby over into the back and find one in her purse. "Now don't you lose this nickel, too," they would warn, even when you hadn't lost the first nickel, because you never had one. Little sister always got a penny, but Mom didn't give that to her until during the Mass at the offertory. Otherwise she would eat it before the collection came around.

The church was a solemn place on Sunday mornings. People came in walking softly and did not talk. They dipped fingers into the holy water font by the door and crossed themselves. Even creaky old people struggled to genuflect before getting into a pew. They did not acknowledge each other. The Mass was not a social event. People said silent prayers. Old ladies said the rosary, lips moving as they slipped the beads through their fingers. Here and there men knelt, their bare heads bowed, absorbed in communication with their creator. Ladies sat and read the Bible. Often we saw a young girl kneeling like a statue, her eyes riveted on the crucifix over the altar. Old men sat with their white heads bent over, hands resting on walking canes. The faith of these people was open, their spirituality plain and uplifting.

The lights were dim in the church so the little fire in the red glass of the sanctuary lamp, which indicated the presence of Christ in the Blessed Sacrament, was bright in the semi gloom. Sometimes, in the middle of summer, when the sun was at a high angle above the spruce trees in the churchyard, it shown through the stained glass windows and made the people glow with colors of red, blue, and green. The church was deathly quiet. When we got into the pew, we put the kneeler down slowly so as not to make a noise. If it slipped, the sound of its crash on the oaken floor echoed like a rifle shot among the pillars and the arches of the church. But everyone kept right on praying except for one or two busybodies who looked around and frowned and shook their heads.

After a while the church bells began to ring to tell the loafers outside that it was time to come in. An altar boy came out of the sacristy door. One by one he lit the candles on the altar with a shiny brass candle lighter. He returned to the sacristy and shadows from the dancing flames flickered on the wall behind the altar for a few minutes. Then someone turned up the lights. It was time for Mass. It started with a parade of servers and the priest in full array entering the church from the sacristy at the side of the altar. One of the servers pulled the tassel on a golden rope that hung by the door; there was the *ding-a-ling* of little bells, and the faithful stood up. The big pipes of the organ, high in the back, shook the church, and the choir began the opening hymn.

The nine-o'clock Sunday High Mass at the Church of Seven Dolors in Albany, Minnesota, was a grand show for a kid to watch: all the shiny vestments, the gleaming chalice and ciborium, the solemn muttering and bowing and blessing, tall candles flickering in the background. The priest swung a golden censer, sending great puffs of smoke drifting upward. The air was heavy with the scent of incense, flowers, and candle wax. The altar boys, looking appallingly pious, were always bowing and ringing little bells and carrying around books that were entirely too big for them.

But, alas, the Mass was just too long. It lasted forever and ever, amen. The priest droned long mysterious prayers in Latin. The choir sang brutally long songs like "Gloria in Excelsis" and the "Credo." The priest read the Epistle and Gospel in English, but that could just as well have been in Latin, too, because it was Bible-English, which no kid could understand, as it was all so loaded with "thees," "thous," and "shalts." The ultimate torture was the sermon. Sitting quietly and pretending to listen as the priest went on and on about things of no consequence was beyond the abilities of any boy.

Yet a boy had to behave like a perfect angel in church. The seating was strategically arranged so the eye of a big sister, a parent, or (worst of all) a nun could be on you at any time. Children sat up front in the middle of the church. My older sisters were in the pews to the left, where the single young ladies sat. My older brothers were on the right with the young bachelors. All the parents with their babies and toddlers were in the middle, not far behind us. Immediately behind us was a double row of Benedictine nuns all clad in black and glowering down on a boy like crows on a fence watching a mouse. We could get away with nothing. I say "we" meaning farm kids. A town boy went to Mass every day and developed skills far beyond anything we could ever hope to achieve. He could deliver a vicious kick under the pew while sitting perfectly still and straight, hands folded angelically in front of him, eyes riveted on the altar in saintly innocence.

It would only be fair to reveal here that it was not only the children who had a hard time listening to the sermon. Moms were busy planning the Sunday meal and poking their nodding husbands so they wouldn't fall asleep and topple out of the pew. Many farmers, like my dad and older brothers, had been up since five o'clock. Often they went out into temperatures of thirty-below to do morning chores. They chopped frozen silage for the cows. They fed and milked cows, fed hogs, hauled manure, and came into the house hungry. They had to fast for Communion. They got dressed for church with stomachs growling. "Nothing by way of mouth from midnight on" was the dictum of the Church. Not even a cup of hot coffee or a swallow of water was allowed. This was a huge sacrifice for a man whose idea of breakfast was half a dozen fried eggs, a pile of bacon, and several thick slices of bread soaked in the bacon grease, topped with butter, and washed down with a gallon of coffee. Townfolk, whose shops were closed on Sundays, got up late and made their leisurely way to church. Missing breakfast was nothing for them. For a farmer it was starvation.

The main concern of a boy attending Mass was to sit, stand, and kneel in conjunction with the congregation. The last thing in the world a kid wanted was to call attention to himself by getting out of sync with the other worshippers. Nothing was more embarrassing than to be left standing when everyone else was kneeling or, worse yet, sitting. There was always some daydreamer who was left kneeling with eyes half closed and head tilted to one side when everyone else was comfortably sitting. Then a buddy gave the unfortunate lad a poke, and he would look around and quickly sit down with face blazing red. The little girls rarely made such a mistake. They watched out of the corners of their eyes and went along with the majority, but they were happy to participate in the snickering when a boy blundered.

At Communion time I entertained myself by watching the adults line up to receive the Host and noting how funny some of them walked and what astonishing hats the ladies wore. The married ladies wore veils over their faces, but I could still tell who it was. The men brought hats to church, too, but they left theirs in the pews hanging from hat clips. Farmers, who never had need for a suit except for church, often wore what had belonged to their fathers and grandfathers—shiny and worn and ill-fitting. Legs stuck out of trousers and jackets hung loosely as from a wire hanger, or were stretched tight with the vest buttons unable to latch. Some ladies smothered us with perfume as they passed, and some men with an overpowering whiff of cow barn.

It took forever to distribute Communion in those days. Usually there was only one priest to pass out the Host. He stopped in front of every recipient.

A server held a little gold plate under the recipient's chin in case the priest dropped the Host or a crumb fell. The priest placed the Host slowly and carefully on the tongue, and each time he did, he said this entire tongue twister prayer: "*Corpus Domini nostri, Jesu Christi, custodiat animam tuam in vitam eternam.*" Then server and priest turned and moved to the next person, and repeated the whole thing. Some Sundays, when attendance was heavy (and it usually was), it took an eternity to finish. Halfway through Communion a boy was fit to be tied. First he knelt on one knee, then on the other. He rested his chin on one hand, then on the other. Once in a while, when he was desperate, he would rest his butt on the bench behind him. This was considered very bad form, and usually he would do that only when he could see Mom and Dad in the Communion line.

Finally after Communion we got to sit for a moment while the priest and servers washed the dishes. The priest said the after-Communion prayers. And then at last—alleluia!—the priest sang "*Ite missa est.*" No sweeter words ever fell upon a boy's ear than "*Ite missa est.*" I didn't know a word of Latin, but I knew those words meant it was the end of the Mass, and when the choir sang "*Deo gratias,*" I could not have agreed more.

The social part of attending Mass took place outside the church after the final hymn. People stood in little groups and laughed and talked of crops and weather. The flow of the conversation ran in the same vein every Sunday, varying only a little with the seasons. For many the social part was extended to gatherings in front of Ebnet's Meat Market. Mike Ebnet had a reputation for making the best baloney in the midwest, and he opened his store every Sunday after Mass so the farmers could stop in on the way home and get rings of boloney for the noon meal. A line of farmers formed in front of the little shop on the main street, and baloney was passed inside and outside the market. Here the conversation was livelier than by the church. The spices of gossip, exaggeration, and swearing—not proper in the shadow of the church—were admissible. The "pretty young bride," so described at the church, became "the hottest little heifer in the county," and about the husband it was said that "the poor bastard has his hands full with that one." Language like "darn it" and "son-of-a-gun" became "damn it" and "son-of-a-bitch." The five-pound northern pike which had been described at the church now became a forty-pound vicious monster that had to be fought for an hour to get landed.

Chapter Four

IT WAS AUGUST near the Feast of the Assumption. The grain harvest was underway in Stearns County. In late July the dark green fields of oats and wheat had turned to light gold, and the plants bowed their heads under the burden of the heavy kernels. Dad and my older brothers had rolled out the great grain binder, a clever machine that cut the grain and tied it in little bundles. The binder, pulled by horses, rolled along on a big bull wheel which was connected to the gears that drove the various parts. The bull wheel drove the sickle which rattled and shivered through the grain and cut it low to the ground. The grain fell on a rotating canvas and was carried into a device that tied it in neat bundles and kicked it out into a basket that rode alongside. Dad sat on the back of the binder. He kept count of the bundles in the basket and dumped them in the field whenever there were six bundles, which was enough to make one shock. He had several levers in front of him to adjust the height of the cut according to the type of weeds in the grain and the amount of droop of the heads. The reins of the horses were draped over his shoulder, within easy reach for when he needed to stop or turn corners. The horse closest to the standing grain wore a little wire basket over his mouth to prevent his reaching down and grabbing mouthfuls of the grain as he walked along.

I knew I could make a shock as well as any adult. You took two of the bundles Dad had dropped from the binder and set them up in the stubble, leaning against each other so they wouldn't fall. Next you took two more and set them up the same way next to the first two but leaning in, slightly against the original two. You put the last two bundles on the other side in the same way. A good shock could stand a high wind. All farmers knew how to make a good shock, but Dad thought I was still too little, so I carried water in a one-gallon syrup can to my older brothers and sisters, who got to do all the fun stuff. Later, when I actually had to help with the shocking, it was amazing how quickly the romance drained out of it. I had never considered that shocking grain was back-breaking torture. All day long you were bending over to pick up and to set bundles into place. I did not realize how the sweat, produced by this labor in the intense heat of August, burned in your eyes and made the dust and chaff stick to your skin and made you itch all over.

On this particular day in August the shocks were standing in the fields cured by a week of sun and wind, ready for the thresher. My little brothers and sisters and I were standing by the tool shed, leaning against the wall and looking up the shady driveway to catch the show. We knew the threshers were coming. Dad had just come home and warned Mom, who was now bustling in the kitchen to make summer-sausage sandwiches and get out cookies and set up the coffee. Dad put beer in the milk house holding tank so it would be cool.

The threshing crew was a group of neighbors who helped each other at harvest time. Today was our turn. Except for Christmas, this was the most exciting time of the year for a kid, and we did not want to miss anything. After a while we heard a far-off rumbling, like metallic thunder. The threshing machine had steel wheels. When it ran on a road it shook over every little stone and pothole, so that its big blower drum and other hollows of tin rumbled and echoed. Soon it came trundling down our driveway and into the yard, pulled by a bright-red Farmall H tractor with Oswald Fisher driving. This was the biggest thing I had ever seen. It was higher than a horse and half as long as the barn. Adding to its length was a grain box attached to a hitch at the rear. The grain box was a big wooden box on four wheels used to catch the grain from the machine. Following the machine, pulled by another tractor, came a long elevator used to drive the grain up into the granary.

Then came teams of horses pulling hay wagons. Those headed into our fields and began loading. It was like a parade on the Fourth of July. The farmers were colorful characters, all of them. Some wore torn straw hats, some greasy baseball caps. Most wore washed-out bib overalls. One radical rebel wore one of those new-fangled coveralls. All smelled of the sweat of man and horse. Some were clean-shaven, some had beards. One smoked a pipe, another cigarettes. All were sweaty, grimy, grinning, and waving at us like they were having the time of their lives. We raised our hands halfway and shyly waved back, and we *were* having the time of our lives.

Dad told Oswald where he wanted the straw pile. Oswald lined up the machine so the wind would not blow the dust and chaff back into the grain box or onto the men pitching the bundles into the carrier. The men maneuvered the machine until it stood level and chocked the wheels with firewood. One of the men lined up the tractor in front of the machine. Dad stretched the main belt from the machine to the tractor and slipped it on the pulley. The man backed up the tractor until the belt was tight. He set the brakes. Dad rolled a big stone in front of the tractor wheel on the belt side.

A load of bundles was already pulled up next to the machine, the horses standing with eyes half-closed. They were used to the commotion. Sometimes a horse would shy when the machine started up, but mostly they looked bored and stood like statues, occasionally stamping one front foot.

Oswald gave the signal all was ready. The man on the tractor opened the throttle a quarter. He engaged the clutch. The belt shrieked as it slipped on the pulley, and a puff of white smoke drifted into the air. Then the belt caught, and suddenly the monster machine came to life. Belts began to turn on pulleys, chains rattled on their sprockets, and shaker arms moved up and down and back and forth. The cutting knives over the carrier began clawing the air, waiting for the bundles. The straw blower fan hummed at the far end. The man on the tractor gave it full throttle. When the machine reached the proper speed, the carrier apron began to rotate, and the men on top of the load began pitching bundles into the feeder. The carrier pushed the bundles past the cutting knives, which sliced the string and opened the bundles. The loose grain disappeared into the throat of the monster. A second later the straw flew out the far end. A few seconds after that, the grain holder dumped, and the first half-bushel of oats was augered into the grain box. The threshing season at the Henry Bloch farm was underway.

The arrival of the threshing crew completely changed the quiet farmyard for a few days. The air was filled with the constant droning of the tractor and rumble of the big machine, and with the German expletives of the teamsters as they swore at their horses. Words Mom and Dad never allowed, like *verdammt, zum teufel, verflixt,* and *verflucht* sailed in the air like barn swallows.

It was exciting as Disneyland. We had to tie Sport to a ground stake by his dog house because all the action made him crazy. If Dad was in a good mood, he would let some of us stand near the washtub of beer by the tractor to watch, and we met the men who came to drink. You could get a feel for the character and the mood of a man by the way he tilted his battered hat. Some had it tilted way back and smiled at the world in the full sunshine. Others had it pulled down low and glowered from the shadow of the brim. One man could open a beer bottle with his teeth. Another could empty an entire bottle down his throat without swallowing. All chewed wads of tobacco like ruminating cows. One man chewed Copenhagen like Dad, but with greater abandon. He had a circle worn on the bib of his overalls where his snuff box rode. He took out the box, tapped on the lid several times, opened it, took out an enormous wad, and shoveled it into his mouth, stuffing it way back into the left cheek. Then he licked his fingers with a slobbering tongue as if it was the best chocolate ice cream. This was amazing. Dad chewed, but he took only a dainty little pinch and put it behind his lower lip.

Whenever they stood around and talked without a beer or sandwich in hand, it would be with both hands deep in their side pockets, leaning against a tractor wheel or a post, if there was one nearby. I admired them for this talent of resting. My father never relaxed like that. He was always busy. If Dad put a hand in his pocket it was to get out a staple or a nail, or to fish out a dirty Copenhagen-stained toothpick to clean his teeth—no fooling around for Dad. If he leaned against anything, it was to push a wagon, or to move a cow aside. If he leaned on a post, it was to straighten it. These men leaned on anything, and they were so relaxed, they might have been taking a nap. When they found nothing to lean on, they would stand wide-legged and hook their thumbs on the suspenders of their bib overalls or rest their folded hands inside the bib.

Almost all of them had a red or a blue bandanna in a rear pocket, with one corner of it hanging out for quick access (though they never did anything quickly). The bandana was used to wipe sweat and dust from one's brow, or to wipe chaff from the corner of a horse's eye, or to blow one's nose when there were ladies present. (Normally that operation was accomplished by squeezing the nose between thumb and forefinger and then flinging the product to the ground with a snap of the wrist, and then wiping the finger on an overall leg.) Nor was quick access needed to cover a sneeze. For a sneeze, one turned politely to the side, bent over at the waist, and exploded into the grass like a water balloon.

They did not talk of wars or politics, but of crops and cows. They compared the fullness of last year's oat kernels to this year's. They argued about which beer was better—Hamm's or Grain Belt—and whether the premium beer was better than the original. One man thought Cold Spring Beer beat them all because it was made right here in Stearns County, where the water was the best. Another man said Cold Spring Beer was for cheapskates, and that his horse produced a better brew if you fed him good oats. They all defended their horses, which they cursed daily in the fields, and they defended their tractors while they wished they could afford a decent one.

Full loads of bundles constantly replaced the empty ones as they pulled away from the machine and headed back into the fields. If the man pitching in the bundles went too fast, the tractor would roar a complaint as the governor opened up. That was a warning that it was nearing maximum capacity. Sometimes the man was thinking of other things and, ignoring the warning, kept pitching and bogged down the machine. The tractor suddenly stopped dead. In the reigning quiet everyone looked toward the pitcher on the load.

"This stuff is too damned wet," he would alibi.

But everyone knew it was not the fault of the rain that fell last week, but the fault of the pitcher. Oswald went quietly around the machine and opened up the side panels to clear the straw. If the straw spout was blocked, too, it was a big problem because it had no panel to open. Then they had to telescope the spout to its shortest length and push the straw out with a long stick. When all was ready again, they ran the machine empty for a few seconds. Then Oswald nodded to the man on the load and all proceeded as before. When a grain box was full, the spout was switched to another box and the full one was taken to the elevator, where the grain was sent up into the granary.

Whenever a teamster left to get another load of bundles, he took a bottle of beer with him, which he said was for the "spiker." The spiker had the hardest job of all. He helped load out in the field. He helped one teamster finish up his load and then he walked to the next one to help him. He pitched all day. The teamsters got a rest as they sat on top of the bundles and drove home. They rested at the machine while they waited for the load in front of them to finish. The spiker got no rest unless something broke down on the tractor or the threshing machine. Even then he had to rest out in the sun, unless by chance he was near the edge of a field and there was a tree nearby. Whether the spiker ever got that bottle of beer, I don't know. He certainly deserved it.

Besides the great show they put on, another advantage of having the threshing crew over was the food. Mom suspended all the normal washing of clothes and scrubbing of floors, and she cooked from morning until night. She and my older sisters made every meal like Sunday. The kitchen table groaned under the tubs and platters of meats and vegetables. Pies and cakes stood all over the cupboard. Baskets of chocolate chip cookies streamed from the house. Every few hours, they carried out a washtub of sandwiches and gallons of coffee.

When evening came and the dew began to dampen the shocks, everything stopped. The farmers went home to their chores and the world was quiet again. They did not start early in the morning because the shocks were still wet with dew. But Mom was up before the sun getting more food ready for the day. When the sun climbed a little and the wind came up, teams appeared out in the field like magic, and I could see bundles sailing onto the hayracks.

The shocks disappeared quickly from the fields and by the end of the second day little was left. The next morning they cleaned up the rest and then the teams that finished at the machine did not return to the fields, but went up the road to the next farmer in the threshing cycle. We stood to the side and watched them leave. One farmer, seeing us watching, waved his hat, laughing and sang at the top of his lungs, "*Wenn ich komm, wenn ich komm, wenn ich wieda wieda komm* (when I come again)." We stood in wonder as he sang. Dad never sang. It seemed a kind of insanity.

I hated to see them go. But later, when I was older and had to do my share of the work, I leaned on my pitchfork and rejoiced at their departure.

Chapter Five

WHEN WE GOT underfoot in the kitchen, Mom would say, "Why don't you go outside and play in the ground?" The "ground" she referred to was the fine loose dirt that was provided by our chickens. Chickens like to take dust baths. They scratch the ground to loosen it, and ruffle their feathers and lie down and shake themselves around in the dirt to get it sifting through their feathers. We loved to play in those areas. This ground had no lumps or rocks, and was easy to move around. We made hills and valleys and roads and paths. We built a farm. We made flat areas for cornfields, and made straight lines in them to look like those made by dad's corn planter. The occasional lump of chicken shit was of no consequence. We simply picked it up, along with some dirt, and flung it out of the play area.

We had sticks and stones for toys. We broke twigs from the spruce trees and set them along our roads and between the fields to serve as trees. We used stones for horses, pigs, cows, and cars. The larger black stones were horses. The small brown ones were pigs, and the in between were cows. A big fancy stone with an odd color like white or purple was a definite car. LeRoy was good at finding cars. I was best at finding pigs and cows. Pigs had to be smooth and round. Cows had to be oval.

The old log house had a leaky roof, and after a rain dad would sometimes go up there and pull out the worn-out shingles and replace them with new. Those pieces of old shingle were prizes, easy to split lengthwise and to break. They made the best fences and sliding gates. We were always searching for pieces of shingle until that great year of 1950, when we pulled down the old house. After that we had an endless supply.

We usually didn't let the younger kids play in our plot of ground. They couldn't tell a cow from a pig. But they could play in others plots close by. One day Vernie and Julie, our younger siblings, were playing right next to us. Janie, the baby, was there too, but she was too little to understand the game. She sat and smiled and tried to eat the dirt. Vernie and Julie both yelled, "Oh, no pooie! No. Not good. You can't eat that. Bad. Bad."

Leroy took a handkerchief from his pocket and cleaned Janie's mouth. It didn't get very clean because it was the same handkerchief we used to shine our horses and cows. But Janie appreciated the attention so much that in a minute she came toddling over to our farm and sat down on a corner of Leroy's cornfield. We took her to Vernie and Julie, set her down, and told them to keep her there or we were going to tie her to a tree. Julie said, "No, you're not!"

"We are too," said Leroy.

"Are not," said Julie.

But Leroy, who was highly skilled in this verbal game and old enough to be bored by it, decided to cut it short. Instead of the required, "Are too," he came back with, "Yes, we are, and if you don't behave we'll tie you up, too."

That was too much for Julie. She threw down her sticks and headed for the house saying, "I'm telling."

Leroy had a quick mind. He knew she meant telling Mom, and since Dad was just back from town with the groceries, he would hear it. Leroy quickly picked up his best stone and ran after Julie explaining to her the advantages of remaining to play some more, one of which was that she would have a new car, and besides we were just joking. Julie slowed. He kept the stone in front of her. She stopped. She looked at the stone. It was shiny quartz with gray lines in it. She took it and turned it over in her hand. She looked at him suspiciously, but slowly turned and came walking back. Leroy looked at me. We had just avoided getting killed. After that we did not threaten to tie babies to trees.

There was a deep pond in the pasture behind the machine shed. Mom did not want us to go there, because we couldn't swim. But it was a magnet. LeRoy and I sneaked out there whenever Dad was gone and when Mom was busy in the kitchen. We watched tadpoles and caught frogs. I knew about the metamorphosis of a tadpole long before I went to school. Often we saw little black clouds of baby bullheads boiling in the pond. They stayed together in tight groups, all turning and diving in concert like miniature flocks of blackbirds.

We lay on our backs and watched the clouds change their shapes against the blue, and we followed the flight of the red-tailed hawk as it circled over the wheat fields. The air was drowsy there with insect sounds and sweet with the smell of the neighbor's new-mown hay. From the oak trees by the machine shed there came the occasional drumming of a red-headed woodpecker. Sometimes a bumblebee buzzed as it searched the red clover close by, and often dragonflies glittered in the sunshine as they skimmed over the pond. A "slough pumper" would sound off from among the reeds and make that mysterious sound like the working of the old water pump.

Another place Mom did not want us to visit was the stock tank. It was in the cow yard, right behind the milk house where Mom could not see from the kitchen window. It was an enormous steel tank, about a dozen feet across and three feet high. Cows and horses drank there. We liked to fish there. Dad put bullheads in the tank every summer. Without bullheads a green scum formed on top of the water and the animals had to snuffle around for a clear spot when they came to drink. The bullheads kept the water as clean and clear as our drinking water. We used to catch those bullheads on a string with a worm tied to it. We used a piece of wire for a sinker. The bullheads were very stubborn and would hang onto the worm and fight like crazy until we lifted them clear of the water. Then they let go, and we put on another worm. It was as much fun as going fishing with Grandpa and Dad.

Actually, it was more fun. Fishing with Dad was serious business. If Dad caught you daydreaming or looking at anything other than your bobber, he would yell at you. You weren't out there to watch the gulls or the cows on the bank. You were there to get fish for food for the family. "Mom is expecting fish for supper," he would say, so that you felt guilty if you watched the loons diving for minnows or the little green heron preening on the log.

ALL SUMMER LONG the children of Henry Bloch went barefoot "because it saved shoe leather." We walked barefoot on rocks and gravel, in the chicken barn and the pig pen, and at grain-cutting time we carried water barefoot to the shockers in the stubble field, where the spikes of oat plants were strong and sharp enough to draw blood from the softer skin by the ankle. By late July the soles of our feet were as tough as the soles of shoes. Even in late fall when the frost was on the grass in the morning, Leroy and I walked barefoot into the pasture to get the cows. By the time we reached the herd, my feet would be numb with cold. The cows were lying on the grass and we had to poke them to make them get up. When a cow rose, we quickly stepped onto her warm bed, and it felt wonderful, like holding our feet in a warm oven. But as we herded the cows homeward, the frosty grass quickly made ice of our toes again.

One morning as we headed home, I said to Leroy, "I wish there was a nice, warm cow bed right here. My feet are freezing."

"Oh, look," he said, "do this."

When you wake up a herd of cows and start them walking home, every few steps one of them will stop and produce a smoking hot cow pie she has saved up during the night. There in front of Leroy was a nice big pie, steam rising slowly above the grass and into the light of the morning sun. He stepped in it with both feet. "Ahhhh," he said, lifting his face and closing his eyes in ecstasy.

My mind rebelled, but my feet begged for relief, and they won. I found another pie and stepped in. The warm, semi-liquid substance squished up all around my feet and in between my toes. Leroy was right. *Ahhhh!* It was not the last time I warmed my feet in a cow pie.

All went well with the bare feet until the summer we tore down the old house. When the men pried up the shingles, often shingle nails, reluctant to surrender to the pry bar, let loose all of a sudden and went flying as much as fifty feet through the air. They'd land in the grass or gravel, sitting on their big flat heads, points up, waiting to trap a barefoot kid. After my little brother and one of my little sisters had been stabbed with rusty nails and Dad had to take them in to Dr. Baumgartner for tetanus boosters, he allowed us to wear shoes around the yard. It was cheaper to buy shoe leather than booster shots.

NO GAME, NO TOY, no movie could bring joy to a little boy's heart like those hundreds of baby chicks that came every springtime. Just as the last little patches of snow were melting in the pasture, there came a day when Dad fired up the stove in the brooder house. It had to read exactly ninety-five degrees in there. Next day he went to Jesh's hatchery in Albany and returned with boxes of baby chickens, which we released in the hot brooder house. The delightful, fluffy little golden balls, happy at their release, ran around bumping into each other and pecking at everything they saw. They snuggled together for warmth and the ones at the edges fell over and tumbled in the straw and charged back into the pack. Here was another of those farm miracles: those clumsy little balls of yellow down grew into pure white, fierce, fully-feathered, fighting roosters and fat, contented, clucking hens in only a few short months.

For entertainment we did not have scary movies, Disneyland, or the Macy's Thanksgiving Parade. But we had the train! The Great Northern railroad ran right through part of our farm. It crossed our driveway on the far side of the apple orchard, close to Highway 52. It was close enough to our house that sometimes, as a train passed in the night, I could feel the bed tremble. What could be more wonderful for a kid than this huge, black, steam-spouting monster roaring down the track? The coal smoke boiling from the stack streamed backwards and went rolling and tumbling along as it dissipated in the turbulent air over the cars. And as it approached our crossing, it set up the most horrendous howling scream that rang in my ears and echoed in the forest. What a gorgeous crashing, thundering, fire-eating giant!

"Train's coming!" would come a shout when someone heard the whistle far to the east as it rolled out of Albany. We kids made a mad dash up the driveway and stationed ourselves at a designated spot dictated by Mom, which was a place just beyond the line of willows by the railroad right-of-way and distant enough from the tracks to be safe. We stood there and waved wildly with both hands to get the attention of the engineer as he approached.

If he saw us he would reach up and pull the rope and give us a blast from his whistle, and it made us happy. Sometimes when the fireman wasn't busy he would wave, too. On hot days they would lean out of the window and wave, and we were delirious. We stood by the track with the sound of the engine roaring in our ears watching the jets of steam blasting out her sides and the pumping of the drivers on its enormous iron wheels. We could hardly breathe when we felt the earth shake as the whole procession thundered by.

On those trains we saw things we would never have seen otherwise. We looked especially for the flatcars loaded with farm machinery that gleamed in the sun, bright and beautiful in reds, greens, and yellows. The machines were new and polished, and the sun shone from their glistening metal sides. Tractors, binders, corn pickers, plows, harrows—we knew them all, though the ones we normally saw in the fields were dirty and rusty and in no way resembled what was on the train. They were as wonderful to us in summer as a Christmas tree was in winter.

At the end of the train there was always a red caboose with a majestic conductor inside. His job was evidently to sit in his little cupola, with windows all around so he could watch for kids to wave at. Sometimes he was standing behind the caboose on a little porch that had been put there for waving. If we kept waving, he kept waving, too, as he grew smaller and smaller as the train rolled down the rails to Freeport and on into the distant world. We were left standing in profound silence, sorry the show was over.

When Leroy and I were with our sisters, we stood back by the line of willows like good little boys. But when we were by ourselves we would stand closer and closer, and see how dizzy we could get, and we would sometimes stagger when the train went by. We were strictly forbidden to play on the railroad tracks, but who could help it? We had contests walking on the rails to see who could go the farthest without falling. We laid pennies on the rails, and then hunkered down in the tall grass and waited for the train so we could watch the wheels run over and flatten them.

Even more forbidden than playing on the railroad tracks was playing with the guns that hung in the tool shed. There they hung between the rafters as in a shrine: a .22 rifle, an old pump BB gun, and the mysterious *Schrotgevehr* (shotgun). We liked the shotgun best. It was a long-barreled 12-gauge single-shot. There was an alluring magic in the sleek, oily, silky steel of the barrel, that incredibly smooth feeling when you broke it open, and the musical "*clink*" as the ejector leaped from its seat. Right there on Dad's tool bench, within easy reach, were shotgun and rifle shells. But no BBs. Dad figured we would never fool with the rifle or shotgun, but thought we might try the BB gun, so there were no BBs around until we were old enough to know which end to point with. Sometimes when Dad went to town, we set up the stepladder and took down the guns just to feel them. And we took out one of those beautiful shotgun shells to wonder at the power within, but we didn't dare load up.

And so those guns just hung there. When we looked at them we wished Dad would take one down and shoot something. Other dads shot pigs and cows at butchering. They shot ducks and pheasants in their pastures. Or they went up north and shot a deer. Dad never did any of that stuff. We began to suspect Dad did not actually know how to use a gun. They were there just for looks.

Then one warm spring night, we were playing outside later than normal. Uncle Al had stopped in for supper and was still there. Uncle Al and Aunt Margaret always stopped in "for just a minute" right at meal time. They were "not really hungry," but since Mom insisted, they would "have a little something." Then Uncle Al would eat like a wolf, and Aunt Margaret (who once told me I would never amount to anything, which I resented at the time, but as I grew older, found she was right) would eat like a horse. She was wide as a barn door and could consume enough to keep two farmers at harvest time. After supper Al would settle in and tell lies for hours and bore everyone. Sometimes Dad fell asleep in the middle of one of his outrageous tales. We kids had gone outside to play tag and baseball and to fight over who was it, and who was out, and who was never being fair. We did not have any big fights on warm days, because all the windows on the house were open and if Dad heard loud yelling and wailing outside, he stepped out on the porch to ask, "*Seid ihr alle übergeschnappt?*"

That literally means, "Have you all gone crazy?" But really it meant, "What the hell's going on here? That's enough of this blankety-blank noise. I don't want to hear another peep out of you." It usually put an end to whatever game we were playing. Dad never actually said anything like "hell" or "damn," but we knew how to interpret his bland German so it meant that and more. The closest he ever came to cussing was the invocation of the name of Mr. Sam Hill.

"What the Sam Hill is this?" he would yell, scowling down when he caught us making a teepee in the barn with the pitchforks, or when we were sharpening a brick on his big grindstone wheel. I didn't know who Sam Hill was, but Leroy and I were both well acquainted with that name before we were six.

By the time Uncle Al and Aunt Margaret left that night, it was dark. The girls had gone inside long ago, because they didn't want to get bats caught in their hair. LeRoy and I didn't worry about bats because Dad cut our hair down to the skull. We were lying on the lawn counting stars. It was a peaceful night. The air smelled good. The lilacs were blooming down by the smokehouse.

Dad came out, not to yell, but to spit out his chew and to see if the new moon was visible in the west. We got up and headed for the house. We knew in a second Dad would tell us to get to bed. But Dad was standing very attentively with his head cocked to one side, listening to something far away. I could hear only the regular sounds of the night: a chorus of frogs from the pasture, the twitter of a sparrow not yet settled in the boxelder grove, the snort of an animal from the cow yard. Suddenly Dad turned on his heel and made a beeline for the tool shed.

"Get the flashlight," he said over his shoulder.

Something was up. We dashed inside, grabbed the flashlight out of the junk drawer, and caught Dad before he made it to the shed. He took the light and went in. Then, it happened. He reached up between those rafters, and down came that shotgun! We held our breaths. He broke it open and rested it over the crook of his left arm. His right hand went into the shell box on the bench, and out came two deadly, waxy-red and polished-brass jewels. He dropped one shell into his pocket and slipped the other one into the chamber of the gun. He snapped the gun shut with the relaxed speed and ease of a veteran, and out the shed he went, on a mission. We closed the door and ran after him.

"You kids get in the house," he said as we walked by the front steps.

There was iron in the voice, and we didn't ask why. We could hardly contain ourselves as we told Mom what was happening. Mom sat at the kitchen table with her darning basket, mending socks. She barely looked up over her glasses at us. She acted as if this was routine behavior for Dad. But we knew better. A momentous occasion was at hand. All of us (except Mom, who continued to darn socks and pretend all was normal) pressed our faces against the screen of the open window, trying to see out into the night and to hear a sound that might carry a clue to what was happening. At first we could see the bobbing of Dad's flashlight up by the chicken barn, but then everything was dark. And quiet. I could hear the clock tick on the kitchen shelf and the leopard frogs from the pond. There was starlight, but the yard was dark. All quiet.

When the shot came, we jumped. It thundered from the chicken barn and hurled itself against our window like a gust of wind. It rolled off across the fields and into the echoing darkness. Then silence again. Deafening silence. The darkness gave no hint of what was going on. The clock went right on ticking like before. Mom kept right on darning the darned socks.

"Mom, did you hear that!"

"I'm not deaf. I think they heard it in Albany," Mom said. She snipped off a thread with her scissors, turned the sock right-side out, and picked up another from the table.

In a minute we saw the bobbing flashlight again and heard the crunch of Dad's shoes on the gravel. He came in and set the shotgun in the corner. When he saw us all looking at it, he said sharply, "*Halt die Pratzen ab,*" which in translation means, "Keep your claws off," but which really meant, "Keep those grubby mitts of yours off, if you wish to see the light of day again."

Dad washed his hands and went into the kitchen.

"Well, did you get the bear?" Mom asked, bending further over a sock and chuckling to herself.

"Yeah, stinkbear," Dad said, and looked at her from the corner of his eye. "Where's Lawrence?"

"Already in bed," Mom said. "His asthma's acting up."

"He can bury it tomorrow," Dad said, and then, "You kids get to bed."

He got his paper and sat down in the rocker.

My sister Beats asked in a low voice, so as not to disturb Dad, "Mom, what's a stinkbear?"

"Oh," said Mom, "he's just trying to be funny. He meant *stinkkatze*—skunk."

Well, a skunk was a few notches down from a bear, but that made no difference to us. Dad had shot something. He went out into the night, stalked, aimed, and pulled the trigger—like a real hunter. We wished school were on so we could tell others. It would have to wait until fall. And we would have to wait until morning to see the dead skunk. We went upstairs, but we stayed at the top and leaned over the rail to listen, because Dad was talking to Mom about the shooting.

"You'd never believe it," he said, "I shot that thing right under the chicken roost. I thought for sure as I was pulling the trigger that the whole place would go up like a bomb, with chickens flying in all directions. They didn't move. They sat on that roost like statues. The only sound was one little '*kuk kuk kuk.*' Nothing more." There was a rustle of the paper, and then he added, "But it's gonna stink in there for a few days."

And stink it did. When Lawrence got the dead skunk out the next morning it was so bad it watered my eyes. And it smelled not only for a few days, but for a few weeks. At first, when we went into the barn to get the eggs, we sometimes had to run outside to take a breath. However, a chicken barn doesn't smell that great to start with. Leroy insisted Dad had actually improved the smell in there. Even after the skunk odor was gone, it would return, although fainter, whenever it rained or whenever there was a heavy fog outside. It was fainter, but strong enough to remind us of that night in June and the great hunt.

Chapter Six

WE HAD ALL those things to keep us entertained in summer. In winter we had snow and ice, and Christmas.

Because Dad believed in the old adage that an idle mind is the devil's workshop, he was obsessed with keeping us busy, and he usually succeeded in the summer. To him idleness was anything that did not involve manual labor. So in summer he had us perform entirely useless work like hoeing Canada thistle in the cornfields. No other farmer did this because everyone knew it did no good. The thistle just grew back, often splitting into two parts and putting out double the seed. But in winter, when the frozen ground kept us out of the fields, there was so little work that even Dad ran out of ideas. Then we could have snowball fights, we could make tunnels in the snow bank behind the granary and pretend we were Eskimos, and we could go down the hill on the sled and crash into the barn and go crying to Mom.

Around Thanksgiving, Mom would bring out the Sears catalogue and let us look at it and point at the toys we hoped the Christ Child would bring us for Christmas. She knew how to steer our little brains to the right toys (ones she would afford). We tried to be good in December so we would get presents, and Mom encouraged us to look forward to Christmas so we would behave. When the winter sun set red in the evening, Mom would say the red was from the glowing ovens of Santa Claus, who was baking cookies for Christmas.

We believed the Christ Child brought our Christmas presents, not Santa Claus. For us, the month of December was the time of the three great kid-characters: St. Nicholas, Santa Claus, and the Christ Child. St. Nicholas was a nice, white-bearded old man who went around in long robes, a bishop's hat, and carried a fancy walking stick. He brought us candy on the evening of the fifth of December, the eve of the Feast of St. Nicholas. We pestered Mom all day.

"Mom, do you think St. Nicholas will come tonight?"

"Well, if you behave yourself all day and don't make any noise to scare him off, he'll probably come," Mom would say. Mom knew how to take advantage of a situation like this.

After it was completely dark outside, and the family was settled in for the evening with Dad at his paper and Mom at her sewing, and us playing on the floor, we paused and looked at each other with every sound, real or imagined, from outside. If Sport made a noise, or the wind moaned in the oaks, we looked at Mom. But she kept on sewing. The evening dragged on, and right about the time we were beginning to get sleepy and had despaired of getting anything for that year, there would come a thunderous crashing at the door. St. Nicholas came on foot, as quiet as a cat in the snow. He put a brown paper bag full of nuts and candy in Sport's dog bowl right by the house. Then the old saint pounded the door with both fists and a boot so that it shook the house, and he ran off into the night so fast that by the time we got to the door and turned on the light, all we could see were his boot prints in the snow.

A little later that evening, when we were eating nuts and candy, Lawrence or Dorothy or Leona would come in from outside, where they had been "checking on a sick calf" in the barn, and they were surprised and disappointed that St. Nicholas had already been there, and they had missed it. They wondered how in the world the old guy could have come and gone without them seeing or hearing a thing. The grownups said the reason Sport never barked at St. Nicholas was because he recognized him from the year before.

Santa Claus was, for us, a completely different character. Around the first of December Dad read in the *Albany Enterprise* that Santa Claus was to appear on the main street in Albany. It was usually set for the first or second Saturday of December. Dad took us. Mom went along to town, but she didn't stay with us. She went Christmas shopping. She met us later at the car, where presents were concealed in the trunk. Santa and his helper came riding down the street on a hayrack pulled by a team of horses. The helper held the reins and Santa waved to everyone and let out puffs of steam as he ho, ho, hoed down Railroad Avenue. He was dressed in the standard suit of red, trimmed with white, as today. His horse-driving elf however, wore bib overalls, a hunting cap, and a worn plaid overcoat. They parked just off the avenue at the corner by the drug store. Santa had a big sack full of bundles of candy in brown paper bags tied with string. He threw the bags into the crowd, where the parents caught them and handed them to their children. Dad was a little shy about holding up his hand, but we pulled on his trouser leg until he had held up his hands and caught enough for each one. I don't remember ever believing Santa was real. His beard blew off to one side in the wind, so I could see his bare chin sticking out, and his pillows of "fat" were so lumpy a blind man could see with one eye it was phony. But it made no difference. Santa made us happy.

The only other time we saw Santa Claus was at the school play. The students put on a play every year at Christmas time and Santa would come in at the end and ask everyone if they had been good, and if they wanted some candy. That Santa was always the father or brother of one of the families and we could recognize the voice. We knew he was a phony, too.

I fervently believed in and loved the Christ Child who came to us on Christmas Eve. You had to believe. The adults made such a big thing of it. They brought a tree into the house the Sunday before. They trimmed it with colored lights, and it filled the house with the perfume of balsam. They put lights in the window of the kitchen so you could see them from the barn. The radio played special music heard only at Christmas time. On the eve of the big day we filled the wood box for Mom, threw down extra hay and silage for the cattle, and filled all the feeders in the chicken barn to the top. Mom and my sisters were getting everything ready in the kitchen. The atmosphere was absolutely electric. After the supper dishes were done, Mom and the older sisters reset the table like they would for a Sunday dinner, but this time they put a little slip of paper with our names on our plates. That way the Christ Child could pass out the presents without getting mixed up. The presents were never wrapped. Christmas paper was expensive. We went to bed early that night, because we had to get up for midnight Mass. We did not have to be told twice, because we knew if we weren't in bed early, the Christ Child would pass our house completely.

About an hour before midnight the adults would wake the little ones up and we ran downstairs and went to the table. The miracle had taken place. The table was loaded with the most wonderful presents a kid could imagine. Plates were stacked with socks and T-shirts, and they were new! Not hand-me-downs. Each kid had some little presents like whistles and marbles, and at least one big present like a truck or a doll. In the middle of the table were one or two big presents like a sled or wagon that was for all the kids. Everything shining, sparkling new. There was nothing patched up, rusty, or dirty. On the cupboard was a box with big, red polished apples from Washington and another with oranges from Florida. With all the stuff looking and smelling like new, it was the most beautiful sight in the world.

There was no time to enjoy it just then. "That's enough now," Mom would say. "You go upstairs and get ready. We have to go to church."

And after I stalled over my toys, Mom would say to my older sister, who was home for Christmas, "Hildy, take him upstairs and don't let him back down until he is ready for Mass."

While we were getting ready, Dad went out to the car shed and started the car to "warm it up." That was a joke. That old 1939 Chevrolet had a heater that sometimes put out a light sigh of tepid air, but nothing that could ever be described as warm. In the Christmas spirit, however, Dad started it ahead of time and even backed the car up near the house so Mom and my older sisters who were home for Christmas didn't have to walk down to the car shed. (We always called it a "car shed," never "garage.") We all piled in: a mass of winter coats, caps, earmuffs, and scarves, all ashiver with the cold, and all talking at once though chattering teeth. And Dad omitted yelling at us—at least some years. He spent the whole trip to Albany trying to clear a spot in front of him on the windshield to see at least his side of the road. And Mom was constantly wiping her side with a mitten to try to clear some of the frost and fog.

It was hard for a boy to leave that pile of treasure on the kitchen table, especially for church. But church was better at Christmas. The Benedictine nuns who lived in the convent right by the church put up dozens of Christmas trees and an enormous Bethlehem scene at the right sub-altar. There were Joseph and Mary, and the donkey they had brought with them to Bethlehem. There were shepherds, camels, and sheep all around, and at the center of all the Baby Jesus. The smell of balsam fir now prevailed in the church. Everyone came early so they could hear the choir sing Christmas songs before Mass started. By the time the bell rang and the entry procession started, a boy's mind was back home by the kitchen table playing with the new toys on the floor, and it stayed there during the entire Mass.

There was little of the normal socializing after Mass, only shouts of "Merry Christmas" as people hurried to their cars. When we got home, Mom got out of the car immediately and went to the house to start the Christmas Eve lunch. It was always pork sausage with bread and butter. Everyone was hungry, especially those who had gone to Communion. They had been fasting since six o'clock. Mom let us play with our toys for just a few minutes, and then we went back to bed and dreamed about the wonder of it all.

We got mostly the same toys neighboring children got at that time: erector sets, jigsaw puzzles, tinker toys. A new comic book was a grand prize, since all our old ones looked like bits of rags. For me, the most memorable was the year I got the toy pony. All the other kid's ponies I had seen were made of cloth, but mine had real hair and was just like Prince, only brown. Mom didn't let us sleep with our toys because the beds were already too crowded with kids, but I kept him right by my bed at night. During the day I dragged him around with me everywhere I went, out in the snow and into the barn. When summer came I played with him in the dirt and one night I left him outside. There the poor thing stood at midnight when it began to rain. I found him the next morning, fallen down and covered with splatters of mud. The mud came off easily enough, but the stuffing inside was soaked through and in a few days it got moldy. The smell was so bad that when I came around with my pony everyone yelled, "Get that thing out of here!" My sisters got to holding their noses, and Mom said I couldn't play with it in the house anymore. I had to put him in the milkhouse at night. Then Leona got the bright idea to douse him with perfume. The perfume changed the smell. I thought it was much better, but everyone else thought the combination of odors made it much worse. Mom took it and put it up in the rafters in the milkhouse until the smell abated. I could see him up there every day, but couldn't play with him.

As the summer wore on, I forgot about the pony. When I did think of him again one day, I couldn't find him. Years later, Mom told me that she burned the thing along with the trash when she thought I had finally forgotten.

When I started grade school and the other kids told me how the adults were fooling us at Christmas time, I refused to believe it. I was stubborn about it. My dad had no fooling in his heart, and he did not spend money on foolish things like toy ponies. We never got presents at any other time of the year. A birthday present was unheard of. And Mom had to pry money out of Dad with a crowbar for things like clothes and kitchen utensils. We had to beg Dad for a penny to buy a gumball, or for a nickel to buy an ice cream cone on Saturday after catechism. It was hard to believe a man like that would ever think of letting Mom spend money on anything as frivolous as a Christmas toy. So I clung to the belief it was not Mom and Dad but the Christ Child who brought my pony. The other kids laughed at me, but I refused to budge. Finally Mom sat me down and explained that whole Christmas thing. It was a shock. One could never trust adults in those days.

MY PARENTS COULD HAVE sent me to school when I was five, but thinking I might be a bit slow, they held me over until I was six. I had to learn English immediately. Mrs. Finken, the teacher, allowed not a word of German to be spoken on the playground. She wanted us to learn English and she wanted it spoken without a German accent. If I wanted something, I told Loretta and she relayed the request to the teacher. I learned fast, because often Loretta refused.

"Oh, you know how to say that," she would say. "Tell her yourself."

Then I would stand there with my toes curling in my shoes from embarrassment and stutter something I thought resembled a request for permission to go to the toilet. Mrs. Finken, whom I addressed only as "Teacher," would smile and tell me to say it again, only louder, and she would help me along until I got it right. I hated the English language, but I loved Teacher, and would have followed her into hell had she led the way. And she was right in her strict rules, or I would have been yelling, *"Rutsch, rutsch!"* instead of "Slide, slide!" when the play was close at second base.

It was a one-room school with all eight grades under one teacher. The desks were all wooden. The top was hinged so we could open them and put books and pencils inside. All the desks had inkwells in the upper right corner, but we did not use them. We wrote with pencils. All the children in that school were from the surrounding farms. In my grade were two girls and me. I wanted a boy in my grade, and I wish to apologize here and now to Jimmy Gill, who was one grade ahead of me. For a while I prayed every night that Jimmy would flunk a grade so he would be in the same grade as I was. He did. My prayer was answered. I had a buddy the rest of our grade-school days.

I loved Teacher in spite of the fact she was a constant source of torture and boredom on the sunny days in fall and spring. I did not like school in fall when the windows were open, and coming across the field was the up-and-down droning of a tractor. Someone was filling a silo. I could always tell because, as each bundle of corn went into the knives of the blower, the tractor motor opened its governor, leading to the constant up-and-down rhythm in the sound. I was missing that excitement. I felt like I was in jail. I felt the same way in spring. But I applied myself to the studies because I wanted to learn to read. I got good grades except in "conduct." Dad would look at the report card and frown.

"*Was ist den hier los?*" ("What's wrong here?") he would say, pointing at the grade in conduct. And I would have to try to explain the unexplainable. I couldn't use the excuse that Mrs. Finken was unfair. He would never buy it. Dad never noticed the good grades in reading, spelling, and arithmetic. Mom at least mentioned them when she told me I should improve my conduct.

"First grade students, wash your hands!"

That cry went out at noon every day from the back of the school room. The first-graders got up from their desks and filed to the back of the room and lined up by a sink in the corner. Two girls from the upper grades supervised the washing of the hands. One stood by a bucket of water with a cup and poured water on the hands over the sink. The other handed out a paper towel for drying.

"Second grade students, wash your hands!" came as soon as the first grade was done, and so on until the whole school was washed and ready for lunch.

"Teacher, Jimmy Gill won't wash his hands right," came a complaint from the back of the room one day.

"Why not?" asked Teacher, looking up from the table in front where she was teaching a reading class to the seventh-graders.

"He won't use soap," said the frustrated girl.

"Jimmy," said Teacher very kindly, "Why aren't you using soap today?"

Jimmy's neck was fire-engine red. He was looking at his shoes and mumbling to himself.

"He says it stinks like girls, and that boys don't use this kind of soap," said the girl, smiling broadly, obviously delighted with her report.

Now that's what I liked about Jimmy. Not only did he regularly skip school, he was the most stubborn donkey you ever saw, and he refused to let any girls push him around. He would never knuckle under, even when the battle was obviously hopeless. It happened that the girls had opened a new bar of soap just as Jimmy was up for his turn. Jimmy's nostrils, used to the milder aromas of chicken, horse, and cow, were offended by the heavy perfume he had detected before only on ladies at church. At home he used his mother's lye soap, which had a nice, friendly, lardy smell—not at all like perfume—and had the added advantage of curing ringworm, head lice, and bed bugs.

Teacher got up and led Jimmy's older brother, Tommy, to the sink.

"Now, Tommy," she said, "wash your hands so Jimmy knows it's okay to use soap."

After Tommy had put his stamp of approval on the soap, Jimmy washed, but he held his hands at a distance and grimaced as he rubbed, and he dried them ceremoniously with the paper towel like one wiping poison from his fingers. He made a face as he threw the towel in the waste basket.

Most of us had lunch boxes made of metal, rounded on top where the thermos bottle was stored. That bottle was an expensive luxury, and it was a day of woe when you fell with your lunch box, and upon rising could hear the rattle of glass inside. You didn't mind your bleeding hand and scraped knee nearly as much as that rattling sound. And when you opened the screw-top to check, sure enough the glass was shattered and Dad was going to kill you.

The first question at the court trial was always, "Were you running?" There was a cardinal rule: never run while carrying your lunch box. The answer to that question was always "no," unless there existed the possibility a little sister might be brought forth as a witness. We carried that thermos every day for a mile to and from school, over a minefield of plowed furrows and through barbed wire fences. And over one shoulder we carried a book bag Mom had sewn out of Dad's old denim overalls. That bag had a pencil case and the books we needed for homework. It was easy to hook the bag on a fence or to stumble over a rock or clod of plowed dirt, and down you went with lunch box and thermos.

On an old bookshelf in one corner of the schoolroom was a very small library of about two dozen books. Most of those books were old, worn, and boring. But I read one of those books over and over: *Valiant, Dog of the Timberline*, by Jack O'Brian. Teacher told me Jack O'Brian had written several other books about a dog named Silver Chief and I longed to go to the big library in St. Cloud to get more books, but that was out of the question. Dad would never drive all that way just for a book. Then a miracle happened: the adults invented the bookmobile. It was a big van with shelves lining the insides, loaded with hundreds of books from the Stearns County Library. In that one van they had ten times as many books as our little library at school. The van parked right by the school door and we were allowed to go inside and check out any two books. Not only that, but if they didn't have a book you wanted, the driver would make a note and bring it next time. The driver knew all about Jack O'Brian and he brought me *Silver Chief*, *The Return of Silver Chief*, and *Silver Chief to the Rescue*.

I read every dog story I could find. At home I listened to the radio when *Sergeant Preston of the Yukon* was on. Just before supper, if the weather was right, I could hear that program on KLTF out of Little Falls. It faded in and out, and sometimes I had to get down on all fours and put my ear by the speaker to get parts of the program. The story was just like *Silver Chief*, only the hero was Sergeant Preston of the Royal Canadian Mounted Police and his dog was Yukon King. Those two tracked down bad men in the Yukon wilderness during the days of the 1890s Gold Rush. I loved to hear the whining, barking and howling of that dog on the radio, and the cries of "Come on, King, Come on, you huskies!" from the sergeant. I wanted to be a Canadian Mountie when I grew up.

We said the Pledge of Allegiance every day at our school, and we said prayers. We all prayed but Marvin. He was the only non-Catholic. His father had come with him to school the first day and told him he was not to stand up and pray with the rest of us. Marvin could not even join in the Lord's Prayer because we did not add "for thine is the kingdom and the power and the glory forever" at the end, which made the prayer entirely too Catholic. And so little Marvin had the burden every day of declaring himself different. In the eyes of us Catholics he was also declaring himself bound for hell. I did not worry about Marvin, however. He was a very quiet boy who seemed to accept every inconvenience in life without a fuss. I thought he would probably tolerate hell in this same stoic manner. Besides, I knew he could always convert at the last minute before he died, and then go to heaven.

But I did give that matter a lot of thought in regard to Charlie Kelm, our trucker. He came to pick up our animals whenever we shipped to St. Paul for slaughter. He was a card-playing friend of Dad—and a Protestant!

I heard John Garding tell Dad, "You shouldn't ship your cows with Kelm."

"Why not?"

"There are plenty of Catholic truckers. Why not use Nentl or Bredick?"

"Charlie is a friend of mine," Dad said. "I trust him."

"You're committing a sin," John said. "He's going to hell, and if you don't be careful, you'll go with him."

Dad said nothing to that. For a while it bothered me every time Charlie Kelm came to get our animals. I thought Dad was committing a sin. But then I remembered Dad went to confession every few weeks, so he was safe unless he died right after shipping the hogs.

That summer we had to ship the mad bull Mom hated. That monster had gotten grumpy and mean as he aged. He developed a habit of lowering his head and pulling at the ground with one foreleg whenever he saw one of us near the cow yard. Sometimes he charged the fence and crashed his horns into the railings, and he would point his nose high in the air and let out an angry bellow that sounded like the train whistle. Dad liked the bull because he was so good at his business of breeding cows. That old veteran could detect, mount, and deposit in two minutes, and could repeat the performance over and over without tiring. Mom was afraid of the beast. She kept bugging Dad to "get rid of that animal before someone gets hurt." Finally Dad called Charlie Kelm. I was glad because I thought I might be able to go along to St. Paul. Each of us boys, when we were old enough, got to make one trip to South St. Paul with the trucker. Leroy had already had his turn a while back. Dad had said nothing to me, but still I hoped.

They put three ropes on the bull with Dad, Lawrence, and Charlie at the ends. One rope was through the ring in the bull's nose. They kept that rope snubbed to a post or to the truck until they finally got the bull into the loading chute and thought it was safe. They were wrong. The bull made a tremendous leap in an attempt to jump over the side rack. He failed to clear but broke the rack into a thousand pieces. He might have gotten away, but he ran between our two oak trees, and seeing Lawrence by the truck, he doubled back to charge him and so tied himself to the larger tree as he circled it. They finally got him loaded with the use of ropes, pitchforks, and cattle prods.

Charlie was getting ready to go. He already had his hand on the truck's door handle when he noticed me looking up at him. He guessed what I wanted.

He pointed at me. "I don't think I've ever taken that one along yet," he said.

Dad said, "No, you haven't, but I'm sure he'd like to go."

"Get in," said Charlie and he waved his arm.

"Have you got a minute?" Dad asked. "Mom would never let him go like that. Go put on your good overalls."

I ran. My turn had come.

All the way to St. Paul, Charlie talked and whistled and pointed out things as we drove along. He told me stories of other animals that had caused him trouble, and he asked my opinion about things as if I was a real adult.

"What do you think of those tall buildings?" he asked as we drove through St. Paul, and he laughed when I said they could keep a lot of cows in there.

When we got to the stockyards and got ready to unload, Charlie told the drovers in the pens that this bull was dangerous. They nodded sleepily as though they had heard it all before. Our bull marched down the chute and into the yard with his head up, looking around as though searching for a target. The drovers looked bored. Just another bull. Suddenly, without the slightest warning sign, the bull spun around and charged. He almost pinned one of the drovers against the fence. Only the man's lightning-fast fence-vaulting skill saved him. The bull crashed into the fence while the man was sailing over the top. The force of the crash shook the whole pen, and all drovers retired from the field.

"That's a big son of a bitch!" one of them said as they watched the bull from the safe side of the fence.

"Yeah, that's gonna make a lot of baloney!" Charlie said. The yard men laughed, but they were watching intently as the bull moved his head from side to side, daring someone to come near. The men got reinforcements, and soon the bull was going down the chutes to the slaughterhouse.

We ate that noon in a saloon by the stockyards. The place was filled with truckers and yardmen drinking beer and eating hot beef sandwiches. I tried to pay for my meal with the dollar Dad had given me, but Charlie wouldn't hear of it. He waved it aside and said I should buy my little sisters some candy.

I had the time of my life that day. That trucker became my new hero, replacing the Royal Canadian Mounted Police. When I was in bed that night, I thought about how he was supposed to be going to hell. For the first time I questioned my religion. There was no way I could believe this man—this cheerful, generous, honest, hard-working friend of my dad—would be sent to hell by a just, loving, and merciful God. There was no way out of it: on this one point, the priests and the nuns and the pope, and John Garding, were wrong.

Chapter Seven

BARELY HAD I SETTLED into my new life of learning to read and write at school when everything changed at home. Dad decided we needed a new house. When the warmer days of spring came that year, we began tearing the siding off the old log cabin. Dad was worried about having enough money, so we used every possible bit of the old house in building the new. We pried up the boards with great care, straightened the nails, and brushed off the rust. By mid-April, with all the siding off, the cabin looked like something Abe Lincoln might have lived in. It was the first time we actually saw the big logs with their notches and chinking. Log by log we disassembled that old cabin, and Dad sent the logs to the sawmill to make lumber for the new house. That house, which still stands a mile west of the KASM Albany radio station on the south side of I-94, has nails, floorboards, and two-by-fours that are almost one hundred and fifty years old.

As soon as the frost left the ground, the builders came. They dug a huge hole to make a basement for the new house. They put up the block walls and poured the cement floor. I was amazed at the luxury Dad was planning. The old basement had a dirt floor. The new cement floor was even as a skating pond and looked big enough to play baseball. The old basement walls were of large, uneven field stones and crumbling cement, which Dad was always patching. The new walls were of cinderblock, and straight as a gun barrel. An old carpenter from Albany named Grausam came with a crew, and they put up the first floor, which would also serve as a roof that summer. Mom and Dad and my sisters moved into that basement immediately and lived there while the house was built over their heads. We boys spent the summer in the car shed by the granary. It was like camping out. We swatted mosquitoes before we went to bed, and sometimes a mouse joined us in bed.

The overwhelming luxury of the new house did not become obvious until we lived there a while. The house had five bedrooms upstairs and a master bedroom for Mom and Dad on the main floor. We had a real toilet we could flush, like the ones they had at the Catholic school in Albany. And now we used real toilet paper. The plumber told Dad that, if we kept on using the *St. Cloud Times*, it would plug up the septic tank. We also had a big, deep bath tub. At first we could fill it to only four inches of water to bathe, because Dad was afraid of running the well dry, and often we bathed in water that someone else had already used. When we first moved into the new house, the boys had to use the outhouse. This had three advantages (in Dad's eyes): it reduced the amount of wasted water, reduced the number of fights about whose turn it was, and reduced Mom's work in cleaning the bathroom.

My sisters no longer carried drinking water from the milkhouse. We washed with clean well water from a faucet instead of rainwater from a rusty pump that drew from the dirty cistern in the cellar. To wash in hot water, we no longer got the kettle from the stove. All the sinks had two faucets, and we could get all the hot water we wanted from the one on the left, marked "H" for "hot."

In the winter we no longer piled snow against the outside walls of the house for insulation. The new house had insulation built right into its walls, and each room had a register that delivered heat from the basement furnace. In the old house, when someone was sick they slept on the davenport in the living room, where it was warm. I did time there for whooping cough, measles, and mumps. But now we could play hooky from school and stay upstairs in our own beds, where Dad didn't pass by every so often and look at us suspiciously.

There was only one thing I missed about the old house. On the hot days of July and August we used to eat our meals outside on the screen porch. I remembered those cool mornings fondly, when the fragrance of newly cut alfalfa was with us at the breakfast table, and we could eat our bacon listening to the meadowlark singing from a fencepost by the smokehouse.

When our new house was finished, because it was so big, some of the relatives gave Dad a ribbing about the integrity of its construction. Dad's brother John said the roof would cave in under the weight of the first winter snow. But we had lots of snow that next winter and the roof held up fine. And Grandpa said that any big windstorm would send that house into the pigpen. That theory was put to rest several summers later.

It must have been in mid-summer, because we were on our second cutting of alfalfa. It was very dry that year. On Sundays after Mass the priest led special prayers for rain. By mid-summer even non-believers were praying for rain. Farmers were saying the crops would be a disaster in only a few days. Many were ready to give up hope. But I knew it was going to rain real soon. I knew how to read the signs, though I was only ten. First of all, it had been windy the day before, and the oak trees had showed the silver side of their leaves. That meant rain. Lawrence had killed a snake in the cow yard, and Dad told him to hang it on the fence. That always brought rain. And later the same day, Grandpa stopped by, and he noticed the dog eating on the lawn.

He said, "*Es gibt Regen, der Hund frisst Gras.*" ("It's going to rain, the dog is eating grass.") Everyone knew dogs didn't eat grass except when they predicted rain. And that afternoon I heard a slough pumper from the pond, and it pumped three full choruses right in a row—that also meant rain. In the evening the sky had a heavy June haze, and the sun sent wide rays streaking straight down into the fields. When that happened, the farmers said, "*Die Sonne zieht Wasser*" ("the sun is pulling water"), and that meant it would rain for sure within a day. And the next morning at breakfast, Dad said Grandpa might be right about the rain, because the wind had switched to the east and the sky was very red that morning. There was no doubt in my mind: rain was on the way.

It did not look like rain. In fact, we were getting ready to haul hay. Lawrence and Leroy took the flat tire off the hayrack and pulled out the inner tube. They pumped air into it and pushed it down into the water of the stock tank and marked all the places where bubbles came out so Dad would know where to patch. Dad was down by the tool shed sharpening the mower sickle. Every once in a while he went into the alfalfa field to see if the hay was dry enough to bring into the hayloft. He told Mom to make the noon meal early and we would begin hauling right after we ate.

Lawrence and Leroy bolted their food, said their after-meal prayers silently, and left the table to harness the horses. By the time I came out they were already on their way to get the first load of hay, Leroy with the reins and Lawrence staggering around on the bouncing wagon bed to lay out the ropes of the bottom hay sling. Dad and I got our favorite hay forks and went into the loft to get ready. It was stifling hot up there with the sun beating on the dark shingle roof. Dad sent me up a ladder in the back of the barn to throw out the thick hay-rope, which was used to pull up the slings of hay.

When Leroy and Lawrence came from the field they parked the loaded wagon in front of the barn and hooked the team to that hay-rope. Lawrence hooked up the slings and the team pulled them up into the barn on a pulley attached to a carrier in the center of the barn roof. Each sling held a bundle of hay as big as a car. When the big bundle was in the right place, Dad yelled, "Whoa!" and Lawrence yanked the trip rope, dumping the hay in one big pile. Our job was to pull that hay to the side to make room for more.

There was not a breath of air that day. The hayloft felt like Mom's oven when she was baking bread. In between loads, Dad and I came down from the loft to get some air and to drink water. Dad's shirt was soaked through with sweat. Even the cuffs he had turned up were soaked. He sat in the shade by the milk house and sipped water from a fruit jar.

Every time we came down between loads, the first thing Dad did was look to the western sky. Soon I could see why. The low, puffy clouds were growing—and fast. There were at least three big thunderheads looming up far behind our neighbor's buildings and more grew farther back. Their sunny tops were rolling over and over like boiling oil, and they were tossing themselves higher into the sky. I saw Mom come out of the house, drying her hands on her apron and looking at the clouds. She went back in.

Dad said to me, "You better get the cows. We're milking early."

I got the cows, but I couldn't see the big deal. Everything was so quiet and peaceful. A catbird was meowing from the brush along the fence, and the barn swallows were all atwitter, swooping and diving among the cows to get the insects scared up out of the grass. Not even a little rumble came from those clouds, although now lightning flickered in them like flashbulbs going off behind a bedsheet. It all looked too far away to be a bother. We began the milking, and Mom and my sisters finished it. Dad and I went back into the loft when the next load came. Dad was in a big hurry. He had already told Lawrence this was the last load. When the last sling dumped, Dad said to just leave it, and we went outside. The air was still and heavy with humidity and, even though the thunderheads now blocked the sun, it was stifling hot. Lawrence was leaning out the half-door of the barn watching the clouds, and Leroy was letting the horses drink from the stock tank. I could smell their sweaty harness-leather in the still air. They were covered with sweat and they drank with noisy gulps. They kept lifting their dripping muzzles and pointing their ears to the west. Once Prince nickered like he was telling Pearl something. It was getting darker and darker, and now I could hear low grumblings among the clouds. There came a sudden electric feeling to the air.

Dad yelled at Lawrence to get the horses into the barn. He told Leroy to run and close the door on the machine shed, and shouted at me to close the doors on the pig barn and the chicken barn. I ran. It was getting darker all the time, and dad was scaring me. As I passed by the house, I calmed down. Except that the lights were on, all was normal there. I could smell fish frying, and I heard sizzling sounds coming through the window as Mom dropped the filets into hot butter. I could hear laughter and the clattering of dishes as my sisters set the table for supper. Julie was by the steps leaning against the corner of the house, standing on one skinny leg and scraping chicken shit from the bottom of her foot with a broken shingle. I told her she better get inside, but she stuck out her chin and gave me an angry frown to let me know I was not the boss. I think she was crabby because Dad had told her to get in the house, and then Mom had told her to get back out and clean her foot.

As I was going to close the chicken barn, I saw some of the chickens already sitting in the trees. It was so dark they thought night had come and they had gone to roost. I took the long chicken pole and began poking them down, sending them running and squawking to the barn. The wind had come up sharply and I was staggering around like a drunk.

Then Dad hollered at me from up by the house, "Let that go, get inside!"

Leroy and Lawrence were already going in. I dropped my pole and made for the house. I could see a solid curtain of rain coming fast across the wheat field.

As I went up the house steps, a gust of wind knocked me to my knees, and rain began to pour. Dad grabbed my collar, dragged me inside the house and slammed the door. I was already drenched in just those two seconds of rain.

Supper was ready, but no one sat down. Everyone was looking out at the ripping storm. The trees bent down at outrageous angles. The flashes of lightning were constant and everything outside was colored an electric silver. I saw our little red Radio Flyer wagon, made of heavy metal, go tumbling across the lawn like a dry leaf in autumn. Deafening crashes of thunder made the house tremble. The electricity went off. Mom lit a gas lamp. The rain came so heavy now I could see nothing in spite of the lightning. The wind threw waves of rain against the house so that the windows looked like a ship's portholes in a heavy sea.

Mom went into the bedroom and brought out a consecrated candle, blessed by the priest to save us in bad weather. She lit it and set it in the center of the table. There wasn't much talking. I think we were all a little scared, even though that new house did not creak and groan in the wind like our old one used to do. After a while the wind died, but rain continued, now pouring straight down. We ate supper by the light of the oil lamp and the candle.

The next morning dawned clear and calm, and looked normal. I opened a window. The air smelled wonderfully fresh and new. But the same old rooster was crowing from the same old fencepost by the feed-floor. As I put on my shoes I could hear the sparrows chittering through the open window. I thought the world had not changed at all—until I stepped outside. There were great lakes in the pastures and fields where there had never been even a pond before. Our outhouse lay on its side by the brooder house. The hayrack had been blown from in front of the barn and was backed against the side of the tool shed. Bits of leaves and whole branches of trees lay everywhere. The cows were standing up to their hocks in a lake that looked like thick coffee. One of our big spruce trees had folded in the middle, resting its pointed head on the ground. Several trees in the pasture were completely down.

There was not a whisper of wind. In the stillness I could hear sounds from miles away. Softly to the east sounded the "*dong, dong*" from the belfry of the Church of Seven Dolors. From the neighbor to the west, where the storm had stood only a few hours ago, someone was calling cows. We learned later that their cows had stampeded in the lightning storm and, breaking the fence, scattered all over the county. But our new house was still standing, solid as a church.

That storm brought one good result: Dad had to call on Uncle Leonard for help. Several patches of shingles had been ripped from the roof of the barn. Dad was scared of heights and so was Lawrence. But Uncle Leonard walked around up there like one on a Sunday stroll. Leonard was just back from the war in Korea, where he had been defending the thirty-eighth parallel. (That's all I knew about that war: "hold the thirty-eighth parallel," which I assumed was a barbed wire fence across the middle of Korea.)

Leonard was my hero. All my mom's brothers were. There was no place on earth I liked better than Grandpa Douvier's farm, where they all lived. It was boy-heaven. There were no girls. Grandma had died when Dickie was born and the sisters, like my mom, were married and gone, leaving a house full of men. Real men. Broad shouldered, burly, hairy beasts, who smoked, chewed tobacco, cursed freely, drank whisky, and laughed. Around Grandpa was always the aroma of sweet tobacco and of cigar smoke. As he talked, he sent streams of tobacco juice into the grass all around him.

When I think of Grandpa's house, I smell gas lamps, hear the ticking of the old clock, and see spittoons in every corner. The floor always needed scrubbing and there were always dishes in the sink. There were cards on the table, along with packs of cigarettes and cigar stubs. Guns, hunting knives, and plugs of tobacco lay all over. When I stayed there, I didn't have to sit up straight at the table or bother with how to hold a fork. If I spilled something, they didn't scold me, but laughed and clapped me on the back. They let their dogs come into the house, and Tibi, Grandpa's little dog, would dance for them on his hind legs.

They had a wonderful old car shed they used for a shop. The siding had once been red, but was now a weather-beaten grayish-pink. Inside was a long, cluttered workbench, which held the biggest vise I ever saw, and out front was an enormous anvil bolted to an oak stump. Leaning against the outside wall, half-hidden by the burdock and quack grass, were old tires, hubcaps, and barrel hoops. All summer long the big front door was open, and sometimes in the morning they would sic the dog in there to roust out a 'coon or two that had moved in during the night. In the winter they shut the big door and heated the shed with a wood stove made from a fifty-five-gallon drum. The stove had little holes rusted through the sides so I could see sparkles of the flame inside as it burned, and the holes allowed enough smoke to bypass the chimney pipe so that wisps of wood smoke always drifted among the ceiling joists. The place was fragrant with grease, oil, and welding smoke, and riotous with the thunder of hammers, chisels, and swearing.

They kept animals on their farm we never had at home. In addition to the horses, cows, chickens, and pigs kept by most dairy farmers in Stearns County, the Douvier boys had goats, sheep, turkeys, geese, and ducks. For a while they had a ram that would lower his head and charge every time he saw a human in the yard. Anywhere else that animal would have been tied, penned, or even shot, but they let him run free and laughed uproariously when someone got butted. They had a big gander that hated children and ran after us with a wide open beak, hissing and squawking with murder in his heart. They had a big white dog named Pal, who we could sic on the gander, and he would drive him under the corn crib. For a while they had a huge snapping turtle tethered to the gas pump with baling wire, tied to a bolt through the fringe of the shell. They fed the turtle pig slop and leftover pieces of meat, and one night they ate him for supper. Then they missed the turtle, because he used to have daily fights with the dogs. Their animals were a source of constant amusement for them.

Three of them had fought in World War II: Benny, Gregor, and Bill. Benny I never met. He had died in a hospital in England. His girlfriend wrote to Grandpa about how he died. He had gotten malaria and ran a very high fever. After the war the government offered to send Gregor's body back to Minnesota, but Grandpa said, "No. Let him rest in peace where they laid him." Benny still lies in a military cemetery somewhere in England.

Gregor fought in Europe and was promoted in the field to the rank of lieutenant, and later, to captain and then to major. Bill fought in the Pacific and carried scars for the rest of his life. Leonard was drafted later and was in heavy combat in Korea. Lawrence and Val were lucky. They served during peacetime.

Mom's brothers all swore fearfully, and this was another puzzle for a dumb kid. Everyone told me only bad men swore. My uncles were the best men I knew, but they tossed "damn" and "hell" into the conversation as easily as preachers tossed in "God" and "heaven." I put it down as another one of those mysteries that grown-ups knew about but could not explain to a kid, like the one about the three persons in one God and (one that bothered me even more) why a monkey would chase a weasel around a vinegar jug.

Mom's brothers were well-liked by the people in the area. They helped their neighbors whenever they were asked, and often when they weren't. They had done their duty for their country without complaint. One by one they had been drafted as they came of age, except for Dickie, who was crippled with polio, and John, who was allowed to stay and work the farm with Grandpa (in those days the government exempted one son, usually the youngest, from the draft). They were honest, hard-working, and they respected Grandpa. Even mothers with little children forgave the Douvier boys their bad example. Prim and proper old grandmas smiled indulgently when they got drunk on Saturday or swore on Sunday, or when they drove their cars recklessly.

"Boys will be boys," they said, "and they didn't have a mother to tell them what's right. Old Douvier has his hands full just keeping them out of jail."

Syl Scepaniak, the Albany cop, looked the other way when the Douvier boys came to town. Having a great fondness for drink himself, he often joined them in the saloon.

Dad's family was completely different. They took their lives and their religion seriously. They did not drink or swear or raise hell. Dad's brother, Joe, was a priest at Roscoe. He drove his car like a myopic old lady. When he visited our farm, we could hear the crunch of his slow-moving tires on the gravel for five minutes before he appeared from among the trees on the driveway. The dog didn't even bother to move out of his way. Mom could make supper while he decided where to park. He stepped out of his shiny car slowly, with great dignity, and shook hands with Dad, grave as an undertaker at a wake.

But my Uncle Bill, who passed by our farm every day, drove like a mad man. You could see the dust cloud boiling up from behind his rusty Ford from clear across the county. Everyone recognized that fast-moving cloud: "There goes that crazy Bill Douvier. One of these days he's going to kill himself." When Uncle Bill drove into our yard, there was a spray of gravel and a squawking of fleeing chickens. The heifers in the cow yard bolted with their tails in the air, and pigeons rose from the roof of the barn. The Ford skidded to a stop and Bill stepped out, grinning and exhaling thick cigarette smoke through his nose. Dad shook his head and muttered to himself while all his children rejoiced at the commotion.

Of all my uncles, I liked Uncle Leonard best. He was full of rowdiness. He said outrageous things. From the time I was a toddler, he offered me a chew whenever he took out his snuff box. He painted Dad's anvil bright red. When he was usher in Church on Sunday, he held the collection box in front of me until I donated. One Sunday morning when I had just spent a miserable two hours in church, I asked him if he liked going to Mass. He said, "The only part I don't like is that you can't scratch your ass. People are always watching."

When Uncle Leonard came to fix the barn roof that day after the storm, he brought Grandpa along. Dad and Grandpa and Leroy went fishing while Leonard patched the barn roof, and also put a new coat of red paint on the cupola. When he was finished, he came down the ladder and very carefully painted Dad's entire anvil a bright red. My little sister, Janie, stood watching.

Leonard looked at her and said, "Pretty, isn't it?"

She nodded her head slowly in agreement. Then she shook it sideways, "Papa isn't gonna like that," she said with a rising, warning voice.

Leonard said, "What! You think Henry won't like his nice, new anvil? Well, but you like it, don't you? That's good enough for me."

She shrugged, still shaking her head.

I knew darned well, and so did Leonard, that Henry would not like it. Henry would consider that a waste of good paint. Henry would say the painting of an anvil was nothing more than "Douvier *Dummheit*," and that it once again demonstrated that Mom's brothers were all a bit crazy. And that's exactly why Leonard enjoyed it so much.

A train came by, and the younger kids ran up to the railroad crossing to see what treasures it might be hauling. I stayed to watch Leonard (and to show I was too grown-up to run after a train). I asked if he had ever traveled on the train. He said he had, when the Army sent him to Korea. He had gone to Seattle on a troop train and then by ship to Korea. I told him I wished I could go on a train.

"Have patience," he said. "In a few years you'll be old enough to travel, and if there's a war, you'll travel a lot more than you want, and to places where you don't want to be."

I watched the train disappearing down the track to the west. I thought I would like to go anyplace with that train, even to war. I said to Leonard, "I wish I could go in the army and be on that train. I want to go fast and free and see new places."

Leonard snorted. "Free? You think being in the army is free? I wouldn't wish that kind of freedom on anyone."

I asked, "Where does it go after it gets to Freeport?"

He told me about the wonderful places I could see if I got on that train. He said it went through Melrose and Sauk Centre, and then he rattled off names of towns I never heard of. It went clear across North Dakota and into Montana, where you could see big herds of white-faced steers on the great prairies, and buffalo, and antelope. It went through Billings, and climbed up high into the Rocky Mountains and went over the great divide and by Glacier Park, where you could still ride a stagecoach and see real Blackfoot Indians. It went all the way into Seattle out on the coast of the great Pacific Ocean.

I longed to travel. I wanted adventure. I wanted to see all those new things. When I heard the train whistle I felt restless. There was nothing so lonesome in the night as that steam whistle, and nothing that made me want so to go where I'd never been before. Cars zipping along the highway made me want to travel. The sight of a neighbor's lights over the fields at night made me want to go somewhere—anywhere. When I saw a strange road, I always wondered where it went.

But there came along a big adventure about this time (thanks to Uncle Leonard) that I could easily have done without. I went with Grandpa to his farm one day in August to help with the grain harvest. Uncle Dickie and Grandpa did the cutting. Leonard and I did the shocking. The other boys were gone from home. When we drove into the field in Leonard's pickup, I found a beer-can opener on the floor. I had never seen one before.

"What's this?" I asked Leonard.

"Good Lord," he said, "Are you thirsty already? We haven't even started."

I said, "No, I'm not thirsty. I just want to know what it is."

"Church key," he said.

The beer Dad kept at home was always in bottles, but now a lot of beer was sold in cans. To drink from a can you needed a tool to rip a hole in the top. Those can openers were called "church keys." Leonard had several in his pickup: on the floor, on the dash, in the glove compartment. The same was true of most every pickup in Stearns County. You got a free church key when you bought canned beer at the liquor store.

Leonard and I shocked oats all that afternoon. As the sun was getting low and the shocks made long shadows on the stubble, we finished the last field. We had been drinking water out of a big thermos jug all day. In the late afternoon, Leonard asked me several times if I was getting thirsty. I thought it strange because the jug was not empty. After supper, Leonard drove me back home. To get to our farm from Grandpa's we had to go through Albany. The last light of the sun was dimming as we came into town. The road ran under the Great Northern Bridge, where we had to turn west to go out to our farm. Leonard turned east. He rolled along the main street and parked in front of the Dug Out Saloon.

"We'll have a short one," he said.

As he got out of his truck, I considered how we looked. His faded work clothes were shiny with dirt. Along the back of his shirt were white lines of salt where sweat had dried. His Caterpillar baseball cap was dusty and the bib drooped on one side under the weight of the grease and dirt. I was wearing patched overalls and a dirty shirt with a ripped sleeve. I knew what Mom would think if she saw me appearing in public in that condition. I mentioned this to Leonard.

He said, "We're not going to church."

He led the way down the stairs and into the bar, where there was a heavy smell of stale beer and cigar smoke. A dozen men were in the gloom, some standing by the bar, some sitting at tables. When we walked in, everyone looked up.

Shouts of "Hey, Douvier, hey, Leonard, over here, have a drink, come join us," came from every corner. I felt good to be with someone so popular. Leonard waved and grinned and nodded as he called out names.

"Benny, what's up? Charlie, how's it going? Well, look at this, even old Otto gets thirsty on a Friday. *Ach*, and Gunter, I guess they let anybody in here."

The bartender set a pint of beer in front of Leonard and asked me what I would have.

"Give him a beer," Leonard said.

"He looks a little young for that," the man said. "How about a grape pop?"

"Damn it," Leonard said, "If he can shock oats all day like a man, he can drink like a man. Give him a beer."

I would have preferred the grape pop. The bartender had hit on my favorite, but all the men at the bar agreed with Leonard and echoed, "Give him a beer." The bartender shrugged, pulled a pint, and slid it down the bar, where it stopped in front of me with the foam running down the side. Someone from down the bar yelled out, "Who's that with you, Leonard? Are you finally admitting you have a kid?" and they laughed.

"This?" said Leonard, not at all fazed. "This guy here?"

Everyone was looking at me. Leonard put his hand on my shoulder. He drew himself up and, emphasizing each word with a nod of his head, declared to the whole bar, "This is my nephew!" And then, as if no one believed him, he said even louder, "Yes, it is. This is my nephew!"

I would not have been prouder if President Eisenhower had just introduced me to the U.S. Congress. Leonard added, "He's come here to have a beer with his uncle." He pointed at himself. "That's me." He grinned broadly, and everyone laughed.

I had barely started my beer when another came sliding down the bar at me, and one for Leonard. "From Charlie," the bartender said, and Leonard raised his glass to Charlie and drank to his health with, *"Bester Gesundheit."*

Down went that beer and I realized that, while Leonard was ready for another, I was still on my first, and what's more, I felt near full.

"Drink up," Leonard said.

"Drink up," the men around me said, and they clapped me on the back.

The beers kept coming with alarming speed. I couldn't hold any more. When no one was looking, I poured some against the side of the bar, where it ran down into the carpet. I slyly pushed one in front of Leonard and he downed it without noticing. I was still behind. Everyone in the bar seemed concerned I was not getting my fair share of the beer, and they kept pushing more on me. I went to the bathroom and poured some into the urinal. When I told Leonard I had to get on home, he declared we were leaving immediately, and kept right on talking and drinking. I was getting dizzy, and my stomach felt bad. I felt like the beer might reverse itself and come out the wrong way. Every time I said we had to go, Leonard would say, "As soon as you finish your beer," and then someone would buy us another.

When Leonard dropped me off at home that night, the house was completely dark. I was glad Mom and Dad were in bed, because on the way home when I tried to talk to Leonard, I noticed my tongue was thick. And as I went in the house I walked funny and bumped into things. I crawled up the steps to keep from making noise. When I lay down on the bed, it seemed to tilt at different angles and revolve about the room like a merry-go-round—only it wasn't fun. I felt sick, I was scared, and I swore I would never drink again. I renewed that oath the next morning when I found I had a bad headache, a stomachache, and I felt weak like I had the flu. I dragged around all morning, and Leroy asked me if I was sick. I said yes and told him what happened.

He said, "Welcome to the club, all you have is a hangover."

I felt a lot better then. Only men had hangovers.

Chapter Eight

A VERY SCARY TIME came to Stearns County. I was in the fourth grade. Even going to school was scary. It was because of polio. One great advantage of growing up on a farm and going to a little country school was that we were sheltered from the troubles, fears, and cares of the world. The problems of the war, racism, poverty, and epidemic diseases passed us by. We never even heard about the Cold War duck-and-cover drills city kids practiced to prepare for an atomic bomb attack. Our parents didn't think it was worth scaring the kids about something so remote. Not one family in our school had a bomb shelter or a plan against an air raid.

Polio had been around for years. At school we had seen the evidence every day. Mildred Finken hobbled around painfully with a grotesque brace of iron and leather on her leg. But now it became an epidemic and reached into almost all the regions of the world. It came to Stearns County hard and fast that year. What scared me most was that I could see how worried Mom was. Her worst nightmare was that one of her children would get the disease. Mom's little brother limped from a bout with polio. Mom saw the pictures and stories in the *St. Cloud Times* every day and heard reports on WCCO about the spreading disease. My two youngest sisters, Delores and Eileen, were still babies. Mom hovered over them with a worried look. They called the disease "infantile paralysis" because people thought it was the littlest who were most at risk. Mom prayed desperately for a cure. That whole summer was filled with horror stories about polio as thousands and thousands of cases popped up all over the country.

The grown-ups knew polio paralyzed the muscles, but they had no idea what caused it or how it spread. Some parents kept their children out of school so they would not have contact with children who might be carriers. Sunday Mass attendance declined in spite of the mortal stain it put on the soul. The seats in the Alo movie theater in Albany were vacant. Since the disease flared up most in summer, parents thought the virus might be living in the lakes where children went to swim. The swimming beach on Middle Spunk Lake in Avon, which was crowded other summers, was now empty. Many thought mosquitoes and flies were carriers. In some towns, when there was a reported case, they doused the entire town with DDT. Around Albany some of the farmers shot all the pigeons on their farm. In one town they shot all the cats. Moms and dads who went to the St. Cloud Hospital to visit their stricken children had to wear masks over their faces and put on gloves. Some burned the clothes of their afflicted children to keep it from spreading. Fear flared in the faces of parents any time their child complained of a headache or nausea.

It was really scary to be a child then. We knew if you got polio, you might never run again—or even walk without those hideous braces. If it got way down deep into your insides, you couldn't breathe, and the doctor put you inside a metal tank they called an "iron lung." One look at a picture of a child jailed inside one of those iron lung things, and you were forever deathly afraid of polio.

Late that year came some headlines announcing a breakthrough. The papers said that if you gave your kid a Gamma Globulin shot, it would give "significant protection against the paralyzing effects of polio." Mom wanted to get us injected, but the GG shots were not available right away. During the coming months my mom kept praying and studying the paper for news about the shots.

I hated to get shots. I really hated them. I was as much afraid of the needle as of polio. A hypodermic needle those days looked as big as a cannon to me. They were not the dainty, superfine pins they have today. The approach of a doctor or nurse armed with one of those pipes caused any kid (and many an adult, too) to grow weak in the knees. I prayed the GG shots would never get to our town—but Mom prayed better. The GG shots came to Albany, and Mom made it clear we would get ours as soon as possible.

They took us to the high school in Albany, where we sat in a big room and waited. The nurses had hung up sheets to make little cubicles where the shots were administered. There was a gurney in each room, like in a hospital. Lord, I was scared. The amount of serum they shot into you depended on your weight. If you were a skinny little kid you got only a skinny little shot, and they put it in your arm. If you were a stout kid you got more, and you had to get on the gurney and take it in the butt. If you were a big, heavy kid, like me, they shot you twice, one on each side. The injection itself was painful enough, but when I got up from the gurney, I found I could barely walk I was in so much pain. It felt like they had stabbed me on each side with an icicle—and left it there. It was the worst pain I had suffered in my life. I tried not to cry, but I know Mom could see tears in my eyes when I came dragging out of that sheet-room. I stood with my parents waiting for the rest of the kids to get shot.

Mom kept combing my hair with her fingers and saying, "It's gonna be just fine. The pain won't last long. All will soon be okay again."

She was right. All would soon be okay. It would be okay because of that doctor of miracles, Saint Jonas Salk. Because of him I would never get another GG shot against polio. When the Salk vaccine came to Albany, I think it was the happiest day of Mom's life. She had no worry about the safety of the shot like some parents did. The fact that Salk had injected his own children was enough for her. America's children lined up all across the country, and Mom was pushing us to the front of the line. It was not a happy day for me. I saw the big needle coming again. Some of the kids thought that it might be an oral vaccine with no needles. I never held out hope for such a miracle. I knew that when adults said "immunization," they meant "needlelization." But even that miracle happened. Only a few years later when we got our booster vaccine, they just handed us a sugar cube to suck on. No needles! That was the happiest day for me. The polio scare was over.

WHEN YOU GROW UP on a farm, you want to be like an adult. You want to pitch grain bundles, milk cows, and haul hay. It never occurs to you that this is anything but entertainment. Even when you see Dad in his sweat-stained shirt wiping his dripping brow and leaning on his pitchfork for a brief rest, it doesn't occur to you. I did not want to be a baseball or football hero, I wanted to learn to milk a cow. But there were some jobs I hated, and the worst was butchering.

Butchering a few chickens on a Saturday afternoon for Sunday dinner was considered girls work, but the boys and Dad helped when there were more to butcher. When I was little, I wanted to help. First they wouldn't let me. The day they did was the day I learned to hate butchering. It was on a Saturday afternoon in the summer, and Mom was butchering a few roosters for Sunday dinner. Dad sharpened the hatchet for her. He put it in the vise and ran a file upward along the edge, testing it with his thumb until he was satisfied.

"Here, bring this to Mama," he told me, and he put it in my hands with the blade pointing away from my face. "Hold it like this," he said, and then he shouted after, "and don't run."

Trying to remember all the instructions, I carried the hatchet slow and solemn like an altar boy carries a lighted candle in church. I handed it to Mom down by the brooder house, where they had some roosters in a crate. Mom and my sisters had caught the roosters by hooking one leg with a long piece of wire that had been bent into a hook big enough to go around the leg but not big enough to allow the foot to slip through. Mom took the hatchet. One of my sisters held a rooster by wings and legs. She laid the chicken's neck on an oak stump, and Mom steadied it with her left hand and chopped off the head with her right, accurate as a lumberjack. My sister held the bird neck-first into a bucket, where it bled out. A dying chicken has remarkable strength, but I didn't know that. I pestered Mom to let me hold one. They kept telling me I wasn't old enough, but I kept begging. After a while they patiently showed me how to hold a chicken. The trick was to be able to hold both legs and the ends of both wings all together in one tight grip. The chicken couldn't move unless it got one of those members free. My rooster was very tame as I held it on the stump, but as soon as Mom chopped off the head, one wing got loose and then it was over. The strength of that bird I remember even now. It got away from me and there ensued one of the most horrible scenes of my childhood. There went the chicken hopping, flopping, and dancing crazily with feathers flying and blood spraying among my mother and sisters who were all scattering, yelling at me for being stupid. I dived after the bird but it dodged and weaved blindly. Even without a head it was smarter than I was. Finally I fell on the bird and right then it gave up the ghost. The chicken and I lay there covered with blood.

I never wanted to help butcher again. Butchering hogs was even worse. When we were really little, Mom sheltered us from hog butchering by keeping us in the house at play. Later we could watch from a distance. I hated even watching, because the hogs screamed so like humans. The first time I was forced to help, it was my job to stir the blood so it didn't coagulate. I had to stir and add salt for the first few minutes as the hog bled out. It was a cold morning in October, and the steam from the blood was rising and making little sunshiny wisps as it drifted upward to my face. Dad was next to me, wiping off his knife.

"Stir," he said, and he threw in a handful of salt.

The smell was not so bad, it was just that I could never separate that steaming smell from the screaming and the stabbing.

I said, "Aaach, I hate this."

Dad gave me a cold, narrow look with those flinty blue eyes of his. He said, "If you want to eat, you better learn to kill."

That sunk into me like lead, and I hated it more.

Then he added with less venom, "*So hat Der Herrgott es bestellt* (That's how God ordered it)."

That didn't make me feel any better. Why did God make me have to kill, and then make me hate it so?

"Stir," Dad said again, and added more salt. Then Dad did something I never forgot. He raised the hand with the butcher knife and licked the warm blood from the back of his hand.

When he saw me making a face, he said, "Good, but needs pepper and salt. Stir."

I stirred. Too slow and clots formed. Too fast and I swirled blood over the side, which was almost as bad as letting it clot. The killing was over, and that was the worst part for me. The rest was just hard, dirty work: dipping the hog, scraping off the hair, hanging it in the oak tree, gutting it, and finally cutting it into roasts and steaks. I hated the whole thing until the meat was sizzling in the pan. Finally, I had something to be happy about. I liked fresh pork liver the way Mom made it by dipping it in flour and frying it in butter and lard. And my mouth watered as I anticipated Mom's pig's-tail soup, which she made from the tail and the feet. That was my favorite soup, and to this day I prefer it to anything else on a cold day.

There was another kind of killing that broke my heart when I was little: the killing of baby cats. Dad limited the number of cats on the farm. A mother cat could have half a dozen at one birthing. Out of the litter, we had to kill all but the healthiest one. We usually kept a female. Only one male was needed. It was a hard thing to see a kitten killed, but it kept our cats healthy. If you've ever seen a farmyard where dozens of shrunken cats go staggering about vomiting all over the place, their dull coats caked with signs of diarrhea, slowly dying from distemper or some other feline ailment, you may understand why Dad killed kittens.

Our cats always appeared big and strong. I always thought our cats could beat up the neighbors' cats with no trouble, although our tomcat had scars that seemed to indicate otherwise. We had a big, old tomcat named Kater, which means "tomcat" in German. He was all covered with marks from fighting cats on neighboring farms. Most of his tail was gone. One eyelid drooped lifelessly at the corner. His ears were short from having been frozen several times in his younger years, when the sap of youth drove him into the bitter winter nights to roam the country for females in heat. The tops of those stubby ears were ragged with claw marks. He had a gash in one shoulder that Dad said likely came from trying to mate with a bobcat. He was the father of all the young cats on our farm, and on a good many of the surrounding farms.

Kater was not a friendly cat. He did not like being petted, but did not pass that trait on to his sons and daughters. They were all friendly. Of those, our favorite was Nigger. She was by far the best cat we ever owned. I did not know that the word "nigger" was disparaging until I left home to go to high school. Until that time I would have felt highly complimented, had anyone applied the term to me. That cat was a super acrobat. She was the only cat I ever saw that could catch adult house sparrows in mid-air. House sparrows were a pest on the farm. As a sparrow sailed by, that cat would crouch low and make a mighty leap. She would go tumbling through the air and land on her feet with the sparrow in her mouth. Then she would look around fiercely in every direction, as all predators do when they have just made a catch.

Leroy and I loved little kittens, so we sometimes tried to sabotage Dad's killing rule. Nigger was a vicious killer of sparrows, rats, and mice, but she was a tender mother with her kittens. One spring she had five little ones between two hay bales up in the loft. Leroy and I found them when we were throwing down hay. We thought it was a smart place to hide. Dad would never find them up there. We began petting the skinny, blind little bundles. We liked especially the black-and-white one. She was an exact copy of her mother. Lawrence warned us, "Don't get attached to those kittens. You know Dad. He'll want me to kill most of them." We begged him not to tell Dad, but Lawrence said Dad would know.

Every morning when Dad was done milking and was walking back to the milk cans with his milk stool in one hand and his milk bucket in the other, the cats ran alongside begging him for milk. While he poured his milk into the strainer, they circled and meowed. Some sat up on their hind legs and pawed the air. Dad would bend over and tip the last of his milk into their bowl. The cats all gathered 'round and lapped up the milk. This was, I thought, the only time Dad ever glanced at a cat. I never saw him pet one. But the very morning after we discovered the kittens in the loft, Dad already knew. When he came into the barn for milking, he grabbed his milk stool and bucket, and as he walked by Lawrence, told him to be sure to kill Nigger's kittens except the healthiest one. He also told him that the kittens were up in the hay loft. Leroy and I were astounded. How did Dad know she had kittens, and how in the world did he know where they were hiding?

Before breakfast, while Lawrence was slopping the pigs and Dad was already in the house, we went up into the loft and moved Nigger and her kittens to the very back of the hayloft, over the lean-to shed that housed the young stock and the bull. Lawrence rarely went back there because the roof was so low. Leroy and I threw down hay from that loft. We made her a nice nest in a corner, and petted her and the kittens until they were all settled in and nursing.

Lawrence would be looking for the kittens right after breakfast. He did not dare defy Dad, but there was no way he would find them back there. He would report to Dad that the kittens couldn't be found. After breakfast, Dad and Lawrence loaded the cream for dad's trip to town. When Dad opened the door of the car to get in, he reminded Lawrence about the cats. As soon as Dad left, Lawrence went to the hay barn ladder. He began his climb. He looked back and saw us staring after him.

"I'll leave the black-and-white one," he said, and disappeared into the loft.

Almost immediately we heard the *thump, thump,* four times as Lawrence hurled four little bodies against the loft wall. We looked at each other in horror. Nigger had moved them back!

WHEN A BOY GROWS UP on a farm he wants to do work like his big brothers. And then when he is obliged to do that work, all the charm and fascination drains out of it, and he wishes he were a kid again and could go play. My infatuation with adult work had a short life.

I always wanted to turn the crank on the cream separator. It made a little clinging sound like a bell when you turned too slowly. When you got it up to the proper speed and the sound turned to a *click*, it meant you could release the milk into the separator disks to spin out the cream. My older brothers would let me turn the crank until I was red in the face and puffing like a steam engine, and then they would elbow me aside and say, "You have to eat a lot more potatoes before you can do this job."

I liked to turn the crank on the cornsheller, too. It made the toothy plates inside the machine turn in opposite directions to shell the kernels from the cobs as they rolled between the plates. But when I turned the crank, the ears got stuck inside and my brothers had to turn on the big flywheel to get them through. They would push me away and say, "You better go help the girls do dishes."

When I was strong enough to do a good job on those same cranks, the jobs took on the unpleasant grind of donkeywork. It made my muscles ache and my mind go numb with boredom. And how foolishly I had envied older siblings the job of cleaning eggs! When I had to clean eggs, I realized it was nothing more than the stinking work of scrubbing off the straw and dirt that was pasted onto eggs with dried egg yolk and chicken shit. Those eggs had to be polished clean as fresh snow and then gently placed pointy-end down into the big egg cases. Dad took the eggs to town to sell to Mr. Jesh at his hatchery. You could blow an entire Saturday afternoon just to finish half an egg case. And there was no end to it. The chickens continued to lay day after day without mercy.

As soon as any work was required of me, it lost all its shine. What was amusement became drudgery. What was exciting became tedious. It took me very little time to hate milking cows. I used to think it would be great fun to get up early in the morning to help milk, but in a short time my brothers had to spur me out of bed with threats of bodily harm. Milking had to be done twice a day—day after day! We were up at five in the morning—every morning—just to milk those stupid cows. I began to bitterly resent cows. The young heifers tried to kick you. Even the contented old ones would sometimes lift up a hoof and nonchalantly set it down on your shoe and mash your toes to a pulp. And then, as you hammered her on the ribs with your fist to get her to move off, she would look around and stare with her big cow eyes and wonder what you were fussing about. I also began to notice for the first time that cows did not smell good, and pigs did not either. I became aware the hay we threw to the cows was dusty, that manure smelled like manure, and when you left the chicken barn, half the bedding was pasted to your feet.

As the drudgery of farm work became more apparent, the Great Northern Railroad kept calling to me that there were other things to do, other places to see. Every day now a fast passenger train with the name EMPIRE BUILDER written in big letters on its side came zipping through our farm with its flaming orange paint, black trim, and big, long windows. We could see people laughing and talking, drinking beer and smoking cigars as they smoothly sailed down the track to wonderful places I had never been. The trains were getting prettier all the time. More and more the grimy old steam-driven engine was being replaced by the sleek, streamlined diesel. The new trains were quieter, and the whistle was different, too—a sonorous, harmonica-sound rather than that piercing wail. Instead of a stream of black, heavy coal-smoke boiling from a tall stack, a mild blue haze with a pleasant aroma of diesel drifted from little black boxes on top of the engine.

Another thing added fuel to my restless fire. My oldest brother, Sylvester, came home from the Army on leave. He was stationed in Alaska! Like Uncle Leonard, he had ridden the train over those mountains, and had been to places I had only read about in the geography book at school. He had been on his way to Korea on a troop ship, too, but they changed his orders and made him a U.S. Army baker in Alaska. He had a big colorful map of the state, and he traced with his finger all the roads he had traveled. Sylvester could say the days of the week in Chinese and he would say, "*Como te llamas,*" to ask your name in Spanish. He looked so neat and clean and proud in his uniform. I wanted to be like him. I wanted to go to Alaska and do all the things he did.

I still liked the farm in the evening, though, when the chores were done and quiet had settled onto the place, when the shadows were long across the pastures and the lights were just coming on in the house, when the wind had calmed for the night and the birds flew to roost in the trees. Drowsy-eyed cows lay in the yard chewing their cuds, the horses stood nose-to-tail to take advantage of the mosquito-chasing swish of each others tails. It was the peaceful hour of the day. But then from far across the fields would come the faint lowing of a neighbor's cow or the whinny of a horse, and it made me feel lonesome again, all hollow inside, and it made me want . . . I knew not what. Just something else, somewhere else.

There were few options open to us. Our parents wanted their sons to grow up to be farmers and their daughters to marry farmers. Dad and Mom were not educated beyond grade school. They thought you had to be smart to go to college, and they weren't so sure about us. There were, of course, all kinds of options open to us, but we didn't know that. We could have been lawyers, but thought you had to be intelligent for that. We could have been doctors, but thought you had to have special hands. We could have been rock stars, but thought you had to have talent. Any of us could have been a surgeon, a baker, a politician, but we thought those professions beyond our reach.

One other path lay open to us besides farming: the religious life. That profession did not have the unreachable mystique of those other professions because Dad had a sister who was a nun and a brother who was a priest. My oldest sister, Pauline, was already a Franciscan nun at the convent in Little Falls. Mom once mentioned to me I might be a priest like Uncle Joe. I began to think about it, but I was not imagining a priest like my parents. They were thinking of a nice, quiet, country priest baptizing babies in a little farming community in Stearns County. I was thinking of a missionary priest deep in the jungle of the Belgium Congo where I would convert tattooed Bantu chieftains who wore bones in their noses and big plates in their lips. When the pope gave me some time off, I thought, I would paddle down the great Nile and visit the tombs of pharaohs inside the pyramids. I would ride camels over the Sahara Desert and see mirages and visit an oasis.

Much of the farm work was actually getting easier, but that counted for nothing with me now. Dad was modernizing (at least by his standards). We still shocked our grain instead of combining, and we still hauled most of our hay in slings instead of bales. We had no milk machine yet, or barn cleaner. We made our wood with crosscut, ax, and maul. But Dad had put electric motors on the cream separator and cornsheller, and he was letting us use the tractor more, which he did not like to do. It sucked up expensive gas. The cost of gas was sometimes as high as twenty cents a gallon. But the horses were getting old and a new team would cost money, too.

I had it in my head that any place was better than a farm. I wanted to get away to the bright lights of the big city or to the jungles of Africa. Mom and Dad were not getting along like they used to. At night when we were in bed they seldom talked to each other. The soft tones of their talk coming from below, which had lulled me to sleep so often during my childhood, were gone now. When they did talk it was likely to end in the raised voices of argument, and there was no lullaby in that. Sometimes when they had a spat during the day, I saw Mom crying.

Those arguments ripped a hole in the fabric of my childhood, much like the new highway ripped a hole in our farm. What is now Interstate 94 steamrolled over our farm and flattened our ancient woods, our orchard, and the tall spruce trees that, for decades, guarded our home against the bitter winds of winter. The farm seemed cruel and hard now. Cruel in all that butchering, cruel in the killing of the kittens, cruel in the trapping of innocent gophers in the grain fields.

Cruel, like when old Prince lay out in the pasture and could not get up anymore. We tried to help him that afternoon, but it was no use. He lay in the hot sunshine and couldn't even move himself to the shade. His old bones and muscles had given up. Dad said he might be better next day. But next morning that greasy man from the dead animal service came out with his stinking truck. We went to the pasture where Prince lay on the wet grass, barely breathing, his bewildered eye reflecting the clouds in the sky. I liked that old horse, even though at any time a slash of his big hoof could have sent my soul into eternity. I liked to hear the clomp of his big hooves on the railroad-tie floor of the barn, and the hollow crunch he made when he was chewing his alfalfa. I had often stroked the velvety softness of his nose and listened to the rush of his breath. Now, there he lay, with the dew on his mane and with droplets of water on the dandelions Dorothy had braided onto the temple ring of his halter. And there he died when that dead-animal ogre shot him, and then dragged him onto his filthy truck with his blood-fouled winch.

That horse gave us his all. How he would lean into his collar with all his might!—and push and strain until every muscle rippled under his shiny coat, and how he kept at it until his body trembled with fatigue. Now he was trash.

I was tired of it all and wanted out. This was no longer home to me. So when Dad asked me, during my last year of grade school, if I wanted to go away to school and study to be a priest, I jumped on it with both feet. Yes. I promised I would work hard. Yes, I wanted to be a priest.

"You won't have to butcher pigs that way," he said with a half-smile.

To start the process, I had to have an interview with the pastor in Albany. His name was Father Odilo (with the accent on the first syllable), but he was better known among the parishioners as "Father Oh-so-slow," because he had a habit of drawling out his words as he read the Mass. Father Odilo warned me about all the hard work of studying at school. He said that to be a priest I would first have to become an educated man. I would spend the next twelve years in school and would have to have degrees in philosophy and theology before I could be ordained. This was all Greek to me. I had not the slightest idea what philosophy or theology meant or what a degree was. I just sat there and nodded. I was greatly relieved he never asked me why I wanted to be a priest. I did not want to let him know it was to get out of farm work.

The Stearns County farmer valued the priest above even the veterinarian. A man could be an idiot, a fool, or a staggering sot, but if he wore the Roman collar he was esteemed above the doctor and the banker. I felt guilty about wanting to be a priest so I could get out of the drudgery of farm labor. One Saturday as I was walking out of catechism class, Father Landelin clapped a hand on my shoulder.

"I hear you're going to be a priest!" he said with great enthusiasm.

I liked Father Landelin. He was the young assistant at Seven Dolors and was always cheerful and smiling, not grumpy and frowning like the old pastor. Suddenly I couldn't stand the guilt, and I confessed the whole thing about my tainted motivation to go to the seminary.

He just laughed the whole thing off. "Oh, that's fine," he said. "That's how God calls you. He isn't going to appear before you in a blazing vision and tell you you are chosen. Your parents are willing to send you, and you'd rather study to be a priest than milk cows. That's the Lord calling. Don't worry about such things." He gave my shoulder a squeeze and added, "Just promise God you'll do your best to answer the call."

That night in my evening prayers I did, and I felt better. I dreamed even more of missionaries and Africa, and of traveling on trains and ships. I was ready to leave home on a great adventure. It was the end of my childhood.

Part II

Chapter Nine

ON THE SOUTHERN SHORE of Lake Onamia, just to the south of the great Mille Lacs Lake of Minnesota, there was an academy for boys who were being groomed for the priesthood. Gnarled old Dutchmen ran the place. They spoke with thick Dutch accents and wore medieval robes of black and white, and the Roman collar. These were the "Canons Regular of the Order of the Holy Cross," an ancient order of Catholic priests and brothers. They were widely known as "The Crosiers," and their academy as "Crosier Seminary." They came to Minnesota in 1910, along with several dozen Catholic Dutch immigrants. Strange Dutch names appeared among their ranks, like Van den Bosch, Van Zutphen, de Venster, and van Hees.

Only a boy raised on an isolated little farm, in a religious family, and schooled in a small country school can imagine the awe with which I entered the sacred walls of their institution. These men were not just priests, but special priests, who had given up the whole world to live in a community of contemplative monks. On the breasts of their scapulars they wore the distinctive mark of the Crosiers: a Maltese cross, with the horizontal arm being white and the vertical arm a blood red. In their little chapel of St. Odilia, they chanted their prayers in Latin. They sang their canticles and hymns in the archaic strains and mysterious rhythms of Gregorian chant. They carried thick breviaries with them and daily muttered the long prayers of the Divine Office. Every day they gathered in the chapel for prayer sessions which they called Matins, Vespers, and Compline. They did not confine themselves completely to the contemplative life, however. Some of them had parishes, and most of them helped secular priests on weekends; some gave spiritual retreats for clergy and laity, and taught in the classrooms of their academy. But when they were home, they kept the monastic life.

I started high school there in the fall of 1956. I had never seen anything like this. The whole place and all the people were strange and exotic. The buildings were of red brick and tall as churches. There were little steeples and spires with crosses at the corners, and from the main steeple over the chapel, Westminster chimes sounded the quarter-hours. There I was, suddenly thrown in with boys from New York, Chicago, and Detroit; some from New Mexico, Kentucky, and North Dakota. Boisterous, self-confident boys, mostly from families far wealthier than mine; many had traveled in big cities and in foreign countries. There were a few kids at the school from small farms, but most of them had gone to parochial school in their hometowns and had been around city kids and learned their ways. Few students were as timid and silent as I was.

They were so much smarter! They had seen the Grand Canyon and Yellowstone Park, had been to operas and plays in fancy theaters, and had seen the tallest skyscrapers in big cities. They had ridden in trains and airplanes. Some of them had taken dancing and music lessons. And they were so skillful. Some played saxophone and trumpet. Some played the drums! I was jealous. I did not consider that, while I was fishing and watching herons hunting frogs, they were sitting at a piano going through long, boring drills.

There was a universe of difference between us. They could throw a baseball a mile, make a football spin like a rifle bullet, and throw a basketball through a hoop no bigger than a milk bucket. They could dribble that basketball down the court while running alongside at full speed. I got confused when I attempted to dribble the ball standing in one spot. Even the skinny runts among them were skilled from years of playing baseball, football, and basketball in city lots.

They all wore shorts when they played sports. I didn't have shorts, and later when I did get a pair, I felt naked wearing them. I had never heard of a jockstrap. It seemed an obscene garment to me. I was embarrassed to be seen in one, but others routinely strolled around the dorm with nothing on but a jockstrap and socks. Their clothes fit better and they always knew what to wear. They knew the names of movie stars and the words to the latest songs. I didn't know who Elvis Presley or Johnny Cash were. I had never eaten a White Castle hamburger. I didn't know what a Dairy Queen or a McDonald's was.

They seemed very sophisticated, and they looked down their noses at country bumpkins. I was a clumsy bundle of muscle from years of pitching hay and manure, shocking corn, and milking cows. When I played football or baseball with them, I felt awkward and stupid. I thought I had no skills at all. It never dawned on me that I had experiences and abilities they had never even thought of. Did they know what to do if a sow couldn't deliver? Did they know what mastitis was—or what to do about it? Would they be able to help a birthing cow with a wrong presentation? Some of them, if asked to feed a calf, would not have known at which end to present the pail. I could set up a grain shock that would stand in a forty-mile-an-hour wind. I could back a wagon with a tractor up a winding driveway. But those skills did not matter. Farm skills were worthless—a source of amusement. At Crosier Academy the biggest insult you could dish out was "stupid farmer."

"You stupid farmer, can't you get anything right?"

"Hey, plow boy, you can stop running now, that was a foul ball."

"Hey, hayseed, purple doesn't go with green."

What mattered was how cool you were. I didn't even know what cool meant. To me a cool cat was Kater on a frosty night. To them a cool cat was an aloof boy with a turned-up collar and a ducktail, one who knew what was going on—not like me, in other words. But I liked it when they told me about the places they had been and the things they had done. And I liked the neat way they had of saying things, using phrases I had never heard before.

"No sweat," meant it was easy.

"Don't sweat the small stuff," meant "Don't worry about it."

"Wise up, clown," meant "Don't do that again."

"Not bad for a harelip," meant you had made a nice play.

"Big hairy deal," meant you were talking about something boring or making a mountain out of a molehill.

"Hang it up," meant quit.

I was always having to ask what these things meant. I could figure out some of the meanings, like "funny as a rubber crutch," or "you're up shit crick without a paddle." But the sayings that came from watching TV and listening to popular music left me mystified, like "no comments from the peanut gallery." I didn't know what a peanut gallery was. I had never heard of Buffalo Bob, whose TV show had a "peanut gallery," and who had a puppet named Howdy Doody. When they said, "see you later, alligator," I thought they had made up something clever. I didn't know it came from a popular song.

They played mean jokes on each other, jokes I had not seen before. They entertained themselves by setting tacks on the chairs of other students, and they considered it a great triumph and huge amusement when someone sat down on one. The more experienced student, who had been around this tack-setting trick for years, had long ago developed the habit of tipping his chair forward before sitting. Any tack fell harmlessly to the floor. That evasion was at times overcome by the use of scotch tape. Other veterans never sat down before carefully examining the area, so that even the scotch tape ploy did not work on them. For those excessively cautious ones, they had developed the use of the ruler. The tack was Scotch-taped to the end of a ruler, and after the cautious boy had looked over his chair and was sitting down, just as the cautious buttocks were about to contact the chair, the ruler with the tack was inserted into the gap by the boy sitting behind the victim. The victim would leap into the air with a squeak and would look angrily at the boy behind him, who sat twiddling his thumbs and smiling while staring at the ceiling. The ruler had already been passed off three or four times so by then a boy in the back row had it under his desk.

They would slap each other on the back like they were good buddies, but were really pasting a sign that said, "Kick me." I had never heard of short-sheeting a bed, but these boys were all skilled at it and practiced on each other, and had a good laugh. I have to admit, I thought it was a fine trick, but was not amused when it was played on me.

One day I made a stupid play on the ball diamond. One of the players yelled, "Hey, dummy, why didn't you throw to first?"

Another player, a boy from Chicago, said, "He's a farmer from Albany—Stearns County Syndrome."

The first player asked, "What's does that mean?"

The Chicago kid said, "It means his dad and mom are cousins, maybe even siblings, and they put beer in his baby bottle instead of milk."

I held a grudge against that kid forever.

They called each other names like "turd face" and "zit face," but weren't bothered by name-calling. Insults did not bother them. I was hurt when they used those names on me. I wanted desperately to fit in, but I didn't want to set tacks or call others names. More than anything, I wanted my fellow students to like me. I was like a love-starved child. I tried to make friends even with boys I found repulsive. I was so desperate to be liked I would do just about anything to ingratiate myself, especially with the upper-classmen or the monks. If someone was washing a car or planting a tree, I would help without being invited. If someone was sweeping the sidewalk or scrubbing the lobby floor, I would pitch in. The other boys formed little gangs of friends, little cliques, but I didn't seem to fit in any of them. It was a good thing there was not a clique of drug users, bank robbers, or friendly ax-murderers at the school. I would happily have joined any group, no matter how disgraceful or villainous.

At first the academic work at Crosier was the worst kind of mind-torture. I sometimes couldn't figure out what the homework instructions meant, and had to ask other students. For the first time in my life, I handed in assignments that were not complete. In a short time, it was obvious I was behind in my classes, especially in Latin. Father Delmar Hesch called me into his office. He asked me a hundred questions about grade school, my family, and all kinds of questions about English and Latin. When we were done, he told me I would be taking some remedial classes in the afternoons when the others were at recess. He said my problem came from the fact that I did not know the names of the English words, and I didn't know the parts of a sentence.

"If you don't know what a noun, adjective, or verb is in English, how can you learn Latin?" he asked. "You have to know the meaning of prepositional phrase and subordinate clause as clearly as you know the meaning of finger and hand."

He must have noticed how dejected I was as I left his office, because he called me back and told me not to worry. He said this was not happening to me because I was stupid, but because my grade school training was a little weak in that area.

"You'll be caught up in no time," he said.

I asked him if any of the other boys would be joining me in the remedial classes. He said no. He immediately knew what I was driving at. Some of the other boys had grades worse than mine.

"Their problems are not like yours," he said. "Don't concern yourself with anyone's grades but your own."

Again he must have noticed my dejection at the mention of my grades, because he added, "In fact, don't even worry about your own grades. Just do the best you can. It will all work out. You'll see."

The remedial classes lasted only two weeks, and I really did not hate them much. They were kept short. I got to know two college students who tutored me, and I got to know Father Hesch. I liked him as much as I liked my grade school teacher. He was the youngest member of the Crosier faculty and looked even younger than he was. He was short, had a boyish look, and wore glasses. He looked like a bright little boy who was pretending to be a college professor. I thought he was the smartest one on the faculty. He was our English teacher, and he sensed how embarrassed I was in English class when I didn't know the answers. While I was catching up, he didn't call on me unless he was sure I knew the answer. I knew he was doing this, and I was deeply grateful.

AFTER A FEW WEEKS at Crosier I was griped by a wretched homesickness. As we drove up to Crosier in early September, Dad had warned me about "*heimweh*," but in my excitement, I didn't believe him. Nothing could be sillier than me missing the farm after having ached so to leave it. But now the homesickness struck me like a horrible flu. I dragged it around like an anvil by day. It lay on my chest like a stone at night. I missed the old barn. I wanted to bury my head in the warm side of a cow and pull the milk from her udder. I wanted to hear the ring of the empty bucket as Mom took the first few strokes from her cow at six o'clock in the morning. I thought it would be grand again to hear the *click, click* of the separator as it spun the cream from the milk. I missed everything. The smell of the silage and the hay, even the manure. I found myself longing to engage in the very pursuits that only a few weeks before I had despised with all my heart. I wanted to be home to help pick the potatoes, husk corn, and fill the silo.

On Saturday afternoon I daydreamed of Mom's kitchen, with the smell of cinnamon and baking bread. I sat at my desk during the long study hours and stared listlessly at my books while I pictured the chickens scratching in the yard and the cows coming home to drink at the stock tank. If I forgot my pain for a moment, it was brought back to me afresh by any familiar sound. The barking of a dog or the song of a bird gave me a stab of homesickness. When Father de Venster came down the study-hall aisle rattling his big ring of keys, it reminded me of the rattle of trace chains as the horses pulled the hay wagon. By coincidence, the Soo Line railroad track ran near the Crosier buildings at the same distance that the Great Northern ran by our house back home. If I woke up in the night and heard the wail of that train, I turned over in my bed and cried.

But never for even a second did I consider calling my parents. I knew what my job was: study to be a priest. I had promised God. I had promised Dad! I had seen how Dad kept on working at a job in spite of heat or cold, in spite of pain from blisters or cuts. I had seen how Mom did her job no matter how sick she was, no matter how hard it was. I was their son. I had a commitment, and I would stay with it. As the weeks dragged by my sickness got better.

ONE AFTERNOON SHORTLY after my arrival at Crosier, all the freshmen were called down to the music room to try out for the boy's choir. I had never imagined myself singing in a choir. I did not want to try out, but they gave us no choice in the matter. One of those old Dutchmen, Father Van den Bosch, was sitting at the piano in front of the room. Van den Bosch pointed at the first student sitting in the front row.

"What's your name?"

"James Baron."

"Well, Mister James," said Father Bosch, stroking a few keys. "Run up and down the scale for me, please."

I was amazed at the gibberish that came out of the mouth of James Baron: "Do, re, mi, fa, sol, la, ti, do. Do, ti, la, sol, fa, mi, re, do."

Father Bosch, a mousey little guy with very short white hair, smiled broadly and said, "Very good, James."

Must be Latin, I thought. That James was an extraordinarily bright boy. He always knew the correct answers in class. But to my great discomfort, when Bosch pointed to the second boy, he merrily sang the same song, and so did the third. With no hesitation, one after another, the boys sang the same thing. Suddenly it occurred to me that when the finger came to me, I would be expected to sing. The finger was advancing steadily. One boy named Hoolihan sang with a loud voice that filled the room. He held the "doooo" at the top for several seconds and put a little tremolo into his voice before making a magnificent descent to the lower "doooo." It was beautiful. I tried feverishly to pick up the words. *Do, re, ti. No. Do, re, mi, la, ti.* The finger kept advancing. The room was suddenly stifling hot. I wished I were sitting in the back row so I would have more time. I thought I pretty well had it down when the finger got to me. I knew enough to fake it. I took a deep breath. Suddenly I couldn't remember if it began with re, or ti, or do. Oh, yes, it was do.

"Dooo," I began, "re, mi, la, la," I panicked. Was it re, or la? I couldn't remember anything. Now I didn't even think my starting "do" had been right.

"I—I don't know that s-song," I finally blurted in total defeat.

There was a roar of laughter that filled the room. I blushed like a hot beet. I think even my hair turned red. Bosch held up his hand.

"That's okay," he said kindly. "We don't have to have any particular song. Here, I bet you can sing this," and he began to sing while picking the notes on the piano, "Are you sleeping, are you sleeping, Brother John, Brother John."

I was enormously relieved. That song was easy. In grade school Mrs. Finken had often had us sing that song as a round. So I sang. Bosch sang along on the first few words. My face was burning red, my voice timid and broken, but I made it through all the way to the "ding, ding, dong" at the end.

Father Bosch nodded, "Very good," he said, but I knew he was just feeling sorry for me. I wished I could crawl in a hole. To make things worse, as we left the classroom, boys were laughing and slapping me on the back.

The next day, the PA system announced that the list of the boys in the choir was posted on the bulletin board and the choir would meet at 5:00 p.m. I didn't check the board until another student yelled at me, "Hey, Bloch, did you see that you're in the freshman choir?" I figured he was joking, but when I went to check, there it was! The second name on the list after James Baron: Donald Bloch. I was amazed. And I was just as amazed that Hoolihan with the tremolo voice was not on the list.

EVENTUALLY, AS I MADE friends, I came to realize the other students were not that much different from me. They had similar fears and desires. I soon caught up in my studies and began to learn some of their athletic skills. As I stopped feeling sorry for myself, the homesickness melted away. But little patches always remained like snow in a cold springtime, and I never felt completely at home at Crosier. I never felt free. When I graduated years later, I was not sorry to leave even though I thought I might never see some of my buddies again.

The best buddy I had at Crosier was a boy in my class named Fleischhacker, who came from a background similar to mine. He was from St. Martin, a small town not far from Albany. He was from a large family and was raised on a dairy farm. He was the one boy who could talk German, liked to play cards, and knew how to play Solo, Skat, and Schafskopf, the games farmers played back home. He had connections at Crosier. He was related to Brother Roman, who lived in the monastery.

There was a student from Saint Cloud named Ahearn who I found most entertaining. He knew everything about baseball. He could recite the names and positions of all the players. He knew Mickey Mantle's batting average. He knew Casey Stengel was insane and should be locked up. He knew why Whitey Ford was in a slump. He looked as innocent as my little brother, but he was always up to something. He often sat next to me in chapel, where he was a bundle of restless irreverence. He constantly inserted the wrong words into the prayers and the hymns. He would sing "*Tantum ergo*, make my hair grow," or "Hark, the hairy old angels sing," with eyes raised to heaven, an angelic face of blessed rapture. He knew just how loud to sing so those around him could plainly hear his words, but so the monks in their pews up by the altar could not. He sang with such daring, and prayed with such zeal, that it made it all the more funny. He liked sitting next to me because he knew he could make me laugh. Most of the city kids were immune to his clowning. They had heard it all before. But it sent me into spasms of snickering, and I received many a dark look from the stalls of the holy monks. They noticed my ungodly behavior, and at the same time couldn't help noting the contrasting saintly demeanor of that nice Ahearn boy. Right at the Consecration he would whisper that Father McNiff (the rector of the school) had a big booger hanging from his nose. He would often note gravy or tobacco stains on the celebrant's vestments, or would speculate that the abbey prior had a hangover again this morning.

Among the students at Crosier were many strange characters in whom I took great delight. Many of them became my friends. But there were also Crosier students whose strangeness made me uneasy. They were effeminate, mincing boys who laughed constantly at secret things I did not understand. I had no idea what made them different, I only knew I was uncomfortable around them. Since I had never seen a boy act like that before, I assumed it came from living in the city too long. I thought they must be "over citified." Their ideas of entertainment were generally different from mine. Of the movies shown once a month in the gym at Crosier, they liked *Singin' in the Rain* and *Interrupted Melody*. I liked *Moby Dick* and *Spirit of Saint Louis*. They liked opera and Bach. I liked Bing Crosby and Tex Ritter.

And they liked to serve Mass. I had never served Mass before I came to Crosier, and didn't like it. I didn't like being up in front of the whole congregation. I felt I was under a microscope and my every move was scrutinized. I didn't like wearing that cassock and surplice; it felt like I was wearing a dress. I was always bungling the names of the tools they used: paten, ciborium, cruet. I did not look forward to being a priest and saying Mass in front of hundreds of people. But there were many seminarians who loved the idea of dressing up in those shiny vestments and officiating in front of a crowd. They could not wait to get their hands on the smoking censer and the sparkling monstrance. They loved the idea of marching down the aisle in a big cathedral wielding the aspergillium and tossing holy water all around over admiring faithful.

A student in my class, Gilman, was a good friend. I could talk to him about anything, and he was very smart. He was also very independent. He studied only the things he was interested in. His interests did not always correspond with the interests of the Crosier professors, so he was not highly regarded by some of the faculty. The feeling was evidently mutual. When I asked Gilman what the word "rector" meant (as in Father Rector McNiff), he said it was a modification of the word "rectum." He knew I was a naïve farm boy and liked to shock me. He was much more sophisticated than I was. He was more knowledgeable about the world, because of his wide exposure to city kids. His parents owned a fishing resort near Fifty Lakes, Minnesota, and he had spent his summers cavorting with vacationing kids from Minneapolis and St. Paul.

One day while I was talking to Gilman, I noticed some of the effeminate boys chasing each other and poking and giggling.

I said, "I don't understand those boys."

Gilman asked, "Why not?"

I said, "They act more like my sisters than like my brothers."

"Oh, hell," he said. "You know why, don't you?"

"No, why?"

"Those guys are homosexuals."

I must have had a blank look on my face. He laughed and shook his head, "You don't know what a homosexual is, do you?"

I said I wasn't exactly sure. He explained it to me, throwing in details. I had never heard of nor imagined the existence of such a thing. I said, "no, it can't be true." It would mean God had made a mistake. I said I didn't believe it.

"Have you ever heard of a faggot or a queer?" he said, sounding exasperated.

"No, well, queer—"

Just then Father Zachman came along the walk. I liked Zachman because he often spoke to me in German, and he reminded me of my maternal uncles.

Gilman said, "Hey, Father, this guy doesn't believe there is such a thing as a homosexual."

Zachman frowned at me and drew heavily on his cigarette. He hissed the smoke out through his teeth. "They're letting anybody in here now," he said. He walked away, mumbling, "I wouldn't be surprised to see a two-humped monkey with tail feathers come in the front door."

That didn't exactly clear things up for me. I looked from the priest to Gilman. I raised my eyebrows and gave a shrug.

Gilman shook his head, "Boy, you sure are a hick," he said.

I was not insulted. I didn't know what a hick was, either.

Chapter Ten

I THINK IT COST $400 a semester to go to Crosier—or was that for a year? I don't remember. Either way, it was a lot of money for Dad to pay out of the farm earnings. I helped earn a few dollars of that money by doing odds and ends around the monastery. Mostly I peeled potatoes. That's how I got to be friends with Dick Bela. Bela was from New Mexico. I had noticed him in church because he always kissed his thumb when he made the sign of the cross. I had never seen that before and considered it a marvelous innovation. Bela was a potato-peeler too, and we spent a lot of time together in a gloomy, cave-like room that we called "the dungeon" in the basement of the monastery. It was not hard work at all. We had a machine that sanded off the peelings by spinning the potatoes in a drum that had walls as rough as course sandpaper. We spun the potatoes until the peeling was just gone, but no more. Then we dug out the eyes with a paring knife. We soon figured out that the longer we sanded, the fewer eyes we had to carve out. But we had to take care, because Brother Hilary watched us closely and had a fit if he thought we were wasting potatoes. He could tell by looking at our finished potatoes, which he examined every day like a jeweler does diamonds. Sometimes, if he was in a good mood, he gave us ice cream. Bela came to think he owed us the ice cream, and he devised all kinds of tricks to steal ice cream when Hilary didn't give it.

One day when Bela and I got to talking, we forgot the potatoes spinning in the machine. When we opened the door to let them tumble out, they were nothing but marbles. We couldn't put the marbles in with the other potatoes, because Brother Hillary would see them right away. We couldn't throw the marbles in the wastebasket, either, because Hilary checked that. We made four little bags out of Brother Hilary's empty sugar sacks and filled them with the marbles. Bela put two bags in my pockets and two in his. After we had washed down the machine with the garden hose and filled the potato buckets with the right amount of water, we called Brother Hilary for his final inspection. I was nervous. I was sure Hilary was taking side glances at my bulging pockets. But Bela was smiling and joking with Hilary as he did his inspection. Brother Hilary scooped his hands through the peeled potatoes and wiped them on his apron. He gave the wastebasket a kick, grunted, and nodded approval. He gave us each an ice cream, and we were out of there. I was greatly relieved when we stepped into the cool air behind the monastery, but Bela had hugely enjoyed the whole thing. We took a walk out to the cemetery where the dead monks lay along the shore of Lake Onamia and emptied our pockets behind the tombstones.

Bela and I became good friends. He was a Latino, although in those days they weren't called Latinos yet. He hated when I called him a Mexican because he claimed to be Castilian, which meant nothing to me but everything to him. Even though he came from a small town, he was a city kid. He became very upset one day when he saw me back down from a fight. Some of the Crosier students were bullies and they knew how to intimidate. They had practiced all their lives. They knew a shy farm kid would not fight. They were aggressive as fighting roosters and would wave a fist in your face at the drop of a hat. If I made one of those boys angry (and that was easy to do), he would step up and put his ugly, red face right in front of mine so close our noses almost touched. Then he would scream, "You wanna fight? Huh? Hah? You wanna fight, farm boy?" That was enough to make me back up.

I could not risk a fight. The monks could boot you out of school for fighting, and in my case, they could do something even worse: they could tell my father. Bela said it was all a game. "The bully is just as afraid as you are," he told me. "He doesn't want to fight, either. He just knows you will back down if he looks ready and confident. He's bluffing! Don't let him scare you, and even if you are scared, never, never back down." Bela showed me how to protect myself in a fight by keeping my fists up in front of my face and my elbows down to ward off blows with my forearms. He showed me several wrestling holds, and he told me I had an unusually strong grip in my hands. It must have come from milking cows. He said, "You can use that to your advantage. If you are in a situation where someone wants to fight, grab him by the arm or hand and squeeze. He will feel that power and it will take the fight out of him."

Bela's tip saved me several times. A little time after that lesson, a bully got in my face. I grabbed his wrist, squeezed, and held on like a snapping turtle. I said through clenched teeth, "I don't want to fight, but I won't back down, ever." There was no fight. It was over right then. The angry boy, all bluster one minute, walked off like a lamb, though he did allow himself the luxury of mumbling something over his shoulder that "if it happens again there will be consequences." But the swagger was gone out of him.

Most of the food served at Crosier I liked, but they had the names of the meals all mixed up. They called their evening meal dinner. That was supper to me. They called their noon meal lunch. That was the meal I knew at home as dinner. We ate "lunch" out in the field as a snack between regular meals. Breakfast was the only meal they had correctly named, and that was the only meal I didn't care for. I was shocked to find that they used thin milk on their cereal instead of cream. There never was a pitcher of cream on the Crosier table. Even when there was pudding! No cream! At home there was always a big, porcelain cream pitcher in the middle of the table, and if we ran out, Mom would fill it again. It was thick stuff, the same as Mom used for whipping. On cold winter mornings, Mom would serve up hot oatmeal and we ladled on brown sugar or honey, and butter, and then poured on generous amounts of cream. When we had pudding for desert she would mix sugar and vanilla into the cream, and we poured that on the pudding until the bowl was full to the top. Now I was eating an anemic breakfast of dry cereal and thin milk. It tasted like paper and water. A real farm breakfast like fried eggs, hash browns, and bacon or sausage was served only on rare occasions like Holy Days. We never got blood sausage or liver sausage, and the mere mention of such dishes made the city boys gag. Strangest of all was that some of these boys had been taught at home that it was impolite to finish all the food on your plate! They always left a dainty little portion and thought it a disgrace when I used bread to mop up the last drop of juice on my plate.

Sometimes I ate too much. Brother Hilary, the cook, made a lot of dishes I had never had before. He never made anything as good as Mom's potato dumplings but he made great chili. I got to eat all the chili I wanted, because many of the other students refused to eat theirs. They said it had "gristle" in it. I liked the gristle. One night I had a bellyache. Brother Hilary had made liver and onions—another dish I could have all I wanted. I had feasted like a king on the big pieces of liver and piles of fried onions amid the jeers of other boys. I even stuffed in a little extra just to show them. Two hours later I was still stuffed. My stomach felt heavy as a bowling ball. During chapel that night I tried to think of which saint was in charge of bellyaches, but nothing came to me. When we were getting near lights-out, I was still hurting. It was the quiet time of night when we were not supposed to do any talking, but Father Hesch was not around, so while I was brushing my teeth, I whispered my trouble to the boy next to me at the sink. It was Ed Sjogren, a boy from Waite Park. I liked him because he was always cheerful and funny, and I knew he would never snitch about talking. He laughed about my stomachache and said it served me right for eating food fit for dogs. But he took pity on me.

He said, "I know what will put you right. Go to the infirmary and have the guy give you some Alka-Seltzer."

Jim Thoenes was running the infirmary that night. When I asked for Alka-Seltzer, he brought out a glass tube stacked with big round tablets.

"Here," he said, "take two."

As I walked back to the dorm room to get a glass of water I contemplated the tablets in my hand. I marveled at their size. They were monsters!

Boy, I thought, *these city boys take some mighty big pills.*

I would not be outdone. If a city boy could handle a pill like this, a tough country boy could, too. I took a glass of water, popped one tablet into my mouth, and washed it down. I figured I would save the second tablet until later in case this one didn't do the trick. That was a stroke of luck for me.

Oh, it worked! I began to burp. I mean, a whole string of burps. Burps upon burps. There was no stopping it. I had no control. I hung over the sink, thinking I might throw up. I didn't know what was happening to me. I had tears in my eyes and Alka-Seltzer foam coming out of my nose. I was gasping for air. In a little while it settled down, and my stomach actually did feel better. But not better enough to be worth all that. I handed the other tablet to Ed and told him what happened. I told him what I thought about his Alka-Seltzer idea and where he could put that second tablet.

"My God," he whispered, "you swallowed the tablet whole?"

"What was I supposed to do? Stick it up my . . . ?"

He was overcome with joy. He spent some time rolling around on his bed to recover. He explained to me—whenever he could get some air—how a normal person goes about taking Alka-Seltzer. Long after lights-out I could still hear bursts of snickering coming from the darkness in the direction of Ed's bed.

I hated that dormitory living. There was no privacy. You could not pick your nose or "scratch your ass," as Uncle Leonard would say. And in the night the noise of other students often woke me. A boy named Dehler snored loudly. He rattled the windows with impossible shattering snorts and rumbling growls and snarls. Pat Fish, who slept a few beds from me, advertised his nightmares by holding loud conversations with midnight devils, often yelling out names and shouting hellish orders at full lung and calling upon the ghosts to leave him be. Somebody was always in the washroom banging the doors on the stalls and crashing down the lids of the commodes. Sometimes I would wake up to the sounds of someone laboriously retching into a toilet. I got my best sleep toward morning. But if it was a cold night, that was the time when suddenly the place would erupt in a tremendous clangor. The radiators began to bang as they warmed from steam sent up from the boiler. There were loud crashing sounds like a lunatic plumber sledging the pipes in a fury. About the time the pipes and radiators were warmed up and quiet again, and I had dozed off once more, the wake-up alarm rang with the skull-piercing clamor of a fire bell. Then there was a crazy stampede as everyone grabbed their towels and sprinted for the washroom to be the first at one of the sinks. It was all very depressing.

At least my grades were improving. But I had to work hard for my grades. I wasn't like Baron or Rheinardy, who never had to study, absorbing the lessons by some kind of osmosis. The knowledge came into their heads just by having the textbooks lying on their desks while they read novels over them to pass the time. I had to work at my lessons with the resolve and determination of a farmer plowing new sod. I used up all my study-hall time and often took a textbook to bed to read before lights-out. When I got good grades, I felt I deserved them, not like in grade school where I often thought Teacher was giving me a good grade just to be nice.

As I gained confidence it was easier to make friends. It was also easier to make enemies. I was such an idealist I could not forgive weakness in others. We were studying to be priests, after all, and I expected students at Crosier to be aspiring saints. When someone cheated at cards I brooded about it for days. If someone lied to me, I was so deeply offended I found it hard to talk to that person again. I despised bullies. What kind of a priest could a bully make?

Above all, I detested a thief. When I was home at Christmas, Mom had made me a pair of mittens. I had told her about how I was learning to play hockey. Mom made the mittens with thick wool she cut from an old winter coat, and sewed a patch of leather on the palms. The thick wool made the gloves feel warm and also served as a cushion against the hockey sticks of the other players; the leather made for a good grip on the stick. I was fond of those mittens. When we played hockey and other students were pounding their hands together or holding them under their arms for warmth, my hands felt fine.

One afternoon as I was dressing for hockey, I opened my locker to get the mittens. They were gone! I was certain I had put the mittens right there on the top shelf where I always kept them. I was obsessed with finding them. I was crazy, I was angry—convinced someone stole them. I spent the afternoon searching in a daze. I wandered back along every step of the trail from my locker to the hockey rink. A group of students were playing hockey and shouted at me to get my skates, but I couldn't play. I watched them for a while, thinking about how Mom would feel if she knew I had already lost the mittens she had labored over for hours. I decided I would not tell Mom that someone stole them. She would not believe that a boy studying to be a priest would steal a pair of mittens. She might think I had lost them and was making up an excuse.

Then I saw them.

Among the sophomore class was a scrawny little bully who—as Gilman declared—"had crawled out of some hole up on the Iron Range." We called him Pestilencio, a corruption of his real name. Some just called him "The Pest." I saw him skating around out there waving his hockey stick and having a grand time. With my mittens! There was no doubt of it. There wasn't another pair like them in the world. As he skated close by the fence where I was standing, I recognized the brown wool that came from Dad's coat. This was like a red cape to a bull. Anger swept over me like a gasoline fire.

I screamed at the top of my lungs, "You have my mittens, you damned thief!" That stopped the game. You did not swear at Crosier, but I was out of my mind. The first to say anything was the thief himself. "What are you yelling about?"

I repeated that he had my mittens, stabbing my finger at him (but leaving off the part about damnation). He dropped his hockey stick and held up his hands with great drama and shock.

"These mittens?"

I lunged against the fence, trying to grab one of his hands, but he was too fast for me. He appealed to his buddies.

"You guys have seen me with these before."

No one said anything. A buddy of his came skating up to the fence. The Pest poked him with the mittens. "You've seen me with these mittens before. Remember? I bought them last year in Chisholm."

"He's a liar!" I yelled. I wanted to add that my mom made those mittens for me, but I knew that might bring a shower of scorn, with the sophomores shouting, "Oh, Mommy made them for him. Isn't that cute?"

The buddy looked doubtful. The thief poked him again. "I bought them in Chisholm at Christmas time."

"Yeah, those are his," said the buddy, and he skated off. The other students did the same, waving dismissive hands at me and yelling, "Let's play." They went on with their game.

I went back to the school thinking to tell Father Hesch. But then I would look like a little tattletale. I walked around brooding. In a little while another confrontation took place, by accident. I came out of the back door of the school. From my right came Father Divi (Father de Venster), and from my left came the group of students returning from the hockey rink, the thief at the front. Father Divi was the study-hall prefect. He sat every night at a high desk in the middle of study hall, turning his head like an old owl. Everyone knew him to be a wise old Dutchmen who couldn't be fooled. Seeing that swaggering thief coming toward me relit my rage like a flash of lightning.

I pointed and yelled, "Father Divi, he stole my mittens. There—he has them on his hands."

That was reckless. The thought flashed in my mind that the rest of the sophomore group might back their classmate. But they did not. As Father Divi came up frowning, they all filed past and went quickly into the building. They were leaving the thief on his own. That buddy of his was willing to lie in front of me, but evidently not so eager to lie in front of a priest.

"Vat iz da drouble here," asked Divi with his thick accent, and as always with a cigarette in his mouth that bobbed up and down with his words, raining ashes on the front of his scapular.

I repeated my accusation. The thief began babbling as fast as he could get the words out. He repeated his story about buying the mittens, only this time he got them in Hibbing instead of Chisholm. He said he bought the mittens last year just before Christmas, the twenty-fourth of December it was—no, it was the twenty-third, now that he came to think of it. He got them for his brother, but they didn't fit so he was wearing them himself. He was so sincere and remembered so clearly! But he included his conversation with the clerk at the store with such detail that I thought anyone could see he was making it up.

Finally he added, almost in tears, raising one of the mittens toward me, "And now he wants to take them away, Father. I have no idea why."

What a phony. He would not have looked guiltier if he had a neon sign on his forehead flashing, "Liar, liar, liar." I had no doubt the wise old Dutchman would see through this and restore what was mine.

But Divi looked puzzled, his brows drawn tightly together. He looked back and forth at the two of us, and I could see he did not read the neon sign. Then the wrinkles on his forehead relaxed as he thought of something.

"Do you haf a receipt?" he asked brightly, looking at me.

My heart sank. "No," I said. "My mother made those mittens for me."

But the pesky thief was quick. "I think I might still have my receipt at home, Father, in my dresser drawer!"

I had to give him credit. He was the fastest liar I had ever seen.

I appealed to Divi, "This wool part is from my dad's old coat. You can't find mittens like this in a store."

Father Divi took one mitten and turned it inside out. He would be able to tell from the cutting and the stitching whether they were homemade or store-bought. I thought that was brilliant, but it did not help me. Mom's stitching was so even and the cutting of the seams so precise that it was hard to believe it was not done by a professional.

"My mother is very good at sewing," I said weakly.

I knew it was over. Divi handed the mitten to the thief and stated with the judicial solemnity of King Solomon that he was ruling in favor of the present possessor of the mittens who would henceforward retain possession until such time as "someone" would be able to produce a proper receipt or other proof.

I felt triple betrayed: by the Pest for stealing, by his buddy for backing him, and by this priest for not seeing through such an obvious liar—a priest, a wise man of God! Later, when Divi met me in the hall on the way to the evening meal, he shrugged and spread his hands palms up.

"Vat could I do," he said. "It vas one manz vord against the utter."

I could not let it rest. It was almost as bad as when I was homesick, only now I wasn't sad, I was angry. I had to do something, and it came to me next morning during Holy Mass: I would steal them back. That evening when the bell rang for chapel, I hid in the washroom. When everyone was gone to church and the dorm was quiet as a tomb, I came out and stood at the end of the sophomore bed rows as quiet as a deer before entering a clearing, listening and watching. Sometimes sick students had permission to skip chapel. Sometimes a monk worked in the office at the far end of the dorm. But there was no one. All was quiet.

I moved as fast as I could without making a sound. I went to the Pest's locker and slid up the bolt. It clanged as it hit the top stop, and I ducked down between the beds. Now I could feel my heart pounding as I squatted, and I felt out of breath like a runner at the finish line. I knew I could get kicked out of the seminary for this, but I couldn't help myself. I went through the locker. Nothing. I looked under the bed. There was nothing. I started to search the bed when I saw them. He had stuck them under the radiator by the wall. Just a little corner was sticking out, but that was enough for me. I knew those mittens.

To that point, I had been a cool burglar. But now I lost it. I grabbed the mittens and ran. I left the locker door open, I left the bed disheveled. I threw the mittens in my locker and turned to run for chapel when it occurred to me that the Pest could simply steal them again. So I put them in Bela's locker under his stack of socks. No one would ever look for them there, and if Father Divi asked, I could honestly say, "I don't have those mittens."

I never wore them again. They were stained, dirty, and all pulled out of shape. I didn't want to send them home to Mom to launder, because she would see what a horrible job I had done taking care of them. I couldn't stand the thought of putting my hands inside them where the Pest's filthy, thieving fingers had been. I washed them in the shower, but that didn't help. I didn't like the mittens anymore, and I lost my enthusiasm for hockey. I finally traded with Bela: his gloves for my mittens, and he felt he got the better of the bargain. I didn't tell Mom what had happened to them until many years later.

For a long time after that, I still raged silently anytime I saw the Pest around school. His presence made me miserable. But he eventually dropped out of school, and later his buddy dropped out as well. I rejoiced tremendously over those happenings, but when I think of it now, the fact is those boys might well have made better priests than some of the pious seminarians who stayed and were ordained, and who did things worse than lying—or stealing mittens.

Chapter Eleven

A S THE ACADEMIC YEARS went by, things got easier for me. I came to regard the monks as fellow humans and not as gods. Unlike many students, I did not find the rules too stringent and the monks too strict. My dad was far more rigid, far more demanding, and less tolerant of weakness than any monk or student at that school. I thought I was where I belonged, but was never entirely content. I still often felt like an outsider. At times I felt the urge to travel and see the world. Sometimes I still got a little homesick.

A good deal of my discontent came from my starry-eyed, romantic idealism. I did not like the Church the way it was, and I wanted to reform everything. I thought the Church and the clergy should be poor like Jesus was. I thought the wealth of the Church was not Christ-like and should be sold off. There was too much gold and silver, too many shiny things meant to dazzle the eye of man, not of God. The clergy ate better food, wore better clothes, and drove better cars than the farmers did back home. They gave themselves fancy titles, like The Right Reverend, His Excellency, His Eminence, or His Grace. The bishop in St. Cloud, who called himself "His Excellency, Peter W. Bartholome, D.D. Bishop of St. Cloud," was known by the farmers as "Cadillac Pete" because he drove a big, flashy car. The Albany pastor drove around in a sparkling, late-model car that was always waxed and polished. I saw all these superficial trappings as an enormous problem—never seeing, never even suspecting the immense sepulchral corruption moldering underneath it all, and which was a far greater problem.

I had arguments with other students who said that if priests had to live the way I proposed, the seminaries and the churches would be empty. They said the flashy buildings and gaudy ceremonies were what attracted the laity to the Mass, and that my proposals would ruin the Catholic Church. But I was sure priests should be at least as poor as their parishioners.

After we were at Crosier a while and it appeared we might be in for the long haul, and wouldn't likely get booted out, we got to choose a spiritual director from among the monks. Whenever we had a problem of any kind we could go and whine about it to our spiritual director. Not that it did any good, but it was a nice gesture from the faculty. Most of the students wanted Father Hesch, or Landwehr, or Sheets. They were young priests and full of fun. They would come out and play football with us and were buddies with the students.

I chose old Father Van den Bosch because he was the most mild-mannered monk at Crosier. He was quiet and humble. He mostly stayed in his cell or went for slow walks by himself along the shore of the lake. I thought he was a saint. He seemed always at peace with himself and with the world. But he had the irritating habit of answering all my questions with another question and then leaving it to me to figure it out. If I could have understood a tenth of the guidance he tried to give me, my entire life would have been much easier, and certainly happier. But I was young and stupid. It was many years later, and Bosch long dead, before I understood the wisdom the man had offered me.

I told him my ideas about poverty for the clergy. He smiled. "The Catholic Church is run by old men who are set in their ways. Little changes come slow, big changes are nearly impossible. When you are young, your idealism blinds you to practical considerations. Ten years from now your world will seem much different. Do you think you are the first young man who has ever had such ideas? Do you think the ideals of your youth will stay with you all your life?"

I told him of my lust for travel. I said that when I was at home on the farm, I wanted to ride the Great Northern to the Pacific Ocean and now that I was at Crosier, I dreamed of catching the Soo Line to anyplace it went.

He said, "Your longing is not for travel. It is for God. No matter where you go, you will want to be somewhere else. When you find God, your longing will stop, you will be at peace. Do you think a train ride can give you peace?" Another time he said, "You will want to be elsewhere, until you are totally here."

Whenever we talked of God, he would say, "You must think of God, not as a being, but as Being itself."

When I complained about a student or monk at Crosier he would give this response, "We are all one in God. Which person here do you think is without the spirit of God in him?"

He was a fountain of wisdom, but I heard only riddles. However, I nodded and pretended to understand. I revered the old man, though I thought him slightly mad. He was a mystery. There was no way for this wise old monk to communicate with an ignorant farm boy who had never gone deeply into the spiritual life, who did not know young ideas fade with time, and who still pictured God as an old man with a long beard, watching from the clouds. I did not value at the time the peace and contentment he talked about. I valued adventure.

IN ROME A GROUP of clergy ran the Catholic Church, the Roman Curia. They were fat, old Italians who shut themselves in the dark of the Vatican and saw little of the outside world. They were mostly satisfied with the Church the way it was and saw no need for change. But then, at the beginning of my junior year, a light came on in the darkness: John XXIII became pope. He, too, was Italian, fat, and old, but he was not a Vatican insider. He was a reformer. He was a sharp contrast to his predecessor, Pope Pius XII, who had been born right there in Rome into a rich, old aristocratic family that had close ties with the papacy and with the Vatican wealth. Pope John was from a small country village in northwest Italy, far from the Vatican. His family worked as poor sharecroppers, and he had a dozen brothers and sisters. I immediately looked upon him as a fellow farm boy, and I was sure he would see things my way. A rustic, jolly Santa Claus was replacing the cool, aloof patrician. I was convinced John XXIII would change the Church to fit my vision. I saw myself saying Mass in little cinderblock churches built by the local bricklayer. I saw myself praying over a chalice made of copper and tin, hammered by the local blacksmith. I saw myself wearing vestments made of burlap and denim, sewn by a farmer's wife who learned her skill patching her husband's overalls.

My wish to become a priest increased—and then skyrocketed when the Crosiers established a mission in New Guinea. Immediately I wanted to go. It was a place on the other side of the earth, so mysterious there was no established name for it. The Crosiers called the specific area "Asmat." That was also the name of the natives there. But over the years the natives kept changing their name and also the name of their government and of their country, so no one really knew where they belonged. I don't think the United Nations figured it out. The western half of New Guinea has been known as Papua, as Irian Barat, and as Irian Jaya. It had other names in the past, including Netherlands New Guinea, West New Guinea, and West Irian. Some now called it West Papua. The capital, in the opinion of many, was Jakarta, but that was over on the north coast of Central Java.

The Crosiers made their headquarters at a "town" they called Agats. The surrounding region was all lowland rainforest and mangrove swamp. The natives still lived in the Stone Age. They spoke an unknown language and could not read or write. The land was so low all their buildings were set up on stilts to stay above the flooding of the Bian and Maro rivers. Some of the Asmat neighbors were still headhunters and cannibals. I still wanted to go. I was too stupid to mind the reports of insufferable heat and mosquitoes, of man-eating crocodiles and snakes. I wanted to go even more when I found they were sending my favorite teacher, Father Hesch. He left for New Guinea shortly after school started in my junior year, and I never saw him again.

Now I really wanted to be a priest. It was no longer just fulfilling an obligation. I looked at my studies now as a means to that desired end. I was happy to go to class. I pored over my Latin, religion, and other courses with vigor. My grades improved to the point where I often made the honor roll. I got along much better with the other students. I thought of them as fellow seekers of the same goal. As I gained confidence, I gained friends. I no longer cared so much about fitting in. The funny thing was that when I was new at Crosier and was desperate to make friends, I had few. Now, when I didn't care so much, I had many. I was elected class president my senior year. But that office was really nothing. It gave no power or prestige—at Crosier, all that belonged to the monks.

The year 1960 came, and I woke up to world events. Until then I had taken little interest in anything but my immediate surroundings. But the exhilarating mixture of Pope John XXIII, Nikita Khrushchev, and Jack Kennedy was too much to ignore. Politics became a major topic of discussion at Crosier. That was because a Catholic was running for president—Senator John "Jack" Fitzgerald Kennedy, who we called "JFK." Just as Pope John was about to change the Catholic Church, so Kennedy was about to change politics in America. Just as Pope John was a complete change from the stuffy old Pius XII, so Kennedy would be a complete change from stuffy old Dwight Eisenhower. Eligible students couldn't wait to go vote. The thought of Kennedy winning the election inaugurated a happy euphoria among Crosier students and among young people in the whole country.

We all listened to the radio and watched TV whenever we had the chance. I read the daily newspaper in the library. For the first time I knew the meaning of NASA, of sonic booms, and of Vanguard rockets. I followed the Russian space program as they sent up dogs, mice, and a pair of rats to see if a human might be able to live up there in orbit. Khrushchev made it plain to the world that the space race was a contest between the capitalistic system of the United States and the socialistic system of the Soviet Union.

In the spring of 1960, I graduated from Crosier High School. That was an event of no consequence for me, because it changed nothing. In fall I would come back to the same school to continue my studies, except I would be in college. The only change would be that, for the first time in years, I would be out of the big dormitory I hated so much. College students stayed in rooms with four beds and two sinks. I would be in a room with three other students. Toilet and shower were still down the hall. Privacy was still hard to come by. The other change was that many of the students I liked best, like Bela, Gilman, and Sjogren, had dropped out of the seminary along the way.

But big changes were occurring in my life. I turned eighteen that summer. I went with Dad to the Post Office in Albany and, as required by law of all eighteen-year-old males, I registered with the Selective Service System. I got a wallet-sized piece of stiff paper called a "draft card," which I was required to carry with me to prove I had registered. Later I got a letter from the draft board which told me that, because I was going to school, I didn't have to go into the army yet. I was classified as 2-S (the student exemption) and was warned to inform the draft board if I left school. They would immediately change my status to 1-A.

For the first time in my life, I got to vote. Young people went crazy with joy when Kennedy won. The Kennedys, Jack and Jackie, were young and handsome. They looked like movie stars. Khrushchev was old and ugly. He looked like a troll that hides under a bridge and eats children. But Khrushchev was a flamboyant publicity hog, and he kept the race between the countries going by constantly challenging, even taunting, President Kennedy in public. The whole world watched the bantering between Khrushchev and Kennedy and the contest between socialism and capitalism.

In the spring of 1961, the Soviet Union made history by launching the first manned spaceship. The United States was still testing the waters by sending up monkeys. It was almost a year later before we got our first man into orbit. We shot John Glenn up there and he made three trips around the earth, showing the nations that we could do it, too. But we were still behind. The Russians were sending up more men and they were staying up there longer. Khrushchev kept pounding home the idea that this space race was proving once and for all that socialism was superior to capitalism.

I was completely in tune with the times. My hero, John Kennedy, was *Time's* Man of the Year for 1961. The next year, my other hero, Pope John XXIII, was their Man of the Year. President Kennedy took up the challenge of Khrushchev and did him one better. He proposed that the United States send a man to the moon within a decade. That changed the space race to a race to the moon—a race America would win by a mile. Pope John saw that the Catholic Church would have to adapt itself to the fast changes in science and technology. The Church would not be caught behind like it had been at the time of Galileo. Pope John also saw that the Church would have to be less dogmatic in order to reach out to non-Catholics. He wanted to make the Church "more Catholic and less Roman." That suited me fine, but I did not realize where all this would lead.

I graduated from Crosier in the spring of 1962 with a degree in Liberal Arts. This meant I knew a little about a lot, and knew nothing of any practical value. I used to tell people the only thing worthwhile I learned in six years at Crosier was how to type. But that is not true. Through my daily exposure to the monks I learned a lesson of far more value than all the Greek, Latin, physics, and math. It was a lesson many Catholics never learn: priests are just human beings— not gods, not saints, not angelic—just human beings. A priest loses his temper, makes mistakes, and is as insecure as anyone else. He is a normal sinner.

Father Brennen was a hot-headed Irishman. He smoldered like a volcano and blew up sporadically for unpredictable reasons. He once kicked me out of class for saying I did not see why the Mother of God had to be a virgin. I did not say Mary wasn't a virgin. I didn't say I didn't believe she was a virgin. I just said I didn't see that it should be absolutely necessary. Why couldn't God be born of a regular woman like my mother? Father Brennen erupted. His face grew red as hot lava and he yelled at me to get out of his class. He shoved me out and slammed the door behind me. But Father Brennen's eruptions were short, and he quickly cooled off to the placid old Irish blarney stone he normally was. And then he was sorry. He was always extra nice to me after that incident.

The hostility that developed between Father Lindusky and me did not start from my side, of that I am certain. It developed while I still had a child-like awe for anyone wearing the Roman collar. He was a lean, hollow-eyed and hungry-looking man, like John the Baptist in the desert. He had a dissatisfied and distasteful look like he was eating the locusts but not the honey. He was also a snob. He was the music teacher and choir director. He had written several pieces of music and considered himself quite an artist. He liked to hang around with the effeminate students, and from the beginning I had the feeling that he did not like me. It took me a long time to admit to myself I did not like him, either.

Father Lindusky carried a heavy, seething kettle of carefully concealed anger, which he did not allow to boil over freely and openly like Father Brennen. Lindusky harbored his anger, secretly fermented it into a venomous brew, and then uncorked at you in the privacy of his office. He kicked me out of music class one day for falling asleep. We were listening to one of Bach's impossibly long organ fugues, or cantatas, or some other of his soporific Baroque pieces. Lindusky came over, tapped on my shoulder, and very quietly asked me to leave. The following Saturday, after I had almost forgotten about it, he called me into his office. He closed the door and cooked over. I think he took my inattention in music class as a personal insult. Bach was a favorite of his. He raged about my lack of respect and about my not appreciating the value of an education. He got all red in the face and the veins on his neck stood out like purple vipers. He said I would be booted out of school if I did not shape up. He cited the fact that Brennen had kicked me out of class, too.

He went on to say he knew I was against letting students listen to opera on Saturday afternoons and I had better change my attitude. This last came from a remark I had once made about one student commandeering the entire student lounge every Saturday afternoon so he could listen to opera on Minnesota

Public Radio. The student, a pale, skinny kid from New York, was a pet of Lindusky's. When he wanted to listen to opera, playing checkers and cards and watching TV had to cease. We all had to leave the student lounge unless we wanted to sit quietly and listen to the bloody yelling of the fat lady on the radio. I made my remark in front of some other students and someone must have tattled.

When Lindusky threatened to have me booted out of the school, I went to Father Bosch and told him my troubles. The little smile, which was always at the corner of Bosch's mouth, deepened.

"You are not in danger of getting kicked out," he said. "You have, among the faculty, the reputation of being a good student and not of being a screw-up. A personality conflict with one person is nothing. Let this be a learning experience. Do you think this is the only time in your life you will have such a conflict?"

"But Father Lindusky says I am at the very edge of getting the boot."

"And what do I say?"

He loved to end a session with a question. He gave me his serene nod, accompanied by a slow wink like an old turtle. That was his signal I was dismissed.

The pious monks of the Sacred Order of the Holy Cross followed the Rule of St. Augustine. They took the three hallowed vows of poverty, chastity, and obedience. But they took no vows of patience, tolerance, and benevolence—virtues which would have served far better in teaching young men. I will always be grateful to the Crosiers for teaching me that a man with a Roman collar can cheat and lie and be a horse's ass as efficiently and skillfully as any man.

I was not sorry to leave Crosier. I hated the dormitory life of the high school, and my two years of college, which should have been happy and free, were like living under the eye of a warden, because Lindusky was there. I gladly said goodbye to that old Dutch bastion. But I would long remember the tall brick buildings standing in pale December sun on the east side of the town, and for many years whenever I heard Westminster chimes from a bell tower in winter, I would feel a little stab of sadness as it reminded me of my homesick days at Crosier and how the chimes played Christmas music from the tower of the Chapel of St. Odilia.

Chapter Twelve

I N THE CENTER of Stearns County there stands among the granite hills a mighty fortress of prison-gray, a sentinel of the Everlasting. The deep-throated thunder of the reverberating bells that swing from this lofty rampart rolls across the Avon hills and dies in the forests among the sturdy oaks and the ashes. This is the Abbey Church of the monastery of the Benedictine monks of St. John's. The monks have been there since before Minnesota became a state, when the Chippewa and the Dakota were still fighting, and when the Red River oxcarts still slogged through Stearns County on their way from Mendota to Pembina. The monks contemplate the same scriptures and propose to follow the same prescripts that ruled at Monte Casino over a thousand years ago, when the great Saint Benedict himself was abbot there. The ponderous, spartan walls of the formidable abbey church and the black-cowled apparitions, bent in meditation, who wander the woodland trails radiate a sense of undying and indestructible serenity.

I spent five semesters there—a short time by those Benedictine standards, but long by mine. I entered St. John's seminary for my third year of college in the fall of 1962. It was for me the best of places, and the worst of places. I started there riding high. Life was good. Finally I had privacy. I now had my own room—my own little private cell with bed, desk, and sink. I was able to better concentrate on my studies and I found I liked the other students better when I was not suffocating from overexposure. And I had my first car: I had bought my brother's 1949 Ford sedan—with overdrive!—for fifty dollars. That first year at St. John's was the happiest of my entire academic career. I began to feel a happy contentment that had eluded me. Everything was going my way that fall. Kennedy was staring down Khrushchev in the Cuban Missile Crisis. Pope John was calling together the Ecumenical Council, Vatican II. Change was in the air. The St. John's monks had just finished building the new abbey church. It was an unbelievable colossus compared to the little cinderblock church I had in my mind as an ideal, but its stark appearance and unadorned walls matched the simplicity I thought was needed in the Catholic Church. I was convinced the Catholic Church was taking a turn in the right direction and I supported every change. Anything new was good.

I studied philosophy. I had to have a BA in that subject and then I had to go on to get a degree in theology in order to be ordained. I could talk like a regular intellectual now. I slung around words like "conceptualize" and "empirical," and blabbed of theory and principle, and natural law. Soon I was perfectly capable of putting out a sentence like: "Let us hypothesize for a moment in order to formulate a pragmatic deduction regarding this apparent dilemma." At times I could say something like that without blushing. In my juvenile ignorance I had a feeling of superiority from studying subjects like ontology, cosmology, epistemology and any other "ology" conceivable—subjects my father knew nothing about. Words like "metaphysics" and "esthetics" rolled off my tongue as easily as "cow" and "horse" had done before. I began thinking of myself as quite an intellectual. I even bought a pipe, though I never could stand the foul taste no matter what kind of tobacco I burned in the thing. I now wore the collar and the robe like a genuine monk. We were required to wear that costume to all classes so as not to get us mixed up with the lay students. That way it was unlikely any student would ask us to go out to get drunk or to chase after the girls from the College of St. Benedict in St. Joseph.

There was no train close by now to beckon me. The only time I felt a restlessness crop up was whenever I saw the lay students sitting on benches by Lake Sagatagan holding hands with pretty girls and nuzzling their necks. I did have one big surge of wanderlust when all the magazines that fall put out articles about why everyone was moving to sunny California. California was fast becoming the most populous state in the union. *Life* magazine put out a special issue about the "golden state" with a cover picture of a Yosemite waterfall glowing like liquid gold in the evening sun. That stirred the wandering embers in my soul for a while, but they died down again as winter came and I settled into the St. John's study routine. The food was good, the company was good, and I didn't have to work very hard to get decent grades.

I was pedaling merrily along like a happy kid on his tricycle thinking all was right with the world. But I was in for a rude awakening after that first year. The wheels came off my tricycle of contentment one by one. It started with the death of Pope John XXIII right after school let out in the spring. When the fisherman's ring was pulled off that dead hand, a lot of hope was pulled out of me. And when the white smoke rose from the pipe of the Sistine Chapel, it came from burning votes for another Vatican insider. Pope Paul VI took the papal reins. He was a man from a privileged Italian family and a long-time pal of that stuffy old Pius XII. I could only conclude that the Catholic Church was not going to change much. What was God doing?

I was unhappy all that summer. I locked horns with Dad a lot. Actually, we had been going at it for quite a while. Dad represented the old, outdated past. I was the brilliant young college student. I was convinced I was at the pinnacle of my intellectual development while he was in full decline. I completely trusted my university professors as the fountain of all knowledge, and just my short exposure to them made me an expert in everything. Since I already knew everything about psychology and philosophy and so forth, I thought it only reasonable that along the way I must have miraculously absorbed great knowledge about the husbandry of cows, the care of farm tractors, and the cultivation of crops. By now I was so smart I was not only telling Dad how he should be treating his wife, but also how he should be running his farm, no matter that I had never in my life had a relationship with a woman or taken care of an acre of land. No matter that Dad had been married for fifty years and had sweated a good living for a dozen and a half people out of his small farm.

Several times when we had an argument, Dad would finish it off by yelling at me, "You think you know a lot because you have read a few books, but I'm telling you that the man who is a day older is a day smarter."

At the time I considered that statement of Dad's to be one of the dumbest things I had ever heard. It was the empty babbling of an uneducated fool. Youth, arrogance, and stupidity are a merry drink when stirred together into one thick-headed shot glass. In only a few short years, the United States Air Force would pound into my head the wisdom of that saying. I soon realized Dad was using his own words to express an old adage and a fundamental truth of human existence: experience is the best teacher.

The next wheel came off my tricycle with the crack of a rifle in Dallas, Texas. I was standing by the billiard table in the seminary recreation room, leaning on a pool cue while my buddy, John Sandel, was trying to make the eight ball in the side pocket. I knew he would not make it, and if he did he would scratch down in the corner. John tapped the pocket with his cue and aimed. We never found out. Another seminarian came in, all excited. He rushed to the TV and turned it on. President Kennedy had just been shot.

It's one thing when your hero dies of old age like Pope John did, but quite another if he gets shot down like a dog in front of God and everyone. It makes you feel like the end of the world has come. It was horrible to watch the TV. Walter Cronkite choked back tears and had trouble getting it out when he announced, "The president of the United States is dead. I repeat . . . the president of the United States is dead." I gaped in sad confusion at the TV coverage for the next few days—as did people all across the country. Schools let out. Children walked out of classrooms weeping. The streets were empty in St. Joe and Avon, and in all the little towns across the county. Shops and banks closed. Trading on the stock market halted. People cried openly in the streets.

Everyone watched TV in the following days: the procession of the horse-drawn caisson trundling the casket to the Capitol Rotunda with the weary *clop, clop* of hooves on the pavement; the funeral with the big black horse and the empty saddle; the slow, breathless *thump* of the muffled drum. People wondered, "How could this happen?" I wondered with them. Where was God? This was part of a divine plan? What plan? It made no sense. Evil was triumphing over good. Some nut with a rifle could kill the Catholic president? The question, "Is there a God?" began to haunt me. My faith began to wobble like a newborn calf standing up for the first time. Any bad news in the world enforced the doubts. The day after Thanksgiving the TV announced a plane crash in Montreal that killed over a hundred people. What plan? Earthquakes, car accidents, soldiers killed in Vietnam posed the same question.

The last wheel left my tricycle of contentment when my brother Leroy announced he was getting married. I was stunned. He was only a year older than me, yet he was ready to take on the great responsibility of wife and children? I felt like a child by comparison. I began to suspect that in the seminary I was not maturing like a normal human being. I began to feel that, secluded behind seminary walls, I did not know what was going on in the real world. By the following spring I was a basket case of confusion. In one year I had gone from a cocky, know-it-all college intellectual to a muddled, tortured soul, feeling his way in the dark like a blind man.

What was I doing studying philosophy, anyway? To be honest, of all the courses at the university, philosophy would likely have been my last choice, and Greek second to last. I was no philosopher. Who was I fooling? I was a farm boy and thought in terms of fence posts and barbed wire, picks and shovels, bricks and mortar. My brain revolted at abstractions and concepts, hypothesis and theory. Why do old men try to teach young men this stuff? Even old men do not understand it. Why torture the brains of the young? I got good grades only because my memory was good. My understanding was wretched. The Stearns County farmers would have laughed at some of the things I studied. It was all invisible mind-stuff with no practical value. Plato said that this world we live in, this world of soil, rocks, and trees, was only imaginary and that some fuzzy, foggy world he made up in his head was the real thing. To that they would say, "bullshit," and that would be the end of that philosophical discussion. The problem with Descartes was he had too much time on his hands. No farmer ever thought of having to prove his own existence. What Descartes lacked was a herd of cows to milk.

I wondered now if I should be a priest. How could I, with all my doubts? During Lent and leading up to Easter I prayed to God for some light, some sign I was where I belonged. On Good Friday they had an awful earthquake up in Alaska that killed another hundred people who seemed to be just minding their own business. What kind of a sign was that? I kept on with my studies and graduated with honors. I looked forward to theology. Surely the study of God would bring me some answers.

My brother's wedding that summer did not help. It wasn't the wedding it-self, but all the circumstances around it. I was the best man, which meant I held close company with the bridesmaid. I had to pose with her for pictures and dance with her at the bridal dance. Because I knew nothing of dancing and was a natural kangaroo-foot, we went to dances together to practice. Electrical joy raced through my veins when steering her around the floor, that soft warm body against mine, and she yielding gently, smoothly—ea-gerly. We drank together (though I needed no practice in that, and it was not part of the ceremony). Several times when we were alone, we made out in the backseat of my Ford like we were both going to the gallows. We raced in my old clunker along the highways, and walked by the Sauk River. I had never looked so deeply into the eyes of a grown woman before. I felt her breath on my face, and pulled into my lungs the scent of her perfumed hair.

I realized the full impact of what I was giving up. It wasn't just that brides-maid. It was the celebrating, the drinking with buddies, the racing in cars. Ex-citement, adventure! I was not ready to return to the seminary that fall. I struggled for the last several weeks of summer vacation. A few days before school started, I drove to Albany and went to the Seven Dolors Church to get a reading from God. I sat in the back pew and tried to think about how I started down this road. The sun was already low on the western side of church and dusk was gathering in the corners. Little fires from vigil lights flickered in front of statues and they made gloomy shadows quiver on the walls. All was quiet and peaceful. I thought about all the time I had spent there when I was little and had not a care in the world. I did not want to return to the grind of school. Why did I need theology? I had enough "ologies" to last me a life-time. Could someone with my kind of doubts be a priest? *Mother of God, give me some help here.* I was afraid I would jeopardize my eternal soul if I rejected the call of God. And there was inside me that strong sense of duty from Mom, and that bullheaded determination to finish the job from Dad. I knelt and looked up at the cross. I swallowed hard, but I got it out: "Thy will be done."

I was refreshed. I returned to school feeling optimistic that the study of theology would clear my head. I was studying the most important topic for all human beings: God. Back within the walls of the seminary and in my own little cell I felt some peace again. I was away from the dangers of the world. I buckled down to my studies. But this did not last. Again TV news stories began to cycle in my brain. It may sound funny, but I believe the main reason

I did not become a priest was because of the Berlin Wall. Every few days now there were stories about people from East Germany dying in attempts to get over that wall. Those people were risking their lives, their fortunes, their children to get to the West. They faced the barbed wire, the machine guns, the dogs, and died bloody deaths at the foot of that wall in a frenzied try for freedom. I realized what I wanted most: freedom. I began to think of the seminary wall as my Berlin Wall. I began to view my life in the seminary as life in an unreal world, and that my calling to the priesthood was unreal.

To prove to myself that I had at least some freedom, I rebelled against seminary rules. Alcohol was against the rules. I kept a quart of Christian Brother's brandy in my locker. When other seminarians came to visit, I offered them shots. I began skipping functions just to show I could. Radios were against the rules. I bought a cheap transistor from Big Ed, a lay student in one of my classes. I played tinny-sounding music in my room and often held that little radio to my ear at night in bed to hear the news from the other side of the wall.

The November winds took the leaves from the trees and made the reflection of the Stella Maris chapel shimmer in the water of Lake Sagatagan. Winter was closing in. I walked along the icy shore. Three Canadian honkers flew over heading south-west. They must be headed for California! Sunny California with long-legged blonde girls walking on golden beaches with the blue ocean waves rolling soft foam over their feet. For the first time I had a specific destination—I wanted to go to California. If I had had the money to put enough gas in my old Ford I would have left right then.

Winter storms came and I brooded in my room. I wanted to be on my own. I wanted to live my own life, not the life others had mapped out for me. For the first time I admitted to myself that I wanted to quit. I was afraid. Some great force was calling me, but was that force God or Satan? I talked to my spiritual director at the seminary. He said it was the devil. He said the devil used the material things of this world to entice young men out of the spiritual life.

"Material things never make you happy," he said.

That didn't seem right to me. My car and my little radio made me happy. I talked to other priests, including my uncle who was the pastor in Roscoe. They all said the same things. It was normal to have doubts. It was the devil who was tempting me. They were all sure God wanted me to be a priest. They all had the same advice, the same platitudes and bromides. I had heard these since I was a baby—generic solutions to all Catholic problems:

"Trust in God and He will point the way."

"If you love God, you will do the right thing.

"Let the Holy Ghost be your guide."

Advent came. All the hymns and canticles of the season had the haunting quality of wanting, of longing, of missing something. "O come, O come, Emmanuel" echoed among the baffles and buttresses and down into the halls and crypts of the Abbey Church. The sad longing was reflected outside. The trees were bare, the birds didn't sing. Flowers were dead. Snow fell and all was white and gray. All color gone. The sun, through a low haze, showed no brighter than a quarter moon. I stared out the window, the season a mirror of my barren inside. The season's liturgy was all about longing for the coming of the Christ. I was longing, but not for the Christ. I didn't care about Christmas. I cared about freedom.

I wanted to leave, but did not have the guts to make so momentous a decision without the approval of some higher authority. I was afraid I would make God mad and get sent to hell. There was at St. John's a monk named Kieran Nolan, who had just returned from Europe where he had received his Doctorate in Theology at Tübingen University in Germany. I was impressed with that degree. He must know all the latest information about God. He must have answers to any God problems. Father Kieran's office was behind an enormous black oak door in the middle of a dark hallway in the monastery. I made my way there one morning, determined to enlist his help in my conflict. I knocked. A voice from inside said something, but I couldn't tell what it was. I knocked again. I could hear a chair scraping on the floor and in a moment the door opened. A plump little Benedictine monk stood there smiling, radiating health and contentment like the morning sun. He invited me to come in and have a chair.

Kieran listened to me for a long time. I told him about my doubts. I told him about my passion for travel and my desire to be on my own. He asked about my family, my childhood, grade school, high school. He asked detailed questions—questions about Mom and Dad, about the farm, even about my hometown of Albany.

I kept thinking, *What does all this have to do with helping me make a decision?*

After a while Kieran was silent. He was looking out the window. Snowflakes floated down softly in the monastery courtyard. The calm and peaceful scene was a sharp contrast to the war going on in my brain. Several times he took a deep breath, but always he kept watching the snow.

In a little while he looked at me. I expected another slew of platitudes.

"You can't stay," he said. "If you go on here, you will always feel deprived." He spoke as though this should be obvious to anyone. "You'll have to get away. You've never had a chance to live life on your own terms. You've never seen what people are like at their worst. You need to experience some of these things. Here you see only the bright, polished side of life. There are lessons out there you must learn. How can you give up the world, and dedicate yourself to the priesthood, when you don't know what the world is? The farm was a sheltered place. Your tiny grade school was a sheltered place. Crosier was a sheltered place, and so is this seminary. You can't stay. Leave."

Since it was only a few weeks to mid-term, he advised me to finish the semester and then go.

"What will you do?" he asked me. "Go home?"

"No," I said. "I can't go home. I'm disappointing my parents. I can't face them now." I told him I would soon have to go into the service because the draft would get me as soon as I left school.

"You're right, you can't go home. You would learn nothing new."

Kieran said the service was a good way to see the world, but that I should avoid the structured life of the military as long as I legally could, so I could give myself some time to live on my own.

"Do you have money?"

I said I had twenty-two dollars.

"Then you have to go down south; hitchhike. It takes money to live in the north country because you have to have shelter from the cold. Down south you can sleep outside. Be a hobo until you can't stand it. "

He rummaged in his desk, pulled out a ten-dollar bill and gave it to me. "That will help get you started. You can stop and work when you have to, but don't stay in one place long, or you will become dependent. Get the wanderlust out of your blood. You can always come back to the monastery. Take a year—take two. Find out what the real people are like."

Kieran was calm, confident, and straightforward. He entirely relieved me of the responsibility of the decision. He did not say it might be a good idea, or maybe you ought to. In my lifetime no one ever relieved me of so heavy a burden as did Father Kieran Nolan.

I thanked him. I stepped out into the hall and swung shut the great door to his office. And there in the hall I collapsed against the wall and cried for sheer relief. I was glad no one was around and the hall was dark, for my body was racked with choking spasms from my sobbing. I thought surely Kieran must hear me in his office. But he did not come out, and in a little while I recovered and was able to leave. I felt drained, I felt lightheaded. I felt wonderful. I felt free.

At first I tried to keep this from the other students, but sometimes at night when brandy was warm in my belly and a good friend was there, it slipped out. Those buddies of mine did not tell me I was jeopardizing my soul or that I was throwing away my vocation. They were only concerned about throwing away my draft deferment.

"The Army will suck you up like a vacuum cleaner."

They all seemed to know more about the draft than I did. To see if they were right, I went to see the recruiter at Selective Service Office Number 117 in St. Cloud. I showed the man my draft card. He checked my number on a roster.

"Let me see, number 21 117 42 112," he read from my card. He looked up. "If you leave school, your ass is mine." That was his assessment of my situation. "The draft board will change your 2-S classification to 1-A. That means you're ready for immediate induction."

I was already twenty-two years old, which made me an old man in the eyes of the draft board. They drafted men from eighteen to twenty-five years of age. They drafted the oldest eligible man first, before he had a chance to escape by growing past draft age. The Vietnam draft lottery system that became so famous later had not started yet. For me, leaving school meant entering the military.

The recruiter told me things were heating up in Vietnam; I would almost surely do a tour there. I didn't care. I was so eager to get out and see the real world that, if it meant going into the Army, fine. And if they sent me to Vietnam, fine. At least I would be traveling, seeing a new land. It never occurred to me that the military was the last place a man should go to seek freedom.

When I was leaving his office, the recruiter shouted after me, "You can sign up with the Navy or the Air Force, if you don't want to be in the Army, but you better do that soon."

The recruiters from Army, Navy, Air Force, and Marines came to campus from time to time. I went to see them all. I signed up with the Air Force because their recruiter said I would be able to delay my entry for half a year, and if I qualified for their pilot program, even longer.

Word got around the seminary fast that I was leaving. Fellow seminarians began to show up at my door to give me advice on how to avoid the draft.

"Go to Canada," they said. "They welcome you there with open arms."

They said you could flee to Canada without money. There were some priests in Duluth who had good connections in Toronto. They would arrange to get me up there, would get a nice apartment, and put me into a good job. This was not called "draft dodging." It was "seeking sanctuary."

The lay students in my classes had lots more ways out of the draft, and they were just as eager to give me advice. "The Army will kill you," they said. "If they don't march you to death, they'll send you to Vietnam, where the commies will use you for target practice." The "stay-in-school" strategy was their favorite. As long as you were a full-time student making "satisfactory progress toward a degree," you were safe. Anybody could fake that by taking a few easy classes and doing a minimum amount of studying.

Big Ed sat next to me in one of my classes. He paid absolutely no attention to the prof. He said he already knew what would be on the tests. He read books with false dust covers and played sink-the-battleship with me. He thought I was a total moron for leaving school, but then he also thought I was a total moron for having entered the seminary in the first place.

Big Ed advised me to become a criminal. He said, "The Army won't take a felon. If you go out and commit a crime, and get yourself convicted, they won't take you. The best way to do that is to shoot an eagle. That's a felony. You're supposed to get a year in jail, but they won't keep you more than a few weeks."

Another way out was to be a teacher. Many students came to St. John's seeking degrees in engineering, botany, or philosophy, and left with degrees in education so they could get the teacher's draft deferment. Seeing me disinclined to become a criminal, Ed said, "Okay, go into education. For you it would be easy. Take a few teaching courses, and you'll have your certificate. Then you get yourself hired at a little country school where the kids haven't yet learned they can spit on the teacher. The worst part of that job is you have to pretend you like the little bastards. But you can handle that by just staying drunk. You can sober up when the war is over."

"I don't want to be a teacher. I want to travel."

"Travel in the summer."

"They don't pay much."

"Yeah, but you don't do much! All summer off, Christmas vacation, spring break. You get paid plenty for working only half the time. Education is the way to go, buddy."

I told Big Ed I didn't want to be a criminal or a teacher. In a few days he had a better scam. He had a friend in the Cities who could arrange it. There was a church group in Minneapolis that lined up draft dodgers with pregnant girls.

"You can't go wrong on this one," he said. "It's a winning situation for both sides. The pregnant girl gets an instant husband, and you will get an instant exemption from the draft. If you're married and your wife is pregnant, you get a 3-A classification, which means you stay home and play with the wife. Let the stupid ones slog through the jungle and worry about bamboo snakes, snipers, and sleeping in mud. And look here, some of these girls are not schnauzers."

After a while, my buddy John Sandel came by my room. John didn't have to worry about the draft. He had a 4-F classification because of his flat feet.

"My feet are so flat, my heels and toes never touch the ground," he said.

He asked me, "Why won't you even consider a move to avoid conscription? Is this a moral issue with you, or are you so wrapped up in seeing everything in the world that you want to see a war as well?"

"No," I said. "That's not it, exactly. My uncles served in the military without complaint. They saw it as a duty to their country. If I become a draft dodger, it will be an insult to them. I would essentially be telling them that they were stupid and could have run away like I'm doing. There is no way I will dishonor my mom's brothers."

"What about the conscientious objector route?"

"That would be the same."

John said, "They'll send you off to a foreign land to shoot at strangers who have never done you the least bit of harm. And those people will shoot back. They will shoot to kill."

It all did no good. Let the chips fall where they may. The Air Force recruiter told me that to qualify for their pilot training program, I would have to pass a battery of physical and psychological tests, all taken in Minot, North Dakota.

"I don't have any money to put gas in my car," I said.

"Oh, you won't need a cent," he said. "You'll be going by train, and the Air Force will pay for everything, including your meals."

By train! I couldn't sign on the dotted line fast enough. I had no objections to being a pilot. At home on the farm, when an airplane flew over, we all ran outside to watch, shading our eyes with a hand and following it across the sky until it was out of sight, but none of us ever thought we might be able to actually fly in one of those things, and certainly not in the driver's seat. Here this man was offering me a free train ride and a chance to drive airplanes.

The recruiter got on the phone to the air base in Minot and made arrangements so I could do the tests during Christmas vacation. I was really getting excited now. I would get my first train ride—the start of a great adventure. I didn't even care if I passed the tests. If I passed, I might be a pilot. If not, I would spend four years in the Air Force doing something else, something new, something unknown—something outside the walls of the seminary.

I was in a complete joyful fog that Christmas vacation. The train ride to Minot was in a howling, blinding blizzard that rocked the car as it rolled along the tracks. Out the window I saw nothing but snow, but at least I was finally on the Great Northern Railroad going somewhere. At Minot Air Base they passed me through physical and mental tests for the pilot program with no problem. Wait. One small problem.

A very young doctor sat on a chair in one corner of the examining room. When I walked up to him, he took my papers and said with a deep, bored sigh, "Turn around and spread 'em," I did. I only knew what he meant from watching the man in front of me.

"Humm," he said.

He poked at my tailbone, "You feel this?"

"Yes"

"Does this hurt?" more poking.

"No."

He signaled another doctor to come over. "Hey, take a look at this."

The other doctor asked me, "Do you have pain when you sit on this part?" He poked, too.

"No."

Now I had two doctors back there looking and asking questions. I had never been particularly proud of that part of my anatomy, and all this attention made me feel somewhat uncomfortable. In Stearns County it was generally considered impolite to carry on a conversation with people while showing them your naked rear end. I considered this posture a good deal undignified.

"Have you ever had a complete physical before?"

"No."

"You are aware you have a pilonidal cyst?"

"I have never heard of such a thing."

Another poke and, "This area has never been infected?"

"No."

"Oh, hell, pass him. Pilonidal dimple. Uncle Sam needs cannon fodder."

The young doctor wrote on a form. He said, "I'm going to pass you, but you have a pilonidal dimple. I have to give you a waiver. That thing is deep and may give you a little pain at times when you're pulling G's in the airplane."

I wasn't concerned. I didn't know what pulling G's meant, and I was a tough farm kid who wasn't afraid of a little pain. While he finished the waiver the doctor asked me what college degree I had. I told him I had a BA in philosophy with a minor in Greek.

He stared. "A hell of a lot of good those will do you when you're dodging SAMs over Vietnam."

I didn't know what SAMs were, either.

After Christmas vacation I returned to school, finished the semester, and left on one of the coldest days of that winter. It was one of the happiest days of my life. God Almighty, I was so glad to go into freedom and adventure, into the vulnerable unknown. Yet, as I drove out and looked back toward that great, gray monastery church, I felt a pang of regret. There was that safe, impregnable castle. There was the hiding place of my youth, the secure fort—the rock of ages cleft in the granite hills.

Part III

In the Big Rock Candy Mountain
You never change your socks,
And little streams of alcohol
Come a-trickling down the rocks.
The boxcars all are empty
And the railroad bulls are blind,
There's a lake of stew, and whiskey, too,
You can paddle all around 'em in a big canoe
In the Big Rock Candy Mountain.
                                    –Haywire Mac McClintock

Chapter Thirteen

I HAD JUST LEFT THE SEMINARY, and now I was a bum. I did not know where I was going, where I would eat, or where I would sleep. I followed that dubious vocation until the Air Force took me under its wing (excuse the pun). I hitchhiked into nowhere. I did not take my '49 Ford; I could not afford gas. I did not take a camera; I could not afford the film. I did not take a razor; I did not want to buy blades. I had a tiny suitcase, which doubled as a chair when stood on end, and an old Army sleeping bag of Korean War vintage that said "good to twenty below zero." I wore a khaki shirt and blue jeans, and an Eisenhower jacket my brother Sylvester had given me when he got home from the Army. I did take my little transistor radio, and hoped the batteries would last. I left my sister's place in Minneapolis on a bitter cold morning. She refused to take me to the freeway where I wanted to hitchhike south. It was too cold. She dropped me off at the bus station. So I started my trip by spending a fourth of my money: I bought a bus ticket to Omaha and stayed overnight at the YMCA two blocks from the Omaha bus station.

Next morning, Omaha was foggy, drizzly, and cold, and I shivered and longed for sunny California. I almost made the mistake of turning west and heading directly there, but luck was with me. I might have been hitchhiking in numbing cold for weeks to get over the Rockies. I was in a gas station asking for directions to the main road when the man behind me tapped me on the shoulder.

"Where you going?" he asked.

"Any place warmer," I said.

"How about Kansas City?"

"Fine," I said.

"Put your stuff in that white Buick," he pointed to a huge, handsome automobile in front of the station.

In a minute we were rolling down the highway in a nice, warm car. The man was not talkative. He preferred listening to music. That was fine by me. I watched the strange land rolling by the window in complete contentment. I was on my own—independent and free. Buck Owens was singing "Together Again," and the man turned the radio loud. We sailed along smartly at first, but in a little while we were barely creeping. It had been a wet, drizzly night and now it was getting colder. We hit patches of heavy fog that slowed us down, and then stretches of bare ice. The whole highway became ice. We were boxed in by traffic. The driver cussed the weather. I didn't care. The scenery was all beautiful to me: the little homesteads along the highway silhouetted against the gray fog, skeletal windmills turning slowly, faded barns and houses with an occasional light showing fuzzy in the mist, farm roads deeply rutted, the ruts full of water, leafless trees that dripped water from their spider-leg branches, their tops hidden in the haze.

The driver turned down the radio. "Dreary morning, isn't it?"

I said, "Yes," though for me it was not dreary at all. It was exciting, wonderful.

At times it took us ten minutes to go a mile. The slower we went, the more talkative the driver became. He switched off the radio. He told me stories about St. Joseph, Missouri, where he had been raised. He said Jesse James had been shot not far from his house. He said his grandfather had been a hostler for the Pony Express that carried mail from St. Joe to Frisco, and he had a lot of stories about the pony riders and the Indians. He apologized for moving so slowly. I explained that time was nothing to me, and I had never felt so free.

It was getting dark when we got to Kansas City. When the man offered to drop me anywhere in the city, I foolishly said, "Twelfth Street and Vine" (an address I had heard on my transistor radio in a song about Kansas City). And so, with darkness approaching, I stood in the middle of the city with no place to stay. The shops were closed, the streets were mostly empty. Nothing was like in the song. There were no crazy little women there, and no one drinking a bottle of Kansas City wine.

I wandered along Twelfth Street and was amazed to find so many girlie joints: The Can Can, Folly Burlesk, The Pink Door, The Shake House. This was the big city! A man at each door waved men inside for a free peek. I looked, but I didn't go in. It cost too much and they were dreary places that smelled bad, the customers looked unkempt, and the girls old and caked with makeup. Along that street I picked up the wonderful aroma of someone frying liver and onions. I followed the scent to a café called McCabe's Lunch. A sign in the window said, "Large Bean Soup: 15 cents, Coffee: 5 cents." The place did not look clean, but it did look affordable. I stuffed myself with liver and onions for ninety cents. That included coffee. The waitress freely gave me refills, and she was not insulted when I asked for more butter, more crackers, and more salad dressing. I also got an extra helping of fried onions, which the cook personally delivered, ladling it onto my plate out of a black cast iron pan that sizzled and smoked.

I learned my first hobo lesson: the best places to eat are little places where local people eat every day. That's where you get good food, cheap food, and local color. The customers sitting at McCabe's lunch counter talked like old friends. They yelled at the cook and the cook yelled back. The place was so small everyone could hear the remarks, and they all laughed and added their own. I could tell from the crude conversation they knew each other well.

"Hey, did you shit in the coffee again?" asked a customer.

"Aw, shut up! You're cheating the undertaker the way it is," said the cook.

"Watch that mouth, or I'll come back there and beat your head with that dirty frying pan."

"Oh, I'm scared. I'm shivering like a dog shittin' razor blades."

"Well, at least your fat ass will be shivering when I kick it."

The jukebox played nonstop. You could get six plays for a quarter, two for ten cents, and one for a nickel. The people were very friendly to me, like I was a regular. I asked the waitress where I could find a cheap hotel. The whole place answered, and argued. They finally agreed on the Brown Oaks Hotel when I made it clear that cheapness was of utmost importance. The Brown Oaks was close by. I got a room there for two dollars, and found out why hobos sleep outside. I spent the first ten minutes killing cockroaches (though at the time I did not know what they were). In my log I described them: "These are huge bugs, flat as a nickel, and they zip around the room like mice." The bed was so dirty I spread my sleeping bag on top of it rather than trust the yellow-spotted sheets.

I woke up next morning with a dilemma. I was never going to stay at another hotel like this Brown Oaks, but I didn't have money to stay at fancy hotels and it was still too cold to sleep outside. The radio predicted warmer weather. Wichita wasn't far away and I had friends there, so I headed west. I caught rides until I arrived at Topeka in the late afternoon. I thought I better stay overnight. I was still three hours from Wichita. I walked around downtown asking about a place to stay and a cheap place to eat. A man named Fred took me to a Salvation Army soup kitchen, where we ate for free. Then he offered to take me to his house, where I could spread my sleeping bag on the floor and sleep as long as I wanted. He said he lived in a duplex with his brother.

What luck! But that lucky feeling melted away as Fred and I walked toward his home in the Topeka slums. First I noticed how often Fred refreshed himself from a hip flask he carried in his coat pocket, and it dawned on me that this jolly man was fairly drunk. Then he told me he lived with his brother, and that his brother had been in the state penitentiary for thirty years. Next he told me I would see some strange things at his place, but I should just ignore them. He did the strange things to humor his brother, who was kind of a nut.

Their home was one room, which served as kitchen, bedroom, and toilet. There was a big double bed, but only the nut was allowed to use it. Fred slept on the couch. The nut had stretched a curtain across the middle of the room to separate the couch from the bed, and whatever was on the bed side of the room (the stove, the toilet) Fred was not allowed to use; and since the refrigerator was on Fred's side, the nut would not go near it. Fred used a hot plate to make coffee, and he urinated into a pot, which he was then allowed to dump into the nut's toilet. I slept in my bag on the floor in a corner on Fred's side of the curtain, behind a chair (I put the chair there after meeting the nut). As far as I could tell, the nut spent his time sitting on the edge of his bed drinking from a brown, unlabeled bottle. I left early the next morning, stepping lightly on the creaking floor to keep from waking either of the two nuts.

"YOU CAN ALWAYS stay with friends if you run out of money," was advice I got as I left the seminary. But if you want to be a hobo, do not stay with friends. The cardinal virtues of a hobo are freedom and independence. When you stay with friends you are not free nor independent. You do as expected, not as you wish. When you stay with friends, you are more a leech than a hobo, and there is a big difference, though many might argue that. The mark of a hobo is self-reliance, frugality, and love of freedom. A human leech is the opposite.

I had no manual to guide me and had never talked to anyone who had made such a trip. I had to learn as I went. I kept a log and made notes about a few of the rides I got and some of the people I met. Often I got a ride simply because the driver wanted someone to talk to. Some were in a hurry and wanted me to drive while they studied the map. Some wanted a driver so they could get some sleep. For me even those rides were exciting, because I was on the road and going somewhere. I made notes about the people, but

I soon learned it was hard to make a flat statement about anyone. From afar humans all seem about the same, but when you sit down next to one and have a talk, you find they are all wonderfully, blessedly different. One great lesson I learned was that in this country, when people think you need help, they give it—freely, lavishly, nobly. I also found the same man can be savagely greedy one minute and honorably generous the next.

One morning I was hitchhiking out of Tulsa. It was hazy, but the sun peeked through, and there was no morning chill. I saw a gauzy brightness on everything. All was fresh and new to me. I saw oil wells, great claw hammers slowly see-sawing in the pastures like sleepy donkeys nodding their heads. I kept telling myself, *I'm in Oklahoma! Oklahoma, where the wind comes sweepin' down the plain.* I was thinking I would go east to Nashville to see the Grand Ole Opry. I caught a ride with a white-haired black man in a battered old car, but he soon turned west. I liked the man, so I stayed with him. He dropped me on a dirt road south of Sapulpa, near where his daughter lived. I did not really know where I was going now, but I did not care. The weather was warm and it was springtime. I sat on my suitcase and listened to my radio.

I was dialing around trying to find a radio station for some local color when I heard the roar of a motor on the far side of the hill. The sound filled the countryside, and there appeared on the hill all the local color I could want. The sound of the truck told me it had no muffler. As it topped the rise, I could see two strands of wire hopping along underneath where it had once been. A shredded confederate flag fluttered from a broken antenna. I saw two cowboy hats bouncing inside with a big dog in the middle. I didn't hold out my thumb because they were filled up, but they stopped anyway. Both cowboy hats got out.

The driver leaned over his fender and said, "Lookin' fer a ride, are ya?"

I nodded slowly, not sure. I figured I might be riding in the back of that dirty truck. But they yelled at their hound and he jumped out. The passenger pointed to the truck bed and said, "Up, up, up."

When the dog didn't respond immediately, he quickened him with a boot. The dog made a beautiful leap up into the bed of the truck, skidded and bumped against the side and gave a yelp. Both men doubled with laughter, and the passenger slapped his knee. He took my sleeping bag and threw it into the back with the dog, taking as much care as one might with a sack of manure. I put the suitcase in myself, thinking he might bust it. The driver lounged lazily against the truck, enjoying the morning sun. His left eye was almost shut in a squint against the smoke from the cigarette that dangled below it. That squint, I found, was always there, and so was the cigarette. His hat, once some shade of off-white, was all dirt and grease, his clothes faded from many washings. When he drew on his cigarette his cheeks caved in under the vacuum. He inhaled deeply with great contentment and allowed the smoke to come from his nose in slow wisps.

He jerked his head to indicate to me to get in. They gave me the honor of sitting in the middle, where their hound had been slobbering on everything. The passenger squeezed in next to me, pushing me well against the shift lever. He was taller, darker, and wider than the driver. He had large, staring eyes that looked like he was surprised.

The driver was talkative, and I had never before heard such an accent. He said "thang" in place of "thing," and drew out the word as if it had two syllables. The word "that" sounded like "they-at." For "tire" he said "tar." As we approached a crossroad with a stop sign, I noticed the rumble of the motor remained at full bore.

"Stop sign," I pointed.

"Ahm fixin' to run it," he said, and he blew past the sign like it was the green flag at a car race, with never so much as a glance at the mirror to see if a cop might be around. They didn't introduce themselves. They never asked my name or where I was going. When I told them I was on my way to Nashville, they said they were on their way home, as if I knew where home was. But as they got to talking about coon hunting, shooting pool, and drinking beer, I felt more relaxed. They didn't seem that much different from my mom's brothers.

We stopped at one of four buildings in a little town and parked the truck by a red gas pump, turned light pink from Oklahoma sun and dust. The driver started to pump gas into the truck while still pulling on his cigarette, but a fat little man with a sweaty gray T-shirt came out and cursed him and shoved him aside, saying this was not a "help yourself" gas station.

"You damn cowboys think you own the place," he said.

The place was a gas station, hardware store, bar, café, and whatnot. The sign by the door said, "Dentist Here Tuesday Morning." I followed the cowboys inside. The hound came in after us, and yelped to high heaven when the screen door banged on his tail. Again the two men laughed as though it was the funniest thing they'd ever witnessed. One of them went behind a low bar and brought out three beers and we drank. When the fat man came in, he collected money for gas and beer. We ordered hamburgers for each of us including the dog, who seemed to know what was coming for he stood with his front paws on the bar and moved his head all around, sniffing and wagging his tail with intelligent appreciation.

There was a pool table in a back room—well, sort of. It was made of slate and had a few patches of faded green felt, and there were pockets along the sides, but the bumpers had no bounce, and there were chunks missing. We played eight ball and drank beer while we waited for our meal. They never asked me if I was in a hurry to get going. The fat man kept hollering out the back for some help, but no one ever came. The cowboys were poor shots. They had not played all those long hours at the seminary like I had, but they were good at taking advantage of the eccentricities of that table. The hamburgers were long in coming and the cowboys ordered more beer. When the hamburgers came, we had to have another to wash them down. I didn't like to spend my money because I didn't want to go broke before I got down south, where I could depend on sleeping outside every night. But I was from Stearns County. If someone buys you a beer in Stearns County you are under a sacred obligation to buy him one back. And if he buys another, you must buy another. You can't get out of it. It is an ironclad rule that has no bending.

As we drank and played, we became friends. The driver of the pickup was Jim Jordan. He smoked a steady stream of Camels and when he lit up, he always offered me one. The other man was Bob Baker. Baker was a half-breed Indian. He smoked Lucky Strikes, but not at the prodigal rate of Jordan. I had a pack of Salems in my shirt pocket, which I mostly used to show smokers I was not against smoking. When I lit up a Salem, both of them declared they were "girlie" cigarettes that only a Yankee would smoke. I told them my name was Don but they kept calling me Yankee anyway.

"You ain't so bad, Yankee," Jordan would say when I bought a round of beer. As time wore on they both got more emotional, hanging on my shoulder, saying things like, "You're the best gawd damn Yankee I ever seen," and once Baker said (much to my discomfort), "Why, hell, I like you better'n my girlfriend."

Baker's tongue got so loose that at one point he confessed he loved me as much as his best coon dog, and that up until now he had never done more than spit on any Yankee's boots.

"Hey," Jordan said. "Let's introduce this Yankee to Sundown."

Immediately we shucked our pool cues, downed the beer, and left. We drove some back roads looking for a man named Sundown Forest. We stopped at a bar, but no Sundown. We stopped at a friend's house, no Sundown. We drove out to Sundown's farm, a dilapidated place with buildings that had sagging roofs and missing shingles, siding so cracked and dry I could see right through, and so in need of paint that one could only guess at the original color. All the buildings, including the house, had coon hides nailed to the siding. There were coon dogs all over the place, some tied to the corners of the buildings, some running loose. But no Sundown. We never did find him, and I was sorry we didn't. They described him as the guttsiest little son-of-a-bitch in Oklahoma. They said he could make you cry with his harmonica, make you laugh until your sides ached with his antics, and make you stare in amazement at his dancing. They added (as though this was really important): "He knows every nigger within a hundred miles from here."

They decided Sundown must have gone over to Beggs, which they described as "nigger town." We headed that way and went into the rottenest, dirtiest bar I had ever seen in my life and had a beer. The bartender was a broad black woman, who had all her little kids behind the bar and was taking care of feeding and disciplining them while she slid beers across to the customers, who—except for us—were black. We didn't stay long and left in kind of a hurry. I had not noticed any hostility in the bar, but the two cowboys said the black men in there were "fixin' to kick the shit out of us," and that the only reason they hadn't thrown us out when we walked in was because we were friends of Sundown.

It was getting late. "You'll have to stay with us," Jordan said. "In the morning I'll take you to the highway."

That was fine. I was so tired I would have slept on the floor in the Beggs bar. We drove along back roads among the hills and pines and came to a little place in the woods. Everything was covered with red mud, red dust, red dirt. A hundred hounds—well, a dozen—came jumping, dancing, cavorting all around, dizzy with delight at having their master home, their big ears flopping as they moved, bouncing like puppies around their mother.

Jordan said, "Ma's done gone."

There was a pot of cold stew on the stove. We lit a fire under it. Jordan went to the cupboard and took out a bottle filled with a clear liquid that looked exactly like water.

"Let's give this here Yankee some shine," he said. He splashed some of the liquid in a glass and we passed it around, each taking a swallow as we sat at the table. There was absolutely no flavor—or if there was any, it was completely covered by the raw, torturous burn of pure alcohol. It sucked the breath out of my lungs and left me gasping and watery eyed. I could think of no reason under heaven why a human would take another sip of that stuff, but when the glass came around I sipped. The cowboys took big gulps, smacking their lips and grunting with contentment. I longed for a try at the stew on the stove, but it was more than an hour before we got to it. They told stories of Sundown Forest and of coon hunting.

My hunger was gone now, and I felt like my stomach had turned upside down. The floor rolled and pitched like a boat in a stormy sea. Finally they remembered the stew. I ate, and after a few swallows, I felt better. We finished the entire pot, a mix of onions, potatoes, carrots, and "coon shanks." The cowboys pulled off their boots and went to lie down in a back room. I rolled into my sleeping bag by the cookstove. The fire had died, and the room was cool. The hounds on the front porch moaned occasionally. A barred owl kept calling in the trees down the way. The stove made soothing little clicking noises as it cooled, and I was out like a light.

The next morning Jordan took a small ham from the smoke house and fried slices of it in a black pan, which sent savory smoky smells through the house, but they did not entice Bob Baker. Jordan yelled for him to get up, but he never appeared. After we ate, Jordan took me to the main road by Muskogee. He dropped me on the shoulder and talked to me though the open window.

"I got to tell you somethin', Yankee. You all be more careful who you ride with, hear? We was gonna roll you yesterday."

I stared.

"You understand what I'm saying?"

I shook my head.

"We was gonna hit you on the head and take your money and your clothes, don't ya' see? I knowed you was a Yankee the minute we come over that hill, an' I says, 'Lets roll that ol' boy.' But you turned out to be a good guy. We took a likin' to ya, so we didn't do it."

"I had no idea," I gulped.

He laughed. "Well, you watch yourself. Might be others out there. And if you ever come by here again, we'd be proud to have you stop by. You can sleep at the house anytime you want. If Ma's home she'll kill you a chicken."

The motor roared, and the truck rumbled off. I stood gaping by the road.

Chapter Fourteen

IT WAS IRONIC the Okie cowboys thought they had *not* robbed me. They had in fact succeeded in relieving me of almost all my money. With paying my share of the beer and hamburgers, and kicking in a couple of bucks for gas, I was nearly broke. I walked along the road near Okmulgee. There was a big lumber truck by the side, the driver checking his tie-downs, on his way to a sawmill by McAlester. I asked if I could ride with him just to the Little Rock highway. He said his company didn't allow it. Then he said I could climb up and lie down between the logs. Then he could say I'd sneaked up there when he wasn't looking. He said he'd stop at the Little Rock highway, and I could sneak back down.

I found this an attractive offer and didn't hesitate. It was a warm enough morning, but once a forty-mile-an-hour wind blew over those logs, it wasn't so warm. I huddled behind my suitcase, using it as a windshield. I felt so cold I was thinking of crawling into my sleeping bag, but the sun climbed higher and soon it was warmer. It seemed like forever before the man stopped his truck. When he saw me getting down, he looked shocked. He apologized profusely for forgetting about me. We had crossed the highway long ago and were at McAlester. He laughed when I said I didn't care, as long as I was farther south, where it was warmer. He showed me on his map where we were.

The old bear of a lumberjack came up with a good suggestion: "Forget about Nashville. If I was you, here's where I'd go." He tapped his map at New Orleans. "They're fixing up for Mardi Gras down there." He said "Nawlins." Had he not pointed at the map I would have wondered what place he was talking about.

I caught two long rides that day. Before late afternoon, I was at a gas station near Shreveport, already halfway to New Orleans. I'd learned to get out at gas stations whenever I could. They were the best places to get rides. I had access to the station's bathroom and cover if it rained. At a gas station I could strike up a conversation with a driver while he pumped gas. People could pick me up there before they got up to cruising speed on the highway. A man whizzing by on the freeway does not like to take time to stop.

The station by Shreveport had a sign in the window that said, "Help wanted," and below it in parenthesis it said: "temporary." I asked about the job and had barely finished my question when the man said, "You're hired." I was subbing for the boss's son, who was taking a short vacation. I spent several days pumping gas and handing monkey wrenches and needle-nose pliers to a cranky, old mechanic who ran the place. He was a black man, and was grim, tough, determined, and so serious and devoted to work he reminded me of Dad. He never rested. He was silent except when he needed something. I had fun with him. I did not resent his grumbling and ordering me around. I was getting paid—and I wasn't his son. I delighted in his talk, which was always low, abbreviated, never a "please" or "thank you" or "nice morning, isn't it?"

"Han' me dat prybar," he'd say, or, "Doan make it too tight, you bus' da tred."

He had a funny accent. For him the name of the town was "Sweeveport" and the wife made "swimps" for dinner last night. I had almost no expenses at that station. At night I slept in a lounge chair in the owner's office. I survived mostly on the donuts left on the counter from the day before and bags of salted peanuts, too stale to sell. When I did eat at the restaurant across the street, I'd have a bowl of soup for a quarter and ate all the crackers and butter I could lay my hands on. I liked to eat there and listen to the waitresses. They called me sweetheart and honey with slow, sleepy drawls. They often didn't pronounce the "r" at the end of a word: "Well, Ah nevah!" or "Baked potato takes forevah." They carelessly threw in an "all" behind the word "you" and used the word "reckon" in place of "think": "You all reckon it's going to rain today?" They had a dreamy leisure and sing-song inflection that sounded like music.

The week before Lent I was thumbing on the road south of Shreveport. I was on my way to Mardi Gras Town, and rich. I had over twenty dollars in my boot. In warmer country now, I'd spend no more money to sleep. I'd sleep in a culvert if I had to. My suitcase had everything I needed: two pocket books, a spare shirt and trousers, a floppy denim hat, a washcloth, a bar of soap, two changes of underwear, a pair of wool socks, and a dozen sheets of toilet paper. I had a tan clip-on tie I sometimes hooked on my shirt collar in an attempt to look like a respectable hitchhiker. I traded my nylon parka at the restaurant for two small jars of peanut butter. Any little empty space in my suitcase was filled with nickel bags of salted peanuts (part of my salary). I had a wool sweater rolled up in my sleeping bag. In my pocket I carried three vital instruments: Sylvester's U.S. Army P-38 can opener, a teaspoon, and my Dad's old pocket knife. Mom gave me that knife when Dad got a new one, the fall I started grade school, in exchange for a promise to quit complaining about school.

My radio was packed away now. The batteries had gone dead. I'd sell that when I got the chance—and I would miss it a lot. Often in the mornings before I got out of my sleeping bag or during the day when I sat by the road, I had turned on that radio and listened to local stations. I had always thought KASM in Albany, Minnesota, must be the worst radio station on earth, and their morning radio personality, Cliff Mitchell, was off his rocker. Sleepyhead Cliff (as he called himself) entertained dairy farmers in central Minnesota every morning as they milked their cows. "Gooood morning!" he used to holler into the mike. "Good morning all you good-looking gear-jammers, de-juicers, flapjack flippers." (He meant truck drivers, farmers milking, and housewives making breakfast.) "Gooood morning!" Ringing a cowbell, he'd continue. "Get up! Ball and squall, run up the cotton pickin' wall!"

I considered him the corniest broadcaster, and the station the most boring. I was way wrong. I found stations of that kind all over the country, and many a lot cornier. But traveling, I found them informative, interesting, and entertaining. They gave me a connection with the everyday people of the countryside—the small stations began broadcasting at sunrise and shut down at sunset.

All through the first part of my travels I could get a powerful station out of Des Moines. It played great music but didn't have local color. As I moved south accents on the small local stations got thicker and the mode of expression stranger. In Omaha I listened to a station out of Shenandoah, 940 on the dial. Around nine in the morning the program was called "Coffee with Florence." Florence read the local paper and made comments on what she read, adding little stories she picked up from local gossip. She read from the obituaries: Mrs. Hilmar A. Bloom had died. She added, "And do you know how old she was? She was eighty-two! You'd never have guessed it! She sure didn't look that old, now did she?" Then Florence had some really hot news: "Martha broke the glass cover of her popcorn popper. Now she has to go to Bethany to get a new cover 'cause they don't have 'em at the hardware store in Shenendoah."

I SAT ON MY SUITCASE, read *Cannery Row,* and stuck out my thumb. Passing cars sent a warm rush of air over me. Sometimes people honked loudly as they swished by, but I paid no attention. It was warm in the sunshine and I was drowsy.

From somewhere far, far away I thought I heard a soft voice calling, "Do you want a ride?" Then I heard it again. I looked up and realized I had been sleeping. A car was parked just beyond me. A lady leaned out the window waving me over. I got in and met a middle-aged couple, Lee and Hardy Gieger from Shreveport, who were so nice to me I later spent pages writing about them in my log. Lee seemed convinced I was near death from starvation. They were going only as far as Natchitoches, a two-hour drive at most, but we stopped twice to eat and drink, and they refused to let me pay for anything.

When we got to Natchitoches, they refused to drop me by the road. They took me to the bus depot and bought me a ticket to New Orleans. I tried to tell them I didn't need a ticket, that I was an experienced hitchhiker, but to no avail. In my log I wrote, "They were so nice to me I almost cried." I asked why they were being so good to me. Lee said their fifteen-year-old son ran away from home. He was missing two days and they were going crazy with anxiety. Finally he called. A black man had picked him up and made him call his mom.

Hardy said, "I don't particular care for niggers, but if I ever meet that man I'll throw my arms around him."

They tried to give me money so I'd call my mother, but I refused it. They finally gave in when I said I'd write her first thing in the morning. I got on the bus and found a seat next to a pretty young girl, Judy Ferguson, from Long Beach, California. I made her talk the whole time about the ocean, the beaches, the people, and the sunshine. She gave me her grandmother's phone number and said I should look her up when I got to Los Angeles. She thought what I was doing was very exciting. I noticed the same attitude in others. Girls often thought it all very adventurous, glamorous, and boys wished they could be doing the same thing. But Judy became very concerned when I said I did not have a place to stay in New Orleans. She had made her reservations months ago, and said by this time there was not so much as a broom closet available anywhere in the city. I think she must have been rich because she was staying at the Roosevelt, one of the fanciest hotels in New Orleans. Others on the bus were also going to Mardi Gras. They agreed with Judy and told me to look out for pickpockets.

It did not take long on the streets of New Orleans to find out Judy was right about getting a place to sleep. All hotels, motels, lodges, flop houses, slop houses, and spare bedrooms were booked weeks ahead. I slept that first night in a stack of fiberglass insulation piled up in a corner on the second floor of a big building under construction. I rolled into my sleeping bag and slept "snug as a mouse in a cotton gin," as one old lady had wished upon me as I walked off after asking her about a place to stay.

The following day I realized the insulation bed was a mistake. It made me itch. I spent most of the day checking out eating places and a place to sleep. New Orleans was food heaven. The air along Bourbon Street was all aromas. I never saw so many restuarants. Many had signs advertising Mardi Gras specials of oysters, shrimp, and steak. They had piles of Creole food on tables in front of their places, and you could buy a huge platter of red beans and rice topped with a big, meaty pork hock for less than fifty cents—and good luck finishing the plate. I ate piles of red beans and rice in New Orleans, and after that first day, I always ate at Brown's Restaurant.

The recommendation to eat at Brown's came from a beggar—really a thief. There were blind beggars all over the city at Mardi Gras time. A very young one, no older than I, had a cup for donations in one hand, in the other a white stick. A little dog followed him around as he tapped along, singing in French.

A blind couple walked together. She played the accordion, and he held out his hat for donations. They leaned against each other for support. A tall black man stood by the door of a bar with his cup. He had a sign on his back and chest that read: "I am blind. My days are darker than your nights."

I thought those beggars were all for real and felt sorry for them, until I met Jackson that evening. It was drizzling, and he looked pitifully bedraggled in his wet clothes. I was dry because I stood under balconies and awnings along the street. Jackson purposely stood in the drizzle. He was having a successful time of it; his clothes were soaked through and people felt bad for him. He made his way on crutches and rested against buildings as though exhausted, but he accosted everyone who passed. If they didn't give him money, he hobbled along beside them begging until they got embarrassed and shelled out.

Jackson made an assault on me, but I convinced him I was a hobo and had nothing to give him. He changed from beggar to Good Samaritan. He told me how easy it was to get money during Mardi Gras. His crutches were a prop, his club foot rags stuffed in his shoe. He told me the best food—and cheapest— was at Brown's Restaurant. He said I could sleep on the floor of Ann's Bar.

"I'll show you," he said. "Both places are at the same street corner. But first, watch me put the squeeze on this rich couple." He stepped right in front of a nice-looking couple and began begging in a pitiful voice, surprisingly loud so everyone around could hear. The man waved him aside, but Jackson followed, stumbling along with the crutches. The couple stopped, the compassionate lady scratched in her purse, and Jackson came back waving several dollar bills.

We went to Ann's Bar, on the corner of Conti and Burgundy. Every corner on Burgundy had a saloon: the Red Carpet, Golden Pumpkin, etc. This bar was the shabbiest. The first thing I noticed was a man lying on the floor by the wall. He was out cold and the front of his pants was wet. We sat at the bar. The bartender gave us each a glass of wine for a nickel, which Jackson, the beggar, paid. He bought another glass for a man named Johnny, who leaned against the wall holding a bloody dishrag to a cut on his cheek. The bartender laughed as he told us Johnny bragged about being an ex-fighter, but a liquored-up, skinny little punk had come in, got into an argument with him, and decked him with one punch. The bar window was broken and taped. The bartender said a tipsy sixteen-year-old girl had driven her fist through it last month, and it cost her daddy twenty-four dollars for the window and forty-four for the doctor.

In came the "blind" young beggar with the little dog. He was a fraud, too. Jackson bought him a drink and they compared notes. They were thick as thieves.

When Jackson went to the can, the bartender told me Jackson spent all his money on muscatel. Right now he was flush with dough and the most generous man in the world, but when he ran out, he'd rob me. The bartender agreed Brown's was the best place to eat, and pointed it out kitty corner across the street. I sneaked out and went there to eat. There was no way I was going to sleep on the floor of Ann's Bar with those winos. That place was too rough for me.

At Brown's Restaurant I stuffed myself with rice, beans, and pig's tail for forty-one cents. The black mammy cook gave me a free piece of bread pudding wrapped in waxed paper to take along. After that, I ate there every day. One day she served sow's ear on rice with a soup that had chicken, wieners, and potatoes—all you could eat—and bread pudding with coffee for desert: all for ninety-six cents. She said I was only the third white man who'd ever eaten the sow's ear, and the other two were city folks who didn't know what they were eating. For me, raised on blood sausage and head cheese (which has in it the ears, the snout, and the lips, too), it was nothing. Another day she had red beans and rice with chitlins, and she stood over me smiling as I wolfed it down. She said, "Fo' a white boy, yo' sho' knows how da eat."

The sun was just setting when I left Brown's that first night. The drizzle had stopped. I still had no place to sleep. I started to look around, even in the alleys. On a street corner I saw a girl standing alone watching the crowd. She looked bored. She was very shapely and had clear, dark eyes, black wavy hair, and skin like a tan olive. She appeared very exotic to me after the pale-skinned, blue-eyed blondes of Minnesota. She was greatly amused to see me carrying a suitcase and a sleeping bag. She was very friendly. I talked with her for a while. We laughed at the antics of the people on the street. When she talked, she stepped very close to me, and I liked the way she looked me straight in the eye. She was Cajun, she said, and that's why the dark hair and eyes.

For me she was Longfellow's Evangeline: "black were her eyes as the berry that grows on the thorn by the wayside." I was having a great time with her and imagined us falling in love. She asked where I was staying. I said I had no place. She smiled and told me she had the perfect place for me. I was such a greenhorn it wasn't until she told me it would cost five dollars and five more for anything oral that I realized she was a prostitute. I was greatly disappointed and told her so. She laughed at my stupidity and called me a baby. When I told her I didn't have any money, she turned, scornful, and said she suspected I liked boys better anyway. I hoisted my sleeping bag and walked off.

I saw her again later. By then the street was dark, everything still shiny wet from the drizzle. The lamps glowed dim in fog come up from the river. She came toward me along a narrow sidewalk, her arm around a man who wobbled and staggered. When she saw me with my sleeping bag over my shoulder, she beckoned and grabbed my elbow. "Come," she said. I could feel her breath by my ear. "You can sleep on our floor. The girls won't mind. There's a bad, un-healthy fog out tonight. Here, help me get this drunk to the house."

I took the man's other arm. He cocked his head at me, smiled, then looked surprised. He started to jerk away from me, then realized the hooker was on his other side. We went into a big house. She showed me where I could roll out my bag, in a corner by a long couch. She and another girl took the drunk up-stairs. I lay on top of my sleeping bag and was comfortable, and grateful. I won-dered if these were the "real people" Father Kieran wanted me to learn about.

I fell asleep, but not for long. The place was a beehive of people coming and going, banging up and down the stairs. The house smelled of booze, body odor, and tobacco smoke. I kept waking and dozing. Once I woke to what sounded like a fight upstairs—much thumping and swearing. A woman screamed at someone. I heard glass breaking and more swearing. It was quiet for a moment, then someone staggered downstairs, threw himself on the couch, and began to snore like a chainsaw. I rolled up my bag and left. I never saw that Cajun hooker again, but I always remembered she was nice to me, and her eyes were black.

There were still a few people on the street, most of them liquored up. I walked down toward the river, thinking I might make a little shelter among the cargo boxes on the docks. Then I saw the bus depot. Why hadn't I thought of it before? I could store my gear for a quarter in one of those coin lockers and sleep in a chair. From then on, my suitcase and sleeping bag spent a lot of time in public lockers in the towns where I traveled. But you can't sleep in a bus depot for all the noise of loudspeakers and rude, shouting people. Besides, it was creepy. The restrooms stank. The walls were dirty, scribbled with disgust-ing messages soliciting oral sex. Next to the condom machine, someone had written in green crayon, "Bust one and win a baby." Somebody else had written, "This gum tastes funny." Over the urinals: "Please don't eat the urinal cakes."

I got my sleeping bag and walked down toward the docks. On the way I got lucky again. I made a discovery that helped me the rest of my time on the road. Out of the darkness a sudden shower of rain sent me scrambling for cover. I got under the awning by a gas station closed for the night, and there, behind the station, was a black 1949 Ford just like mine, except the front end was mashed in. I'd slept in the backseat of my Ford before. I tried the back door. Open. The inside was in perfect condition, clean and dry. In a minute I was rolled up in my sleeping bag on the backseat listening to the *drip, drip* of rain drops from the Spanish moss that hung from live oak branches. It was cozy in there, like a hunter's cabin. I slept so soundly the sun was already clear of the oak trees and blazing in the window when I woke. I knew I'd made a great find. In those days every gas station had a mechanic, and they all kept damaged cars behind the station. They fixed up those cars or used them for parts. Usually they didn't bother locking them. In the coming months those cars were my night shelters in many a town across the south, the west and up into Canada.

When I dumped my sleeping bag at the bus depot, a tall, black Voodoo preacher stopped me by the door. He said he had come all the way from Africa to "help" the people at Mardi Gras time. He had with him a very great-looking white witch. They planned to walk up and down Bourbon Street and sell supernatural potions, roots, and talismans to make sick people well and healthy people fall madly in love. I explained to him I couldn't fall in love right now, because I'd be going into the military soon and might have to go to Vietnam. He understood this completely and wanted to sell me a little amulet to keep me from getting killed in the war. I declined. He didn't understand. As I walked away, he prophesied loudly I had not long to live, the way I was going about it.

I walked down to the river. Leftover fog drifted lazily around the houses and sometimes made shiny columns where sunshine struck between buildings. The houses along the shore all sat up on stilts. Seashells were piled up in heaps like sand piles. They used the seashells on their roads like we use gravel in Minnesota. A black man fished for catfish. He lived in one of those stilt houses and did nothing but fish all day. He said he made a good living; he sold the fish to restaurants and got thirty cents a pound, and if he dressed them out he got seventy cents. During Mardi Gras he got even more.

I explored the docks on the waterfront. Ropes as thick as a man's arm were wrapped around posts. There was a pleasant smell of tar and hemp and saltwater. Big, slow ships moved like a dream in the hazy harbor, and long barges with tugboats pushed them. They signaled each other with horn blasts. One barge came all the way from Minnesota. A tiny tugboat pushed it toward the dock, the motor muttering. Behind me, coming across the rooftops—church bells. Then I remembered it was Sunday, and the bells were calling people to Mass. I followed the sound up a hill until I saw the belfry tower.

The Mass was short. I expected the priest to rain fire and brimstone on the excesses of Mardi Gras, but he seemed quite happy with the entire affair. He was young and perhaps somewhat vain, for his beard and hair were very carefully trimmed and he walked up and down making large gestures as he preached. He told about how Jesus loved sinners like Mary Magdalene, and how He changed water into wine. I got the impression that sinning during Mardi Gras was okay, as long as you repented by Ash Wednesday and went into denying the flesh after that. I sat in the back of church and thought about how peaceful I was inside. I was not sorry about leaving the seminary—and I never was later, even in my bad times.

When I left church the priest was talking to an old man. I joined the conversation and introduced myself. I told the priest about quitting the seminary and hitchhiking to see the country and the people. He said he had just the thing for me. He had planned a boat trip that afternoon into the bayou country with this old man, but something had come up. He asked the man if it would be all right if I went instead. The man consented and without thinking, so did I.

"Don't worry," the old man said about his boat. "She's a bit leaky but she floats just fine."

I didn't relish going into mosquito country with an old Cajun in a leaky boat. I wanted to go back to the French quarter and watch the "real people" carry on. Thinking back, that Sunday boating in the swamp with an old man who loved every lizard and snake was the highlight of my stay in New Orleans.

New Orleans is surrounded by a big swamp. The Cajun, gnarly as the bayou oaks, knew something about most every plant and animal. The little motor pushed the boat very slowly, giving plenty of time to look around. The motor purred low enough so we at times surprised a moorhen or a great egret. We snaked our way between huge cypress roots and under branches of ancient live oaks. The live oak does not grow straight and tall like our northern oaks, but bows and twists, and drapes itself heavily with Spanish moss.

The swamp, in some places where live oak branches hung low, closed-in cave-like, haunted by eerie shadows from the swaying moss and dark forms gliding under the water. In other places the swamp was a tall, open cathedral, a ceiling of arching cypress branches curving high overhead, shafts of sunlight coming through openings and lighting the trunks like pillars in a church. Once we saw a pair of alligator eyes blinking between knobby cypress knees but the eyes disappeared with the slow wave of a tail and a green swirl of duckweed as we approached. That was all I saw of an alligator. The old man said so few were left I was lucky to see even that much. But the place was teeming with other animals and birds. We passed a camp belonging to hunters who trapped muskrat, otter, and beaver. They also trapped the nutria, which I had never heard of before. The old man called it "river rat." It was like a giant muskrat. Those hunters sloshed in the muck every day among the water moccasins and rattlesnakes. I firmly resolved to avoid that line of work.

As we headed back out of the bayou, the old man asked me about myself. He listened without comment until I told him I would likely be in the Air Force by Christmas. He frowned and shook his head. He had read in the paper the war was going badly and the U.S. was now bombing North Vietnamese towns and villages, and that President Johnson was sending thousands of Marines to fight there.

"I think we are headed for big trouble," he said. "I wouldn't want to be a young man right now."

The old man clucked his disapproval again when I asked him to drop me off in the French Quarter. I was hungry for red beans and rice.

"The place is a den of thieves," he said.

I said, "I know. But I have to find out what real people are like."

"Those aren't real people. They're Mardi Gras nuts. You don't need to know what they're like. Your home is the seminary. There you were in your Father's house. You were on the straight and narrow path. Now you are the prodigal son. Go back home where you belong. They'll receive you with open arms."

"Not now," I said."

"I'll pray for you," he said.

The streets were abuzz with peddlers of candy, hot dogs, and ice cream. The merrymakers were dressed up like characters from books. There were cowgirls and cowboys, two different versions of the Lone Ranger, and a green Robin Hood with his Maid Marion. A big, fat man dressed in white with a baker's hat sang "Hot cross buns!" I did not buy any. I was sure they were not as good as Mom's cinnamon rolls. A butcher walked around steeling his knife and bragging about a steak house on Burgundy Street. Lots of young people shouted and twirled, and some staggered. Right in front of me a silent, headless horseman dressed all in shiny black rode by on a coal black pony. It was beautiful.

I walked through the French Quarter. The houses and shops were a hundred years old. The people dressed in old-style clothes, the ladies in long dresses and the gentlemen in coattails. I heard Frenchmen chattering in the old tongue, Mexicans sputtering Spanish, and strange, dark people talking unrecognizable languages. Sometimes I heard the *cling-clang* of a trolley car, the next minute the low moan of a fog horn from the river. It had the flavor of a harbor town with the salt smell of the sea and sailors swaggering by with their giggling girlfriends.

All over were street venders yelling about hoagies, jambalaya, and salt-water taffy. Bartenders came right out on the sidewalk in front of their taverns and poured zombies they sloshed together from fruit juices and black rum. They let you have a swallow for free. Rollicking sounds echoed up and down the street as little two- and three-man bands walked around. Horns everywhere played "When the Saints Go Marching In." I had never imagined a circus like this.

Above the narrow streets, ladies leaned from the wrought iron rails of second-floor balconies, shouting to people below. They threw down flowers, and sometimes candy and clouds of confetti. Several young men under one balcony yelled up at two pretty girls. As I drew nearer I heard them chant, "Show us your tits, show us your tits." I was aghast at such rudeness and disrespect. The girls kept shaking their heads no, but they did not leave the balcony. I almost made a total ass of myself. I was about to go and rescue the girls from this embarrassment by telling the boys they were entirely out of line, when one of the girls stopped me dead in my tracks. Snickering and giggling, she honored the boys' request by ripping open her blouse in a brazen, spectacular display, and the other, not to be outdone, immediately followed suit—and her display was even better. On the street every man cheered and tossed coins up onto their balcony. I walked on, shocked, and a good deal disgusted that people would act like this. Real people. I was learning.

The French Quarter also had its strip joints. These were much classier, and the girls far better-looking, than in Kansas City. They had guards at the doors, too, who allowed men a free peek inside. Club Flamingo, Chez Paree, Blue Angel, Gunga Den, Sid Davilla's, Sho-Bar, and plenty more. For bait the doorman described in detail what the girls did in their show. The Chez Paree had a girl named Candy Bar. She was a "cowgirl" who stripped down to nothing but gun belt and boots. At the Blue Angel was a very pretty girl named Lilly Christine who took off her clothes and played with herself. At Sid Davilla's was a fat girl named Blazee Starr and a thin one name Pussy Galore (the movie *Goldfinger* had come out a few months before). The Sho-bar had a girl named TNT Red, who dressed like a sweet and innocent little school-girl but then lay on the stage and performed acts that would have got her kicked out of class, out of school, and out of Albany, Minnesota, if she had tried her act there.

All Bourbon Street was crowded with people, Many already dressed in the outfits they would wear for the Fat Tuesday parade. There were chimney sweeps with long brooms, hunters dressed in fringed buckskin, mimes, and pirates like Blue Beard and Jean Lafitte. The rest of the day and all day Monday was crazy like that. Then came Fat Tuesday. If you combine a ticker-tape parade, an insane asylum, a New Year's Eve celebration, a St. Patrick's Day drunk-out in St. Paul, and a University of Wisconsin-Madison homecoming, you might have some idea of Mardi Gras day. I got to the parade route early that morning, but throngs of people were already choking the avenues and side streets in anticipation of the parade. Some had been out all night. Every crazy person in the world was in New Orleans. The parade avenue was so choked with people I couldn't imagine how a parade was going to get through. All around I could hear the sound of drums and horns. Several times that morning people shouted, "Here they come!" and people pressed forward and mashed each other to get a look, and then it turned out to be a false alarm.

When the floats finally came, it was a sight. It appeared that sometime during the night all the weirdoes from the French quarter had joined all the nuts from the rest of town and mounted floats to put on a parade. The spectators pressed back to give them room to pass. I was being squeezed from all sides, sometimes by pretty girls who didn't seem to mind a bit. Many of the spectators were dressed like the people on the floats. They wore masks and false beards, long noses, and costumes like clowns. They were wild with delight, like children. They jumped up and down and yelled at people on the floats to throw them something. Their requests were constantly granted. Candy, beads, flowers, rings, cigarettes, cigars, peanuts, caps, handkerchiefs, and all kinds of trinkets went flying through the air, followed by clouds of confetti. There were stampedes to get at the trinkets, and pushing and shoving, and always laughing. I was caught in an ocean of people and allowed myself to be rushed back and forth with the waves.

Every crazy costume bedecked someone that day. Every crazy stunt possible was tried, and every quart of liquor was employed. There was a float labeled "Dante's Hell." It was a mass of screaming devils, all almost naked and painted red and black, brandishing pitchforks and stabbing at each other and at the crowd. They had fearsome witches with them who stirred brews in garbage cans, sending up streams of dry-ice steam that trailed behind the float. The devils and witches dipped big mugs into the garbage cans and passed them to spectators, or they just threw the brew over the crowd, and people tipped back their heads and stuck out their tongues to catch a drop. The devils were kissing the witches and running around in the crowd kissing the fairest maidens along the way—and the maidens kissed back. But there were also some painted devils darting around in the crowd, and I saw that some of those were pickpockets. They worked in teams. I was glad I had stashed my gear and had my money in my boot. Those were some clever devils, very nimble and fast with the fingers.

It was hard to believe that this kind of celebration ever had a basis in religion, especially as a lead-in to the season of fasting and abstinence. It was just too much for me. By mid-afternoon I was staggering from fatigue. A woman next to me, who was constantly yelling and drinking out of a glass, grabbed a handful of hair on the back of my head, pulled me against her, kissed me full on the lips, then laughed like a loon and went on yelling. There was no pleasure in it. Her breath was heavy with cheap whiskey and her lips as cold as the ice in her glass. I found it revolting. Even the thrill of female bodies pressing against me was wearing thin.

I was thinking about where I could take a bath. I had been "bathing" by swabbing off with a wet washcloth in public bathrooms the last several days.

Now I struck upon an idea. Judy Ferguson, the girl on the bus, had told me she had booked her room at the Roosevelt Hotel through Tuesday night, but that she had to leave Tuesday evening. I headed for the hotel. The Roosevelt was right by the French Quarter. The man at the desk said that Miss Ferguson had just checked out. I went up to her room, hoping she was still packing. I knocked. The door was slightly ajar, and I went in. She was gone. I looked up and down the empty hall. All was silent. I hung out the "Do Not Disturb" sign. I locked the door. Half a bottle of champagne was sitting on the TV in a bucket. It was warm and gone flat, but it tasted fine to me. I ran a tub full of steaming water. I soaped up with perfumed soap and lay back and sipped champagne and read magazine articles from the *Roosevelt Review*. I could have wept with the luxury of it all.

I came out of it suddenly when there was a knock on the door, a soft cry of "Maid," and the sound of the door being unlocked. I grabbed a towel and surprised the maid coming in. I told her we had decided to stay one more night and there was no need to clean the room. She seemed happy with that. She dropped off some clean towels and left. I stayed in that tub until I was all wrinkly, and then I slept away the night.

I left the city of New Orleans the next day having learned several lessons about people: they do not take their religion seriously, they freely mix the sacred and the profane, and they are preoccupied with sex and drink. I learned some lessons about myself, too. I learned my moral character was no better than that of other men. I did not pass up the Creole hooker or several other women in New Orleans because of my high moral values. It was from want of money and from fear of disease. I also found I was capable of theft. As I left the Roosevelt, I stopped by the traveling desk for directions. The travel agent was asleep at his post. There was half of a bacon-lettuce-and-tomato sandwich on his desk. I spread a city map over the sandwich and pretended to be studying the roads while I checked for danger. I folded a corner of the map over the sandwich. When I left the hotel, the sandwich somehow came along. The map was free, and now the sandwich was, too. I ate it sitting by the road. I did not repent, even on Ash Wednesday. I justified my theft by saying I was hungry, he was not. I justified eating bacon by saying that I did not remember it was Ash Wednesday when I stole the sandwich.

I now realized how much easier it is to be a saint while secluded in a seminary or behind the walls of a monastery. I saw that the business of being a saint was made infinitely more difficult when there was actual temptation around. My admiration for saintly monks declined, while my admiration for saintly city-folks grew.

Chapter Fifteen

AFTER NEW ORLEANS, I knew where to store my gear and where to sleep. And I knew where I could take a very comfortable shower any morning I felt like it. In those days hotel rooms did not have the automatically closing doors they have now. Guests walking out of their rooms in the morning did not bother to close the doors. They had their hands full of luggage, and the open door acted as a signal to the maid she could come in and clean the room. If I wanted a shower, I would go to any large hotel early in the morning, go to an upper floor and walk down the hall until I found an open door. I would listen for a moment by the door, and if I heard nothing, I would walk in as if it were my room. If I found someone, I would say, "Oops, wrong room," and leave. If there was no one, I looked for hints that the room was abandoned: luggage gone, closet doors open, no clothes on the hangers, some drawers open and empty, the door key lying on the bed or the bureau. I hung out the "Do Not Disturb" sign and took a nice, warm, leisurely shower.

As a bonus, I often got free food guests had left—treasures like parts of sandwiches, donuts, and candy bars, and always a half bag of potato chips. I was too young then to worry about germs. I did not need my drinking glass wrapped in cellophane, nor did I look for a personal message from the hotel manager on a strip of paper across the toilet seat letting me know that all germs were destroyed and it was safe to park my butt. I washed my socks in the sink, wrung them out, and later dried them by the roadside in the sun. When all my clothes were dirty I washed a load. Every town, even the smallest, had a Laundromat then. I could wash a load for a quarter and dry it for fifty cents.

A hobo does not carry a map or a travel guide. Those things make you greedy for routes and destinations. I must go here, I must see that. What good is a map when a local man gives directions? He doesn't say, "Turn left on County Road 27. Go two miles to County Road 50." No, he says, "Go until you get just beyond where old McGowan's sawmill used to be. Turn there and go awhile 'til you get to the big white pine on the left." If you let a travel guide book direct you, you're liable to turn down rides not aimed at exactly the right destination. You might sit all day waiting for that one special ride. The exhilaration of hitchhiking comes from the unknown: the next driver, the next road, the next town. If you knew all that beforehand, you could just as well stay home in your rocking chair and watch TV.

An old man should not be a hobo. The vagabond road is for a young man to travel—young enough so everything is still fresh and new. The same trip in old age would be dull. By then you've seen it all before, somewhere, sometime. But for a young man—I was no more than a boy, based on my experience—it was wonderfully exciting every day. All of it: oceans and mountains, narrow valleys and broad plains, swift antelope and sleepy bison. And most of all the people. But even if you're young, today hitchhiking is no longer available to you. Carjacking has put an end to it, made drivers wary.

I never worried about getting lost. The drivers who picked me up were always glad to tell me where I was. They'd happily pull over to the shoulder and get out their maps to point at towns and trace roads with their fingers. Not to say drivers always knew where they were. I was sitting on my suitcase eating peanuts somewhere north of Houston one afternoon, enjoying the warm sun, the jingle sound of a meadowlark calling from a fencepost behind me, and thought in Minnesota they were likely having a snowstorm. I was way out in the country where a rancher had dumped me when he turned off onto a rutted dirt trail—no sign of human habitation. All I knew was San Antonio and Dallas lay somewhere to the west.

A red-faced man pulled over and waved me to his window. "Where does this road go?" He was in a hurry.

I shrugged. "I don't know."

"Well, where are you going?" he asked, exasperated.

"I go wherever they take me," I said.

He swore. He called me a damn fool and laid rubber as he went smoking down the tar way. I was thinking of going to Dallas to see where Kennedy had been shot, or to San Antonio to see the Alamo. I sat and read *Cannery Row* for a second time. A car went by flying like the wind. A loud screech of the tires caused me to look up. Two young ladies in a white convertible had just skidded to a stop a quarter mile down the road. Another screech sounded as they backed, and tire-smoke drifted from under the car. The driver yelled, "Get in," jerking her thumb at the backseat. They didn't bother to open a door. There was very little room back there, but I did not hesitate. These girls were driving the greatest little car ever made: a Ford Mustang. I threw in my stuff and vaulted over the side. My bottom had barely hit the seat when we were off in another neck-snapping screech of rubber.

I'd never been near one of these magnificent machines, except in a showroom at the dealership in St. Cloud. This was pure heaven: sitting back in a fine new Mustang convertible, two pretty girls in the front seat, their perfumed hair flying in the wind, the warm air of springtime rushing past my ears, heading west. The girls weren't going to San Antonio or Dallas but were headed for a basketball game in Austin. One of them had a boyfriend playing in the game.

They were having a grand time, these two, drinking grapefruit juice and vodka out of coffee mugs. They didn't have an extra mug, but they told me to go ahead and drink right out of their big thermos. They called me "sunshine" and "sweetheart." I loved southern girls. Northern girls didn't ever do that with a stranger. When one of them reached back a cup for me to pour another drink, she called me "sugar pie." It felt great. Only one problem: those two little darlings were drunk. They were spilling their drinks, laughing and slapping the dashboard. The driver had the distressing habit of entirely disregarding the road ahead and almost turning clear around in her seat to tell me about her Mustang. She didn't know much. She knew she had over 200 horses under the hood and a V-8 engine. But she had no idea what the V stood for, nor the eight. She only knew the thing made noise, moved the car and made the wheels squeak. She had no idea the cost. She thought her daddy paid a thousand dollars. I knew it cost over three. She knew she had the most comfortable bucket seats and would squirm her little bottom deeper when she mentioned it.

The two did not have a care in the world except running out of grapefruit juice. We stopped to buy some, and they showed me how to mix it in the thermos with vodka that came from a bottle in the trunk. When the driver almost turned the wrong way on the highway, I delicately hinted that she might be getting too drunk to drive. She was not insulted in the least. She pulled over and said, "Okay, sugar, you drive. You might as well earn your keep."

She got in the backseat and spread herself out like the Queen of Sheba, dangling her feet over the side or resting them on the back of my seat, lit a cigarette and made a great show of smoking it. She raised her cup in salute and waved her feet at trucks going by, unaware of the way the wind blew her skirt around. Drivers waved back, honking long and loud in appreciation. I'd never seen young girls act like this. She pushed my hat over my eyes. When I complained, she took it away and put it on herself or on her partner. The two laughed at everything. They both looked at themselves in the mirror, laughing and spilling their drinks. They spent a half-hour entertaining themselves with my hat.

They suddenly turned up the radio to full blast because Roger Miller was singing, "Dang me, dang me, they oughta take a rope and hang me." They asked me if I liked the song. When I said I had never heard it before, they wondered if I was from Mars. When they found I didn't even know who Roger Miller was, they about fainted. They judged I must be the biggest square on the planet and had a great laugh. Everything I said sent them into stitches. They asked me to name my favorite song. I tried to think of a popular song and finally said I liked "Folsom Prison Blues." This sent them into convulsions.

"That's only about ten years old!" They gasped and were doubled over with laughter, slapping each other on the back for several miles while singing parts of "Folsom Prison Blues" and trying to sound like Johnny Cash.

WHEN I LEFT AUSTIN for San Antonio, I was picked up by Texas State Representative Ralph Scoggins, on his way to the San Antonio Airport to pick up his wife. He was as pleasant a man as I'd ever met. In less than two hours, by the time he dropped me off, I felt like asking him to adopt me. He gave me his card and said if I ever got into any trouble while I was in Texas, I should show the card and say Representative Scoggins was a close friend of mine. If that did not help, I should call him personally.

I saw the Alamo, and I saw Carmen Maria Georgina Soler-Baillo Caminero.

How do I remember that name after all these years? I was in love. I confess: in those days, I fell in love with anything that wore a skirt and was nice to me, but I would have married Carmen right then if I had money, a house, and a car. Carmen was everything I was not—mature, sophisticated, confident, and wise beyond her years. She had been born in Cuba and hated Castro like poison. Her parents had sent her and her little brother to the United States but were not allowed to come because they were doctors. Castro did not allow professionals to leave the country. Carmen cried when she said her parents loved their children so much they were willing to give them up and send them to the United States rather than force them to live in a communist society. She did not know if she would ever see them again.

Carmen was part of a group of volunteers that worked in the poor Mexican section of San Antonio. They had a house in south San Antonio and daily went among the Mexicans to help them with their problems. I spent several days going out with them. Carmen took me around to see the town. She said the Spanish section was more Mexico than United States. It had little automobile traffic, kids played baseball and flew kites in the street. The highline wires were draped with kite strings and tails. Little girls played a game I had never seen before. They tied a ball or a piece of wood on a string which they loosely tied to one ankle and got the ball going around in circles. With the other foot they leaped over the string every time it came around. This came out later as Skip-it. An American company thinks they invented it. Mexican kids did it long ago.

From Carmen I first learned about the heat in jalapeños, and about the great taste of refried frijoles. We ate in the Mexican section at night. Carmen was fluent in Spanish and spoke English with a beautiful Cuban accent. She was at home anywhere she went. The Mexican music played at night around the Mercado by norteno bands sounded like old-time German music back home in Stearns County, only better. Mexicans used the accordion and concertina in much the same way, but in the background they laid down a wonderful thumping rhythm with a bass guitar in place of the labored, grunting sounds of the tuba.(I never liked that fat, overgrown horn.) Mexicans used the polka rhythm a lot but kept the songs current with constant revisions. While Germans at home still sang with Lawrence Welk about rolling out the same old barrel since World War II, Mexicans sang about illegal border crossings, drug killings, and separated lovers and families. They had blood, prison, and murder in their songs.

On St. Patrick's Day Carmen talked me into spending a few quarters to call home. Mom said a big blizzard blew outside. Roads were closed, schools were closed, and cars were stuck all over the place. In San Antonio, it was eighty-five degrees and the sun was shining. Carmen decorated herself with a green scarf and a gaudy green bonnet. She pinned it on her dark hair and stood with one hand on her hip with her chin stuck out high.

"Well, how do I look?" she asked me.

I wanted to tell her she was perfect. I wanted to tell her she was the most beautiful thing I had seen, but I didn't have the courage. I said, "You look nice."

She responded dramatically by tossing her head, saying, "Hah, you say that to all the girls." She always made me laugh. I wanted to marry her right then.

I don't know why Carmen was so nice to me. Maybe because, though she was my age, she looked upon me as a child who needed help. I could have stayed in San Antonio longer, but I knew how quickly one can wear out a welcome. In a few days I said I had to get to California by Easter, but that I would be back later in the year. She must have seen my moral struggle, because when she dropped me on the west side of town, she gave me a picture of herself, on the back of which she wrote in Spanish, "Never lose faith in your ideals."

DON'T HITCHHIKE IN TEXAS. You'll never get out of there. You can hitchhike in any direction all day long and through the night, and the next morning you'll still be in Texas. It took me forever to get to El Paso. I almost died of thirst along the way. About ten miles east of Fort Stockton, intending to make Van Horn by sunset, I sat beside the main highway (the only highway) at the top of a long, rising grade. Mostly trucks were on that road. I could hear them groan as they shifted down for the climb. I waved at some of them when they passed, but didn't hold out a thumb. I didn't expect a ride from a semi. I waited for a car, but nobody stopped.

I was thirsty. All I had to eat that day was salty peanuts. I'd already drained my water bottle. It was very hot. No shade trees, only that sad excuse for a plant called sagebrush. Not a wisp of cloud blocked the sun, only a dozen black vultures in the sky, circling slowly in the distance, black spots against the blue. I wondered if some dummy like me had died of thirst out there. The road shimmered from the heat; I couldn't see a vehicle clearly until it was almost upon me.

I got desperate. I changed my mind about flagging a truck and thumbed everything that came along. I even tried a school bus. Nothing stopped. But again I was in luck. Suddenly I heard the "*Bang! Flibbidy, floppity, flop, flop, flop,*" of a flat tire. A big semi stopped just short of me. The driver got out, circled his rig, and kicked at one of his tires, calling it several unkind names in Spanish. (I did not understand, but I could tell a curse from a compliment.) I asked if I could help. He said, "No!" He had done it a million times by himself, he said. Besides, he wasn't allowed to pick up hitchhikers. He was sore, but he did let me drink from his water jug. I went back to hitchhiking. When he was done with his tire and back at his cab, he paused for a minute with one foot on the running board. He watched me thumbing by the road. He spit. He jerked his head and waved for me to come. "Get in," he yelled.

A few days later I was thumbing out of El Paso, still heading for California. I thought I'd pass through Santa Fe on the way. I wanted to see that town of the old west. But I had to shift gears. The man who picked me up informed me I was already halfway across New Mexico! It seemed impossible, but El Paso, Texas, is farther west than Santa Fe, New Mexico. That was one time I should have looked at a map, or I should have studied geography better in school. But no matter. I went to Las Cruces.

Las Cruces, a short skip from El Paso, took me all day. The first ride I caught had car trouble. I spent most of the day waiting with the driver at a gas station. When I got to Las Cruces, I walked to the west side of town where there were a lot of big truck stops. I spent the night, as it was getting too late to go on. People don't trust hitchhikers in the dark. Besides, it was too cold to stand by the road. In the back of a parking lot I found a truck marked "Allied Van Lines, Inc." It wasn't locked. From the dust on the gearshift I judged it had not been used for weeks. I climbed in and made it my bedroom.

The next morning I saw the most glorious sunrise of my life. It came up from behind the Organ Mountains that guard the east side of Las Cruces. The air was biting cold, and frost covered the hood of the truck. I sat up in my sleeping bag to look. The sky was completely pink, then slowly got bright orange as the sun rose behind a high mountain peak. The whole world was in daylight, but the sun was still behind that dark mountain, sending out great shafts of light like the second coming of Christ. Suddenly it came blasting over the peak in blinding glory, warming the truck in a minute. Water dripped from the hood.

It was still early, but cars already moved on the highway. I got up, put on my jacket, and wandered out. I had barely settled down when two young men came along in a big Buick. I held out my thumb. They zipped by at fifty miles an hour. As they passed the passenger opened his door and waved for me to get in. He shouted, "Come on, get in!" which of course was impossible at that speed, but it did make me laugh.

But in five minutes I had a ride—a man on his way to Deming. Silver City and Bayard were just north of there, and two of my classmates at Crosier were from Bayard. When I told the driver I was going to stop at Silver City, he said, "Oh, you want to see where Billy the Kid and Pat Garret hung out."

The driver did not like Pat Garret. He said, "Garret was a cheat and a coward. He got what he deserved. You know he died back there in Las Cruces, right outside of town, shot between the eyes while taking a piss."

My old Crosier buddy Dick Bela was studying law in Austin. Another classmate, Alvin Trujillo, was in Bayard. He took me up to see the ancient Gila Cliff dwellings, driving his old flivver. We had to cross the west fork of the Mimbres River several times—through the water, not over bridges. We got stuck once. I got out to push and lost a little pocket notebook in the water. That notebook had some of my most interesting stories—some were true.

I hitched a ride down to Lordsburg, then turned northwest into Arizona. I got to Duncan late in the evening. I was dropped right by the courthouse. Seeing a light inside, I entered and asked the sheriff if I could sleep in his jail. He gave me a cell by myself with a bed and a toilet. The former inhabitants had drawn pictures and written their names all over the walls. Johnny Gray must have been there often, or had done a long stretch there, because his art, proudly signed, was all over—rivaled only by Woody from Silver City. When the place was dark and I lay on the cot, I could see stars shining between the black iron bars of a small, high window. I thought how confined a man must feel locked in there for a time, seeing this tiny sample of the vast glory of the night sky, and thinking of the vast space and the boundless freedom outside.

I PRACTICALLY SKIPPED ARIZONA. I didn't even see the Grand Canyon, though it wasn't on purpose. Out of Duncan I got the longest ride of my hitching in the States—over 200 miles—all the way to Phoenix in one stroke. (That distance was nothing compared to rides I'd later get in Canada.) I rode in a pickup with a quiet little man who drove along looking at the scenery and humming to himself as if he were on vacation, though he claimed to be on business. I saw my first saguaro cactus that day, a giant beauty standing all by itself, towering above a mass of mesquite and sagebrush. The driver laughed at my admiration for it. He said there were millions in Arizona.

I caught a ride north out of Phoenix to Flagstaff, thinking I'd go see the Grand Canyon, but a man from Denver moving to Las Vegas picked me up. I rode with him into Vegas.

Las Vegas was a good hobo town in those days. You could get a free breakfast in most of the big casinos and sometimes a free lunch. You could sleep in the big comfortable casino chairs (as many of the gamblers did when they got tired). But I didn't need their chairs; I stayed with Vince.

Vince Laubach and his brother, Bob, ran a little corner grocery in Las Vegas called the Family Market. I'd never met Vince. A former Crosier student told me he was from Stearns County, so I went in to meet him. Behind the counter was a man with broad shoulders and a very broad smile. When we compared notes, I learned his father had once owned the farm just south of my father's. They had sold out and moved to Las Vegas for his dad's health. His parents had recently moved to Twenty-Nine Palms, California. You couldn't find a kinder man than Vince. He invited me to stay at his apartment on East Stewart. I could sleep on his couch. He took me in without hesitation, based simply on the fact I was a farm boy from Stearns County. When he found I'd never played a slot machine, he reached into the cash register, pulled out a handful of quarters, and shoved them into my hand.

"Get out there right now and play," he said, pointing to the machines in front of the store. As I went out he yelled after me, "Anything you win is mine."

If I had won anything, I would've certainly given it to him. I felt guilty to be spending his money, but every time the machine was friendly and gave me a few quarters, it turned hostile and, in the next few minutes, took them all back—plus a few more. It see-sawed back and forth like this until, before I knew what it was up to, it had robbed me of all that Vince had given. I went back in, and Vince laughed and acted very surprised a person could lose money playing those machines. He asked his customers if they had ever heard of such a thing, and they all went along with his joke and said it was hard to believe.

For a few days I helped at the store, sweeping and making deliveries. When I had free time, I walked around town looking at the casinos. At least a dozen were crowded near the corner of East Fremont and North Main Street. They were all about the same: noisy with slot machines and gambling tables, crowded with smokers and drinkers all hypnotized by poker chips and dice. I was surprised how many old ladies sat in front of slot machines pulling the levers. Some looked very bored, pulling lazily at the handles, cigarette hanging from a corner of the mouth, half-closed eyes staring, barely noticing when they won a few nickels. But another kind jerked the handles with great energy and watched with eager eyes as the reels spun in the window. Each time their shoulders slumped as the machine delivered no coins, but when it did deliver, they cackled like witches and looked around to see if anyone noticed.

The bright lights of Las Vegas burned all day, even in bright sunshine. Signs read: Golden Gate Casino, Monte Carlo, the Club Bingo, the Pioneer Club, Phil Long's California Club. The Pioneer Club had an enormous lit cowboy over it, which gestured "come in" all day long and drawled out, "Howdy Partner" every five seconds—okay at first, but very tiresome after a while. I logged Diamond Jim's as my favorite. I had the courage to play blackjack there and made three dollars, though I knew nothing about the game. Three dollars ahead, I chickened out and quit playing. At Diamond Jim's I first saw a scopitone, a jukebox that cost twenty-five cents for a single play, but you wouldn't only hear the recording, but see it acted out in beautiful color on a screen. They kept playing over and over a song called "Cake Walking Babies from Home." You could see the band playing the music while pretty, leggy girls danced in front. I thought it was miraculous.

Once at Diamond Jim's I saw a man dragging a lady out. He had a hold of one arm, had dug his fingers into the clothes on her back and was pulling and shoving her along, saying, "Use your brains for a change! We're going home." She fought him tooth and nail, yelling, "God damn you, I got ten dollars back there, you son of a bitch." They should have gone a block down the street to the "Lowest Priced Divorce in Town." (That was a shocker. In Stearns County when someone got a divorce it was kept as quiet as possible.) Near that "divorce chapel"was a wedding chapel where you could get married for ten dollars, including flowers. A pawn shop touted, "We Buy and Sell Wedding Rings."

The Lucky Casino had its name on a big sign with an all-red background. The doorman said it was the biggest neon sign in the world. The Hotel Fremont had a sign, "If you're the outdoor type, the Hotel Fremont is for you." I don't know what they meant by "outdoor type." Liberace was playing, and he did not strike me as the outdoor type. I saw lots of hotels and casinos—the Sahara, the Tropicana, the Starlite Club, and the Mint, but I never had the time nor interest to see them all. One night I took a girl who lived near the Family Market to the top of the Fremont Hotel. We drank whisky and enjoyed the view, when suddenly she said the Mint was on fire! I said they were likely just putting on a show with red, glowing lights, but she said I was blind or stupid or both. The waiter came and informed us the girl was right (about the fire). He said the Mint had a big fire, but the fire department had it under control and it would soon be out.

The slot machines were not just in the casinos. Every grocery store and gas station had some. They always gave change in quarters so you'd play their machines on the way out. They had them nicely lined up by the door. At the bus depot people played while waiting for a bus to take them to the casino. In some men's restrooms they had slots by the urinals so you could (as Vince put it) get rid of money and urine at the same time.

One day Vince had two grocery deliveries for me: for Mrs. Montgomery and Alice Chaney. Vince said, "They're nice old ladies, but one likes to take drugs and the other likes to drink and is a bit blunt in her speech." I brought Mrs. Montgomery her groceries first. She lived in a big trailer in the middle of a trailer park. She was bedridden. A lot of bottles stood on a tray by her bed, most of them morphine products. She had syringes close by and had needle marks on her arms. The shades were pulled and no lights were on. Depressing.

Next I went to old Miss Alice Chaney. She was tipsy and wheezed from asthma, but she was a tough old broad, and funny. She told me to put the groceries away on the shelves in the kitchen. I said I wouldn't know which shelves they went on. She said, "Oh, fer Christ sake, if you're that dumb, just put them on the counter by the sink."

I had to laugh at her spunk. I put the groceries on the shelves as I thought best. A sign on her cupboard: "How to get thru the day: keep a smile on your face, a song in your heart, and a pint in your pocket." She attempted to write out a check. We tore up the check—it was illegible (she took my word for it). I wrote out a check for her, but we scrapped that one too because she messed up the signature. We got the next perfect, and I put it in my pocket. She decided she needed a drink and told me to go get her a pint of vodka. I had no cash, so we made out another check for five dollars, which I was to cash at her bank.

I said, "I don't know my way around town. I'm not sure I can find the bank."

She said, "Oh, hell, I'll go with you."

"Okay, ma'am, whatever you say."

"Quit calling me ma'am, god damnit! Call me Alice like everyone else."

"Yes, ma'am." I said, and she gave me a dirty look, so I added, "I mean, Alice."

When she saw the car I was driving (Vince's spanking new 1965 Impala Supersport), she said, "I don't know if I want to drive in this piece of junk. Don't you have a Buick?"

But she got in and appeared quite comfortable. Off we went to the bank, where she stayed in the car. I had no trouble cashing the check; the teller said the old lady was loaded (he meant with money). We went to the nearest saloon and got a half-pint of vodka for $1.50. She insisted I keep the other $3.50, even though she had already given me a dollar for helping her get dressed to go downtown. She had gone into her bedroom and was fussing around in there. She yelled, "Hey you, kid, what the hell's your name anyway? Oh, yeah, Don, come in here a minute."

I felt a bit uncomfortable, but went into her bedroom. She was arranging her hair and putting on her lipstick in front of a little wall mirror but having trouble holding steady and wanted me to watch her so I could catch her if she fell. She did okay, though. I only once had to grab her by the arm to steady her a bit. Then she told me to close the snaps on the back of her blouse, and she stuffed a dollar in my pocket for the help.

When I left her off at her house, I thought about how only a few months ago I would have considered this bizarre behavior for human beings, and disgusting, too. But I had changed. Those two seemed a lot more normal now, and I got a big kick out of Alice. Here was a woman who didn't believe in following the rules laid down for women in society. She swore like a lumberjack and told you exactly what she thought with never a bit of sugar coating.

After a few days I was ready to leave Las Vegas. I felt I was imposing, even though I did odd jobs for Vince. I had seen enough of Vegas and was restless to see California. Smoky casinos, extravagant shows, comics, stars, drunks, flashing lights, ringing bells, music, noise, noise, noise . . . like the New Orleans Marti Gras, Vegas was too much for me. Really, I liked New Orleans better. New Orleans was friendly and gay. Vegas was sly and calculating. New Orleans gave you warm hugs while taking your money. Vegas took it with cold, metallic precision.

When I got ready to leave, an opportunity for adventure presented itself. A man came to repair one of the slot machines by Vince's grocery store. I was watching because I wanted to see what the guts of one of those things looked like. The man said he sold and repaired machines all over Nevada. He asked me if I wanted to go along on a trip for a few days and help drive his car. I said yes.

That's how I met Moe Trenkle. Moe drove around in a 1964 Pontiac Bonneville, pulling an enclosed trailer. He had a smelly little lapdog that did not like me. She snarled and showed her teeth as I got in.

"Don't worry about my little sweetheart here," he said, scratching the dog's ear. "She thinks she has to protect ol' Moe. She doesn't bite."

Moe looked liked a hobo gangster with his stubble beard, uncombed hair, and wrinkled, baggy clothes. He always wore a felt hat low over his hooked nose. His great pot belly sagged heavily against his belt. His dog didn't help his image any. She was a dirty, snappy little bitch of uneven coat and shed patches of hair everywhere she rubbed. She was always rubbing.

I thought Moe might be hauling his bed in the enclosed trailer, but when I asked, he said, "Nope, just slot machines and parts." He fixed slot machines, and by "fix" I mean both ways—repair, and the other kind of fix (to pay more money or less according to the owner's wish). I figured that out from watching. He knew all about slot machines—the old cast iron, mechanical kind that needed no electricity. There were a lot of those old machines in Nevada. The new electric ones were coming on fast, but there was still plenty of work for men like Moe. He had a business card that said, "Atomic Coin Company" and under that, "Rebuilt Slot Machines of All Kinds." It should have said,"Except those blankety-blank new fangled electric ones." Moe hated the new machines.

Moe had me along to help carry slot machines and drive his car when he got sleepy. I was a bit nervous at first driving this gangster's big automobile in traffic with the trailer behind. It always seemed like the hood ornament was somewhere down the street in the next block and the trailer was lagging behind in the preceding block. I felt like I was piloting the *Titanic* through glacier fields. It didn't help that Moe would sometimes suddenly wake up and shout, "Stop, god damnit. Where the hell do you think you're going, kid?"

When I told Moe I was from Minnesota, he said, "Oh, I've been there often. You ever been to Stearns County?" I about fell out of the car.

Moe had been a bootlegger during Prohibition. He had hauled Minnesota 13 (a Stearns County corn whiskey) from Minneapolis to Cheyenne. I told him my grandpa used to make moonshine. That sat well with Moe. He liked Minnesota moonshiners. They had given him his start in life.

Moe got started hauling whiskey for a peddler in Cheyenne. He got paid for his load and his mileage. After he had some money, he went into business for himself, selling moonshine in the small towns of western Nebraska. He paid twenty dollars for five gallons in Minnesota. When he got to Nebraska he made the five gallons into ten by mixing it half-and-half with distilled water. This left his whiskey at about ninety proof. Pure Minnesota moonshine ran about 180 proof; the really good stuff as high as 200 proof. Moe printed labels that said: "Top Quality Minnesota Corn Whiskey" or "Minnesota's Best Grain Alcohol." He sold it for two dollars a quart.

Moe said, "I got my driver's license the day I turned sixteen. I drove my first load the next week. Made regular runs to Cheyenne. I took a few loads to Chicago. Never got caught. I was sixteen but looked twelve. When the cops stopped me, they were more worried about my driver's license than my trunk. I made good money and have those Stearns County farmers to thank." He punched me in the shoulder, "Anybody from there is all right by me."

I didn't tell Moe I had studied to be a priest. I wanted to retain my status as a good guy. I stayed with him about a week and we traveled over most of Nevada. I often hinted we should stop and look around when we were near a place I recognized from my reading, but Moe would say, "We're not on a sight-seeing tour." I wanted to stop at Virginia City. I knew Mark Twain lived there when he wrote for the *Territorial Enterprise*, but Moe zipped right by without so much as a glance in that direction. I didn't hold this against him. I saw more of Nevada than many natives did.

It would have been a wonderful trip—perfect for me—had it not been for two things: his damn smoking, and his damn dog. He smoked all day, dribbling the ashes on his shirt, sometimes having coughing fits, and routinely threw the smoking butts, filter and all, into the ashtray and let them burn down. When we got up north near Idaho, it was too cold to open the window. I almost died in there.

At night he stayed in cheap little one-bed motel rooms. Moe and his dog took up the bed. At first I slept on the floor of Moe's room, but after a while I slept in the backseat of his Pontiac, where I did not have to deal with Moe's dog and Moe's snoring. Every night on his bed Moe drank deeply of Wild Turkey (he called it "Thunder Chicken"). He cursed women and cops, double cursed his bad luck until he fell asleep. His snores rumbled in the room like a truck engine. Whenever he was drinking he'd caress his dog and talk baby talk to her and say, "Are you Daddy's little Pookie, ye-ess, you're Daddy's little Poookie," and other sickening stuff. The dog often licked his mouth. She liked whiskey, too. All day while we were on the road, the little cur slept in his lap, and when Moe took a pull on his half-pint of peppermint schnapps, he let her lick the cap and the bottle mouth. Then she spent the next five minutes licking her chops.

In the larger towns we stopped in the back of casinos. Moe went in and talked to the bosses. Sometimes Moe took his tools and opened up the back of one of their machines and tinkered with the gears and springs. Then he went around front and put coins into the machine and pulled the handle until he was satisfied. If he was not satisfied, we would load the machine into the trailer and leave the casino a new one. Those old cast iron machines were wearing out. There were too many moving parts in the guts. Pulling the handle made the three reels spin and it also wound up a little motor that put the brakes on the reels and kicked out the coins when there was a winner. There were just too many reels and tumblers and springs and gears and gimbals. Moe said it was easy to cheat those machines, though I never figured out how.

One night just outside of Carson City, Moe got a motel room. It was teeth-chattering cold, so I slept inside on the floor. Moe had turned up the heat way too hot in the room, but he turned it off completely before he went to bed and started up his rumbling snore. The room cooled fast. Soon I was snug in my sleeping bag. I slept until near morning and woke up to hear the dog pacing and making whiney sounds. Pretty soon she started scratching on the door. I thought, "I'm not getting out of this nice, warm sleeping bag for that stupid dog. Let Moe take care of it." Moe kept on rumbling, and the dog kept scratching and yipping. Then she got real quiet and began making straining sounds. I wondered what she was up to. Not for long. The chilly air was suddenly overwhelmed with a foul stench. I knew I had made a mistake. I pulled the bag over my nose and slept on. Moe slept late in the mornings, and I often got up early and walked around the town, but that morning I stayed in and pretended to be sleeping until I heard Moe get up and curse the dog.

"What happened?" I said, all innocent like, as Moe cleaned up the mess.

I could tell there was something shady about Moe's business. He carried a very fat wallet stuffed with hundred-dollar bills. He was always paid in cash. I never saw a receipt or paperwork. He always made me wait by the door of the casinos while he talked to a boss. Some casinos were "off limits—too many cops around." Moe had connections with casinos from Lake Topaz up to Reno.

Reno was just like Vegas. Even the names of some places were the same, and it too had its wedding chapels and blinding lights. Big signs said that Jim Nabors (Gomer Pyle) was entertaining at Harrah's, Lorne Green was at the Nugget, and Jimmy Durante was coming soon. One sign along Virginia Street had statues of five blazing showgirls—they must have been twenty feet tall, with ten-foot long legs—framed in bright running lights and standing over a huge sign that read: Primadonna Casino.

From Reno we went east. We left pretty, green valleys and entered the dry alkali desert of the high Mojave. There were hardly any trees. The air was dry and thin, and so was the population. Everything and everyone looked dusty. It was hot by day, cold by night. Moe was eager to get to Jackpot. He wanted to play poker at the Lucky Seven Casino, where he had friends and where he "always won money." But we ran through several snowstorms as we climbed into the Sonoma Mountains, so Moe said we better stop until the weather cleared. We slept that night at the Sonoma Inn in Winnemucca. As we got near Wells the next day, Moe dozed in the passenger seat, holding his big belly and his dog in his lap. The wind whistling around the windows, the tires purring on the road, and soft music on the radio all made me sleepy. I was thinking I had better pull over when Moe suddenly woke up, poked me in the ribs and says, "By God, kid, let me tell you about a little experience I had here in Wells one time." Then he told me this story:

It was late at night, I was headed north to Jackpot. I decided to get a motel in Wells, but I hauled my ass all over town and everything was full. So I heads out to find another place, and I see this blond lady (actually Moe said c--t; the words "lady," "girl," and "woman" were not in his vocabulary) standing by the road. She had two suitcases with her. It was a cold son-of-a-bitch that night. I mean, a guy had to be a damn hard-hearted bastard to pass her by even if he wasn't looking for some pussy. I pulled over and asked where she was going. She says, "Idaho."

And I says, "I'm going there, too, but I'm going to stop at the first vacant motel and get some sleep."

So she gets in, and she's a nice young thing, see. I go a few miles and there's a motel. I says, "I don't know about you, baby, but I'm a-gonna go to bed here."

She says, "Okay, I'll go to bed with you."

We go in and she says, "You don't mind if I take a bath, do you?"

I says, "Hell no, baby. You go ahead and wash that pussy nice and clean."

Well she just laughed about that. So while she was taking a bath I says to myself, "This here is not just an innocent little girl. She is too free and easy." I had a roll of cash on me: $2,800 in one hundred dollar bills. I had seventeen dollars in my wallet and a bag of quarters in my pocket. I hid the roll of hundreds behind the bottom dresser drawer, and left my wallet and the quarters in my pants pocket. After we fucked a few times, I went to sleep like a log. When I woke up, that damn bitch was gone! I checked my pockets. Sure enough, all the money gone. I opened the drawer and there was my $2,800 all nice and safe. I'll be a son-of-a-bitch, that was close! She never knew what she passed up. I learned my lesson. I know these bitches all over Nevada. I never trusted one again."

It was true Moe knew a lot of women all over Nevada. He had no respect for women, yet some seemed to like him. They came over to talk whenever we entered a casino. Moe poured on the flattery something awful, but he kept one hand on his wallet.

When we got to Wells, we ate. A hooker came in and boldly sat down next to me and tried to talk me into going with her for twenty-two dollars.

I asked her, "How do you know I'm not a cop?"

She said, "Honey, don't you know prostitution is legal around here?"

Moe knew her. She was from the Hacienda Club. Moe told her to buzz off and she left, calling him all kinds of foul names, most of which fit him. I kind of liked her except that she was stupid enough to think Moe was my father.

About three o'clock in the morning we got to Jackpot, up on the Idaho border. The poker room at the Lucky Seven was closed. They weren't doing well. There were five big casinos in that town, but not a house. I mean, not a one! People lived in trailers. We went into Cactus Pete's Nevada Club and got a place to sleep. Before we went to bed, we went to Diamond Jim's for a drink. A young Indian in there was totally drunk. He spoke English, but I couldn't understand a word, his tongue was so thick. His drinking buddy finally dragged him out of there, and I watched them in front of Diamond Jim's. They stood by a car and seemed to be having an argument about who was going to drive. The Indian took off toward the casino across the street. When his buddy tried to stop him, the Indian turned and took a couple of surprisingly fast swings at him, any of which would have felled an ox, but he missed completely. His buddy let him go and came back into Diamond Jim's.

He said, "I'll kick his ass clear into next week as soon as he sobers up."

"Ugh, too much firewater," the bartender said.

The Indian got halfway across the street and fell. He lay there pawing at the dirt like a turtle on its back. It was a cold night and he wore only a thin summer shirt. His buddy said, "I hope he freezes."

A couple of young men on the street went over to help him. They got him on his feet and headed him toward the car, but suddenly he had another fit and started swinging one roundhouse after another, going like a windmill, sending his helpers diving out of reach. The momentum of one of his swings sent him stumbling, and down he went again. One man reached down to give him a hand, but the Indian aimed a vicious kick at him. That did it. They left him there and came into Diamond Jim's.

"After about ten minutes in that cold," they told his buddy, "he'll beg somebody to pick him up."

"I hope somebody runs over him," his buddy said.

They waited a while and then they all went back out. The Indian was passed out now. They loaded him in the back of the car and drove off.

We would have slept late the next day, but Moe's stomach was bothering him so we got up early to get him some Alka-Seltzer. I looked around the town a bit and could not figure out what in God's name they were thinking when they built the casinos way out here. The Stardust was practically empty, and the 93 Club, which had most of the business that morning, had only a few slot machines going. But Moe said, "You should see these places on weekends. They're always filled up." Moe said Senator Estes Kefauver was an idiot, and got everybody in the country riled up about slots. Pretty soon they made them illegal almost everywhere. When they busted up the slot machines in Idaho, they built a big log cabin full of the one-armed bandits just across the Nevada line—Cactus Pete's in Jackpot. Gamblers stampeded from Idaho every weekend and kept the reels spinning and the dice rolling. The town was growing.

We went to the Lucky Seven to eat breakfast. The Lucky Seven had no business. No one was at the slots. We sat at a table with the owner, Curly, and two of his girls. Curly was nice-looking and so were his girls. He informed us he had been robbed the night before. Someone had broken in through a hole in the back of his place where there used to be a fan. The thieves got away with $8,000. He figured it was somebody local because they knew their way around. He had fired one of his dealers lately and suspected it might be him. He said the sheriff had just left and was coming back to take fingerprints.

Moe forgot his poker game. We headed for Twin Falls, Idaho, to make a delivery. It was illegal to take a slot machine across state lines, so he asked if I wanted to stay at Cactus Pete's or go along. I said I'd go. As we drove out of Jackpot, I remarked it was too bad someone had robbed the Lucky Seven.

Moe looked astonished. "You don't believe all that bullshit, do you, kid?"

"What do you mean, all what bullshit?"

"That stuff about him getting robbed."

Now I was astonished. "Why shouldn't I believe him? I'm a complete stranger in town, and he comes and says he's been robbed. Why would he be lying?"

"Let me tell you something, kid. I'll bet you as sure as I'm sitting here he robbed himself. Yes, sir, he took that money himself. I know it. He's fixing to skip the country, so he robs himself. That way he can stall his creditors a while longer and make a few hundred as he packs his bags. When the pressure to pay up gets heavy, he'll dump the joint back into the former owner's lap, run off with the money, and probably take one of those girls with him."

I didn't know who to believe. Curly sounded so sincere. Curly said everything was just beginning to go well, he was meeting his payments, and all seemed fine until the robbery. But I suspected Moe must be right. He was a smart old badger and had been around the block, while I was a stupid kid. Moe suggested I buy the Lucky Seven. He figured it'd cost about $65,000. He thought I should get a loan from Dad for the down payment. He told me about the expenses: bartenders got about $140 a week, dealers got $150 or a percentage of the table, there was a $500 yearly tax on each slot machine, and a $150 tax for each blackjack table. But each slot machine, Moe said, would make about $3,000 a year. I said I'd think it over. That was a lie. I could just imagine Dad lending me money to buy a casino in Nevada.

We went up to Twin Falls and delivered two machines at what looked like somebody's home. We set them on a back porch, covered them with a horse blanket, and left without seeing anyone. Back to Wells that night, Moe was hugging his dog and his Thunder Chicken. He said he knew all along no guy from Stearns County would be afraid about a little slot-machine smuggling, and he called me a "good son-of-bitch."

As we headed east patches of alkalai looked like snow, but I knew it wasn't snow because the sun was blazing hot and the highway shimmered with watery-looking heat waves. The air conditioner on Moe's Pontiac couldn't keep up. We baked in that Bonneville oven, and Moe's little sweetheart panted like she was dying. We stopped at Wendover, on the Utah border near a vast alkalai desert called the Bonneville Salt Flats. I wondered again how they could sustain a town in this god forsaken land. True, it was not far from Salt Lake City, but Mormons didn't drink or gamble.

We stopped to eat at the Stateline Casino, right on top of the border. The waitress told me that originally the town was just a service station, but the casino did a pretty good business. There was an airbase nearby where the government stored munitions. The base had been used to train pilots during the war for the bombing missions on Hiroshima and Nagasaki. She told me, yes, Mormons do gamble, they do drink, and they do other naughty things that would make Brigham Young blush.

I wanted to go see the salt flats, but Moe said BS on that. The waitress said we ought to go see "Jukebox Cave" nearby that had ancient Native American paintings on the walls. During the war the airmen had put down a cement floor in the cave to dance on. They held their parties there at night, because it was nice and cool and they could burn lights inside the cave without violating wartime black-out rules. I wanted to see the cave, but Moe said he'd seen plenty of Native American paintings. None of them were any damn good. He was in a hurry to get back to Vegas.

We didn't stop much on the way back. When Moe dropped me off, he left the car running, saying a quick good-bye like he was in a big hurry. His cigarette hung from one corner of his mouth, his dog was asleep in his lap. I thanked him. As he drove off I said, "See you again, Moe." I never did. Nor that dog.

WHEN I FINALLY LEFT Las Vegas (or Lost Vegas, as Vince called it), I was a passenger in Vince's car. He was going to visit his folks in Twenty-Nine Palms. We took the southern route through Piute Valley, and turned west through the Mojave. This land is the opposite of the lush, tropical land of palm trees and ocean beaches I had always imagined for California. Vince wanted me to see the beauty of the desert, but Lord, it is a fiery wasteland of sand and cactus that made the alkali desert of northern Nevada look attractive. I much preferred Minnesota's great forests, hills, and ten thousand lakes.

Vince wore his religion on his sleeve, and was always saying a quick prayer for someone or something. As we drove along he decided we should say the rosary for the poor souls in purgatory. He unhooked his beads from the rearview mirror and began leading. He put so much syrupy expression into the prayers it made me laugh. Sometimes I laughed so hard I could not give the response right away, and he'd look at me sternly from the corner of his eye, frown and shake his head until I answered.

We turned south, climbed through the Sheep Hole Mountains and went west to the peaceful village of Twenty-Nine Palms, California. We stayed at Vince's parent's house that night. They were just as nice and generous as Vince, and treated me like royalty just because I was from Stearns County. His mom was like my mom—she fussed constantly in the kitchen and kept asking if I wanted anything. She put together a big sandwich and a sack of cookies for me to take on the road. But she refused to hand them over until I sat down and wrote Mom a letter to say everything was fine.

Vince headed back to Las Vegas, and I headed for the beaches of Los Angeles. I almost said I never saw Vince again, but I did—twenty years later I saw him on TV. He was working for the federal government and was blowing the whistle on all the waste and corruption in his department. That was just like Vince. He was even more idealistic than I was. I was working for the Drug Enforcement Administration by that time, and I said to the TV, "Vince, if you were working for DEA, your whistle would be worn out."

Chapter Sixteen

D O YOU KNOW the Joshua tree? I admired it like I did the saguaro cactus in Arizona. Rooted in sand, they stand month after month with not a drop of rain. It gave me a feeling of permanence, like the burr oak of Minnesota. I contemplated it when I slept in the desert one night not far from Twenty-Nine Palms. It was a moonless night. Desert darkness is not real darkness. The stars are so bright that even without a moon you can see. And desert silence is not like city silence. You can hear a coyote yip from a mile away and hear a dim answer from even farther on. And the loneliness of the desert is not like regular loneliness. It's not the choking torture of homesickness. *If I die out here,* I thought, *no one would ever know.* I felt a flow of pleasure at this loneliness. I didn't feel desolation and emptiness—and certainly not abandonment—not like I felt at Crosier. This loneliness I could understand, even enjoy. I much preferred sleeping alone in the desert to sleeping in a dormitory with a hundred boys. I felt closer to God in the desert than I ever had in St. Odelia's little chapel or the colossal concrete Abbey Church at St. John's.

It was harder to get rides in California—on the freeway nearly impossible. Drivers would not stop. I kept to the coast. Good Lord, what a beautiful highway!—for scenery, I mean. It must be the best in the world. The signs along its sides gave it different names: U.S. Route 101, El Camino Real, U.S. Highway 101, Star Route 1, and California State Highway 1. Drivers called it the "Pacific Highway" or the "Coastal." It ran north-south all along the California shore overlooking the Pacific Ocean.

Because it was harder to get rides, I considered riding the bus, but I'd have to take off time to work. On the road I made a dollar here and there doing little jobs. Once a man gave me two dollars to wash his car at a gas station while he read the paper and smoked a cigar. One day in east Texas a man paid me to watch his gas station while he went to the hospital. His wife had just had a car accident. In Van Horn I spent an entire night cleaning grills at a barbeque joint. In Los Angeles I helped a city worker pick up trash. It was easy to get little jobs then. People still trusted each other. But jobs took time. I wanted to travel.

I never resented being checked by the cops. After all, I looked like a bum. I *was* a bum. The only time I ever felt harassed by a cop was one morning out of Long Beach. He stopped across the road from me. He was on his radio. While he was talking, he crooked a finger at me that I should come over to him. I hated this man before he spoke a word. Nothing improved. He looked too young to be a cop, and too arrogant.

"You got a driver's license, buddy?"

The "buddy" sounded like "shithead."

"Yes," I said. I couldn't bring myself to say "Yes, Officer," even though he was scaring the hell out of me.

"Let's see it."

I felt like saying, "I'm not driving," but I was afraid.

"We don't like hitchhikers around here," he said. "Where you going?"

I tried to sound as definite and sure as I could. "To Salinas to see a friend."

I don't think he heard; his radio chattered. He grabbed the mike and started talking. Then he turned to me. "I got your name," he said as he handed the license back. "If there's trouble around here I'll be looking for you. You got that?"

"Yes, sir, ah, Officer." I felt great relief. It sounded like he was done.

He was. He pulled a squealing U-turn, and sped back up the road.

That night after I was safely rolled up in my sleeping bag on the beach in Santa Barbara (with no police around), I resolved if I ever met that cop again I'd give him a piece of my mind. I thought of dozens of things I should have said, and departing gestures I should have made, and then I felt better.

In Santa Barbara you could walk on water. They had a pier there that reached so far out that, when I stood at its end, I felt I was in the middle of the Pacific. One of the main streets of the town, State Street, ran right down to the beach and out onto the pier that had the same name as my home county—it was "Stearns Wharf." I stayed out there to watch a bloody red sun sink into the Pacific haze, and to drink in the scent of seaweed the evening breeze brought on-shore. I liked the feel of the wind and the smell of the salt water. I watched the harbor lights come on and the stars brightening over the ocean. When it was completely dark, a night watchman came along and told me to get the hell out of there. I slept in some bushes by the beach, but it wasn't as comfortable as the desert; the wind was damp and it didn't quiet down at night. It kept blowing and rolling the rushing water onto the sand. I wasn't used to that noise, and it wasn't soothing like everyone said. It kept me awake a long time.

The next morning after the sun came up it got warm fast. I fell back asleep and stayed there until noisy beachgoers woke me. I lay there thinking maybe I should ride the freight trains up the coast. I saw a hunched old man come down to the beach. He sat on a bench and smoked a cigarette, sometimes erupted in coughing fits like Moe Trenkle. I sat by him and asked if he knew anything about California law about riding freight trains. I wanted to get to Monterrey, but I said Seattle. I thought Monterrey might be only a few miles away.

He rattled off trains and locations. I was soon lost—Southern Pacific, Frisco, bus to Oakland, ask the switchman, the Western Pacific, Stockton, ask the brakeman, the Chile Pepper, Portland, the Great Northern, Seattle. At the end of it all he added, "And that's the only way to go. Any other way's gonna take too much time." I put him down as a retired railroad man, as he knew so much.

I stored my stuff at the bus depot and walked around town a bit. I came back to the beach in the late afternoon and heard someone call behind me. When I turned, I saw the same hunched old man trying to catch up to me.

He said, "Hey, kid, stop, stop. I'm sure glad to see you." When he caught up he breathed hard for a while and had a coughing fit. He said, "If you got a little time, kid, I'd like you to walk to the store with me. I have to pick up a jug for a friend, but I'd like to give you some advice on the way."

I was agreeable. He'd impressed me with his knowledge of trains. We got a quart of Swiss Colony Tokay and sat down on a street bench. He drank and passed it to me. He told me about how dangerous it was to ride the trains telling me of robberies, knifings, and murder. There's no law on the train, he said. Only hobo justice, and that's no justice at all. He said he had worried about me all day after he'd given me the rundown on the trains.

He said, "I thought, now why in the hell did I send a green kid like that on those trains! He don't know nothin'. He'll get himself killed. Now listen, you don't have to ride the train. A good, clean kid like you? Shave and get a job, buy a bus ticket, walk, but don't ride the trains."

His name was Frank. I learned in the following days he was Frank Ward, master bum, hobo, conman, crook, seven-time loser, and chain smoker with terminal lung disease. He didn't ask my name. He called me "kid" from the start and stuck to it. When the Tokay was half gone he announced he must take the rest to "Starky at the jungle." Some of Starky's money was invested in the bottle. We walked down the tracks of the Southern Pacific and found a place back among the trees where a half-dozen men lounged on the beaten grass like tired farmers resting in contentment after a long day haying. Starky took the bottle. When he hefted it, he fixed Frank a cold eye.

Frank said, "The kid here was thirsty."

Starky looked at Frank. With one side of his mouth pulled back he said, "Yeah, I bet."

Starky was not the only man with money in the bottle. Another man, Jack, had contributed. With a few gulps each, Starky and Jack drained the bottle. When Jack tossed it on the grass, another man grabbed it and tipped it over his mouth to get the last drops. I wished I hadn't taken a swallow from that bottle. I didn't enjoy it like these men. I made a show of turning my pockets inside out and gave Starky the change I found there. I don't think it amounted to fifty cents, but it was received with a great show of gratitude. Starky vowed I would have the first swallow out of the next bottle, which would appear whenever there were enough contributions.

These men had made themselves a sleeping shelter out of a tarp tied to limbs of an oak tree. Holes in the tarp had been patched with bits of blanket. The entire thing was weighted down with rocks at the bottom edges. Three of the hobos had a lively crap game going under the tarp. They rattled the dice in a coffee mug and threw onto a piece of cardboard. They had shell corn for money. They said I could sleep there, if there was room. Frank took me aside and said I could sleep on the floor of his hotel room.

We sat around the ashes of a dead campfire and talked. No introductions. If a name was used, it was always a nickname. Rarely did a bum go by his real name like Frank did (and even his real name was Francis). A bum would rather give you the fillings out of his teeth than his name, but they didn't mind telling stories about themselves. Jack said he was divorced and running from the law to "keep from paying that bitch all that alimony." He had one squinty eye, and he mostly stood with his head cocked to one side and his mouth open. He had the look of someone who did not understand the question. Most of the others were reluctant to talk at first, sizing me up.

A pale man arrived with another bottle of Tokay, and it got passed around. This man had white hair and light-blue eyes. They called him "Albino," but he wasn't a real albino. As the bottle went around, a black man called "Big Boy" came and sat next to me. He had one hell of a purple, swollen eye and his upper lip was split on one side and leaked a red-and-yellow fluid when he talked. The lip was puffed up and obviously very tender. When he drank, some of the wine escaped from the sides of his mouth and dribbled on his shirt. He said he sure needed that "medicine." He drank before me. When he passed the bottle to me, though my stomach lurched at the thought, I had no choice but to tip up and drink. Albino brought out a can of beans and began to open it with his jackknife. I took out my P-38 can-opener and showed him how to use it. This was a big hit. Many of them had never seen a P-38.

Either the wine or the P-38 loosened them up. Everyone found food in their pockets and packs. Soon we were eating baloney, crackers, raw onions, liverwurst, and cold bacon, most of which was stolen from grocery stores or taken from restaurant garbage cans. After we ate, out came pipes, cigarette makings, and cigar stubs. Everyone smoked. Albino passed his tobacco can and papers to me. I rolled a most misshapen cigarette, but I did manage to keep it going once it was lit. In the gathering darkness I thought no one noticed, but later at the hotel Frank said, "Hey, kid, I didn't want to embarrass you out there, but you better let me show you how to roll a butt."

I got my gear from the bus station and moved into a corner of Frank's room. The room was upstairs in the back of an old wooden hotel, not far from the beach. Frank told me to enter by a back door and use the stairs so the manager wouldn't see me. The floors and stairs creaked and groaned, were dirty, and the curtains dusty. At night I could hear the wind whistling through the cracks in the window. Frank would sometimes wake me in the night with his coughing, and I'd pray he didn't die on me. Then I'd hear the clink of his lighter in the dark and knew he was lighting a smoke to calm his cough; it always worked. But his smoking was a worry, too. I knew if anything in that dry building ever caught fire, the whole place would go up. But I preferred sleeping there rather than in the damp wind on the beach or by the noisy tracks in the hobo camp.

By day I hung around the hobo camp or lay on the beach and wrote in my log. I was totally ignorant of the sea. I didn't remember about tides, and one day I woke up and found the waves lapping at my feet and my log book floating on the water. It made some of the Santa Barbara hobo stories unreadable. The hobos loved to tell stories as they lay around and drank Tokay. I overlooked the bragging and swaggering and sopped up their stories with a hunger they enjoyed. My interest spurred them to greater heights of exaggeration. Whenever they tried to pass off self-serving tales as fact with their fellows, they were ridiculed into silence. They didn't have that problem with me. I was green as grass. So, for a while in the camp, great invention made the life of Julius Caesar look dull by comparison. Often bums gathered around to listen, not to hear the story, but to see how far the narrator could go before I showed signs of skepticism.

At night I listened to Frank's stories. He seldom stretched the truth, although he blamed society for all his problems. He never bragged about how good he was at anything—even cooking beans. Frank wasn't supposed to cook in his room, but he had a hot plate on which he cooked pinto beans almost every day. When he ran out, I went to the grocery and bought more; that man knew how to make pinto beans better than a Mexican. I never got tired of them. At the store I also got myself a sack of Bull Durham tobacco and papers to roll cigarettes. Frank told me carrying tailor-made cigarettes indicated the smoker had money, which could attract attention from a robber. You never let people know you had money. Big Boy, the black man with the smashed face, had made that mistake. He had "come into some money" a few days ago and bragged about it. He got drunk and fell asleep. Some bums were robbing him when he woke up. They clubbed him until he was persuaded that they needed the money more than he did.

The hobos seemed to respect Frank. They looked up to him as an old master of their trade, but they didn't trust him. One time Starky and I went off to take a leak in the bushes. Starky said, "Watch yourself with Frank, kid. He'll skin you alive."

They all called me "kid" because most of them were more than twice my age—many much more. When one asked me why I was a bum at my age (he thought I might be running from the military, since I still had my brother's Eisenhower jacket), Starky told him to mind his own goddamn business. I told them I'd be entering the Air Force later that year. That set off an argument about serving in the military. The man they called Phil (a nickname for Felipe, but he said it was for "Fill" and pointed to his open mouth when he said it) had left the army during the Korean War when his service time was only half finished. The army was still looking for him. He'd been a hobo on the California coast for more than ten years. He said it would be foolish to take the grind and grime of the military when I could live this life of ease by the tracks, and he stretched back on the grass with his hands behind his head, smiling in great luxury. Felipe was a short, very dark Mexican who enjoyed his life immensely.

I liked Felipe best of all the hobos. He was an enterprising bum. Every day he went about Santa Barbara and collected newspapers. He read them, he slept on them and under them, he burned them for fuel, he used them as towels and toilet paper, and sometimes, when it was cold, he stuffed them in his shoes for socks. Felipe got his clothes from a funeral home in town. He went there every few days to look through the garbage. The others thought it bad luck to wear a dead man's clothes. But Felipe said he'd rather wear a dead man's clothes than a live man's. A dead man wouldn't come looking for him.

Frank insisted I should go into the military, but Starky agreed with Felipe, saying war was immoral. Starky was a religious man—of sorts. He believed the Palm Sunday tornadoes that hit the midwestern states that year were a sign Jesus didn't approve of our involvement in Vietnam. He gave Jesus credit for everything good in his life, but also blame for everything bad. Several times I saw him shake his fist and swear at the heavens to let Jesus know what he thought about the way he was running things. I had to admire his faith, even though I was shocked at his open blasphemy. Felipe, who carried in his pocket a little statue of the Blessed Virgin, said Starky would burn in hell for that. When Starky drank, he became either very animated and dramatic, extolling the virtues of jazz and being alive, or subdued and melancholy, often weeping bitterly about the cruelty of life and the undeserved lot he suffered at the hands of Jesus. Jack found him funny either way. Frank found him dull and vain. Unlike any of the other hobos, Starky spent time holding a little hand mirror in front of his face, trimming his thin beard and hair.

"Don't go," Starky said. "The draft board cannot possibly find you riding the rails. Look at Phil," he said, pointing with his scissors. "He's been on the run for years with no trouble. Half these guys are on the run from the law. Don't go. Jesus doesn't like war." Starky was sure that a time of peace was coming. He said, "The lion shall lie down with the lamb."

Frank said, "The lion already lies down with the lamb, but the lamb's in his stomach."

Felipe liked to ride the trains and did not try to dissuade me like Frank did. Every time Felipe talked to me, he gave me a tip about trains. One day he said, "Don't ride the Pig unless you're in a big hurry and the weather's good." The Pig was the hobo name for the piggyback. The railroads often carried semi-trailers or other big containers on flatcars, sometimes making up an entire train of containers. That was a "piggyback." The reason Felipe didn't like riding them was because you rode outside in the open, were easily seen, and the cops checked them more than some old cattle car. But it was a fast train. Often the containers had iced-down fruit, so other trains waited on side tracks for her to pass. Felipe told me if I had to ride the Pig, I should ride one of the last cars. When the cops checked, they often didn't get to the back end of the train before it started rolling. And I should always have a rain coat, because the Pig did not stop, and it could run through rain showers and cold nights.

He said, "And don't ride the cattle cars. When the train's at full speed the wind comes blasting through the slats. Even on a warm day it is not comfortable. The wind keeps stirring the dust from the floor. Besides, it's too bright in there to hide."

Felipe had gone all up and down the coast back when he was traveling with his cousin. They were like brothers, always together, but his cousin was (as Frank put it) "a reckless bastard." He used to climb up on top of the boxcars, and run along the train just for fun. He was killed when he slipped one morning. The fog had made the tops of the boxcars greasy.

When we walked along the railroad tracks into Santa Barbara, we almost always ran into hobos. Hobos traveled freely along the California coast on freight trains and slept in camps and homeless shelters, which were in most towns. The hobos were familiar with all the railroad yards, hump yards, and switching stations. They knew every soup kitchen, every Catholic mission (their favorites), and every shelter in walking distance from the tracks. Some had secret houses where they could con the lady out of a sandwich, and they knew which houses had good things in the garbage. They often stole from grocery stores, but rarely in their immediate vicinity and never more than a can of beans or a candy bar at a time. They knew which wash lines were within sprinting distance of the railroad track. They knew where there was a chicken coop with no dog guarding it.

Frank spent his days in his room tending his emphysema, coming out only when the weather was perfect or his bottle was empty. I think the hobos were a bit afraid of him. There was a story he had killed a man over a woman years ago and had thrown pieces of him into the San Luis Obispo Bay. Frank himself told me about armed robberies he'd committed and the consequent jail time, but he claimed he never killed anyone. When he talked he had a funny habit of sometimes holding one hand by his mouth and talking out of the other side as though he was passing top secret information. At night Frank would lie on his bed and talk for hours. I'd sit in my corner on my sleeping bag and pretend to be just listening, but actually I was making notes, which I used the next day to write in my log. Frank would often start a story and then go wandering off on a tangent until I didn't remember what the original story was. My notes would remind me of it the next day, and I would lead him back into it. This made for some disjointed notes, but eventually I put together the sketch of his life. The next short chapter is his story. It's written down in the first person, the way Frank told it to me.

Chapter Seventeen

FRANK'S STORY

I WAS BORN MAY 10, 1903, in San Francisco. I am the son of the meanest bastard that ever walked the face of the earth. My aunt used to tell me that whenever she came for a visit. "I can't see," she would say, "How Gramma and Grampa ever had a mean son-of-a-bitch like your father."

For a while he ran a grocery store with a "blind pig" in the back room. He could not get a liquor license because he had a record, see? So he used to sell the stuff in the back room on the sly. He'd let them in the back door—the winos. Even the city cop used to come in there and drink. But it didn't last long. One day when I was coming home from school I saw a patrol wagon in back of the place. It was backed up right against the door and the bulls were loading up barrels of beer and wine. In those days you always got the stuff in barrels if you were running a place. The bulls were buzzing around like a nest of hornets, wearing those long overcoats they used to have and those hats that looked like upside-down pisspots. I stood there a moment, not knowing whether to go in or run away.

I went in. When the bulls were done loading the sauce into the patrol wagon, they loaded the old man and went clopping off to jail. They still used horses on the patrol wagon. This was a long time ago, you know. They let the old man out after a while. He came back home and got back to drinking and to beating me.

Prohibition came, and the old man was in the bootlegging business. He and his two cousins dug a tunnel down in the cellar. They tunneled under the street and tapped into the city gas line to fire the still. They never got knocked down with their still. One time the bulls came. Somebody snitched on them. But they had done a good job hiding it, and the bulls couldn't find a thing. The bulls left, and the cousins went right back to cooking and drinking. They never did make any money on that still. The stupid bastards drank it all themselves.

For a while there, the old man had a barn out at his sister's place. He used to buy old, skinny, broken-down horses for twenty or thirty bucks. Then he'd take 'em out to the barn and fatten 'em up and we'd work 'em a little. That's how I learned about horses. Pretty soon they'd look like pretty good horses again, and he'd sell 'em for maybe a hundred to people that didn't know any better.

What got me started on the wrong track was I ran away from home. I guess about the worst thing a parent can do is make his kid feel like he ain't wanted. I was twelve then, and they caught me and put me in this home for bad kids. The old man gave me up, and they were glad to have me at the home, 'cause they got paid from the state by the number of kids they kept. But I ran away from there, too, and I always got caught. You know how stupid a kid is. He gets out and just runs, and the warden knows just where to look for him. I remember once I made it all the way to the next town, which was thirty miles. I ran through part of the night. I was young then, you see, and could run for hours with no stop.

But all this time I was getting smart, getting a lot of experience. I learned from hearing the warden talk about how stupid I was. Pretty soon I got out and hid right near the place while they looked out in the country, and way out to the next town. In those days they used to deliver bread and milk to front porches in the morning. I would follow the milk wagon until he left some by a house with no lights, and I'd take it to my hiding place. After a few days I got away completely by moving at night. Now the only problem was that I had on this special outfit from the home, see, and everybody could spot it. You know how that is. I rode the freights. They went much slower then, and stopped often. Along the way I stole a horsehide jacket, some cowboy boots, and a black Mormon hat from a farmer by the tracks. You've seen those Mormon hats—wide brims, you know. That afternoon I burned my old clothes in a culvert under the tracks.

Well, and I got a hold of this big .44 with the real long barrel, what they call a "hogleg." I packed it in my pants and had a box of shells in my jacket. I made a lot of scores in small towns. Sometimes I'd just steal a sack full of candy bars and a few bottles of pop. Then I'd hide in the willows along the railroad track and eat candy and drink pop all day. At night I'd walk down the tracks or ride the train, always moving, you see. I learned that much from the warden.

Then one night I tried to make this drugstore in Oxnard. There was a night watchman in the joint, and he sees me crawling in through the window. He busted a couple of caps at me. I ducked down and busted a few back at him, which scared him into next week. He beat it out of there like a jackrabbit. The town was alive real fast so I hid in some straw by a barn. I watched them. They came right by me, but I thought they didn't see me so I stayed. But all the time some were sneaking around behind to get me surrounded, and all of a sudden two men grabbed me by the ankles. The sheriff was there and two deputies—the sheriff in front with a big damned shotgun in my face.

They took me to court and ended up sending me to a reformatory up in Colorado, a place called Buena Vista, not far from Salida. You had to be sixteen or older to be sent there. I was only thirteen, but like a damn fool, I lied about my age in court, I don't know why. Dumb kid, if you know what I mean. Anyhow, it was over for me then. They put me in there with a rough bunch, guys who used to stick up banks and all that. I was there for four years. I wouldn't have been there so long, but I kept trying to break out and they kept adding time. Once when they caught me, the guards shook me down and took my money, which was quite a bit, because I had just made a good score in town. One guard said, "We should let this guy run more often." Ha, ha! But they missed the money in my watch pocket.

They threw me in the hole for a long time. There was little light, and they fed me crap. Then I went blind—I had what they call "night blindness." You know, that's what people get when they don't get the right kind of food. All we got in prison was beans or this lousy mush—no milk, no greens, no anything. Anyhow, they got me in bed and called the doctor. The doc says, "I'll tell you what's wrong with this kid. He's starving. What he needs is some decent food, some milk, meat, butter, apples, things like that." So they kept me in bed a while and gave me some milk every day and pretty soon I was up again and mean as hell.

After a while they decided to parole me to a rancher near the prison. The guy came, and he was a real cowboy. He had one of those buckboards—you've seen 'em. He takes me to the ranch and breaks out the chuck. Man, did I eat. We had thick steaks, milk and butter every day. And he kept saying, "Eat all you want, boy, I know they don't feed you in those prisons." I mean, it was like heaven.

I was a natural-born rider. When we went after cows the first time, he told me, "Hey, you're a pretty good cowboy." But then we started to plow and that was real sweat work. I got itchy feet. I wanted to get some excitement. I was too stupid to know my own good. I was getting forty dollars a month, and this back in '21. Pretty good money for those days.

What really bothered me was that one day this guy told me that, when the warden had paroled me, he had said, "This kid will run away from your place when he gets a chance, but we'll catch the dumb bastard in a day and throw him in the hole." That did it. Yes, I would run away, but they'd never catch me! I laid plans to leave. I got this young mare and put her in the corral and fed her oats every day until she was in real good shape. Then I took a jug of water and rounded up a sack full of bread and meat. I went to bed early that night, got up a few hours later, and sneaked off. I had taken the guy's wire cutters (you need those if you're going cross-country on a horse), and I was looking for his pistol, but he had that in bed with him, so I had to go without.

I headed toward the mountains using the gates wherever I could find one. When dawn came I got off the horse, scratched the owner's name on the bridle, and chased her toward home. You're too easy to follow on a horse. I hiked into the mountains and rested and ate. All the time I watched. Day and night. They came looking, and I moved higher. Listen, kid! When you're hiding, you always stay above them. That way you can look down and watch them, but they have a hell of a time spotting you.

Well, that old warden went back to Salida empty-handed. I caught a freight to Pueblo and kept heading east and north for about a year. I made some small scores here and there. In Kansas City I made a big score and picked up a Smith & Wesson .38 on the side. That was a good gun and I had it a long time. I went up through the Dakotas and over into Minnesota during the summer. I made some of my best scores in Minneapolis-St. Paul.

Anyway, that's how it went. I got into Chicago and that's where I decided to go back home to California. Chicago was real jumpy in those days. It was when Capone was raisin' hell, you know. I wasn't used to that. Cops on every block, checkin' your asshole. I got nervous, and I got cold. I went straight south for warmer weather, and then rode the trains west. I wanted good old California, where it was nice and warm so you could sleep in a boxcar at night.

It was easier to ride the rails in those days. The old steam engines were slow and needed water all the time, so you could get on or off at the stops. We used to leave messages for each other, like where you could get food, where the bulls were bad, where you could find a flophouse. They don't do that anymore, and if you find a message, it could be a joke, or even a trap. We were all young hobos back then, young as you. Now we're all old. I carried just one little bindle. It was a blanket strapped to my back with my stuff rolled up inside. That way both hands were free. You had to have both hands, because we would ride the couplings between the cars and had to have a good grip. Don't ever do that. You get tired fast. We used to ride on top, hanging on to the catwalk. Some crazy bastards would even ride the rods underneath a car.

Once I tried to make this big score in San Jose and there I got sneezed. This time they took me to San Quentin. I made the hole once or twice in San Quentin, but generally I got along pretty good until we tried to blow the joint. They sent my ass to Folsom, where there is no escape. For a time I had a cell to myself. You have a cot and two buckets—one is your shit bucket and the other is full of water for drinking and washing. We worked the stones at Folsom. They put me by myself because I didn't work well with others. They thought that by myself I might work, and I did, too—to stay in shape. I was there for five years. Made the hole a few times again. Finally they gave me eight dollars, some civilian clothes, and fare to Frisco—home.

I got into selling drugs and they caught me with nine pounds of uncut opium. Back to Folsom Prison. This was my longest stretch—nine years flat. I would have gotten out earlier, but I cut this spook with a blade. The spook called me a "mother fucker," so I went to the kitchen and said, "Hey, give me a blade." They tossed me a butcher knife, and I cut the bastard. They put me in the hole for nine months. It's an underground room, see? All concrete, about eight feet long and maybe three feet wide. There was another guy in there with me. That guy did not talk. I swear this is the truth. When I came in he says, "Hello," and when they took that nut out four months later, he said, "Good-bye." In between, nothing. He would not even answer any of my questions.

I did other stretches in little county jails here and there. You know, small-time stuff, drunk and disorderly stuff, heisting booze or cigarettes. Don't get me wrong. I didn't always steal. I worked, too. I once had a job with the railroad, and I often followed the harvest to earn a few dollars. For a while I had a good job at Fort Ord by Monterrey, but I got drunk as a sow one night, chased the bartender around the room and knocked him out with a beer bottle. The army couldn't prosecute a civilian, and the town couldn't prosecute because it was on federal land. The only one that would put me in jail was the FBI. That case was dismissed because the guy testified I had hit him with a fire iron five or six times. Well, in those days I was a big muscular guy from swinging that stone hammer at Folsom. Anybody could see that if I had hit the guy with an iron more than once, he wouldn't be there testifying.

Then I got an honest job picking lemons down by San Bernardino. That's where I got sick, real sick. That's when this lung trouble first started. Maybe it was from the spraying. I was picking lemons, when suddenly I couldn't get my breath anymore. I quit and went to town and stole some beer and wine and got drunk. I was drunk and sick for a couple of days. Then I rode the Pig up to Santa Barbara, where I got a doctor through the Salvation Army. They put me in the state hospital and then they put me on disability. I get a check every month now. I'm supposed to let them know whenever I make some money, but hell, I can't go down there and tell them I got thirty dollars last Friday from knocking over a saloon. So as long as they keep paying me, I can stay here instead of at the hobo camp with the boys.

I like those guys at the camp, but they get tiresome. They don't know anything. I used to read a lot in prison, but most of them don't know Shakespeare from shinola. They're just stupid. Here about a month ago, me and a guy named Jim were lying in the jungle waiting for a train. This drunk stranger comes along with a big bottle and he lies down near us and falls asleep. So Jim and I finish off his bottle for him and we roll him and take his money, and we look at his papers. Listen to this. The guy's name turns out to be Ralph Waldo Emerson. Can you beat that? Jim takes the papers and says, "That's my name now."

I said, "Do you know who Ralph Waldo Emerson was?"

"No," he says, "Never heard of him."

Jim's a good guy, just ignorant.

I says, "He was one of our early American poets."

"Well," says Jim, "that's okay, I'll be a poet."

See? He's too ignorant to know that those papers will only call the cops' attention to him, and he'd be better off with no papers at all.

I came to this hotel because I know the manager. I used to be in jail with his cousin. And I have to have an address—they won't send my disability to a post office box or to the jungle. It's a nice little hiding place. The bulls shake down the jungle all the time, but so far they haven't bothered me here.

Chapter Eighteen

FRANK WAS A FAIRLY well-educated man. He had only gone through the sixth grade in school, but he had an uncle who taught sociology at UCSF. The uncle got Frank interested in the classics, and Frank spent a lot of time reading in jail. The uncle supplied him with books. "I used to memorize the good parts," Frank said, "so I got the words into my vocabulary."

It was true. He could speak perfectly good English, if he wanted to, but mostly he talked like a bum. He liked Milton and could spiel off whole chapters of *Paradise Lost*. His favorite was Oscar Wilde. "That guy can use those simple Anglo-Saxon words and really bring out the beauty of the language."

Frank had never married, but he talked often about the women in his life. I could tell from his features that, when younger, he'd been good looking, sort of like Cary Grant. He once loved a girl named JoAnn, who used to go with him when he pulled a job. And Frank madly loved a girl named Lornie. He had her name tattooed on his arm. She used to visit him at Folsom. She was married now and had two kids. She got married to one of the guys who was with Frank in Folsom, and it was Frank who introduced them. But Frank loved her still.

When Frank came down to the jungle the bums all gathered round, mostly because he always had a bottle with him, but also because he was a great talker. One time we were sitting by the fire passing around a pot of coffee—yes, coffee—no one had a jug that day. A new bum, Floyd, was just passing through, grinning at everyone. They all knew him from somewhere up by Monterrey. He was a typical old bum: ragged, hungry, and drunk. They all shook his hand and slapped his back. We sat down for a smoke, and I passed Floyd my makings while I rolled my own. I watched as Floyd, with speed and dexterity, rolled the most perfect, tight little cigarette I had seen, and he was drunk! I said, "Let's see you do that again," and he did. Starky took it and said Floyd should go into business rolling cigarettes.

Floyd was asking about how to break into a safe. Starky said he should ask Frank. Just about that time, along comes Frank with a jug. You should have heard the cheering! He might have been Santa Claus bringing a sleigh full of toys to poor children. They asked Frank the best way to bust a safe. Frank had been drinking, and he started off like a college professor teaching safe-cracking, but then he wandered afield again and got lost in whorehouses, murder, and the gas chamber.

He said, "Okay, I'm gonna tell you how to break into a safe, just to show you bums how much there is to it, so you don't think you can pull it off yourself. First I'll tell you something most guys don't know. It often saves a lot of work. A lot of the good safes now have what you call a day combination. If you close the safe and only give the dial half a turn—not a full one—you can open that thing again by simply turning the dial back to the last number of the combination. Sometimes a safe will be left that way because the owner's ignorant or just sloppy. You grab the handle and start dialing back. You give her a try at every click, every marker. If she's on day combination, she'll open before you make a full round. But most of the time you have to break in. There are three basic ways: with tools, with explosives, or with a torch.

"Suppose you're using tools. You need hammer, wedges, and pry bar. This method makes a lot of noise, so you can't always use it. Maybe you can use rags to cover the sound. Maybe you can use a copper hammer, it doesn't ring like steel. You just bash in the door of the safe as much as you can. That's to break away the edges so you can get a wedge in there. You drive in a wedge, then another, and another, until you have room for the pry bar. You pry until you have the face off. You tear out the insulation—you know, asbestos and that crap. Now you're down to what they call the hard plate. There's a pin there that holds the door shut. You hit and hit until it snaps, that's all, and you're in.

"If you find you have to blow the safe, you use grease for that—nitroglycerin. Drill a hole over the dial. Stuff it with cotton. Then, using an eye dropper, soak the cotton with the grease. Then stuff in a detonating cap, or an electric fuse works best. Sit behind the safe. When she pops off, rake it in.

"A torch is much quieter, but the trouble is, it throws a lot of light. You can see fire from an acetylene torch for twenty miles. And you have to carry the oxygen and acetylene tanks around. Put them in a nice suitcase. You have to have a good torchman or you'll run out of gas before the safe is open. You get all the cans and buckets you can lay your hands on, and you fill them up with water and set them around the safe. One man cuts and the other man pours water. Otherwise it gets so hot inside the money'll burn. Once you've made a little hole, you fill the safe with water. Yes, the money gets all wet, but who cares? It won't burn and it's easy to dry out.

"Gerhardt Williams (you know, the one we call Al, or Pinhead) is the best safe man I know. Right now he's doing time up at San Quentin. Wesley Gant is even better on the safes, but he's reckless, isn't careful. He's in jail too, because he trusted an ex-cop. That cop told Wesley about this whorehouse up in Salinas. It was supposed to be loaded. It was one of the whorehouses that belonged to Sally Stanford, you know, that bitch that ran for town council in

Frisco a while back. Wesley thought it was a good score so he tries to make it. The bulls were camped inside waiting. He should've known better. Sally was always working with the cops. He did another dumb thing one night before that happened. Wesley and Joe the Burglar were robbing parking meters downtown. They were both drunk and singing and making a lot of noise. A paper boy saw them and a few minutes later the police were there.

"And here's another thing. One day I walked into Wesley's room and he says to me, 'Need some money, Frank? Help yourself, it's in the top drawer.' I open the drawer and it's full, I mean full, of stacks of paper money. Once I saw Wesley with that dumb bastard, Pistol (that's Hightower's nickname, you know). I'll tell you how stupid Pistol is. He killed a priest down in L.A. Don't ever ask why. These guys are nuts. Pistol buried the priest on the beach under one of those big flapjack signs. The bulls offered a reward for information about the killing. Pistol wants to collect, so he goes to the cops and says he thinks the body is buried by the flapjack sign because he saw some black cloth sticking out of the sand there. They go down to disinter the body.

"One bull sets his shovel. The other says, 'Careful so you don't hit the head.'

"Pistol comes right back and says, 'No, the head is over this way.' So they had him right there.

"But the cops shouldn't ever have put Wesley Gant in jail, because it was there that he checked out Nobel's book. Nobel, you know, is the guy that invented dynamite. Wesley studied that book close. When he got out, he came down to the jungle one day and made up some dynamite. Remember that? We were watching and were plenty scared, but it worked fine. From that book he also learned how to extract the nitro from store-bought dynamite. When he gets out, he'll help you blow your safe, but you better do the planning. You be the lookout, you be the brains.

"Roy Gant, I mean Wesley, has been around a long time. Back in 1927, the bank in L.A was made for $75,000. Wesley did that job along with Emmet Perkins. Later Perkins teamed up with a Jack de Santos. He owned a bar up north. His broad ran it for him. They robbed and killed a guy there. Barbara Graham was with the guy, but she just joined up with Perkins and Santos. They heard there was a Mrs. Monohan down in L.A., who had a nephew that owned a big joint in Las Vegas. Rumor was the nephew stored his money at Mrs. Monohan's. So they go down there to make the score, but find nothing. Perkins put out the old lady's lights. Then they heard about a guy that owned a store up in Nevada City. He used to haul his money home with him on weekends. They stopped him on the road. He had four kids with him. They shot 'em all, but one of the kids didn't die. About this time Santos's broad hears her man is hanging around with Barbara Graham, so she squeals to the cops. She knew the whole story. She got on the witness stand, and so did the kid that lived. They gassed all three of them ten years ago: Perkins, Santos, and Graham."

Starky said, "We know all that, Frank. Get back to the safeman. We need one that's not in jail."

Frank said, "I just threw that stuff in for the kid. I just wanted him to know if you see that sappy movie they made about Barbara Graham, don't shed tears. She was a cold killer. Right now I don't know who'd be good on a safe."

IT GOT DARK and the bums kept on telling stories. The steeple clock of a church sounded from the town, and Starky shushed everyone. He counted the strikes.

He said, "The Gray Ghost will be coming through in a few minutes."

A first-class night train called The Lark ran the Coast Route of the Southern Pacific. The hobos called her the Gray Ghost. She was all gray and silver except for a red stripe at the top, and she was always on time. She had a mythical reputation among the hobos for swiftness, punctuality, and for the ability to bring bad luck. You did not ride the Gray Ghost except in a dire emergency.

"If you ride her," they told me, "hold on to that bridge with both hands or she'll blow you right off. When she stops, climb on the roof and lie flat, 'cause the bulls watch her close. But she doesn't stop often. She never goes in the hole. All the trains have to go in the hole for her. That's why she's always on time."

When the bums said a train "goes in the hole," they meant taking a siding off the main track to let others go by. They said riding the Ghost always brought bad luck. Riders were likely to get arrested, struck by lightning, or break a leg. They had examples of all three. And the bad luck followed for days: you may get bad whiskey, fall off a trestle, or get drunk and get run over by a train. They had actual examples of those, also. It took great courage to ride the Ghost, and those who had done it bragged about it like a hunter brags about his twenty-point buck or a fisherman about his twenty-pound walleye.

That night when she came, when we heard the sounding horn down the way, saw the headlight coming round the bend, and the hobos said in low voices, "Here she comes now!"—I have to admit that, sitting there in the dark by the fire, a ghostly chill ran through me as she went flying by in a blur of lights and a clatter and tremble of railroad tracks. It made my hair stand on end.

THOSE WERE LAZY TIMES in Santa Barbara, but the itch to be on the road soon took hold again. I was attacked by that same old restlessness, and it proved to me my problem had not been so much the confines of the seminary; it was that I always wanted to see what was over the next hill. I wasn't even a good bum. A good bum knows when he's got it made in a place, and he stays until it peters out. When I told the hobos I was going to ride the train up to Salinas, they all gave me advice. Two rules could never be broken, no matter how hungry or curious I got: never steal anything that belongs to the railroad, and never, ever break the lead seal on the door of a freight car (although Big Boy had once violated that rule up by Salinas, and the car was full of cases of whiskey). Other rules were mere suggestions. They kept these rules to stay out of trouble with the bulls: don't get on a train until it starts moving, get off before it stops, stay out of sight as much as possible. Frank agreed the best way to catch the train was when it started moving, but not to wait too long. Once a buddy of his threw his bindle into a boxcar, but he stumbled in his first try to get on. By the time he got to his feet, the train was moving too fast, and he had the pleasure of watching the car with all his possessions trundle down the track out of sight.

When riding the trains, wear dark clothes, making you less visible at night, and on sunny days a bull won't see you sitting in the dark corner of a boxcar, because he is sunblind. Don't wear loose clothes that catch on things and throw you under a wheel. To find the train you want, you can ask a brakeman, or better yet, the switchman. They described the brakeman's shack, and told me how to recognize a switchman. But never ask a railroad man for directions when you're drunk. They told me trains going north into the mountains have three or four engines to pull up steep grades. Trains going south over the flatlands only have one or two. If you get on a "through freight" like the Red Hot Chili Pepper or the Pig, you better have food and water along. They don't stop.

The best place to get a meal was the Catholic Missions. The Franciscans had built one every thirty miles along the coast. That was a day's walk (for a Franciscan—three days for a bum). At those missions you could get a good meal of beans, bread, and milk every evening, and the monk serving would sit down and eat with you. They said, "And there always is good old Sally (the Salvation Army)." There were other charities, too, but at most of them you had to "take the ear-beating" (listen to a sermon) before they let you eat.

Jack had a rule that you never go inside a woman's house to eat a handout. "If she invites you inside to sit at the kitchen table, you say you have claustrophobia and that houses make you afraid. If you eat inside and hubby comes home, he'll kill you and dump your body on the track. And besides, that claustrophobia thing will make her feel sorry for you, and she'll give you an extra sandwich to take along. Study the clotheslines. If you see only women's clothes, it's likely the man is out of town. And don't hit on a house that has a lot of toys lying around. That means children, and women don't like bums around their babies."

They said if you really needed money you could get farm jobs, especially up around San Lucas and all around Salinas. Or you could sell a pint of blood. You could get five dollars a pint in Salinas, and if you waited until Frisco, you could get ten. But Big Boy said, "Don't go to San Francisco. It's full of drugs, beatniks, hippies, and queers."

I slept at the hobo camp that night so I could hear when the morning train came in. Frank had actually gone a little misty-eyed when I said goodbye. He wrote down my real name, and said he'd write the Air Force in a year to make sure I was there and hadn't stayed a bum. Then, as I was leaving, Frank called me back. He said, "Just in case you need some quick cash, I'm going to tell you about a real easy score in San Luis Obispo. You can make it when you run out of money. There's a washeteria there right by the tracks, so you can get in and out of town easy. You jump off the train and wait until late at night when no one's around. Hit the change machine. It's standing on the left-hand wall as you come in. The place is not brightly lit. Besides, people don't get suspicious about seeing somebody in a washeteria late at night. They're open twenty-four hours, so it's a pretty easy score. But don't get sloppy about it. And don't work with a broad," he said, as he went off on a tangent again. "A broad doesn't think like a man. She's smart enough, but she'll snitch you off any time for revenge. If you get into a fight, or look at another girl, look out! Here come the cops."

I left camp early in the morning while it was still dusk, and all were asleep except Felipe. He helped me roll up my sleeping bag and sent me off with a warning to "be careful in the hump yards." A hump yard was a yard on a small hill with tracks running down the slope. The engineer pushed cars over the crest and released them down the slope, where switchmen directed them into lines ready to be hooked to an outbound train. The bums always warned about hump yards because a loose car could sneak up on you if you were drunk.

"And don't ride with strange bums," he said, pointing at my sleeping bag. "There are men out there who will kill for a bedroll like that one." His goodbye was: "Don't ride the Ghost."

I crossed the tracks (never catch the train from the hobo camp side—the cops watch that side) and walked through the bushes toward the parked freight train. It started up a clattering of its hitches and began moving to meet me. It was easy as pie. I threw my stuff into the first open door and jumped on. Once out in the country, I sat in the doorway and let my legs swing back and forth, until I remembered they said you shouldn't do that on a train. ("You're an idiot if you dangle your feet. Some of the signals are set so close they can snatch your foot and tear you right off the train.") So I sat off to one side of the door, hugged my knees, and watched the dim lights of houses go by in the dawn. Free. On the road again.

I thought it was so wonderful at first to ride those trains, meandering through the countryside, watching the farms, trees, lakes, and mountains slide by. When you pass a citrus grove, you can smell the blossoms. When you pass a cow barn, you can smell the cattle. You can let the steady *clickety-clack* of the wheels put you into a trance so you forget everything. You don't know where you are, who you are, what time it is. All you know is you are alive—and moving, moving.

But this kind of travel had plenty of drawbacks. When you see something interesting, you can't just get off and browse. You're at the mercy of the train. I would've liked to stop in the Santa Maria Valley to walk among the farms. It was all rolling hills, checkered with fields of gold and green like Stearns County in August. Holstein cows would lift their heads from grazing as we clattered by. But there was no stopping. On and on we went.

The bums had told me to always sleep in the front end of the car with my feet pointing toward the engine in case there was a sudden stop. But the sleep I got was not restful with all that swaying and bumping and wiggling. And I got no exercise. They had told me, "Don't go strolling around in a boxcar when it's rolling. If the train suddenly starts around a curve just as you pass the side door, you'll go staggering out the door and find yourself rolling in the ditch as the train disappears down the track."

My body ached from lack of exercise. At the beginning I did not even get off and walk around when the train stopped. I was afraid the bulls would see me, and also that the train might suddenly take off without me. I learned the latter was next to impossible. The engineer always blew two short blasts on the whistle well before he released brakes. Cars banged such a racket when they got rolling a dead man could hear. The train rolled so slowly at first that a dead man could rise from the grave, stretch out all his bones, and still get there on time.

The first time I was brave enough to get out and walk down the tracks to uncramp, I got a big scare. The engineer blew the highball (the two blasts). I started back for the car where my gear was. Whoa! All the cars looked the same! For a minute I panicked, sticking my head in every open door until I found the right one. After that I studied the boxcars. They were very different. The cars had labels from every line in the United States: Southern Pacific, Western Pacific, Union Pacific, Missouri Pacific, New York Central, Rock Island, Milwaukee Road, Great Northern. Even if you set two cars of the same company side by side, they were easily told apart by other markings like paint splashes, old cargo labels, broken siding, and how faded the paint was.

I had to get to Salinas. The bums talked about it all the time and I wanted to see the area where Steinbeck was born. By the time I got there, I was dead tired. I felt like I hadn't slept in weeks. I expected a little town like Albany, but it was huge, much bigger than St. Cloud. I saw the Cominos Hotel at Main and Central. I thought I once heard Steinbeck had stayed there. I decided to splurge. I got a room for $3.54. It was the best room I rented my whole trip—bath and everything. I slept until evening and then went out to find some food. I walked around until I found hobo-looking characters and fell in with them.

I passed around my tobacco and papers, and soon we were on our way to the hobo camp. And there, who should appear out of the bushes zipping up his pants, but Floyd! He'd ridden the freights up from Santa Barbara right after I met him at the jungle there. Floyd's eyesight was poor. He saw me coming, but he didn't recognize me until I was right by him. Then he gave me his big grin.

"Hello, kid, you want me to roll you one?"

He had just taken a leak, so I said, "No, I've learned how to roll my own now."

Floyd said he was going to a charity place in town where they had decent food. He appeared sober now but said he'd been drunk since he'd come to Salinas. He said in the Salinas jungle someone always had a bottle of burgundy.

We got to the charity place before they opened. Bums were drinking wine in a grove of trees nearby, and some were suspiciously merry. They said the place wouldn't open until 7:00 p.m. but said we'd have to take one hell of an ear-beating before we got to eat. We waited with them and smoked. They referred to this place as "The Mission," but it wasn't at all like those beautiful Franciscan Missions. It was just a plain old square building. Shortly after seven, the men began to form a line. Floyd and I fell in. We stood outside on the sidewalk while the front man tried the door every few seconds.

When it opened, we were greeted by an undertaker—at least he looked like one, dressed in black. He acted like one, very solemn and oily polite. We sat on low plank-and-cinder-block benches. A big wooden podium up front had a light on top. A sign advised "No Talking," and the undertaker suggested a time of silent prayer. From a back room came the clatter of dishes and a maddening fragrance of cooking. The undertaker kept checking his watch. After a while, he closed the door and slid home the deadbolt. He attempted to lower the shade over the window, but it was stuck. He announced that the "Reverend Doctor of the Bible" would be in shortly, and made a gliding exit.

Everyone there was hungry: stomachs growling and feet shuffling, legs were crossed and uncrossed, elbows rested on knees supporting chins in palms, now the left, now the right, occasional deep sighs and clearing of throats. I was surprised the little sign on the podium was able to keep these men silent. I tried to talk to Floyd, but he frowned and held a finger to his lips.

In walked a fat man with an underbite, several chins, and the back of his neck bulged above his tight collar, pushing his head forward so his jaw extended before him almost as far as his belt buckle. Pointing the way with his jaw, he plowed to the podium looking for all the world like a bulldog, and sounding like one, too. He wheezed softly, lugging an enormous Bible. He hoisted it up onto the podium with a swing and a bang. His face flushed with the labor, the Reverend Doctor addressed the congregation.

"Narrow is the gate," he thundered, startling several of the congregation who had been dozing. He said the gate leading to eternal life was so narrow few could squeeze through. This was a surprising topic, since he was by far the fattest man in the room, but he cleared that up by saying he was not talking about the body, but about the soul, and Jesus in this passage was not talking of a real gate, but a spiritual one through which a pure soul could slip. A soul with no sin was as thin as a shadow, but a soul fat with layers of sin would not fit. Therefore, repent! Put off the layers of drunkenness and idleness—the thickest layers, and take on the virtues of sobriety and charitable labor, for those slenderize the soul the most. This Biblical exegesis was most refreshing for me, it was so new.

The doctor moved on. "Man does not live by bread alone, but by every word that issues forth from the mouth of God. Come, my sheep, and I will feed ye spiritual bread and ye shall not hunger, and I will give thee living water and not wine to drink."

So he continued stirring together unrelated Bible passages with the most sparkling ingenuity. He aimed his Biblical creations directly at the idle and wine-besotted sheep in front of him. Some (unaware the Reverend was talking about them) occasionally shouted out an "amen" to show their total agreement. The Reverend was much gratified. He had a definite preference for passages related to food and drink that, had they not been presented in such an unsavory manner, would have served only to increase the hunger of the starving bums. He brought up manna from the desert and milk and honey, and loaves and fishes and plenty of food to feed five thousand. As he preached he sometimes rested one hand on the Bible (to indicate the source of his inspiration?) and pointed the other hand at the ceiling (to impersonate the Statue of Liberty, I thought). Sometimes he clutched the podium with both fists in case it tried to escape. He sallied forth into the audience and, having made an especially moving point, spun on his heel and marched back to his pulpit in silence. An exaggerated pause allowed his point to sink in, and he continued in a dramatically lowered voice.

He wore a shiny, bright green, three-piece polyester suit. I heard whispered speculation about how it might look in the dark. The main focus of the congregation, however, was on the middle button of the vest, which was straining to keep his belly from cascading over his belt. The button was ready to fire across the room any moment. And as the Reverend strolled among his flock, some sheep cowered, I thought, when the button was aimed in their direction.

This sacred presentation was suddenly interrupted by knocking at the door. The Reverend was stunned. The undertaker came from the back room and hurried to the door. A ragged man shouted, "Let me in. I want to eat." The undertaker pointed at his watch, shouting, "Go away. You're too late," and succeeded in lowering the shade. A few kicks at the door from an angry boot, then quiet. The undertaker apologized to the Reverend and asked the sheep to take note that no one was allowed to join the flock if late. Again the undertaker vanished into the back. The Reverend took a breath and continued. The ragged shadow appeared at a window and a terrific pounding came from there. The Reverend tried to ignore him, but the effect of the sermon was greatly marred. He paused and angrily motioned for the bum to go away. The bum gave him the finger.

"Here," said the Reverend with unreserved sympathy, "is a good example of a drunkard who cannot fit through the narrow gate without repentance. Let us say a prayer for him."

Then he raised his face to the ceiling and squeezed his eyes tight shut. "Oh, Lord Jesus, we thank you for bringing us together here and we ask your mercy on this poor, lost—"

"Bullshit!" yelled the shadow at the window.

This was too much. A snicker escaped me. The Reverend looked up with a frown. I composed myself so quickly only those immediately around me knew who it was. The bum at the window left. The Reverend droned on. The bums got more into the spirit of the thing and now spouted ejaculations at the end of most sentences. "Alleluias" and "amens" erupted all around. The Reverend seemed pleased. That spurred them on. The Reverend exhorted the assemblage to guard against false prophets, who, in sheep's clothing, make a mockery of religion, casting scorn upon the most sacred principles of "Gahwd, the Alllmighty," and prey upon the innocent by leading them away from the straight and narrow path and turning them into swine that wallow all day in the mud and filth of drunkenness and idleness. "Amen. Alleluia. Amen." came from all parts of the assembly—from the very ones who had spent the day wallowing.

One man jumped up and shouted, "I love Jesus, I believe everything he says," and he shed tears over this. He ran up to the podium, falling to his knees next to the Reverend, shouting: "I'm saved, I'm saved. Yes, Jesus, I repent. I was a drunkard, but now I see the light." The man gripped the Reverend's leg and cried, "Thank you, Reverend, I was a sinner, but now I'm saved, saved from the fires of e-eternal damnation."

The Reverend, at first startled, was pulling back his leg to disengage, then, realizing the man looked cleaner than most and didn't smell as bad, and probably remembering his florescent suit was washable, warmed to the occasion.

He put a hand on the man's head, extending his other arm as if to embrace his flock. "Rejoice my brothers, for one of my lambs who was lost has been found, alleluia. He has found the narrow gate." (Here he rolled his eyes to the heavens.) "Father, we thank thee in the name of Jeheesus Christ, our Lord. Amen. "

While all this was going on, I heard gasping, gurgling, and choking around me, much of it coming from Floyd. I saw Floyd was doubled, purple with suppressed laughter, and several others were in the same suffocating predicament.

"He does this all the time," gasped Floyd. "He's been saved by every preacher from San Diego to San Jose."

The Reverend was so pleased with the conversion that he called for his favorite hymn, and announced dinner would be served forthwith. Looking forward to the promised meal, all the bums sang lustily the first line of "Shall We Gather at the River," and then many (like me) mumbled through the rest of the verse, having never learned anything beyond the title. The Reverend Preacher shook the ceiling with his joyous outpouring. The bums' vigor abated somewhat as the Reverend swung into a second verse, and at the third, they looked about nervously as doubt crept in about the termination of this blessed event. Finally the Reverend Doctor of the Bible realized he was the only one singing and put an end to the torture by calling for dinner. This brought a loud cheer, markedly enthusiastic, and the Reverend frowned.

The good Doctor of the Bible chose not to partake of our supper of barley soup, beef, bread, and milk. He left rapidly by a side door, but it gave us all great comfort to reflect that the Reverend Doctor was likely fasting to expiate the sins of some wallowing swine.

When we left the mission, Floyd said he was going back to the jungle to sleep. It was a cool and foggy night, so I told him I had a room at the Cominos and he could sleep on the floor. At first he said he couldn't. He didn't want to get me into trouble with the management. I persuaded him. He left saying he had to get his bedroll from the jungle.

I lay on my bed writing in my log for a couple of hours. I figured Floyd had found burgundy again and was staying with friends. I had just turned off the light when I heard a very soft knock. Floyd. We stayed up a while and talked. His full name was Floyd Rundel, and he was about sixty-five (he wasn't sure). He had been a steeplejack painter when younger. He had climbed the highest buildings all over the U.S. He sometimes made over a hundred dollars in one day. But he kept blowing it on women and cars. He said, "I figured it was a job I could always depend on. Why save?"

In Chicago the scaffold he was on gave way. Floyd hadn't shortened his safety line. Down he went. Three stories from the sidewalk the safety line caught him. The spring took up the shock. Floyd was unhurt—physically, that is.

"That took all the nerve out of me. I can't climb a tall stepladder now. I just can't do it. I used to think I was so smart, going where others could not go."

Next morning we walked out to the hobo camp. I had come to Salinas to look around where Steinbeck used to live. I wanted to see Tortilla Flat and Cannery Row. So I left Floyd at the hobo camp and hitched a ride to Monterrey. I went to Fisherman's Wharf and looked at the shops. There was a strong scent of fish and a constant cry of seagulls. Pelicans sailed along the wharf. Some parked on the posts and left generous deposits to pay the rent. I saw a little boy carrying a string of mussels he wanted to sell in one of the markets. I supposed Steinbeck used to do the same. I saw a huge, bronze anchor with its chains. Its sign read: "Brought up from the bottom of Monterey Bay in July 1944. Origin unknown." I found Cannery Row, but it was completely abandoned—dead and empty as a ghost town. I don't think a single one of the old canneries was open anymore. One was being used as a storehouse for cars.

On the street I met a bum (I could spot them now a mile away). I smiled at him, and he immediately hit me up for money. I told him I was broke, but I offered him my sack of Bull Durham and my wheat straw papers. We lit up and sat in the sun by a wood fence and smoked. He must have been convinced I was a fellow bum. "Come along," he said, "we need some liquid refreshment."

We went into a saloon full of people. He introduced me to his buddy. They said they had "something" in the back room, where brooms, mops, buckets, and brushes were stored. A five-gallon pail stood in a dark corner with gunny sacks stuffed inside. One guy watched at the door. The other pulled out the sacks and reached inside, coming out with a quart of wine.

"Drink, friend."

I drank, and it was top grade burgundy. We each had a few swallows and then they put the bottle back.

"When is the last time you ate?"

"Yesterday," I lied. I had a peach about an hour earlier, but I figured that didn't count.

"You got a place to stay for the night?"

"No," and that was a pure fact.

"Listen, go see the monsignor down the street. Tell him you're low. I can't promise you a bed, but a meal you'll get, don't worry."

They told me they did janitorial work for the saloon. The reason they kept the wine in the back room was because the saloon keeper had caught them stealing a bottle one day, and so he checked them over every time they went out the door. They still stole his wine, but now they drank it on the premises.

Chapter Nineteen

I WAS OUT OF MONEY AGAIN, so I had to work. I made the fool mistake of thinking it would be fun to pick strawberries for a few days. The men at the hobo camp in Salinas warned me only a crazy man would do such work. But I knew this about a bum by now: he hates work more than anything and must be starving before he thinks about resorting to it. When forced into work, he hates it like poison and quits the minute he gets his first pay. Some of the bums had picked strawberries. They gave me advice. The farm labor camps were hell, they said. Not as bad as prison but worse than the army.

Strawberries like cool, moist nights and sunny days—not hot days, and with a light breeze to dry off the dew. This was exactly the climate along the coast, and you could find hundreds of strawberry farms within twenty miles of the ocean. Farm jobs were always available there. There was a shortage of Mexicans, who used to do all that backbreaking work of picking strawberries, weeding and thinning onions, cutting broccoli and celery, and any short-handle hoe jobs—all jobs that required the worker to bend down, way down. The pay was low for the amount of torture. Only the lowest segment of the American population took those jobs—hard luck guys who couldn't get a job elsewhere, and winos who couldn't hold a job because they got drunk and forgot to show up for work.

A big sign by Salinas read, "What kind of a good-neighbor policy is this?" The picture showed a Mexican looking with longing eyes across the border at the unharvested crops. He was labeled, "Our Mexican neighbor, who can and wants to do bend-down labor." On the American side of the border was an American, labeled, "An American who can, but doesn't want to do bend-down work."

You could stand on most any street corner in the early morning and get a job in minutes. Or you could go to a designated pick-up area late in the afternoon. Sometimes the farmer asked for your Social Security number, but that was only to comply with the law. You could spiel off any number that came to mind.

The farmer who picked me up asked, "Ever do bend-over labor?"

"I was raised on a farm."

"Get in."

The farmer took me to a camp run by a company called The New Englander. I got to the camp in the evening. The camp buildings were old army barracks. I didn't take anything along to the camp, not even a change of clothes.

The veterans had told me "they would steal your ass if they could unscrew it." I had nothing with me except a lead pencil, a pocket full of three-by-five cards, my knife, and a sack of Bull Durham. I figured I would work for two days and leave. They assigned me a cot in the barracks, and I flopped down to test it. Not bad, a bit lumpy and smelled of mold, but comfortable. It was cool and damp in that building and there was nothing to read. I hated the place already. I wished it was morning so I could go out in the sunny fields. I was pretty sure it was not as tough as the bums had made it out to be, and if it was, I was confident I could take it. I was a tough farm boy.

I could not take it. I lasted—barely lasted—one full day. I left in total defeat and total admiration for anyone who can do that kind of work day after day. I will shock grain, pick rocks, husk corn, peel potatoes, shovel manure, or do any other drudgery rather than pick strawberries. A new guy can pick maybe a dozen crates a day, but he has to work hard at it and by evening he will be very sorry he did not rest more. A veteran will do twice that and be happy. They gave me a choice of getting paid a dollar-forty an hour or seventy-five cents a crate. I chose to get paid by the crate, until I picked one. Then I changed my mind and chose to get paid by the hour.

I left the camp with eight dollars in my pocket and a skin full of sore muscles and aching bones. I told the man who paid me I just could not go back out there again.

I dragged myself to San Francisco. I knew some students there who were at Crosier with me. I rested two days. Then I was ready to go. I took the city bus to the Haight Ashbury District by Golden Gate Park. I wanted to see how real hippies lived. I walked through the district, but saw nothing I had not seen before. The streets were deserted. They were having a big rally in Golden Gate Park, but I didn't know that. I went to a busy street corner and held out my thumb. I was going to Stockton to catch a freight train north. The bums said there was a big railroad yard there.

A young white-haired man on a motorcycle swerved crazily in front of a honking car and slid to a stop by me. He grabbed my sleeping bag and threw it on the gas tank in front of him, and signaled with his thumb for me to get on behind him. I held my suitcase in my right hand and hugged him with my left. He jerked the throttle open and we went roaring down the street, weaving through traffic like he was going to a fire. He drove that bike hard. He drove like Jehu in the Bible. Had he not had such a pig of a motorcycle, I would have fallen off the back several times in the first two blocks. And had I known the driver was insane, I would have jumped off.

When we stopped at a red light (one of the few he stopped for), he said he was going to Sausalito. I said, "Okay," and off we went. I had never heard of

Sausalito. I thought it was the name of a street, but we roared on and on and soon were going over the Golden Gate Bridge. By then I knew I was headed in the wrong direction. Stockton was to the east. After a while he stopped and asked where I wanted to be dropped. I said on the main road going east to Stockton.

He said, "You have to go north or south to go east. The bay is in your way."

"What?" I said, "I better get off here."

"What's in Stockton?" he asked.

"A railroad yard. I'm catching the train north."

"Hang on," he said, and gunned his bike again.

He drove down to the bay and parked on the lawn in front of a large house with faded siding and a rickety front porch. He said I could stay the night. He thought someone would be going to Stockton in the morning.

The hippies I had missed at Haight Ashbury I found in Sausalito. They lived in a kind of commune that included the old house and a big houseboat docked nearby in Richardson Bay. The houseboat was not navigable. It was resting on its belly in the sand. A dozen or more people lived in the commune; the number was hard to tell. Someone was always coming or going. Silver, the motorcycle nut who brought me there, was one of them. Well, he wasn't really, for he was different. Silver was the laziest human being I have ever met—and the most reckless. The only reason he wasn't dead was because he drove such an underpowered cycle that he couldn't get up the speed to kill himself. He wove in and out of traffic and squeezed between cars so close that drivers yelled, "You damn fool," as he passed. You could trace Silver's progress down the street by the missing, puttering, spitting of his motor, and by the angry honking of car horns.

Why the bike didn't run better, I don't know. Silver spent time tinkering with it—cleaning the plugs and gapping the points—whenever he took a break from lying in the hammock on the porch drinking Chivas Regal or sleeping on the beach. But he never cleaned the outside of it. The entire bike was covered with oil, including parts of the seat and handlebars. The other communists were trying to figure out how to ban Silver from the community, for he did not contribute his share of the labor and only contributed to the pool of money when the girls refused to let him eat, but every time it got down to a vote, they let him stay. When I was there, a girl named Kory demanded his banishment because he had made her sheets dirty. She had hung sheets in the early-morning stillness, and Silver had parked his bike next to the washline. Mid-morning a breeze came up from the bay, and Kory's sheets began to wave back and forth, gently caressing the sides of the cycle and cleaning off some oil. Kory was steaming mad, but could not get enough support to ban Silver.

I stayed there two days and argued with them about religion and philosophy. They loved debate more than anything. They were all as young as I, or younger, and I could identify with them in some ways, but mostly they were a mystery. What they really wanted was to get away from Mom and Dad. I could understand that. What was I doing? But I wanted to get away so I could be free to make a living my own way in the world as it was. They wanted to change the world, overthrow the present system, and live in a beautiful new world where they could have sex, take acid (LSD was still legal), smoke pot, and lie around and get high. They said they wanted to be free, but I knew that lying around all day in a drug stupor was not freedom. I had learned that much from watching the bums in Santa Barbara drink wine. I also knew living in a commune was not freedom. Freedom demanded some solitude. Above all, freedom demanded independence. They not only depended on each other, but many of them depended on a monthly check from Mom and Dad.

To them I too, was a puzzle. They thought farm life was "living off the bountiful land" and was like paradise. They wondered why I would leave it. (City kids always think of nature as a generous mother, ready to give of her abundance to mankind. A farm boy knows she's a cranky old battle-ax that gives up nothing without demanding the sweat of your brow and a pain in your bent-over back.) They said I talked like their insane parents, yet I lived like a hobo. I was about to join the Air Force and become part of the hated "military-industrial complex," yet I was a social rebel. I was a "total square," I was "out of it"—trapped in the "totalitarian cage of capitalistic society," and yet I was bumming around on the road like I had taken on a bit of "Zen" (live for the moment), which they much admired. They thought they were making a statement with their unkempt beards and hair, but they could not figure out what statement I was making with mine.

They were intrigued that I could spout Latin, could quote Aristotle, and that I said the "essence of God is existence," or that "God is Being." I did not know what those maxims meant (I was parroting Father Ernie from ontology class), but to them it was very deep and philosophical, and something they had not heard from their parents. They would approve by saying, "Right on, man," or "Far out," with such great passion it made me laugh.

Their talk was a foreign language to me. They never said LSD or marijuana; it was acid and pot, grass, or weed. A marijuana cigarette was a joint. A roach was a joint smoked down to a nub. A toke was a puff. A hit was an inhalation with effect. A buzz or a trip was a high. Silver didn't say he was under the influence, he said he was stoned. Wasted meant really stoned.

One of them they called "Reesey Girl." When I first walked into their kitchen, she was smoking. "Have a toke?" she asked like we were old friends, handing me a very sadly rolled cigarette. I passed. I asked her where Silver was.

She said, "Don't know, probably out selling grass."

"Selling grass? Who the heck buys grass?"

"Marijuana, you dope."

"Oh. I didn't know he was in the business."

"Well, he is. And if you ever need good shit, talk to Silver."

She put the juicy cigarette to her lips, and with a great sucking sound took the smoke deep into her lungs. She held her breath for a while, putting pressure on her lungs, then blew the smoke out through a little opening between her lips and smiled at me.

They did not mind one bit when people called them communists. They said communism was superior to capitalism. I had been taught to despise, hate, and fear communism all my life. They loved it. They thought it was a good system, and when I pointed out that it wasn't working so well in Russia, they said it was because the leaders were corrupt and not enlightened. Mike (or Jesus) had a copy of part of the *Communist Manifesto*, which he quoted sometimes, but without making sense. They called him Jesus because he played that role. He wore a full beard, had hair down to his shoulders, and wore long, flowing robes and sandals. Whenever he walked outside he carried a tall walking stick and smiled benignly on everyone. He was obviously playing a role, but everyone except Silver went along with it. Jesus despised anyone who went to work every day and said they were capitalist pigs. Anyone who wore a coat and tie was said to be wearing a straightjacket. When I said that this country had become great under the capitalist system, they said, no, it became rich and powerful by exploiting other countries, and they pointed to the Mexican farm worker as an example. They had me there.

Most of them had been to college, and most were from rich families. They were privileged children, yet they nursed a deep hatred for the very establishment that gave them their privileges. And they did not seem to realize that when they spent their money on food, clothes, and Chivas Regal, they fed the very monster they hated. The gods of their fathers were all dead. They believed in no religion unless it was some mystical oriental stuff of which they had only a foggy idea: Buddhism, Hinduism, transcendental meditation, or anything that sounded different from what they had been taught as children. When I went into their living room I often found someone sitting in the corner burning incense, sitting in a lotus pose, and muttering to himself or *omm*ing monotonously.

Reesey Girl spent her time in the kitchen. She wore a long granny dress and hummed to herself all day. I liked her, but she was an airhead. She talked this way: "Like you see, I was going like, you know, to get, like groceries and stuff for dinner? And you know, this guy kept like bugging me? I mean really. He was like older than dirt, and like, you know, really dirty, smelly? You dig? It was like, wow, a total drag."

But she could dance! When we were sitting around on the floor in the living room that night, with some weird music playing, candles burning, and censers smoking, one of them said, "Reesey Girl, dance for us." Everyone seconded the motion, and Reesey Girl got up. Her face was not pretty, but she had a gorgeous body, and she moved oily smooth like a cat. Slowly at first she danced, up on her toes, barely touching the carpet. Her movements were whisper-soft, her body floating as light as the smoke from the censer. She whirled and began to move faster. She weaved and snaked with savage contortions that made her sweat. Her long brown hair waved behind her when she turned her face to the ceiling; she moved her lips like she was silently praying to some heathen god. She went round and round, graceful as a doe, fierce like a tiger. Reesey Girl could dance.

I could see they were as confused as I was, but they were not looking for answers like I was. They thought they had the answers. They somehow considered themselves a vital part of world events because they carried signs and shouted slogans on street corners, but I felt that, deep inside, they were not convinced, for they went at their drugs and their drink with reckless abandon. There were so many contradictions in their thinking. They demanded freedom, but hated the United States Constitution, their country's written guarantee of freedom. They had an astonishing hatred of cops, and an equally astonishing love of drugs. They boasted about how well they all got along, but they were always bickering. They prided themselves on their frugality, but drank Chevis Regal instead of Guckenheimer. Jesus would not eat the crust of his bread. He had a big round cookie cutter which he used to cut the middle out of each slice, rejecting the rest (and angering Reesey Girl, who was the baker). They constantly harped about the immorality of war, of poverty, or of anything they didn't like, but practiced little morality in the conduct of their own lives. They were fond of saying violence never solved anything, but were also fond of throwing rocks at the police. They liked Mao Tse-Tung but hated, *hated* Lyndon Johnson (he killed Kennedy, they said). In any argument a quote from Mao was a clincher; a quote from the Bible was mocked.

I did not understand them, but I never blamed them for that. I knew I was the last one to come to for life's answers. When I left them, I pondered for days how it could be that a young man like myself could feel more at home with the old, ignorant hobos in the Santa Barbara jungle then I did with the young, college-bred hippies in Sausalito. At least the bums knew who they were: the dregs of society. These people thought they were the cream of society, and that they would eventually be the saviors of mankind.

Me? I was confused.

Reesey gave me a going away present: a copy of *Mad Magazine* to read on the train. I could have married that girl, but she wanted to run off to Katmandu or Timbuktu and smoke hashish—or was it Tangiers? I forget. But I was meeting the real people.

Chapter Twenty

STOCKTON LAY BAKING in the sun. Heat waves shimmered from every flat surface. Sweat dripped from the end of my nose as I watched the trains from the bushes by the tracks. Twice I had to go back to the depot to fill my water bottle. Then, about four o'clock, I saw a train was ready. *That must be going to Roseville,* I thought. The highball sounded. When she began to roll, I moved in. You normally don't ride on a flatcar because you're like a goldfish in a bowl, but I was so hot I thought I would die in a boxcar. I would have taken a cattle car, because they have slats with wide gaps to let the air through, but they were all shut on my side. I waited for the last flatcar in the line and hopped aboard. I lay down near the back of it, my head on my bedroll, my feet on my suitcase.

The train was moving very slowly, like it was reluctant to get going in such heat. I opened my suitcase to get out my jar of peanut butter. It wasn't there! I had left it in the bushes by the track. Just then an old bum strolled out of the brush and calmly climbed onto the front of my car. The nerve! He gave me not so much as a nod. He sat down on his bedroll in the middle of the car facing the front, like he didn't know I was there. The train gathered speed and soon we were clacking along out in the country. The breeze quickly dried my sweat-soaked shirt and I was feeling good, except for that bum. He sat there like chiseled stone; only his hair moved a little in the wind.

I wanted to get to Roseville, because I knew they had a big railroad yard there and would be making up trains to go to northern California, and maybe on to Oregon and Washington. I had made up my mind to go to the Yukon. I was a bit nervous about riding on a flatcar at first, especially with that hobo statue up there. But the guy was minding his own business. It was a nice ride. The wind fanned off the heat and did not swirl around in little tornados of dust like in some boxcars. I could see everything up and down the tracks as we went. When the engine took a curve I could see the entire train. I waved at the people waiting in the cars by the crossings. I waved wildly to any children by the tracks, often until they were out of sight, for I remembered how it was when I was little.

The man of stone just sat there.

The train slowed, preparing to stop. Slower and slower it went until the thunder of the hitches collapsing against one another rolled up the line, shook our car, and went on back to the caboose. We were parked. I got up and walked to where the stone man was sitting. He heard me coming and half-turned, but he hardly looked up as he asked, "Where you headed?"

"Roseville," I said. "I want to catch a train up to Portland." I sat down by him, and he finally looked at me. He was old, like Floyd, but looked much healthier. He was all freckly, and I could see his hair had once been red, though now was mostly gray.

"Portland? Cold up that way," he said. "You're going to need an extra bedroll. Tell you what. I'll sell you mine for one dollar. I need something to eat real bad."

"Sorry, Red, I'm broke." That was a lie. I had the strawberry money in my boot and a quarter in my pocket. I called him Red, and he seemed satisfied with that. The wrinkles in his face reminded me of Grandpa. I rolled myself a cigarette and passed the makings to Red. He said he was on his way to Roseville, too, and from there he was going to Folsom to visit his brother at the prison. We had barely lit up when the highball sounded from up front. In a minute the hitches began to thunder again, and we were under way. Red was not a talker. He seemed amused that I waved at people, but said nothing.

After we passed through a little town, the train picked up speed and she sailed right along. When we got near Elk Grove (the larger towns had signs by the tracks), the train took a side track and we were stopped again.

We waited. I had no clue how long the train would be stopped, but Red seemed to know. He said, "God, am I hungry." He stood up and pulled a few nickles out of his pocket. "Look, kid," he said, "I think she'll be in the hole a while. If you got any money at all, let's put it together and buy a loaf of bread from that house over there." I gave him my quarter, and he was pleased.

"I lied," I said.

He laughed, "A bum that lies about his money? Whoever heard of such a thing? Watch my bindle," he said, and headed for the house.

I removed my boot and got out two dollars. I put one in my hat and the other in the watch pocket of my jeans. I figured I would tell Red it was my emergency money—if we needed it. I liked him, but not enough to let him know I had money in my boot.

In a little while a train came from the front. It passed by in a big hurry, and immediately here came Red. He thought we were getting ready to move. He had no bread. No one had answered his knock. But he had his pockets full of wheat which he had scraped out of the corners of a grain wagon. He gave me a handful, and we sat there and munched on the kernels, spitting out the hulls. It was delicious. He gave me back my quarter. I shared my water. We munched and spit, and waited.

"She must be waiting for another train," he said, "or she'd have blown by now."

A second train came from the front, and then the engineer blew the highball. The hitches clattered, and we began to roll. At the very next siding she went into the hole again. I had caught a bad train. But this time we were near a house where someone was home. A man was relaxing on a lawn chair in his backyard. A barbeque grill was smoking by him.

"You suppose that old fart would sell us a loaf of bread?" Red asked.

"Try him," I said, and gave him my quarter again. Red walked to the lawn fence to ask for the bread. I hoped the man would give us some of his barbeque, too. I remembered how often Mom had given a hobo a nice thick sandwich when he walked to our house off the Great Northern railroad tracks.

Red and the man hollered at each other for a while, but I noticed the man stayed on his lawn chair. I knew we weren't getting bread. Red came back. We ate more wheat and had a smoke. I got off and walked around a little. I heard someone calling. By golly, there was the man by the fence with something in his hand. I went over and got four big biscuits from him. I gave two to Red. They were stale and had no butter, but the way we wolfed them down you would have thought they were fresh cheeseburgers from McDonald's.

It was getting dark now. The air freshened and the ride was more comfortable. I lay on my back and watched the stars come out. Red slept. Once in a while in the distance I saw a light in a barn or a farm house. I imagined a farmer milking his cows and his wife frying fish for supper. For a moment I wished I was back home, but it passed. I fell into a dreamy doze, a kind of haze—that drifting zone between wake and sleep—the twilight of sleep, like being sleepy and a little drunk on good wine. All peaceful and warm—all was well.

The clash of the hitches woke me as we came into Roseville. I judged it was around midnight. Red knew his way around this place. We walked through part of the town to get to a hump yard where they hooked up the trains going north. On the way a cop jumped us, but it was the usual routine: check IDs, phone in to see if there's a warrant, warnings about what happens to criminals in their town. Red fed that cop a big line of horseshit about how we were on our way to pick peas in Washington. He showed the cop his seamanship papers and all kinds of other junk and the cop was impressed. He talked much nicer to us after that.

Roseville must have been the biggest railroad center on the West Coast. The whole place was a complication of innumerable parallel tracks filled with freight cars. That hump yard was a scary place in the night. Switch engines moved cars around on tracks so close together I didn't think the cars would fit. It was a black night. Anytime my eyes got used to the darkness, a light would blaze out from somewhere for a second and strike me blind. Dark silhouettes swung flashlights and lanterns all over the place. There was lots of crashing and banging as the cars jammed together and the hitches fell into place. And there were ghost cars that rolled along by themselves down the slope of the hump, inaudible in all that noise until suddenly—*bang!*—they crashed into another car and hooked up. I could see immediately that you had to know what you were doing to operate in this yard at night. I told Red to excuse me, but I wanted no part of this. I figured I better stick to being a hobo in the daytime.

On the side where they parked unusable boxcars, we found one open and went to sleep in it. When daylight came, we did not get up. The air was cool. We waited until the sun was shining into the door and saying, "Get up, you lazy bums, hit the road." We walked around until we found a coffee machine, ten cents a cup. We sat on our haunches on the sunny side of a building and huddled over the coffee like it was a private kitchen stove. The coffee steamed in the sun, and we both drank in gurgling slurps to cool it before it went down the throat.

We went back to the yard to find me a train north. At the margin of the yard a black man was sitting on a stack of railroad ties. Red asked him about the trains, but he knew less than Red did. He told Red he had been robbed the night before.

"When the kid leaves," he said, "I'll tell you who did it to me."

"Oh, the kid's okay," Red told him.

So the man told us how this young punk took his twenty dollars, his transistor radio, and his .22 pistol while he was sleeping. He said he thought he was playing nursemaid to a little baby, helping him out, but he was mistaken. He looked at me sidewise like he suspected I might be another baby of that kind. He told us where there was a really good soup kitchen in Dunsmuir, and said there might be a Pig going through to Portland sometime next morning.

I did not want to wait for a Pig or a Chili Pepper. I just wanted to get on a train and move north. Red said he would wait with me until we found one, and then he would head east to Folsom. We found a secluded spot by the side of the tracks. The alluring scent of a bakery came from somewhere nearby. That made us both hungry again. Red said he would go find something to eat. I trusted Red now and told him I had some emergency money. I apologized for not bringing it out before. But Red got a good laugh out of this. He confessed he had money, too. He had twenty-five dollars! But he would not use it. He owed that money to his brother. He had that debt hanging over him for seven years. He said he was going to pay it off now, even if it killed him. I tried to give him the dollar out of my hat, but he refused. He said, "I've gone without money for longer periods than this and never starved yet. We'll both keep our money."

I watched our stuff. In a short time, here came Red carrying a big box under his arm. I could tell by the grin on his face he had found something. I opened the box. It was full of donuts—several dozen! All kinds! Not fresh, but that was of no account. We sat there among the bushes in the sun and ate and ate. We stored the remainder in our gear. The ice track began moving as we ate.

They were icing up the reefers (mostly fruit cars) and it was about to pull out. It was the Chili Pepper, but the bulls were watching her like prison guards, so I didn't try for it. There was another train Red said was getting ready. We sat in the weeds by the track and watched it. We had a good-bye smoke.

When the engineer blew the highball, we shook hands good-bye. But that highball gave Red the bug. "Oh, hell," he said, dropping my hand. "I'll go with you for a while." This was a true hobo. The call of the highball was the call of the wild for him. He loved riding, moving, rolling along.

But I said, "Red, go see your brother." Then he tried to talk me into going to Folsom with him, but I had a call too—north, to the Yukon, to Alaska. My train was picking up speed.

Red gave me a push. "You better get going, then."

I had to run for the train. I aimed at a nice, new Southern Pacific boxcar with a wide open door. As the car passed, I ran alongside, threw in my stuff, and jumped aboard, landing belly-down on the floor of the car.

Right then I realized I had made a mistake. I lay there a second, my hands under me like I was about to do a pushup. In the dark shadows at the front of the car I could see four men sitting against the wall. I could have flopped back off, but it was too late. When I had pitched in my gear, the suitcase had slid out of my reach, and the sleeping bag had rolled toward the back. The train was rapidly accelerating and I knew that, by the time I recovered my stuff, it would be suicide to jump off. I said "Hello" loudly, fiercely, to belie my fear. I got up, took my suitcase, and walked to the back of the car by my sleeping bag. I kicked the bag into a corner and sat down. I put the suitcase a few yards in front of me. I pulled out my pocket knife and set about cleaning my fingernails with the point of the blade. I wished the knife was bigger. Felipe had laughed at it and called it a toy, but he had showed me how to hold it if there was a fight. I stuck the knife into the floor next to me and leaned back into the corner. I pulled my hat down over my eyes and pretended to sleep.

I did not sleep. I watched them carefully, getting strobe-like glimpses from under my hat brim as it bobbed up and down from the movement of the train. I watched them like a cornered mouse watches a cat. One of them was skinny and old, and one was a little Mexican. I could have wrestled with those two, but I was really scared of the four of them together. One of them was a tall, peaceful-looking black man, but the other was a wide, hugely muscular white man with an unhappy face and a domineering demeanor. They called that one Earl, and he was drunk. They were very quiet when I first got on, but soon they began talking, and Earl brought out a gallon jug. He must have slipped it behind him when I jumped on. The jug passed among them with great efficiency so the last man drinking was still wiping his mouth as the next man was sanitizing the bottleneck on his dirty shirt sleeve. But now I noticed the black man sitting in the corner was not part of the group, for the jug did not pass to him, and he was not included in their conversation.

In a short time their efficiency with the jug produced three drunks. They were singing and slapping each other on the back and laughing and rolling on the floor. When Earl laughed it was a savage, brutal sound. I did not like the man. The black man did not, either. He came back and sat against the wall where I was. He was friendly and I offered him a smoke. He said he had planned to get off close to Castle Crag, but the next time the train stopped he was getting away from these drunken bastards. I said I was, too.

Then Earl staggered back to us and blabbered for a while. He directed his talk to me, ignoring the black man. Earl was from Wisconsin and could talk a little German. I answered in German and he was ecstatic. "My little German buddy," he called me. I would rather have been buddies with a warthog. His clothes were dirty and greasy, and he smelled like a goat. He crawled back to his pals and they all ate sandwiches out of a cardboard box. They did not offer to share. They drank some more until there was about an inch of wine left in the jug. Then they lay down and fell asleep. The man by me dozed, too.

I lay down near the door and watched the orchards go by. There were rows and rows of peach trees, and huge well-kept groves of walnut and almond. The sun was hot now, and I took off my jacket and used it for a pillow. I looked over at Earl. He was passed out. The damn fool had wet his pants. It was a disgusting sight.

The sun felt good and I fell asleep. When I woke up, Earl was standing over the Mexican, pulling him up by the shirt collar. "You took it, you swipin' son-of-a-bitch!" Earl was shaking the man and hollering so loud that every cord in his neck stood out.

The skinny old one said, "It was him. I saw him put down the bottle . He drank the wine and some of the meat is missing, too. I saw him. I saw him."

It sounded funny, high and squeaky, like a little girl telling Mommy that little brother had been in the cookie jar. What came next was not funny. Earl walked toward the Mexican with both fists clenched. The Mexican's eyes grew large. He shook his head no. Earl took two clumsy swings at him. The Mexican easily ducked them even though he was sitting on the floor. This made Earl madder. He started kicking. The Mexican curled up and warded off the kicks with his legs and forearms. Earl had on a pair of thick, ugly boots. Blood came from a cut over the Mexican's eye. Earl was like a bull enraged by the red. He fired kicks one after another until the car swayed and he fell over backward.

"Anybody that steals from a bum should be killed," he gasped. Earl had appointed himself judge, jury, and executioner.

We were coming into the town of Chico, and the train was going slow.
"You get off!" Earl yelled.

The Mexican hurriedly nodded agreement and grabbed his shoes. Earl kept yelling at him to get off. The Mexican sat down in the doorway to jump.

I yelled at him, "Put on your shoes, *zapatos*!"

"Stay out of it," the black man grabbed my arm. "Dat man have a knife."

He meant that skinny old buddy of Earl's, and it was true. I hadn't noticed it before, but he had a long knife strapped to his leg, and now he had his pant leg up and was fingering the handle. Either the Mexican was too drunk or too scared to put on his shoes. He sat in the doorway a moment getting ready for his jump, his shoes in his hands, his feet dangling over the edge of the floor deck. The side of his face looked like raspberry jam. His one eye was swollen almost shut. Both lips were split and thickening on that side. Some of the blood had already clotted, and drops hung grotesquely from his chin. He threw out his shoes and swung down running. He ran a few long strides, but his forward momentum was too much and he stumbled and fell. We were right by a crossing and I saw two people in a car looking on, horrified. I stepped back out of sight. I looked at Earl.

"He stole from a bum!" he screamed, as if unable to comprehend the enormity of such a crime.

Hobo justice it was, as Frank had called it, when he said there was no law on the freight train. But it was a hard thing to see a dirty, disgusting bum like Earl be judge, jury, and police. Now those two frauds went to cooking up a big story about how the Mexican had pulled a knife on them and had taken two pounds of ham and all their money. This was their story in case the cops started asking questions. They were afraid the police might get involved if they saw what Earl had done. They were afraid because the Mexican knew their names and knew where they were going. The old man had a warrant out for him, and Earl had a record. The black man mumbled to me that we ought to pitch those two off the train the next time we crossed a high bridge.

The great, flat orchard land began to swell into beautiful green hills. The hills became higher and sharper. I could see the mountains coming. We passed Redding and crossed over Shasta Lake. Lord, the water looked good. We were out of water. The black man's canteen was empty and I had finished off my water bottle hours ago. The sun beat down on the roof of the car and we sweated in there like farm hands. Earl and his buddy had no water to start with. They thought their wine would do them, but that only made it worse. They sat there licking their lips and trying to collect some saliva in their mouths. We followed the river—the cold, sparkling, maddening river. We went through one tunnel after another. I was plenty thirsty and all the time the beautiful Sacramento

River was bubbling away down below. I was hot, and all the time I could see the snow-icing on Mount Shasta in the distance, looking like ice cream—a grand pile of it in the sunshine. All afternoon I smelled that river. All afternoon I watched that mountain and prayed for a stop so we could get water.

We kept climbing higher into huge forests of giant evergreens, and the air got cooler and had a wonderful aroma of pine and cedar. We passed smooth green mountains and rough, jagged, granite-gray crags that looked like iron teeth sticking up out of the greenery. I knew where I was most of the time now. Red had given me a map, and the railroads had put little white signs by every town with the name printed in black letters. Near Dunsmuir we took a siding and—glory be!—finally we stopped. We grabbed every bottle we could lay our hands on and ran for the river. I didn't care if the Dunsmuir sewer ran in there. The water looked so cool and sparkly, and I was sure it ran off of that ice cream mound on Shasta. I flopped down and drank, and ducked my head and washed my hair. It was cold, wet, and wonderful. We filled our bottles and some empty beer cans we found along the shore. As we returned to the train Earl and his buddy began to lay plans to get another jug of wine. They made a big show of pooling their money and asked us to chip in so they could get a gallon. The black man said he was staying in Dunsmuir and I said I was broke. But then I thought of something.

"Wait a minute," I said. "I forgot about my emergency dollar."

I took off my hat and fished around the inside lining until I found the dollar bill. I handed it to them, and made a big ceremony warning them that I would be "right here" waiting for my share of that bottle, and they better not drink it on the way. This made them very happy, as they were always glad "to share a little vino with a friend." They took their cardboard box and went sprinting down the weedy ditch toward the town, happy as hyenas on a scent.

The black man looked at me sadly, "You ain't never goan ta see dem two again, not your dollar needer."

"I know," I said, ginning at him. "That was the whole idea."

That made him laugh, and he said he thought it was a right smart way to get rid of the bastards. Just in case there was an honest bone in one of their bodies, we moved up the line to another boxcar. The afternoon dragged on. We watched up and down the line, but no one came to deliver wine. We ate the rest of the donuts out of my suitcase and drank water, water, water. The highball sounded, the hitches clanged, and we began a slow roll off the siding.

Then another man jumped on board. I had seen him by the tracks earlier, but I never suspected he was looking for a ride. He was clean cut, had nice clothes, and had no bindle with him. He wore a dark-gray blazer, and looked more like a parson than a hobo. He acted very casual, as if he knew his way around trains, but I had my doubts. He did not act like a bum at all. He came right up to us and shook hands and introduced himself. He said his name was John Smith, and that he had chatted with the engineer and knew the train was going to Portland. That's where his home was. Then he told us a hard-luck story about how he ran out of money and was looking for a job, but couldn't get one because his name was John Smith, and people were always suspicious he was lying about his name. (I was, too.)

Now our going was really slow as we got to climbing hard. Many times on the steeper grades the train plodded along at a donkey's pace. We kept winding back and forth on hairpin turns. Sometimes the train turned clear around so we could see the engine coming back and passing on the other side of the mountain above us. The air got much cooler and I put on my jacket. Shortly after the sign for the town of Mott, the black man stepped off with the skill of a veteran and was gone. I wished John Smith had left instead. I liked that black man.

We came to flatter country and picked up speed again, moving right along through the north of California. John Smith and I spent our time admiring Mount Shasta. We got to see it from almost all sides because the Southern Pacific tracks almost encircled the mountain. The sun was low now and we were running along in twilight, but the top of Shasta still glowed in the mellow light of evening sunshine. John Smith waxed drippy poetic about the view.

As it got darker it got colder, and as we climbed higher it got colder. I mean, it was getting bitter cold in that boxcar. We closed the door on one side, but the other side was jammed. We pushed and banged on it. John Smith and I ran against it a couple of times. Nothing worked. It held solid as a weld. I got out my wool sweater, put on my extra shirt and socks, but I was still freezing. So I lent my clothes to John Smith and crawled into my sleeping bag. He put on my sweater, my shirt, my jacket, and my hat. He huddled down in the corner. We went through a snowstorm with heavy winds that rocked the car. Snow swirled into the open door. Then it cleared and the moon came out and it got colder still. We went clattering along, roaring through tunnels, thundering over trestles, jerking and bumping, lurching and swerving.

I slept. The bag was warm, and the sharp air in the car made it feel really cozy in there. It was roughly ten o'clock. Every time I woke up I could see John Smith hunched down in his corner, or standing there shivering and stomping his feet. Once I woke to see tall, moonlit pine trees passing tight by the door so the branches waved from the passing wind of the train. I could smell the piney resin. Another time I woke and could see nothing but blackness at the door but far away bright, snowy, moonlit peaks. All the time John Smith was shivering.

I was so comfortable I hated to do it, but about four in the morning I changed places with John Smith. He was turning blue with cold. Now I stood there and stomped and shivered. But I was lucky. We started to descend and the air got warmer. And then the sun came up and I was fine. John Smith slept until mid-morning. I finally had to wake him, because we came into a railroad yard, and they humped our car. I didn't know where it was going, so I wanted off. A brakeman told us we were in Eugene, Oregon. He said we were lucky we didn't freeze to death riding like that in the mountains at night. Then we were honored with the visitation of a railroad bull who told us to get the hell out of the yard. We were leaving anyhow, but John Smith apologized and bowed and scraped before the cop and promised he would never do such a thing again and almost wept in his immense contrition. We went to a restaurant to get some hot coffee in us. When we sat down John Smith began patting himself all over and found that his money was missing. He implied that the black man had taken it, but I didn't believe that for a second. I said I would pay for the coffee.

John Smith was originally from New York. He was an oily, overly polite kind of guy, and he laid it on thick for the waitress. First he told her how beautiful she looked (she was plain and wrinkly, had a crooked tooth, and hadn't combed her hair in a week). She looked bored, waiting with her pencil poised, and finally said, "What do you want?"

"I sure would admire a cup of your delicious, hot coffee," he said, all buttery.

She turned to me. I said, "I want a cup of coffee too. But not to admire. I want to drink it."

I was trying to give John Smith a hint, but he kept right on spreading himself all around whenever a waitress was nearby. I fixed him like this: when a pretty, young waitress came to give us a refill, and he started his schmoozing again, I said to her, "Say, do you know where a couple of bums like us could get a free bite to eat? We haven't eaten since day before yesterday and we're kinda low."

That let some of the air out of him, but when we left, he still thanked the waitress for her "wonderful hospitality" when he should have been thanking me.

We caught another train north and got into Portland late. John Smith gave me his address—I should say *an* address—I thought it was as phony as his name. I promised him I'd look him up next time I came through Portland. I found lying was becoming easier with practice—and more satisfying, too.

Everything went smoothly the next day. I caught a fast train and made Seattle by early afternoon. I went back to hitchhiking and immediately got a ride to Vancouver. I had planned to stop in Bellingham and ride the bus over the border so I would not get some driver into trouble. But the guy who picked me up said, no problem, and before I knew it, I was standing by the road east of Vancouver, Canada. I sold that driver my transistor radio. I wasn't using it anyhow, and surely wouldn't in the desolate areas I was planning to travel. The man felt sorry for me, I think. He gave me ten dollars for the radio, far more than it was worth. He may have thrown it out the window when he was out of sight.

I felt uneasy now holding out my thumb. I wished I had checked on the hitchhiking laws in Canada. The sun was going down, and I was just beginning to look around for a place where I might lay my sleeping bag for the night when a car, going about eighty-five, stopped on a dime with a howl of tires that echoed off into the distance. Then began one of the prettiest rides I had on my trip, most of it through the beautiful Fraser Valley. The driver's name was Bill Montgomery. He was headed for Kamloops, a trip of over two hundred and fifty miles. He had just had a big fight with his wife and was on his way to see his father. He said he wanted to get a divorce, but he would not do it without his father's approval. He said his old man would "kick the shit" out of him, so he was on his way to have a talk. We drove east in the twilight, and turned north at Hope when the moon was just coming up. The highway running northeast from Hope to Kamloops did not exist back then. Bill consumed sandwiches, beer, and cigarettes as he drove, and he shared them all with me. I had just quit smoking, but not knowing the customs in Canada, I did not turn down a cigarette. (It might have been an insult, you see.)

We followed the Fraser River up to Cache Creek, going through at least a dozen tunnels. That road must have cost a mint to build. Often we drove along the very edge of a mountain with the Fraser boiling in the moonlight a thousand feet below. Bill had planned to drop me at Cache Creek on the road going north to Prince George and to continue east to Kamloops, but it was so late he got himself a room at Cache Creek. He let me sleep in the back of his car. Next morning at first light, I rolled out. I left Bill a note. If I had been rich, I would have left him a hundred dollars for that ride in the moonlight.

I waited a long time for a ride that morning. Cars went by again and again, and I cursed the Canadians for how selfish, stupid, narrow-minded, and mean they were. But I found out it was I who was stupid. A young man picked me up. He said those cars had passed me by because they were local people not going far. When they saw a man with a suitcase, they assumed he was going up north to find work. They figured he wouldn't like to be left by the road somewhere away from the town. This young man was on his way to Prince George—another long ride (almost three hundred miles). And he was just as nice as Bill Montgomery had been. He would not let me pay for my lunch when we stopped at 100 Mile House. When he dropped me off at the south side of Prince George he told me to be careful. Prince George had the highest VD rate of any city in Canada. After he dropped me, almost immediately a man brought me to a road on the other side of town where he said it was much better for a hitch going north. He left me off and in a little while I was cursing him, too. There was no traffic! Fat chance of getting a ride here.

Wrong again! In no more than ten minutes I had a ride from the first car that came along—a ride all the way to Dawson Creek, which was another two hundred and fifty miles. I sat in the backseat; Lenny and Walter in the front. They had a case of beer back there, and it was my job to hand the bottles up front. For compensation I could help myself. Lenny was a heavily bearded French-Canadian (part French, part Native American). He was very proud of his French blood and his ability to speak French. But as he drank he became more and more proud of his Indian heritage so that by the time we arrived at Dawson Creek, I was riding with a full-blood Mohawk, who proved it by letting out occasional war whoops. Walter, also heavily bearded, said his ancestors were from Bohemia, and they were proud only of their ability to drink.

They stopped at Chetwynd. We were out of beer. We went into a big saloon. There must have been over a hundred burly lumbermen in that hall, and more coming in all the time. It was their Friday-night stampede. They all wore thick woolen clothes, thick leather boots, and thick, heavy beards. The air in the room was a dense fog of tobacco smoke and cursing. I never saw such a jamboree of drinking, cussing, smoking, and spitting of tobacco juice. There were only a few women in the place, all of them waitresses, and their bottoms were constantly being patted, pawed, and pinched. Every man had in front of him a whiskey tumbler, a beer stein, or a shot glass. Some had all three. Every man was loud in his talk and his laughter.

We got a case of beer and a basketful of sandwiches and pressed on for Dawson Creek. I asked Lenny why every man up here wore a beard. He said it keeps you warm in winter and keeps mosquitoes off in summer. It was about one in the morning when we got to Dawson Creek. There those two lumberjacks headed east to the Peace River country. I ate a "seaburger" in a café attached to the gas station there. Behind the station were two smashed cars. No one would be using them that night for sure, and probably never. I passed up the first one because the windshield was busted out. The second one had good windows, but the doors were jammed. One back window was partially open and I found I could raise and lower it by grabbing the pane with both hands. So I crawled in and sacked out. I awoke with the sun in my face and knew I had overslept. Two men sitting at the window of the café watched me crawling out of the car window. One man pointed. It looked like they were talking about me and I imagined the conversation:

"Look at that bum crawling out of that old car. I bet he froze his ass in there last night."

"Serves him right. He could be working like everyone else."

"What a miserable life."

"Aw, bums don't know any better. Hell, he's probably happier than we are."

Chapter Twenty-One

I SAT BY THE WEIGHING SCALES at the Dawson Creek truck stop, asking all the truckers going north if I could go along. No! I think they called the cops on me—in a little while two Mounties came and checked me out. They did the same as cops in the states, only they were more polite. One of them called me "sir" and asked me how I was doing before he asked for my ID. I asked about hitchhiking. They said it was okay. They apologized for bothering me. I told them that, on the contrary, I was honored to be checked out by members of the world-famous Royal Canadian Mounted Police Force.

When the wind warmed enough so I dared venture from the shelter of the scale house, I went to the road. I got a rush of pleasure to realize Dawson Creek was the beginning of the Great Alaska Highway (the famous Alcan). A post marked the zero mile and a sign said this was the beginning of the highway. It was 1,523 miles from Dawson Creek, British Columbia, to Fairbanks, Alaska. I was cold there by that famous highway that morning. I shivered and stomped my feet. A black dog came along and sat by me like I was his master. He just sat there, looking around. When I talked to him, he looked up and wagged his tail.

Again there was almost no traffic, but again in a short time I had a ride. Two women picked me up. Both had dyed curly hair: one platinum blonde, the other inky black. They said they were sisters, though they didn't look alike. Blondie drove, Blackie chain-smoked in the passenger seat. They were both disheveled and unkempt, like sheep wintered in a lazy farmer's barn. They looked like they needed sleep, a good bath, a clothes iron, and a home. I think they lived out of their trunk and their suitcases, in the backseat by me. They were both nice and polite to me, but they snapped at each other so I soon believed they were sisters. I said I was excited to be, for the first time, on the great Alcan Highway. They didn't seem to know what I was prattling about. Blackie turned around and looked at me as if to check and see that I was all there. I told them I was on my way to Whitehorse to walk on the Klondike Trail where Robert Service had once been. That impressed them even less.

We got about halfway to Fort St. John when Blondie decided she needed a break. She pulled over and got out a pack of Buckingham cigarettes and shook one out for Blackie and one for me. They both lit up and passed me the lighter—a fancy one with gold and silver inlays.

Blondie turned to me. "Hey, dig that micky of whiskey out of my suitcase."

Blackie refused a drink, but Blondie and I put away most of that pint in a few minutes. Man, that whiskey felt good! It took away every bit of the chill I'd caught sitting in the wind by the highway. Blondie felt refreshed, and off we went to Fort St. John. I got a good look at that town. I was there for about six hours. It was a town with no women. One would as soon expect to find a zebra in that town as a woman, and if a woman did appear, all the men stopped and stared at her as if she were a zebra. Blondie and Blackie would do a good business there, I thought. If the prostitutes from New Orleans would've come up to this country, they'd be rich in a week. About nine o'clock in the morning I was at the Frontier Inn. It was so cold and drizzly I did not want to stand by the road. I hung around the inn waiting for the weather to change.

I got a ride lined up. A man at the inn named George Knight said he would take me to Fort Nelson the next day if I was in front of the inn at exactly nine in the morning. He was all British, with a heavy accent, and he used the word "bloody" to modify most nouns: "That bloody mechanic has been working on my bloody car for two bloody days." Everywhere in town I saw Native Americans. I wanted to know what tribe they were from. Nobody knew for sure. Some said Cree, some Blackfoot, some Beaver. All said, "Who cares?"

I had such phenomenal luck getting rides that after a while it was easy for me to believe some higher power was directing traffic. By mid-afternoon the drizzle stopped, but dark clouds still hung low and a chill wind blew. It was a full half-mile to the road, and I already had a ride to Fort Nelson, but I got restless. I went out to the road anyway. That miserable walk, with the sky threatening and the wind blowing, began the crowning glory, the climax, the high point of my trip. Around four o'clock the sun came out. The whole world changed from dreary to cheery. A man in a loaded-down Jeep panel wagon pulled over. I could barely squeeze my gear in there, it was so full of his stuff.

After we got underway, I asked, "How far are you going?"

He said, "All the way."

I thought he meant all the way to Fort Nelson. The next big town after Fort Nelson was Whitehorse, but that was over eight hundred miles, and I never thought of hoping for that. But no. When this man said "all the way," he meant "all the way." He was going to Anchorage! That was over seven hundred miles beyond Whitehorse—an odyssey of one-thousand-six-hundred miles! He looked like a slob: dirty T-shirt and torn, washed-out blue jeans, moccasins, no socks, a five-day stubble on his face. I had just hit the perfect ride. This man was Captain Richard "Dick" R. Castner of the Alaskan National Guard. He had driven about ten thousand miles in the last month, going all the way from his home in Alaska across Canada to his wife's home on the far side of Ontario. He was on his way back. He said he was tired of talking to himself. All he required of me was company. That was an easy assignment. He was pleasant and intelligent, a man of many interests, well-read, full of fun. He camped outside at night and slept in a sleeping bag like mine, and carried in his Jeep an endless supply of Army C-rations and told me to help myself. What more could I ask? There was never a happier hobo.

I told Dick I was getting off at Whitehorse. I wanted to travel the trails taken by Jack London and Robert Service during the days of the Klondike gold rush. I'd go up to Dawson City and then down to Skagway. Dick shared my sentiments about the Klondike trail. He too was a fan of those two authors. He said Dawson City during the gold rush had more people than were present now in the entire Yukon Territory, which was as big as Texas. He said he'd go with me, but he had an appointment with the Alaska National Guard.

The road was dusty, a very fine dust that seeped through every little pinhole and crack of the Jeep. When we followed behind a gas truck for a while, the air in the Jeep got thick. We tried to pass, but the truck did not want to be eating our dust, so he would speed up every time and hog the middle of the road. I told Dick this was like driving on a bad farm road in Minnesota, but Dick said, no, he was sure this was a much better grade of dust.

He said, "I have become quite a connoisseur of dust. You'll find the Alcan dust of superior taste and quality. After a while you can barely live without it. I often bottle some of it so I can have it with me at the cabin." There were times I did not believe everything Dick said.

It was a bad road. Vehicles had wire screens on their headlights as shields from rocks. There was a constant clatter of gravel in the wheel wells. When we met a vehicle, we could expect a hail of stones on our windshield as it passed. Dick's windshield was richly starred with rock dings and spider-webbed with cracks.

He pushed the Jeep hard for about three hours, then stopped where a brook ran near the road. He set up a coffee pot on his camp stove and sent me down to the brook to get a bucket of water. We broke open a box of C-rations and Dick had the crackers with his coffee. I wolfed down a can of beef and beans. C-rations included everything a bum could want, including waterproof matches and cigarettes—wait—they had no Tokay or burgundy or muscatel. When he was opening the can with a P-38, I asked him where he got it. He opened his glove compartment and handed me a handful of the openers. There was one in every box of C-rations, but the U.S. Army did not call them P-38s. In the brutal poetry of the Army the thing was: "Opener—can, hand, folding. Type 1." Dick said it was called a "P-38" because it took thirty-eight punctures to open a can, but I could easily open one with half that.

It was pleasant by the road with the clear, cold brook gurgling away below, the air fresh and pine-scented, low-growing evergreens all around, and the whole picture framed by snowcapped mountains along the horizon. Dick had an eye for scenery. He picked nice spots for breaks, eating, and sleeping.

When it reached twilight (in the land of the midnight sun in June, there is no such thing as dark), Dick knocked off for the night. We found an abandoned lumber camp and had supper. We spread our sleeping bags on the floor of the cook shack. Dick had an air mattress—real luxury. I slept on the wooden floor. Dick laid his rifle next to him. We talked of Jack London poems and quoted from Robert Service. Dick knew far more than I did. We talked slower and quieter. Pretty soon he was barely mumbling. Then he was snoring.

The sun was up when I woke. Dick was standing in the doorway brushing his teeth. I could see his puffs of breath against the sun. Squirrels chattered and birds called, sounding like a jungle. I went down to the river and washed out my mouth. My God, it was beautiful. The scent of pine was doubly strong, with piles of sawdust all over. We drove about two hours and stopped to have coffee at seven o'clock. You don't think anything of getting up at five when the sun gets up at three.

Dick told me about himself as we drank coffee and ate crackers. He was a pilot in the Alaska Air National Guard. The year before he and his wife built themselves a cabin by Lake Oscar (near Palmer, about fifty miles north of Anchorage) and spent the winter. His wife now stayed with her folks until he could find an apartment. He didn't say so, but I was pretty sure they got into a fight at the cabin. Isolated there all winter, she got a bad case of cabin fever. I couldn't imagine what other problem she could have had with Dick. He could talk for hours about books and music, hunting and fishing. There was hardly a subject I could broach that did not fire his interest.

I said, "It must get depressing here in winter with long nights and little sun."

He said, "No. We have the aurora. Not as bright as the sun, but more pleasant to look at." But I still bet his wife got depressed in that cabin in winter.

Some "towns" listed on Dick's Alcan map were not really towns, just a building with a gas pump in front. On the Alcan a thriving metropolis would have a house with a lunch bar, two gas pumps, and a shack with bunks you could rent for the night. We took a coffee break at Muncho Lake and another farther on when we got into mountainous terrain. We lay on the grass for a while, watching rock sheep and mountain goats move slowly on upper cliffs.

For a while the Alcan Highway snaked right along the Yukon border, so sometimes we were up in the Yukon, and then back down again in British Columbia. When we stopped at Whitehorse, Dick made me an offer too good to pass up. He said if I went all the way to Anchorage with him, he would get me a ride to Juneau on an Air Guard airplane and I could stay at his cabin until the day of the flight. A real log cabin—in the Alaska wilderness! We pressed on.

We slept in a thick grove of black spruce. The ground was spongy with needles. We had Dick's tarp for a roof. A cold fog moved in. In the morning the pines, spruces, and larches were flocked with heavy frost like Christmas trees. Then the sun came up. The trees glowed fiery gold and made a picture as fine as any Christmas card. The Yukon has a rugged beauty I wouldn't try to describe without the help of Jack London or Robert Service. Drab stretches of muskeg and scrub pine, yes, but something about the enormous solitude and vastness gave it a mysterious, magic appeal you cannot forget. Always in the distance the mountains, the blue Yukon Mountains. The exhilarating freedom I often had on the road was somehow magnified by the desolation in that forlorn land.

We got to Lake Kluane, a long lake like Mucho. After driving along the shore for half an hour we stopped for breakfast at a café in Destruction Bay. Dick said we needed a good breakfast because we were going all the way to Anchorage that day, but I knew he was sick of eating C-rations. Two very pretty young girls worked at the café. It must have been a lonely place for them. The nearest civilization was Whitehorse, over a hundred and fifty miles away. After breakfast Dick talked to the owner. One of the girls, a sturdy, black-eyed Inuk, took me down the trail to the lake to show me the geese. We stood close together. I took her hand. She was all warm and snuggly. I could feel the heat of her body through my clothes. We watched the geese and the sun glinting off the water. Dick honked that it was time to go. As she turned, on a sudden impulse I pulled her hard against me and kissed her. She responded warmly for a few seconds, then pushed away and we hurried up the trail. She waved good-bye with a big smile as we drove off. I was glad I kissed her. I never knew her name.

It seemed to me Dick was a too optimistic about making it all the way to Anchorage that day. We hadn't even crossed the Alaska border. I figured we might make it by midnight, if we pushed hard. He was in no hurry, loafing along like he had all the time in the world. We stopped at Burwash Landing, still on Lake Kluane. We strolled idly down to the lake and watched some people launching a boat. It was nearly eleven by the time we crossed into Alaska.

Dick said, "Let's have breakfast."

I said, "You mean lunch."

He said, "What? Lunch? At eight o'clock in the morning?"

There was a three-hour time change! It was early morning once again, and we had only four hundred miles to go. We got to Anchorage early in the evening, and slept in the National Guard barracks. Next morning the scheduler told us it would be at least a week before I could get a flight to Juneau—great!

We drove north from Anchorage to Palmer and turned west to Wasilla, where Dick stopped at the post office to pick up his mail. We went to the meat locker and got a caribou roast for supper. At Eagle Creek we turned into the woods toward Lake Oscar. The "road" was an abandoned logging trail. At Lake Oscar we parked. Dick put on his hip boots and struck off through the swamp along the lakeshore. After a while he came paddling across the lake in his canoe, which we loaded and paddled to the farthest corner of the lake, into a little cove. There on the shore stood a pretty little cabin, the logs still shiny and fresh. It was the coziest little house I ever saw. It had only one room but had everything in it we could need except a toilet.

"I've got to show you my shit house," Dick said and led the way down a little trail. The trail made a bend. There was a little log hut—a two-holer, but with a distinctive feature: the seat was covered with the thick winter fur of caribou.

Dick opened his mail. He had a box from Herter's in Waseca, Minnesota, that held his new rod and reel, which he immediately assembled. The box also had a genuine kangaroo hat band, which he immediately put on his hat. He was astounded when I said I never heard of Herter's. He said everyone around there sent for stuff from Herter's. He showed me his Herter's catalogue, as thick as a Sears-Roebuck catalogue. He said every year the arrival of that catalogue was like Christmas time for the boys in Wasilla and Eagle Creek, and for weeks was the chief talk as they sat drinking coffee at the café.

I got two buckets of water out of the lake. One we used for drinking, the other for doing dishes. Dick showed me how to start up a batch of sourdough to make pancakes for breakfast and how to make a quick maple syrup. We talked until late and hit the bunks. This was for me incredible luxury after all the nights sleeping in cars, on sand, and on rocking boxcar floors. At four thirty squirrels woke me. They chased each other around on the roof of the cabin, and ravens were making a racket. I walked down to the outhouse. A full-grown male moose stood staring at me. We had a staring contest for a minute, then he snorted and bolted. There was a moose trail there, ten steps from the cabin. They came down to the lake every morning and evening for a drink. Two beaver lodges were in sight of the cabin. For some reason the beaver did not like the moose. In the stillness of morning and evening I could hear them popping their tails as the animals came down to drink.

After breakfast Dick went to town to let friends know he was back. I preferred to stay at the cabin. I split wood. For lunch I had a caribou sandwich and homemade beer. For supper we had barbequed rock sheep ribs. Dick brought more strange meats from his locker in Wasilla. He knew I'd never had this stuff before. In the course of my stay we also had moose, bear, and beaver tail. He wanted me to get a taste of the varieties he had. I think he was also showing me how he lived off the land.

One evening a chilly wind blew in. It got dark and began to rain. We retreated into the cabin to read in the lamplight. In all the world there can be no greater luxury than lying on a bunk in a log cabin in the great Alaska wilderness reading Robert Service poems, the cold night-wind making rushing sounds around the corners of the cabin and whistlings at the window, a warm fire cracking and popping inside the cook stove, a pot of caribou stew simmering on the top, breathing the aroma of stew and pine smoke, occasionally holding your breath to listen to a wolf howling in the distance. A log cabin is peace enshrined. It was comfort beyond reason. It was true freedom.

Then came the Monday I had to leave to catch my flight to Juneau. To make it to Anchorage in time, we got up that last morning at two o'clock and paddled across the lake in the twilight. I felt more like crying then I ever felt at leaving any other place—Crosier, St. John's, even home. It was the fourteenth of June, my twenty-third birthday.

I just barely made that flight out of Anchorage. We got there late. Dick shoved me into the back of a cargo plane (one engine was already running), showed me how to work the safety belt, shook my hand, and was gone. He had fulfilled his promise to get me a flight to Juneau. We flew up to Fairbanks, were on the ground a short time, and then flew back down to Cordova on Prince William Sound. When we left Cordova, the captain, a Colonel Stringer, kept her low all along the coast to Juneau so I could see the sights. The high cliffs of the mountains come right down to the ocean there. No beach. All along the waves were dashing themselves against the rocks, shooting geysers high into the air and making rainbows in the sunlight. We flew by a long, high glacier. In one place, just as we went by, a huge chunk as big as a town lost its grip and descended into the sea with an enormous splash. It disappeared in the churning foam for a second, then slowly rose and floated. The co-pilot, a Captain Holenbeck, was back there talking to me. He said the racket of our engines vibrated it loose.

Juneau was as green as Minnesota in June—actually, more so, because of all the moss. It's always misty and rainy, so nothing ever dries out completely. Moss grows all over—beautiful green moss on the roofs, soft and spongy in the woods. I thought I'd look over the town that night and hitchhike south in the morning. I asked which way to the freeway going south. They stared at me. There was no freeway. In fact, there was no road! This was the capital of the great state of Alaska, and there was no road? Okay, I'd catch a freight train. No train. There was no track out of Juneau. Juneau was accessible only by air or sea. For me that meant airplane or ferry, and both were too expensive.

I had to get a job. It cost over twenty dollars to ride the ferry to Prince Rupert. I had five. I saw a Catholic church and made the fortunate decision to talk to the priest. That's how I met Father Manske. He didn't know of any job openings, but he had a place for me to stay "out by the shrine," and he thought he might be able to get me on the ferry in a few days. He took me in his little car for about a twenty-minute drive west of town. He parked by a little log cabin on a hill not far from an inland bay. Father Manske said, "Here's your home, a little hermitage in the wildwood." He pointed out a small island in the bay on which stood a chapel—the Shrine of St. Therese of Lisieux. "It's a good place to communicate with the Almighty," he said.

As we walked down toward the shore, we saw a picture that might have come from Norman Rockwell. The sun was setting very red over the hills on the far side of the bay, and the quiet water was all afire. The island was a black silhouette of tall, evergreens against the red, and a fisherman had anchored his big boat out in the water and was paddling to shore in a little skiff. Boat and man were also black silhouettes in the bay as the paddles dipped and rose, paused, dipped and rose. On the shore a little boy picked his barefoot way over the rocky beach going to meet the boat. A big Siberian husky danced excitedly on the water's edge.

That fisherman was Frank Koch, and he lived near the hermitage with his family. He took me fishing next day and gave me a big king salmon. I lived on it for three days. I had salmon for breakfast, lunch, and dinner. I made it fried, baked, stewed, and grilled. If you don't like salmon, it's because you haven't had it fresh.

I never expected to stay at a place more beautiful than Dick's cabin, but here it was: a snug little hut of old logs, the wooden shingles covered with moss, a wood stove for heat, candles for light, and a nearby creek for drinking water. The people had built a narrow causeway to walk to the island. The chapel, with its roof of moss and walls of stone from the beach, looked like it was just part of nature. The roof had no spire, but there was no need. A spire would have been an anemic redundancy, for above the chapel towered the majestic spires of primeval spruce and hemlock that reached for heaven like the saint herself, and sighed and whispered prayers whenever the wind moved free on the bay. When you walked there among the ancient trees by the chapel you were with God. And the things of God were all around: deer, moose, porcupine—and eagles! Eagles were as common there as blackbirds in Stearns County.

Father Manske asked me to split a pile of wood for him, and I worked on it every day. It was meager to pay for three days in such a place. I would have split the whole forest for the privilege. Then Manske put icing on his generosity by giving me the fare for the ferry to Prince Rupert. That was almost twenty-five dollars! He pretended to be paying me for splitting the wood, but that was far too much, especially since my room and board were free.

THE FERRY HAD JUST come in from the north somewhere. I paid the clerk twenty-three dollars and fifty cents to ride lowest class, and we sailed for Prince Rupert. Right away I was ambushed by an old lady, Mrs. Churchill, the most impossible busybody I ever saw, but a nice busybody. She never rested, or at least she never rested her tongue. In half an hour she knew every person on board and was determined to introduce everyone to everyone else. She cross-examined passengers to milk them of any interesting details she could pass on. It was a twenty-hour trip to Prince Rupert and her tongue clattered the whole time. A retired school teacher, she mothered everyone on the boat like they were her grade-schoolers. A native girl on board had slept through the stop at Juneau, where she was supposed to get off. Mrs. Churchill went around and collected the money for her fare back to Juneau.

When Mrs. Churchill asked me what I did for a living, I told her I was a bum.

She said, "Well, you do need a shave and a haircut, no denying that, but that hardly makes you a bum. Now," she said as if to settle the matter forever, "What do you do for work?"

I said, "I don't. I'm a bum.

She could not accept that answer. "Where did you work last?"

I told her about the strawberry fields in California and how I had left after little more than a day. She asked what I did to pass the time. I told her I traveled. She asked me how I got around. I told her about riding the freights from California to Washington, and about hitchhiking up the Alcan Highway. At last she was persuaded. After that she introduced me to people by saying, "This is Don Bloch. He's a bum."

She mothered me, first when she wanted to give me two dollars for food, which I refused. I should have taken it, because a hamburger on that ferry cost a whopping seventy-five cents (triple what I was used to paying). Then, when I told her I was hitchhiking out of Prince Rupert with the aim of getting to Minnesota by the fourth of July, she lined up a ride for me! She introduced me to a Mr. Wall, who was driving all the way across the continent to the East Coast. Mr. Wall said he would be glad to have the company.

Mr. Wall was retired and traveled for entertainment. He was a boring traveler. He just drove and drove. He mailed lots of post cards along the way. I think he was trying to establish himself as a "well-traveled" man back home. He was not well-traveled. He was not interested in meeting people, not interested in the history, or in looking at the sights. I offered to buy him a beer in Cache Creek, but he wasn't thirsty. I wanted to stop in Kamloops; I thought I'd look in the phone book and call Bill Montgomery's dad, to see if Bill got his divorce, but Wall drove right on through. We filled up with gas in Monte Creek. I read a paper on the bulletin board about a long-ago train robbery nearby. A man named Bill Miner, the "gentleman bandit," held up the train. It was just getting interesting when Wall grabbed my arm and said, "Let's go." I pointed at the article, but he said we didn't have time for reading "tourist propaganda."

What was I complaining about? The man was driving me home, and he was nice to me. He finally got himself a motel room in Calgary, where he let me shower and watch TV until he got sleepy. It was Sunday night and we watched *The Ed Sullivan Show*. By coincidence Ed had on the same knife throwing act I'd seen live a few months before at a casino in Las Vegas. It was the one where a man balances himself on a rope with one foot and sticks knives around a girl rotating on a board. Then we watched *Bonanza,* and I went out and slept in the backseat of Wall's car.

The second night he stopped in Wolf Point, Montana. He got himself a room at the Tip Top Motel. I bought a big bag of Wolf Point's "world famous" beef jerky, and lived on that the rest of my trip. I slept in the back of his car again. The next morning I tried to talk him into going down through the Black Hills. He had never been there, but he wanted to go through North Dakota, which he accomplished without a stop (what excitement!). He dropped me in Bemidji and hurried on his way like he had urgent business. I hitched a ride to Motley and slept in a very comfortable old Buick behind the El Roy Café.

I got back to Albany on the twenty-ninth of June. Mom answered my knock at the door. She stared at my bushy hair and beard and looked puzzled.

I said, "Hi, Mom."

"Oh, for goodness sake," she said. "You could scare a person like that."

She was happy. She gave me a hug, pulled me inside and said to Dad, "Look what the cat dragged in."

Dad was sitting in his easy chair reading the paper. He looked up, nodded, and went back to his reading.

I was home.

Part IV

Up, up, the long, delirious, burning blue . . .
Where never lark, nor even eagle flew.
                          –From "High Flight" by Gillespie Magee

Chapter Twenty-Two

I N THE SECOND WEEK of July 1965, Mr. and Mrs. Henry Bloch of Albany, Minnesota, received a letter from the United States Air Force. The return address read:

Colonel A.M. Dodd
Headquarters Officer Training School
United States Air Force
Lackland Military Training Center
Air Training Command
Lackland Air Force Base, Texas

The two-page letter basically told my parents the U.S. Air Force now had their little boy, and they promised to take good care of him. It briefly described the tranquil life at Officer Training School (leaving out the parts about the blazing hell of the Texas summer, the brutal physical requirements, and the harassing by upperclassmen). I'm sure my dad scratched his head several times as he read some of the things they did mention, like "the present and future technological Aerospace developments," and the "process of the military judicial system." Dad would have stared at that address. He'd wonder why the fools thought they needed that much writing to get their point across. His address was "Albany, Minn.," and that worked just fine. Toward the end of the letter the good colonel comforted Mom with this warm, glowing sentence: "You can rest assured that your son's physical, spiritual, and mental well-being are in capable hands." The letter was dated July 8, 1965, a few days after I showed up at Medina Air Base for training—training I almost missed.

I went to the Air Force recruiter in St. Cloud with letters from the Air Force asking me to express my intentions to begin training in July. When they had arrived at home, I wasn't there to receive them, so they lay unopened on the corner shelf in the kitchen. One of the letters said I had to answer within two weeks or my slot would be filled. It was well over two weeks. The sergeant looked at the letters and said, "Yeah, well, it's too late now."

He made a call to somewhere in Texas. They said I must wait for the next class, which would be in October. In my head I immediately began to hitchhike back to Alaska. I felt relieved. But as I walked out the door, the sergeant called after me. He was on the phone again. He asked me, "Can you go right now?" I said sure, and he confirmed with the man on the phone.

With that, my life of freedom ended. Soon I was on a bus to Minneapolis. The bus ticket and my hotel in Minneapolis was paid for—with meals! They said a sergeant would meet me at the bus depot. Suddenly all my needs were being cared for. I was riding a nice comfortable bus, and I didn't have to hold out my thumb to catch it. I wouldn't have to scavenge for supper, I already had a place to sleep, and I didn't have to worry about breakfast—a wonderfully relaxing feeling. I was honored the Air Force thought so much of me.

The sergeant who drove me from the bus depot to my hotel picked me up the next morning and took me to the office of an Air Force captain at Fort Snelling. There I took the induction oath. I felt a bit intimidated when I swore to "support and defend the Constitution of the United States against all enemies, foreign and domestic." I also swore I was taking this oath "without any reservations." That seemed a bit of a stretch. I'm sure few young men take that oath without any reservations, but I said it anyway. When I finished it off with, "so help me God," the smiling captain heartily shook my hand and said, "Congratulations, you are now in the United States Air Force."

The captain laughed about my beard and long hair. I said I had no shaving gear with me. He said, "That's great. Leave it just like it is. It'll be a nice surprise for the colonel down there. Besides, there's no sense getting it cut now. The Air Force barbers are tonsorial artists and will be delighted to have a chance to restyle your hair and beard."

He seemed to derive immense pleasure from picturing me arriving at the Air Force base looking like I did. He took a picture of me. He said he had never administered the oath to an officer-recruit who looked like a hippie, and he thought he might get the picture into the next edition of the *Air Force Times*.

They put me on a Northwest flight to San Antonio—the first time I had been aboard a commercial airplane. It was wonderful. The food was great, the stewardesses beautiful, the seats comfortable. I sprawled in my seat and thought about my situation. I wasn't free like on the road, but I had no care in the world. I felt destitute without my suitcase, sleeping bag, and spare clothes, but the captain assured me I would be issued what I needed, could buy anything at a store on base, and would be allowed to draw against my wages.

The plane landed in San Antonio well after dark. I was met at the gate by an Air Force sergeant, who took me to a big blue bus loaded with new recruits. We drove to Lackland Air Force Base. The driver stopped me when I tried to get off. I was the only one who had to go on to Medina Air Base.

They checked me in at Medina, and took me up to the second floor of a building where an "OT Captain Ketterer" reigned. He checked his clipboard, said "Room 217," and led me down a long hall to my room. Ketterer was in charge of that hall. My room had a big window that opened onto a quadrangle in the middle of a complex of buildings. In front of the window was a table with one lamp and a chair on either side. There were two beds and two closets. Ketterer checked his clipboard again: "Right bunk," he said. He told me I was assigned the right half of the room, including half the table, and I was not allowed on the left half without my roommate's permission. He'd be along later. He had me sign for one pillow, one olive green U.S. Air Force regulation blanket, two sheets, and a dust cover. I had my own chair, my own bed, and my own closet, which included two big drawers. I had nothing to put in the drawers, true, but I was no longer a hobo. I was in my new home.

My first lesson at Medina was to learn the meaning of the old military cliché "hurry up and wait." They'd sent me down to Texas in a whirlwind of hurry, with not even time to go home and get a toothbrush. Yet when I got there, I had nothing to do for several days. I arrived on the second of July. My school didn't start until the fifth because the fourth and a weekend interfered.

I spent the weekend lying around, reading novels, and going to chow. At chow I stuck out like a sore thumb. Everyone else was close-shorn and shiny-shaved. But the food was sumptuous, lavish, and delicious. They piled it on my plate and kept shoveling until I said, "Enough." I must have gained five pounds those first days. I enjoyed myself tremendously under Uncle Sam's care.

I had no idea upperclassmen were insulted by my presence. At Medina an upperclassman, like OT Captain Ketterer, had rank. A lowerclassman didn't. Come Monday I would simply be called "OT (Officer Trainee) Bloch." The upperclassmen saw me at chow with no name tag. As I was a topic of conversation, they called me "OT Wooly." By Sunday evening everyone on base, including me, knew who OT Wooly was. That set up the drama of Monday morning.

The students at the Officer Training School were organized into a military wing composed of groups and squadrons. This was to simulate the organization of the Air Force. The wing, groups, and squadrons were commanded and staffed by upperclass students (ones who passed the first six weeks of training). The upperclass spent their free time harassing the lowerclass (the greenhorns still in their first six weeks), although at Medina it was not called harassing. It was "training, correcting, guiding, teaching," or whatever euphemism you could put on it without embarrassing yourself.

The control system at the school was based on demerits—at Medina they were called "gigs." Every violation earned a gig. On Friday each week gigs were counted up. You lost weekend privileges according to how many gigs you had. Twenty gigs restricted you to the base. Thirty restricted you to your barracks. Forty and you stayed in your room except for chow. Fifty and you had to hide under your bed—or something like that. I don't remember the whole system, but that was the general idea. More than fifty gigs, and you were put before a firing squad (if memory serves—which is not always the case).

Most gigs were handed out in areas of dress, marching, and grooming. Everyone had to be neat, clean, and the same. You could earn a gig or two or three for wearing your cap (oh, excuse me, your "cover." That's a gig right there for saying cap) at the wrong angle. Ill-shined shoes, unpolished belt buckle, bad shaves, all brought showers of gigs. Upperclassmen passed out gigs with vicious delight, though they made out to be helping you out of the kindness of their hearts so you'd have a successful career in the United States Air Force.

While I was on the road, and especially in California and Alaska, I got used to long hair and beards. Meantime, the military grew a rather strong bias against such tonsorial styles. If you had a beard, you were suspect. Long hair made you a freak. With both, you were a goddamn hippie bum! No question. When I showed up at Medina, unshaven and with hair to my shoulders, it was an insult to the flag of the United States of America and to the Republic for which it stands. As I sat at breakfast reading the morning paper and going through my order of six fried eggs (over easy), pancakes, hashbrowns, and chipped beef on toast, they were scratching their denuded heads and rubbing their mahogany-polished chins, consulting as to the proper way of dealing with OT Wooly so he might realize the advantages of the military way of life. OT Wooly was to be gigged in so tight, he'd be lucky to get air. But they had to wait until Monday morning. OT Wooly was not in officer's training until then.

On Sunday, there was a great influx as upperclassmen returned from leave and lowerclassmen poured in to start school. By Sunday evening the barracks was bursting with men: all neatly groomed, no beards, no long hair. I began to feel conspicuous. I didn't mind looking different from upperclassmen, but the new guys were greenhorns like myself. I resolved to be first in line when the barbershop opened next morning.

We were ordered to the barbershop after breakfast, where we were shorn like sheep. Everyone's haircut the same. The barber cut my hair to the bone, my beard as well, then gave me a razor. When I looked in the mirror I laughed. My own mother wouldn't know me. Next we got our uniforms and boots. We got all shined up, and were ordered to fall out for inspection (or is that "fall in"? It was "fall out" if you weren't out there, "fall in" if you were). Upperclassmen walked around telling us to straighten up, shoulders back, suck it in, heels together. After a while they began to mumble to each other, "Which one is OT Wooly?" He was gone! Vanished. Could he be late for the first formation? Well, just what you would expect of a damn hippie. But no, the count was correct.

They had never bothered to take a good look at me. They'd seen only the hair and beard. Not one of them recognized me. Our nametags didn't help because they had all gotten used to referring to me as OT Wooly, and that was not on my tag. They walked around our formation looking.

"Are you OT Wooly?"

"No, SIR!"

I said, "No, sir," too. My official name was OT Bloch. I wasn't about to become party to their game. The ranking upper classman had an idea. He faced the formation. "OT Woolly, step forward," he commanded. His voice echoed off the buildings. Nothing happened. All was quiet. They had another idea. OT Wooly's barracks leader would know his real name. They sent for OT Captain Ketterer.

"It's Block," he yelled. "B-l-o-c-h."

"OT Bloch, step forward."

We were formed up in alphabetical order, so I was in the first rank. I took one step forward. I was immediately surrounded by a half-dozen upperclassmen, who looked at me in astonishment.

"Look at those shoes! He must have been standing in manure."

"This man has more cables than a telegraph office."

They walked around shaking their heads in disbelief, wondering what this man's Air Force was coming to, when it would recruit hippies and beatniks to serve alongside real airmen. They snorted with contempt and said OT Wooly sure didn't look like much, and it was amazing he thought he could serve with other men, even with stupid, greenhorn lowerclassmen. They began giving me gigs for all kinds of infractions, most of which I didn't understand: half a dozen gigs for "gross cables," two gigs for not having my shoes properly shined (one for each shoe), gigs for not having my gig line in order, gigs for improper shave, for sloppy salute, for one eyebrow bushier than the other, for having my cover at an improper angle, for a nose hair (at least they thought it might be a nose hair), and for infractions too shocking and outrageous to record. By the time we fell out of formation, I had about twenty gigs on my record while most everyone else had two or three. Some had none.

The upperclassmen's generosity with gigs lasted several weeks. I was a constant source of their entertainment. They'd stop me in the quad when they saw the name "Bloch" on the tag and point me out to their comrades. "Look what we have here: OT Wooly," they'd say, and felt they couldn't dismiss me without finding at least one infraction.

I must admit I helped them pile on the gigs. I knew nothing of the military. I didn't know about spit-shining a shoe, never heard of a gig line (the hem of your shirt along the buttons must line up with your belt buckle and your fly), and never heard of a gross cable (bits of thread left on your clothes by the manufacturer or the tailor). My only exposure to close order drill had been watching Abbot and Costello in *Buck Privates*. Marching, I was constantly turning the wrong way and bumping into the man who turned the right way—and delighting the upperclassmen. I didn't know how to do a proper pushup, I didn't know my selective service number, and didn't know how to shave properly.

The upperclassmen practiced what they preached. They were a wonder to behold. They were all in top physical condition, all walked proudly with heads high, chests out, stomachs flat. Their uniforms always looked like Mom had just pressed them that morning; their shoes flashed like mirrors in the sunshine. They clicked their heels and saluted smartly.

My roommate asked me, "What have you been doing all summer? You should have been studying about the Air Force before you came here. You should have been doing pushups and running the mile. You should have had your brother march you around the backyard until you answered to the orders on instinct."

That was OT Snell. He considered me about the most ignorant human being he had ever come across. He was somewhat aloof, but if it weren't for him I would never have made it through the school. He knew everything, and he answered my questions freely with only an occasional snide remark. He couldn't give me gigs for being stupid, a fact he often regretted. He was a totally dedicated Air Force officer. He not only knew all the rules, but *approved* of them. Of course, he was right about my ignorance. Almost everyone there either had some ROTC training, had been at the Air Force Academy, were members of the National Guard back home, came over from the U.S. Army, had already been through Airman Basic at Lackland, or at least had fathers and uncles who had filled them in about what it was like when they had been in the Air Force. Many had visited the base ahead of time and knew the buildings. I wandered around like a Cretan toddler lost in the labyrinth.

So here I was again, just like at Crosier—way behind—in academics as well. They issued us a load of books I could hardly carry without a wheelbarrow—books no one ever heard of. When we went to class, the instructor could as well have been talking Chinese. He let "sink pack" and "you safe" and "sea calf," and also initials like GMT and BX roll off his tongue as easily as ordering bacon and eggs at chow. I had to find out from Snell (much to his dismay) that "sink pack" was really CINCPAC and stood for Commander in Chief Pacific Command. "You safe," he told me (rolling his eyes), was really USAFE and meant United States Air Force Europe, and that "sea calf" was SECAF—Secretary of the Air Force. The initials GMT were for Greenich Mean Time (that cleared up nothing), and he was sure I was the only person in the world who did not know what a BX was, and that I could go outside and ask anyone for directions there. The academic instructors talked about tactical plans and approaches, about strategic views and concepts. They talked of TAC, SAC, and MAC. As I looked around the classroom it seemed I was the only one puzzled. Expressions like bird colonel, field grade, and zero dark thirty meant nothing to me. I lay on my bunk at night with acronyms whirling in my head like alphabet soup in a blender. Even talking to other OTs during cigarette breaks was befuddling. They shortened their language with ASAP, SNAFU, and AWOL.

The Air Force brass said there was no harassment at OTS. I am sure they meant well, but whenever you give some people power over others, there will be abuse. Ketterer did fine. When he showed me how to salute, how to make my bed, or arrange my locker, he gave the impression he was saying, "Sorry, but this is the kind of BS you have to put up with around here." But some, like OT Lieutenant Johnson, were imperious, oppressive, and dictatorial. Johnson gloried in the "skills" he had learned. When he showed you how to make a hospital corner, he went at it as if his knowledge were gleaned from long scientific study. He was the radiant expert, while you were a lowborn imbecile likely never to master anything so complicated—at least not at his level.

If the requirements for storing clothes was not harassment, it was certainly a disgusting farce. You had to wind your socks and underwear into such tight little rolls you could bounce them on the floor or play hockey with them. Your laundry bag was tied to the foot of the bed with a very precise regulation knot so complicated that the average OT, once a knot passed inspection, never untied it again. He put his clothes in by opening the exit zipper at the bottom and stuffing the clothes upward and took out his laundry leaving the bag hang, and carrying his clothes in a paper bag.

I did not like OTS, but then I figured there was probably not a job in the world I would have liked after my months of freedom on the road. Everybody kept telling me, "just stick it out, it gets better in a few weeks, and in three months you'll be a second lieutenant." But there never was any danger of my dropping out. I kept remembering my brothers and uncles had gone through Army boot camp, and I was the son of a father with the emotions and tenacity of a bear trap, and of a mother whose sense of duty trumped all problems.

I thought close order drill was harassment. Even after I had it down, I felt like a damn fool getting into line and marching like a mindless robot just to get to the mess hall. And I always hated standing at attention to be inspected by arrogant upperclassmen. The sane ones would look you over and say softly, "I'll have to give you a gig for that spot on your shirt collar." Or "Take one for heels not touching, you have to watch that. Colonel Dodd will be doing this inspection one day." You felt he was trying to help you. But the dictators were different. They always shouted, so everyone in the ranks could hear their clever remarks.

"I suppose you're waiting for Mommy to come and iron that shirt!"

"You call that a shine? What did you use, a Hershey bar?" (They had memorized all the old military clichés, and employed them at every chance.)

"Gentlemen, I have found the original OT Snafu!"

"Oh, no! Take a look at this man's gig line! I've seen straighter corkscrews."

"Can you believe the gross cables hanging from this guy?"

The way they shouted out their horror, you'd have thought someone had threads hanging from him like tinsel on a Christmas tree. Dictators loved to holler, "Drop down and give me twenty," and you had to flop on your belly and do twenty pushups. The dictators, whenever they felt they weren't receiving proper respect, would threaten to send you to Colonel Dodd. You could hear that kind clear across the quad addressing an underclassman: "Listen here, numb nuts. You better get your fuckin' head screwed on straight or your ass will be in front of the colonel."

It was a mistake to begin a sentence with "Well, sir, I thought," because you would always be cut off with outraged shouting. "You thought! Who told you to think? Worms aren't allowed to think in this man's Air Force. You're not being paid to think!"

Some of the students seethed for hours when they were called names. But that part never bothered me. My father had often called me a dummy using names like *dummkopf, schafskopf,* and *holzkopf.* It was nothing serious. Sometimes their names made me laugh, and they would give me gigs for that. But I soon learned their ways, and was able to rattle off my selective service number like a machine gun and to recite the chain of command as easily as the Lord's Prayer: "Sir, I am OT Bloch, Group One, Squadron One, Flight Seven, Sir!" and was able to recall that Colonel Dodd was the man in charge.

Those first two weeks were an inspection nightmare. Everything had to be just so. Even the crease in your trousers was a matter of huge importance and scientific study. If the crease didn't bend at all, your pants were too short, but if it bent more than a little bit (the "little bit" being defined by any upperclassman), they were too long. It had to go back to the tailor.

You had to shave your chin until it shown like the hood ornament on a new Mercedes. There was one upperclassman with about a dozen stripes on his shoulder boards who used psychology on me:

"OT Bloch, are you depressed?"

"No, sir."

"You were not recently attempting suicide?"

"No, sir."

"Why did you try to cut your throat?" (He closely studied my Adam's apple.)

"Sir, I did not try to cut my throat, sir."

"There are several wounds here that look like knife slashes."

"Sir, those are from a razor, sir. From trying to shave as close as possible, sir."

He said nothing more. He moved on to the next man and examined him.

"Hmm. Uh huh! OT Beaseley here knows how to shave. OT Beaseley, you will teach OT Bloch to shave properly. OT Bloch, you will take two gigs for the cuts on your throat. But don't worry, you will not be getting any more gigs for improper shaving. From now on, OT Beaseley will take any gigs that you incur in that department."

Pretty smart. It worked well. Beaseley was not about to get a gig for my shaving. He had learned from his military father. My father had shaved with a straight razor, and I guess he assumed I'd learn from watching him. Beaseley taught me to pull the skin to one side of the Adam's apple and shave that, then pull to the other side and shave that spot again. That way you don't have to go across the point of the Adam's apple where you get cut. He also pointed out the trouble spots on the side of the throat that need to be shaved up, down, and sideways. I never got another gig for shaving. Neither did Beaseley.

We were warned ahead of time about barracks inspections. One Saturday morning shortly after we started school, Ketterer and some of his buddies did us a big favor. They held a mock inspection, and were they ever funny! They came down the hall in their pith helmets and underwear, marching together and slapping their boots on the floor like Nazi storm troopers. They yelled at us about infractions that made us laugh, like too much sunshine coming through the window, improper nose slope, and unsightly finger length. It relieved the tension in the barracks greatly and allowed us to see some humor in the real thing, though you did not dare laugh during a real inspection.

A real barracks inspection was serious. They checked the knot on your laundry bag and made sure your socks and underwear were rolled tight. They threw a quarter on your bed. If it didn't bounce, the cover wasn't tight enough. They measured the overhang of the sheets with a tape measure. It had to be the same on both sides. You had to make "hospital corners" exactly forty-five degrees with not a wrinkle. If your bed was not just so, they'd tear it up and watch you make it. They snooped into everything except your "panic box," the small box into which we could put personal items. No one was allowed to look in there. If you had a dirty comb, dust rag, or handkerchief, you quickly stuffed it in your panic box when you heard the inspectors coming. If the inspectors stopped at your door, one or both of the OTs in the room had to call the room to attention loud enough to make the windows rattle.

INSPECTOR NUMBER ONE stopped by my bed.

"How many inches is this bed from the wall?"

"FOUR INCHES, SIR!" I shouted at the top of my lungs. I shouted to save time. All the upperclassmen were deaf. If you didn't shout into their faces at full lung, they'd inevitably come back with "I can't he-ear you."

"I'm sure you won't mind if I check," said Inspector Number One.

I minded a lot, because I knew it would not be right, but I shouted that I didn't mind. I knew he would check anyway. The other inspectors gathered to join in with this skeptic. He drew from his pocket a block of wood. Holding it an inch from my nose, he announced that this block of wood was exactly four inches wide. With a smile and a flourish he inserted the wood between the wall and the bedpost. The wood clattered to the floor. The inspectors were aghast (triumphantly so). They stood shaking their heads as if they had just discovered a child's dead body. The conclusion of the entire team, to a man, was that the bed was definitely too far from the wall. I had no reason to believe they were ready to accept my measurement over theirs, so I didn't offer a counter opinion. With surprising enthusiasm, Inspector Number One shouted into my face that I had just earned a gig for having my bed much too far from the wall. I felt like telling him just one lousy gig would be a meaningless addition to the pile, but I let it slide.

The inspectors decided they would give me a chance to adjust the bed. I moved it slightly closer to the wall. Inspector Number One tried to insert the block of wood. It didn't fit. More consternation. With the same enthusiasm I was informed that this time the bed was too close, and that I had just earned myself another gig. Ordinary men would have tired, and given me up for a hopeless case.

An OT normally had to keep track of his gigs and was on his honor to report them correctly. But inspectors were suspicious fellows. One of them had a handy little notebook in which he entered my name, and he put down a stroke for every gig. He showed it to me several times during the inspection, evidently so I would not be in a big sweat about keeping my own tally. I thought this a great convenience since gigs were flying about so freely. I was grateful. However, just before they left the room, they shattered their kindly image. They asked me how many gigs I had just received. I deferred to the man with the notebook, thinking he'd be happy to serve some purpose. This did not sit well and earned me another gig. I took a guess. I figured it was better to guess on the high side. I was over by two gigs. They gave me another gig for overestimating my ability to obtain gigs.

All this attention was quite flattering. After all, many of the OTs went about their business with barely a glance from upperclassmen, while I was frequently the center of attention. However, I noticed no jealousy on the part of my comrades. One morning we had fire drill. The alarm sounded at 0430 when everyone was bound to be fast asleep. It had been a hot night, and I was sleeping in the raw, which was my habit. I knew most everyone slept in T-shirt and shorts, but I saw no reason for extra clothes in this hot weather, and no uniform was specified for the night. I stepped into my shoes, I took my flashlight, I grabbed my dust cover, pulled it over my head, leaving just enough of an opening to see where I was going, and went down the hall chanting "fire drill, fire drill" as did everyone else, and as was required. We went down the stairs and formed up in the parking lot—everything just as we had been briefed to do. We were not allowed to put on clothes, except shoes, and those remained untied.

The upperclassmen were quite pleased how well the drill had gone. They had handed out only two gigs—one to the last OT exiting the building, one to a sleepyhead who failed to cover his head completely. They told us we could uncover our heads and stand at ease while an upperclassman gave a "well-done" speech. Others walked around inspecting to make sure no one had stopped to tie his shoes or to put on his pants. An upperclassman stopped in front of me, and then it began.

"Where's your T-shirt, OT?"

"SIR, IN MY ROOM, SIR!"

"You don't wear a T-shirt at night?"

"NO, SIR!"

I felt I was on good ground here. We had a mandatory "uniform of the day," but I had never heard anything of a "uniform of the night." The uniform of the day was announced first thing every morning at 0500, when upperclassmen woke us up by standing in the hall and beating on garbage can lids with hammer handles (their version of reveille): "Good morning, gentlemen! Today is the twenty-fourth day of July, of the year one-thousand-nine-hundred and sixty-five. There are eighty-eight training days left for the lowerclassmen and twelve days left for the upper. The uniform of the day is dress blues."

That uniform was sacred. Woe to you if you were caught in anything other. But they never announced a dress code for sleeping. There was no written foundation for a single one of those gigs they gave me that morning. I felt completely sandbagged. Upperclassmen began to gather. They were shining their flashlights into my eyes, ears, shoes, nose. One shone his flashlight down the front of my dust cover and shouted, "Oh, my God, he doesn't have shorts on, either!" Everyone else was dismissed, but I had the honor of standing at attention while the upperclassmen happily gigged me for no T-shirt, no shorts, and for sleeping in the nude—all manufactured violations.

THEY THREATENED ME many times with having to visit the green-eyed, fire-breathing monster, the satanic angel of judgment: Colonel Dodd! That visit never came about—except once—and then by accident. The colonel proved a placid pussy cat instead of a dragon. All those gigs had restricted me once again to the base for a weekend. I was on "lawn patrol" that Saturday, sweltering in the sun by the barracks bent over a patch of grass. I was hunting the enemy: an alien object. I had searched for over an hour like a hungry eagle looks for prey, and was shocked—shocked!—to find several gross violations: an inch-long string, five bits of white paper from field-stripped cigarettes, and a gray feather from some very small bird. I heard footsteps coming up the sidewalk. I looked up. Colonel Dodd! He was about to pass, but he stopped and came walking toward me. I hit a brace that would have put a wooden soldier to shame. I snapped a salute, which he returned, but I forgot to unlock mine because I was trying to figure out what to do with the objects in my left hand which I was half hiding at my side. I was glad when he gave me "at ease," because I could put that hand behind my back. They had not given a class on how to salute with garbage in one hand—unless I missed that one.

The colonel asked me what I was doing out there in the hot Texas sun and why I wasn't in town drinking beer. I told him about the fire drill thing. He seemed amused. He asked me other questions about where I had gone the past weekends. I saw a light come on. He frowned and looked at me sideways. "Are you the one they call OT Wooly?"

I tried to figure a way to answer that. I started to say I did not know about that, but I stuttered and came out with a feeble, "Yes, sir."

Now I was in trouble. It would all come raining down on my head. But Colonel Dodd wasn't hostile. He asked me about the school, if I was unhappy here. I said, "No, sir," which wasn't exactly the truth, but I didn't think, "Yes, sir," was the proper answer either. He asked if I realized I had more gigs than anyone else in the class and was setting records. I said I had been made aware of that fact from time to time. He asked if I had an explanation for this.

When I answered, "Yes, sir, I do," he became interested. He asked me to step into the shade. He said, "Let's hear it."

So I told him about Alaska and the long hair and beard and mosquitoes and not having shaving gear, and having to hurry down here or be dropped from the class. I said I believed the upperclassmen had taken the whole thing personally, and I couldn't blame them. If I had to do it over I would have cleaned up before I came. As I talked he looked off into the distance with his lips pursed. Every so often he gave a slight nod, which kept me going. He asked to see what was in my hand. I showed him. That amused him, too.

He said, "Okay, you're done with policing this lawn. Go get something cold to drink. Take the weekend off. And next weekend, too."

He started to go, then turned back and said, "Relax. It's all a game. Play along. Everyone graduates from OTS with the same rank. And don't worry about the gigs. They won't count against you at the end. I promise."

I didn't know exactly what that meant, but it felt good—like a big load was off my back. After that I wasn't afraid of Colonel Dodd. Whenever an upperclassman used that old threat, I thought, *Go ahead, throw me in the briar patch.* I think upperclassmen were more afraid of the dragon colonel than I was.

I ABSOLUTELY DO NOT want to leave the impression I hated everything at OTS. I didn't. I liked three things: the food, the pay, and the Honor Code. Everyone said the military was underpaid. Many of my comrades whined about meager pay, especially when they found themselves broke on a Monday morning after a hard weekend carousing. I didn't do any carousing those first weeks at OTS and always woke up on Monday with the same money I had on Friday night. We received the pay of a staff sergeant—more money than I had ever made in my life, and it amazed me they would give me that much money, feed me, and give me a place to sleep.

I loved the school's Honor Code. How I wished we'd had that code in the seminary! All of us had to sign a paper that said: "I will not lie, steal, or cheat, nor tolerate anyone who does." This was everyone's standard of personal conduct and it was no joke. You could put your entire Air Force career in jeopardy by even the smallest violation of that Code. At OTS you could leave your wallet, sunglasses, or wristwatch lying around. Someone always brought it back to you or turned it in. I trusted my comrades and never felt any of them capable of stealing any of my stuff or of telling me a lie. At the seminary we had no Honor Code, no Honor Committee, and no Honor Court. There was just the vague feeling that young men studying for the priesthood should be good boys.

The weeks went by. Soon I was in the upper class. That was no picnic, either. The physical training and academics were as intense as ever. We were getting ready for our final exams, and the competition was fierce. OT Snell was constantly studying and doing pushups. He said he wanted to make DMG. I didn't know what that was. He said it stood for Distinguished Military Graduate and explained how it could help to have that on your record. I studied and did pushups with him, though Snell said he thought I wouldn't be able to make it with all the gigs. He thought they'd count against me at the end. But I remembered what Colonel Dodd had told me, and I worked all the harder. Snell was very serious about all this. I tried to be like him. I even went running with him during some free periods. The faster you could run the mile, the better your score. They expected us to do at least forty-two pushups in two minutes. We could rest, but only in the up position. Snell showed me how you could help yourself by bouncing off your chest, but you had to be subtle about that because the examiners would be watching for such tricks.

The weather got hotter, physical training sessions harder. I found myself dragging through the week waiting for just one thing: Saturday 1300 hours. Then I was free until Monday morning. When I finally got into town, I went straight to the Mexican section to look for Carmen. She wasn't there. She'd left and no one knew where she was except she'd gone to Florida. I never heard of her again.

We took our exams in history, social studies, and military justice, and completed the notorious final physical. They added up the scores and gave each of us a paper with the tally. They had also graded writing ability, military bearing, and "performance of duties within the OT Wing." They pinned a gold bar to your shirt collar, snapped a salute, and said, "Congratulations, you are now a second lieutenant in the United States Air Force." Snell and I both made DMG, though he was near the top of the list and I near the bottom. Snell said, "Makes no difference, consider yourself lucky." I was happy to get out of the hot hell of San Antonio—though I was getting out just as the weather was turning cooler, and I was going from the frying pan into the fire: pilot training.

Chapter Twenty-Three

I WAS A FARM BOY. I had been around machinery all my life. I had been driving farm tractors since I was ten, and had run all kinds of other farm machinery. I thought I should be able to run this machine, too. It sat on the ramp at Woodring Airport near Enid, Oklahoma, basking in the morning sun. The Air Force called it a T-41. Its civilian designation: Cessna 172. I knew exactly what every control did. I had studied it carefully in my chair at the BOQ (Bachelors Officers Quarters), looking at the pictures in the book. I held my hands and feet as if controlling the real airplane and pretended I was flying. The book said to turn left, you turn the wheel left; to turn right, you turn the wheel right. What was hard about that? There was that extra dimension of up-and-down, but even that seemed pretty straight forward. To go up, you pull back on the wheel. To go down you push. They had added foot pedals that could make the airplane's nose waggle from side to side. That seemed a superfluous addition, but I trusted the engineers knew what they were doing. I figured the most likely reason this whole process of flying seemed so complicated to many was because city boys don't know anything about machinery. I thought for once I was ahead of the others.

It was a calm morning, the eternal Oklahoma wind in temporary suspension, the sky an undisturbed blue from horizon to horizon. With great confidence I mounted my seat in the T-41 next to the instructor. With great discouragement I dismounted an hour later. This flying machine was not like other machines. It was the first of many discouragements I suffered that year.

Rather than being ahead, I was once again behind most of the other students. Some came from families with a flying tradition: Granddad was a hotshot pilot in World War II, Uncle Joe flew over Korea, a brother had just finished pilot training. Some came from homes with libraries full of airplane books. Some had taken flight lessons. Some had their private pilot's license. I was here because I didn't want to get drafted into the Army. They were here because they had been planning and dreaming of flying since they were six. I did have one small advantage: I never got airsick. I never felt even a bit queasy. Some students had to carry barf bags with them when they flew.

I HAD ENTERED the main gate of Vance Air Force Base on "14 Oct 65" (that's how you write a date in the military). On the flightline next to the long, shimmering runways stood row upon row of magnificent jet aircraft—T-37s and

T-38s—resplendent in the sunshine. I was filled with reverence and wonder. The United States Air Force was going to show me how to fly those things. I felt a lump of gratitude in my throat. A large sign read, "3576 STUDENT SQUADRON" and at the bottom it said, "INCOMING STUDENTS RESPORT TO BLDG 604." That's what I did. They assigned me a little apartment in the BOQ. Once again I had a home.

During my flight training, I completely suspended writing my log. I sometimes scribbled myself a note and stuck it in my pocket, but lost many of them. I had no time. I was up to my eyeballs—no, let's be honest, I was way over my head. I was constantly drowning and coming up for the third time.

They issued us a truckload of flight publications. I hopelessly considered I'd have to learn all this stuff in only one year. But the instructors went at it in remarkable step-by-step military order, so that, every once in a while that year, I felt my head momentarily above water. Besides the books, they doled out flying gear: helmet, calculator, knee board, checklist—everything you might need to fly a plane, including a real G-proof fighter-pilot wristwatch, a pair of genuine fighter-pilot gloves and sunglasses, and a flight suit with a thousand zippered pockets to store your junk. A very plump, pleasant sergeant fitted my helmet for me, adding and subtracting padding until it fit perfectly. He showed me how to slip it on "like a real fighter pilot," spreading the ear pieces so you "don't rub your ears off." He showed me how to strap on the oxygen mask by sliding the bayonet connector into the receiver on the helmet and clicking it tight with no leak. In the T-37 and the T-38 we wore those oxygen masks all the time. The T-41 had no oxygen tank.

We had to get thirty hours of flying time in the T-41 before we could go near one of the beautiful jets lined up in perfect rows on the Vance Air Force Base ramp. They hauled us out to the other side of Enid in a standard blue Air Force bus and dumped us at the Woodring Airport. The T-41 was a big disappointment for many. They had signed up for pilot training expecting to do all their flying in jets. That used to be the case, but things had changed. Now we had to start in one of these disgusting little T-41s—merely "kites with corkscrews on the front." I wasn't disappointed. I'd never bothered to check what I'd be flying. I did not know one airplane from another.

The T-41A USAF was also called the Mescalero, but we never used that name, just the "T-41" or the "noisy kite." Like other Cessna 172s, it was made in Wichita, Kansas. The Air Force had paid $7,000 apiece for them. Cheaper than the average Cessna 172, they had a limited amount of avionics. All our T-41 missions had to be flown in VFR (Visual Flight Rules) conditions— the weather had to be nice. IFR (Instrument Flight Rules), means you could fly in the clouds. We had civilian instructors in the T-41. It was not dignified for a hotshot USAF pilot to sit in a little single-engine plane driven by a pro-peller. The head man at the school and the check-pilots, however, were Air Force officers, and not generally happy to be stuck in that job. A student yearbook from that time has little or no mention of the T-41 program. The impression is we trained only in T-37s and T-38s. There are no pictures of the T-41 instructors or mention of their names, and damn few of the T-41.

If you have not flown an airplane, you cannot possibly imagine—and I doubt I can convey here in writing—the problems involved for a greenhorn. Just taxiing the airplane is difficult. While on the ground, you steer with your feet. Your feet rest on pedals that move the rudder (a flap-like thing on the vertical part of the tail). By tilting those pedals forward with your toes, you activate the brakes. Your feet do the steering with a combination of rudder and brake. But that very tempting steering wheel right in front of you (the yoke) makes one forget to steer with the feet. From old habits in a car, you resort to that wheel every time. You desperately try to steer by cranking around that wheel, which does absolutely no good. That wheel has nothing to do with steering until you leave the ground. Meantime your airplane hap-pily meanders unbridled into the alfalfa field by the taxiway. You just flunked.

On a normal afternoon in Oklahoma, a stout wind rips across the flats. The airplane is a weathervane on the ground. With the wind pushing on the wide vertical tail, the nose wants to turn into the wind. You stomp on the opposite rudder. If the wind is strong enough (I should say, "If you're in Oklahoma") you run out of rudder and have to tap the brake for assistance. That makes the airplane stop, unless you remember to add power at the same time. So there you are, jerking along the taxiway banging the rudders, cranking back and forth on the wheel, tapping the brakes, cramming in power, feeling like (and defi-nitely looking like) a fool, while the instructor, arms folded, grins.

But wait. Even when you figure out that you steer with your feet, problems aren't over. That wheel in front of you does have to be turned, but only accord-ing to the direction of the wind. The wheel is connected by cables to the ailerons—the flappy things out on the wings that move up and down with the wheel position. They make the airplane turn in the air. On the ground, if the wind is coming directly from the front, you hold the ailerons neutral, meaning you don't turn the wheel. If it comes more from the right or the left, you turn the wheel into the wind. A wind from the front right is called a right-quartering headwind, and you turn the wheel to the right. The reason for this is because it makes the aileron on the right wing go up and makes the aileron on the left wing go down. While the wind is trying to cause you to leave the taxiway by pushing on the tail, it's also trying to tip you over. With the right aileron up it tends to hold that wing down, and with the left aileron down it tends to hold that wing up, thus countering the wind's attempts. In a tailwind, you have to do the opposite: you turn the wheel away from the wind, not into the wind.

We're not done yet. You also have to concern yourself with the position of the elevator, a small door mounted horizontally at the tail end of the airplane that makes the plane go up and down (in the air, that is). When you pull back on the wheel, the elevator moves up; push forward and it moves down. While taxiing in a headwind you must hold the elevator neutral, but in a tailwind you hold it down.

If you don't understand any of the foregoing, don't worry; neither did I, and I was the one trying to taxi.

The piles of publications they threw at us explained all this, and we'd better burn the midnight oil, or we'd be lost. The system of controls invented by the Wright Brothers—aileron, elevator, and rudder—remain the same and are the basis for controlling every machine from the Piper Cub to the F-18. We had to know the names of the parts of the airplane as well as we knew the food on our mothers' tables. The instructors in academics and in the airplane used aviation words. They talked about yaw, pitch, and roll. They said rudder, aileron, flaps, and elevator. When they maneuvered the plane in the sky, they were turning around the horizontal axis, the vertical axis, or the lateral axis. And we had to have an immediate, clear idea of what those terms meant, or, while the instructor was telling us how to recover from a stall so we would not kill ourselves, we would be trying to remember what an aileron was.

Up in the airplane you don't get a second chance. When flying you can't park the thing to think things over, and you can't back it up. If you miss a turn, it is way back there in the sky, and you'll never have that opportunity again. In the classroom I had little trouble. In the sky I had plenty. But it was not my fault. There was some kind of a curse on the T-41 at Woodring.

MY INSTRUCTOR LEVELED the airplane at 4,500 feet and set the throttle. He touched the trim wheel several times and then took his hands off the controls. The plane flew by itself in the peaceful morning air. Steady as a rock.

"Okay," he said. "Let's try some straight and level. Just keep it like this for a minute. Head for that white farmhouse straight ahead. You got it."

"Roger, I got it," I said. His name wasn't Roger—nor Bill or Pete. "Roger" was the mandatory method of switching control of the airplane between pilots. The man relinquishing control said, "You got it"; the man taking control said, "Roger, I got it." That was about the only thing all I got right that first flight. I took control (an embellishment) by putting my left hand on the yoke and my right on the throttle. I put my feet on the rudder pedals. I was flying a real airplane in God's great blue sky over the United States of America! The steady purr of the motor, the soft hiss of the air over the fuselage, the fields below slowly moving under us, and with me driving—what a great feeling!

When I grabbed the yoke, the nose of the plane went up a little. We were climbing. I pushed forward on the yoke to get the nose back where it had been. I noticed, too, the plane was not quite wings level. No problem. I turned the yoke ever so slightly to the right. Then I noticed that, in correcting for the climb, I had put the plane into a little dive. I pulled back on the yoke to get back to level. At the same time I was no longer lined up on the white farmhouse. I turned to line it up, but the nose just seemed to hang there. Then I remembered—rudder! I stepped on the rudder to make it move. The nose swung quickly but went right by the farmhouse. Then I noticed I was way above my altitude of 4,500. I pushed forward. It dawned on me this plane had taken on a life of its own, turning, diving, climbing, wobbling with no regard for my corrections. The sound of the air over the fuselage was different, and the motor sounded crabby. Every time I stepped on a rudder pedal to try to counter a crazy sideways movement of the nose, the propeller snarled in resentment

"I got it," sang the instructor with unspeakable boredom. The plane settled down immediately. Magic. I wiped sweat from my forehead. These Air Force flight suits were way too hot for Oklahoma. The instructor adjusted the throttle, touched the trim, and said, "You got it."

We were back at exactly 4,500 feet, and perfectly lined up on the white house. I said, "Roger, I got it." But I didn't have it. The plane did the same thing again. Apparently it did not like the feel of me on the controls and bucked as soon as I touched them. When I had the plane it was a crazy wild bronco; when the instructor had it, it was a docile child's pony.

My instructor, Rankin, was a good enough instructor. I liked him even though he blew a fuse once in a while. I was used to that. Dad did it too, so we got along fine. He liked my landings but was never satisfied with my air work. We were assigned a piece of sky in which to do our maneuvers and I had to stay within the boundaries or he flunked me. While I did lazy eights, stalls, forced landings, or slow flight, I had to monitor landmarks to make sure I didn't stray to one side or the other. I had to watch my altitude so I didn't go above or below my assignment.

"Rudder, rudder, rudder," I can still hear Rankin chant. When I turned the plane with the wheel, I always forgot I had to use rudder, too. And he was an irritating stickler for radio calls. Every word had to be in there and in just the right order. I had to say, "Blue Chip Six-Zero, base, full stop." (Blue Chip was his call sign.) If I said, "Blue Chip Sixty," he'd have a stroke. If I forgot the "full stop," he'd make the call himself and lower my grade. When I called for landing instructions, I had to say, "Red Rover, say landing." You couldn't say, "Red

Rover, what's your active runway," or "which way are you landing?" It had to be just so. And God help you if you said "yes" on the radio instead of "roger."

We had a separate checklist procedure for each air maneuver, and we better not miss an item. This was serious stuff. And before we could start anything we did two clearing turns. Lieutenant Coady put it like this: "Don't even fart up there without first doing two clearing turns." You had to "clear the area," that is, make sure you were the only airplane in that airspace. You did this by making two turns, one in each direction. That made sense, but, as with all the military maneuvers, the turns had to be done with such attention to the details that the primary purpose was obscured. To clear the area, instead of just turning the plane all around and looking over the sky, we had to make two precise ninety degree turns—exactly ninety. Altitude had to remain riveted. We had to maintain an exact degree of bank in the turn also. The result was the student, instead of searching the sky for other airplanes, was watching his altimeter and attitude indicator, and *pretending* to be looking at the sky.

The same was true for stalls. Instead of letting us horse the airplane around until we got into trouble, then show us how to fly out of it, we cleared the area, entered at an exact airspeed, held a precise attitude and an exact degree of bank, until we completely forgot what the maneuver was for. But that's the military.

These small, light airplanes with big wings were extremely safe because they glided so well. With the engine off, they glided for miles to a nice soft landing on a roadway or a farmer's field. We practiced "emergency landings" or "forced landings" daily. We'd be flying along when suddenly the instructor would pull the power to idle and say "forced landing." Our job was to find a suitable landing area, spiral down to traffic pattern altitude, and glide to the landing area we picked. This was the one time we were allowed to go below our assigned area. Being high was hardly a problem; we could put down full flaps and slip the airplane sideways. That made it go down like a rock. If low, we delayed lowering the flaps, hoping the instructor would "clear the engine." During approach the instructor had to clear the engine from time to time—bring up the RPMs, then reduce back to idle. This kept the cylinders from fouling, which they tended to do with too much idling. So the instructor could help you out when you were a little low in your pattern by clearing the engine.

While we flew the pattern we constantly checked altitude, wind drift, engine instruments, and, most of all: airspeed. Airspeed had to be perfect, and that made sense. Every airplane had an ideal glide speed where the drag on the plane was the least. The better the adherence to that speed, the better the glide ratio. Do the whole pattern perfectly, but with bad airspeed control and we could still flunk. We flunked if we failed to land into the wind. So before take off we had to know the prevailing winds on the ground and keep that in mind when picking an emergency field.

This may sound complicated. It was. Further, while this went on, we had to run through the checklist for the particular emergency procedure the instructor had named: smoke in the cockpit, dead engine, engine fire—whatever he dreamed up to put us into the forced landing. We had to announce every item out loud to the instructor: "fuel off" (touching the selector), "seatbelt" (touching our buckle), "door open" (which we actually opened). We opened the door on a forced landing because the door could jam with a hard landing, leaving you stuck inside. We also opened it to give us "quick egress" (military for "getting the hell out of there") on the assumption she was gonna blow.

We didn't actually land out of those forced landings. As soon as the instructor determined we had the field made (or not, and had flunked) he said, "Go around." That meant abort the landing: full-power climb, flaps up, checklist, checklist, checklist! It all happened so fast at first it seemed impossible. Actually, there was plenty of time. Later in the T-37 I would look back with great fondness at the slow, easy style of that good old T-41.

OCTOBER CAME and the weather got cooler. The Minnesota Twins were in the World Series that year, but I knew nothing about it. I never listened to radio or TV. I was in a fog of studies. On the last day of the series, when I could have watched part of game at the Officer's Club, I stayed at the BOQ and studied. I totally missed one of the best World Series ever. I was taking life too seriously. It eventually showed in my flying.

In the morning sun, I could see my breath, and guys walked to classes with their jackets on. But the sun was always hot as it climbed over Oklahoma. By noon everyone was back in shirt sleeves. Nights were clear, but by no means quiet. The roar of night flying saw to that. To entertain us at our studies, T-37s or T-38s would take to the skies and thunder away the stillness of the night. To assist in destroying silence completely, the sergeants of the maintenance crews tested engines every night down on the flightline. When they tested the afterburners on the T-38 it made my quarters tremble, and made me scramble to shut the window so I could think. At about 2300 hours things suddenly calmed, silence reigned again, and in a little while you could hear a coyote yipping from the PT field and another would answer from far off on one of the runways. Then I lay down and shut my eyes and counted a whirl of attitude indicators, altimeters, and oil pressure gauges. After a while I slept.

During those T-41 days we rarely went to the O Club (Officer's Club). We were too busy studying. We grabbed a quick sandwich and ate while studying. Only on a Friday night might we go to the stag bar at the O Club to have a drink, not to get drunk, but to watch the other officers getting so. The Stag Bar was a place where we could let our hair down. We did not have to wear a uniform, salute, or call everyone "sir." Students and instructors showed up in sweat-stained flight suits and got skunk drunk. No women were allowed in the Stag Bar. It was always thick with cigarette and cigar smoke, and in those days also from tobacco pipes. On Friday nights young pilots, full of the sap of youth and of whiskey, stood on tables and gave speeches and led their brothers in bawdy song. They puked on those tables at midnight and staggered around the parking lot looking for their automobiles. There was no stigma attached to getting drunk on Friday night. One night I asked a T-38 student with a bandaged hand, what happened. He proudly told me he had been drunk the week before and, while looking for his car, had dropped his keys. As he was crawling around in the dark, feeling for his keys, a car backing up ran over his fingers.

IT WAS A FOGGY MORNING. Visibility was down to less than a quarter-mile. The base was silent. As I walked to class, I was confident we'd fly that afternoon. The Oklahoma sun would come through like always and conditions would be "severe clear" before long. I was near solo time and knew they'd soon let me go up by myself in the T-41 at Woodring. By the time we got to the flightline shortly after noon, we had flying weather again. I was scheduled for the second flight, so I had plenty of time to stand around and get nervous, and the wind had plenty of time to pick up and get gusty. At mid-afternoon Rankin came in from his first flight.

"You're next," he said, happy. "Off into the wild blue."

I felt pretty confident until I came in on the first landing and let the wind manhandle me in the flare like a novice. I was drifting off to one side. When I lowered the wing into the wind, my nose was pointed off into the cactus. So I shoved in the throttle. I went around. I didn't know how to salvage that landing.

"I can do that better," I said, which was stupid, because I'm sure Rankin was thinking, *Well, I surely hope so.*

Rankin said nothing.

I made several more landings, but was not happy with one of them. Rankin said nothing. On the next pattern, when I called base, Rankin said, "Make it full stop."

As we taxied back, I did after-landing checks. I felt I had flunked. Rankin said nothing. As we neared the ramp he said, "Stop." I did, and he got out.

"I thought you might like to take it around a few times by yourself," he said as he tied up his seat belt. Then he shook my hand and said, "You won't need any luck. Just have fun." And he closed the door.

I was glad I was wearing sunglasses because I was misty eyed.

I taxied to the yellow line at the head of the runway. Red Rover gave me the green light. "I said, 'Blue Chip Six Two, roger to the green.'"

I taxied onto the runway. I reached the centerline, I opened up the power. I was off. It was wonderful. I had 145 horses strapped to my rear and was climbing alone into God's great sky.

"Blue Chip Six-Two."

I was busy trimming for the ninety-mile-per-hour climb, so I could not answer right away.

"Blue Chip Six-Two."

"This is Blue Chip Six-Two, over."

"We're using runway one-two, not runway one-seven."

And so began my flying career. The first time I ever flew by myself, I took off on the wrong damn runway!

I thought Rankin would flunk me for that, but the fact was we had done all our dual landings on runway one-seven, and Red Rover had switched runways just as I was ready for takeoff. Rankin, watching from the ground, didn't know about my mistake until later. It was a stupid mistake. I should have listened to the take-off instructions from Red Rover. Rankin passed me. It was the fifth of November 1965.

Two of my best buddies had washed out of the program. With nothing to do, they took up slot car racing. At night they went to the racetrack in Enid and raced their cars against the locals. They'd always stop by my BOQ to get me to go along, but I was always studying. On the day I soloed, one of them had just bought a new XKE, and they were on their way to try it out. This time they were sure I'd go with them to celebrate my soloing. I almost did, but at the last minute, I decided I had better study. That was the Henry Bloch in me: nose to the grindstone, shoulder to the wheel. Work always comes first.

There was a bit of a lull near Christmas. They gave us a few days off for R&R (rest and recuperation). I didn't go home. It was too costly for that short a time, and besides, I thought I should be studying. I went to the officer's club the night before everyone was leaving. The T-37 and T-38 students and instructors were there raising hell in the back room, buying drinks for everyone, singing, dancing and shouting loud, exaggerated Christmas greetings across the room to anyone who entered. At one point Colonel Christmas (yes, that was his real name), came in and called the room to order.

"When you go home," he said, "have fun. Get some R&R. Get all the pussy you want, but don't get in any fights. Don't wear your uniform in public. Not bowling, not to the movies, not at church on Sunday. There's a lot of anti-military types out there, beatniks and hippies, and other scum, who will yell anti-military bullshit, and maybe spit at you. Don't punch them out."

This caused a firestorm. From all quarters I could hear, "I'll kick their ass," and "Fuck them, those cowards."

"I give you fair warning," said Christmas. "Get into a fight and you're in danger of losing your slot in class. Don't come with the excuse they started it. Understand? I don't care if they call you a mass murderer, or butcher, or baby killer."

He left. Then began a riot of swearing and describing of consequences should any long-haired, bearded, hippie-type try something. In a short time they had hung all the beatniks and hippies in the country or relieved them of vital parts.

The club had been trimmed with lights and fir trees. Everything looked like Christmas, but outside there was no snow. Every once in a while above the din I could hear Bing Crosby's voice, "I'm dreaming of a white Christmas," and "I'll be home for Christmas." I left the club when officers began to sing along. I couldn't stand it. The lump in my throat made my voice come out funny.

THINGS WENT FAST after Christmas. I was scheduled for my final checkride in the T-41. I had just come back from a flight with Rankin. *What a horseshit ride,* I thought. *My grandmother could fly better than that, and she's dead.* My air work stank as usual. I thought it'd take another month to get ready for a checkride. Rankin enforced that conviction by ripping me for erratic altitude control in steep turns and almost overshooting the field on the emergency landing.

Then, as he bent over the grade slip and made careful marks on it, he said, "I'm putting you up for your checkride tomorrow morning."

"What? I need more time. How the hell am I gonna pass? You just saw how I flew. I'll flunk."

"Naw, you'll pass. You're a fuckin' genius at landings. That's what saves you. The check pilot will overlook your shitty air work."

"Thanks a lot."

Next morning I went straight to the scheduling board to see who my check pilot would be. I'd dreamed all night of going up with a "Santa Claus"—our name for a generous pilot who overlooked a lot of smaller details and gave you every chance to pass. That wasn't to be. I stared at the board—the worst possible luck! Major Frogface was my check pilot.

I loathed the very sight of the man. Short, Napoleonic with a wide mouth from ear to ear. The mouth got him the name Frogface, but it was never a smile; it had more the grim look of an alligator. He wore thick glasses that made his eyes look big like a frog's, which also made him stand out as the only Air Force pilot at Woodring who wore glasses. Everyone else had 20/20 vision, or better. Frogface was in charge of the T-41 program. He was the absolute boss, and nobody dared challenge him. He was a sour man who barked orders all day like an angry dog. I was scared of him all the way down into my flight boots. The very thought of flying with him made my palms sweat.

When he came to my table, I jumped up and snapped a salute. He simply said, "Let's go." A good check pilot would sit down and talk to you, assure you the checkride was like any other ride. He'd try to calm you so nerves didn't interfere with maneuvers. Not Frogface. We went straight to the plane. I checked the logbook and began my preflight. I was just about finished and about to climb aboard, when a volley of unhappy adjectives erupted from the major. He was astounded that I had overlooked the bad tire on the right main gear.

"If you think this tire's flyable, you haven't learned much. One hard landing and it's gone! Of course, I'm sure *you'd* never make a hard landing."

Oh, he was in a fine mood. We waited as maintenance changed the tire. It was only a matter of minutes, but it made us late for our takeoff time. We had further delays.

"Woodring VOR, Woodring VOR," I can hear it still, but Frogface could not. As part of the preflight cockpit check we had to "tune and identify" the VOR (a navigation receiver), turning up the volume, making sure we had the right station by listening to the Moorse Code identifier, then turning the volume low, just high enough so we could hear the voice identifier. All during the flight, every few seconds, a voice said into your ear, "Woodring V-O-R."

As we taxied out, the major said, "Stop." I did. He said, "Can you hear that VOR?"

I said, "Yes, sir."

"Turn it up so you can be sure that it's saying Woodring."

I turned it up and waited to see if it was loud enough for him.

"Are you going to sit here all day blocking the taxiway?" he said. "Let's go. We're late already."

Frogface kept me on edge by questioning every second check I made. When I was done checking the magnetos, he said, "What was the drop on the left?"

I'd never been asked that before. The magneto check was just to make sure you had no more than a 150 RPM drop on either magneto and that the maximum difference between the two magnetos was no more than seventy-five RPM. I wasn't told I was supposed to memorize what the drop was on the left, nor was there reason to. When I stuttered my answer, he snapped, "Check it again."

When we got to our area, Frogface had a surprise for me. Normally a check pilot has the student do easy maneuvers first to give him a chance to relax and build confidence, but Frogface immediately pulled the power and announced "forced landing." I knew the winds were from the east. I selected a field pointing into the rising sun and set up a landing pattern over that field. I thought I was doing fine, but Frogface kept peppering me with questions.

"Which field are you looking at? You think that's long enough? You better watch your airspeed if you think you're going to pass this ride."

These were all great confidence builders. I got more nervous, afraid to make any adjustments of power or control for fear of offending the major. When I got lower, I saw a farmer's fence at the approach end of the field. I delayed the flaps a bit to make sure I'd come in high, leaving no doubt of clearing the fence. At that time Frogface, who had already cleared the engine, cleared it long and hard so I was way high. I dropped full flaps and pointed the nose down at the middle of the field.

"I got it. Look at your airspeed."

My airspeed was high because the son of bitch had run in the power for five seconds, right when I needed to lose altitude. He initiated a go around, and announced "you got it." I took the airplane, raised the nose to get climb airspeed and cleaned it up (put up the flaps). Before I could get to the climb checklist, he pulled power again. We were so low I had no option but land straight ahead. There was one decent field, but it was short, so I dived for the near end. I was hot and a bit high, but it was all I had. I lowered full flaps and stomped on the rudder to slip the airplane. Frogface took control as soon as I began the slip. He evidently was one of those pilots who did not like slipping.

"I got it. You're high again," he sang out, as if he knew all the time it would be this way and was getting bored with the whole thing. "Let's see if your area work is any better."

I was convinced I'd already flunked the ride. *What the hell does this guy have against me?* He was purposely making this more difficult. I knew I was screwing up, but he was doing everything he could to make sure I did just that. This checkride was a total disaster. But the real disaster was yet to come.

He told me to go to the middle of our assigned area and begin with power-on stalls. I cleared the area, but as I rolled out of the second turn, I saw an object coming toward us from the right (the major's side of the airplane). It was at our level so I reduced power and began a descent. The object was a DC-3 as big as a house. The major was looking right at it. I stuck the nose down some more to make sure we passed well beneath it. He looked at me.

"What are you doing?" he shouted, as though I was holding up a bank.

"I'm going under that airplane there," I said pointing.

His head snapped around, and he jumped as if hit by a high-powered cattle prod. He hadn't seen the DC-3, and it scared the hell out of him. He grabbed the controls, screaming, "I got it!" and banked sharply to the left, turning us belly-up to the DC 3—exactly what my instructor had told me never to do.

Rankin said, "If you put your belly up to the other airplane you lose sight of him, and now you've just put yourself in a position where you know there's another airplane close to you, but you don't know where he is. That's pretty scary. He could be turning right into you and you wouldn't know it until you roll out and look again, and have a nice surprise as you collide."

When the major rolled out of his turn, he was looking all around, shouting in a total panic, "Where is he? Where is he!"

I said, "He's behind us, sir." Which he was. The DC-3 was plodding along at the same altitude and same airspeed and was by now almost out of our area. Frogface turned the airplane back toward Woodring.

"You just flunked this checkride, mister!" he said with venom.

I sat in stunned silence. The major called for landing, and never offered to turn the plane back over to me. I could not believe what had happened. That airplane was as big as a barn, but the major had not seen it.

The major was red, smoking with anger. "I don't give a rat's ass if your daddy was a big, hotshot pilot, or your whole family is just waiting for you to pin on those flight wings. You blew this ride out the window. I'm tired of you spoiled brats coming up here and thinking you can breeze through this program without half trying just because Daddy was a general."

I wanted to tell him my daddy was a Stearns County farmer and my whole family had no idea what flight wings were, but I held my peace. As we flew along, every few minutes he erupted with, "I'll be damned." Whenever he said it, I wished fervently that he was right.

After we parked, the major got out and made a beeline for the flight shack, leaving me to do the post flight, which I did with the speed of a snail—a slow one. I was not eager to go inside. The crew chief came over and asked me how my flight was, and said sarcastically that he was relieved the new tire held up. I knew he didn't think the tire change had been necessary, and normally we would have had a good laugh about it, but I was too down to laugh.

By the time I got back inside, the major had already filled out the grade slip and slapped it down in front of Rankin. He had already told Rankin it was the worst checkride he had ever been on. He had given me an overall grade of "U" (unsatisfactory, flunked, failed, bombed), and had plastered the grade slip with angry red marks, including a line in the remarks-section that read, "Student failed to call out a bogie in his area and he attempted to pass less than 500 feet from the other aircraft."

We all knew this procedure. If any pilot sees another aircraft in the sky he calls it out. "Bogie twelve o'clock" meant there was something in the air straight ahead that might require evasive action as it got closer. The major had given me a U for forced landings. He had also given me a U for power-on stalls, which we never did. And the major did not mention on my grade slip that our DC-3-bogie was on his side of the plane, and that he had been looking right at it, and that the student had every reason to think the major was waiting for the student to make a mistake. Any other instructor would have said, "Bogie at two o'clock," and let the student take the proper precautions.

I made no attempt to tell my side of this story, because I knew it would make me sound like a whiner, and whatever I said would be contradicted by the major, and his word would stand. Before he left, he told me he was sending me up for an elimination ride, and he added (and I quote): "I can tell you right now, you will never make it through this program!"

I thought that was unprofessional behavior for an Air Force officer in charge of a flying school. I think the major must have soiled himself on that checkride, and he was angry I had witnessed his unprofessional panic. The major had also revealed a profound bigotry against "spoiled brats." True, there was occasionally an Air Force brat who entered the program for the wrong reason. He might have felt compelled to keep up a family tradition, or he wanted to impress the girls and figured, "how hard can it be to fly a stupid airplane?" He may have breezed through college cheating on tests and copying term papers. But those guys stuck out like sore thumbs in training. They didn't last long. They washed out at OTS, or ROTC, or the Academy. Or they quit on their own when they realized it was going to be work.

Rankin said, "Looks like you had yourself a really bad case of checkitis."

Checkitis was the term used to describe choking on a checkride. I said nothing. I just sat and stared glumly at the wall. An elimination ride meant if you failed the ride, you were out of the program. The end. Game over. The pressure on a checkride was bad enough, but on an elimination ride it was astronomical.

Rankin said, "Don't worry, you'll pass your elimination ride. This grade slip does not reflect your ability. You must have really upset the major."

"How the hell am I going to pass? Do you think he's going to cool off and be a nice guy tomorrow? You know he'll flunk me."

Rankin smiled, "He can't fly with you."

"Why not"

"The man that flunks you can't give you the elimination ride. There has to be a second opinion."

A glimmer of hope. That meant Lieutenant Coady might be my check pilot. But what good was that? The major would talk to him. A first lieutenant would not go against a major.

I got no sleep that night. I spent the entire night not studying, not going over flight procedures. I had no time for that. I was too busy murdering Frogface. I invented all kinds of clever ways to rig his airplane with dynamite so he went spiraling in and died in a ball of fire. As the night advanced that kind of death no longer sufficed. Now the major started his death spiral at twenty thousand feet so he had plenty of time to think about his sins as he augered in, and now he crashed into a lake so there was no fire. After much suffering, he finally dragged his bloody body onto the shore, where a pack of wolves ate him.

I got on the bus next morning to go to Woodring and a fellow student, Lieutenant Doubrava, said, "You look like shit."

"That's exactly how I feel," I said.

Rankin was waiting at the flight shack. "You got Coady," he said with a smile.

Lieutenant Coady had a good reputation as a check pilot. He was not exactly a Santa Clause but he was easy to fly with and was fair in his grading. I had never heard a bad word about him, even from a student he had flunked. Coady came to my table, returned my salute and sat down. He spent a good twenty minutes going over maneuvers in a calm, reassuring voice, interlacing his briefing with: "Just fly like you have been with Rankin. No sweat. I don't expect miracles. Relax, let's have some fun up there. Rankin says you're good at landings. Show me a couple of those, and you'll be fine."

When I was walking to the airplane with him I had the feeling if I did a half-ass decent job in the area and made a couple of good landings, I would pass the ride. That much I felt I could do.

And so it was. Everything was different. Everything relaxed. We did a few turns, some slow flight, and then advanced to the more complicated maneuvers. I knew when the forced landing was coming because it was all that was left, and I saw Coady looking around on the ground for a good field before he pulled the power. We were back in the pattern early at Woodring with plenty of time to spare. But I felt the pressure again when I did my landings. I knew Coady expected a lot of me there. I wondered if he noticed how my hand trembled as I reached for the flap lever.

After I had done several landings, Coady said, "I got it, and took the plane to pattern altitude." I felt a bit sick. I wondered if he was thinking of flunking me.

As we climbed out, he said, "Okay, Lieutenant Bloch, you have passed your checkride, but we have a little time to kill, so you can shoot two or three landings just for the fun of it."

I will forever be grateful to Coady for that sentence. I relaxed. I made the best landings ever. The wind was almost calm, and there was nothing to it. I kept the nose up and let the stall warning horn beep before I touched down. I held the nose up and lowered it only as I added power. I was doing everything just right. My hand did not shake when I put up the flaps.

"Let's do a no-flap, full stop," said Coady.

"Yes, sir."

I was in heaven. I knew Coady did not have to fudge to pass me.

Chapter Twenty-Four

I N ONLY A FEW DAYS I had completely forgotten about Major Frogface. Only one thing could have accomplished that feat—I was flying a jet now. I was flying with an ejection seat and a parachute like a real fighter pilot, steering the thing with a real fighter-pilot stick instead of a funny wheel. The major was gone from my mind, as far away as Dracula in Transylvania. I hardly ever saw him around the base, and he rarely came to the O Club. However, months later, I did have a short encounter with him one night while drinking at the O Club. I'll get to that.

The transition from T-41 to T-37 began while we were still in the T-41 program. We spent half of our days in academics and the other half flying. Many of the academic classes were aimed more at flying the jets than the props. Some classes were about flying in the clouds (IFR), which we did not do in the T-41. Some were about the effects of high altitudes (like 20,000 feet, where you won't find any T-41s). I had no trouble in academics. I knew how to study, and I knew how to take those multiple-choice tests.

Some of the academic training was entirely new to me. Have you ever heard of a Barney chair? The purpose of this torture device was to show us not to trust our senses when flying in the clouds. Senses will betray you, and your misplaced trust will kill you. The chair was mounted on a pivot so it could be spun like a top. They tied us to the chair with a strong belt so we could not jump out and go crashing about the room when we were sure we were falling and would grab at anything to steady ourselves. There was a railing around the chair for the same reason.

The blindfolded student is put in the chair. The sergeant gives the chair a spin—not much, a slow turn will do the trick. After spinning for a while, the sergeant puts a light finger on the railing to slowly stop the chair. The student is unaware he is stopped. He becomes convinced that he is falling into eternity, and he claws at the railing and hangs on for dear life as his buddies roar with laughter. It is done again with the student bending forward, and when he is told to sit up, he gets even crazier, trying to save myself by clawing at the sky. The reader will not believe this until he has done it himself. It is a fright to watch and certainly frightful to be the one in the chair. I would have clutched a red hot poker to save myself. I learned that the inner ear can play horrendous tricks on you. The illusion is called "spatial disorientation." They made a believer out of me: your senses can lie. When flying in the clouds trust your aircraft attitude indicator—not your feelings.

They put us into a little "altitude chamber" and sealed the door by cranking a wheel like on the vault in a bank. We wore our helmets with oxygen masks dangling at one side. They pumped the air out of that room to let us know what it feels like to be at fifteen, twenty-five, thirty, thirty-five thousand feet. They showed us how to "clear your ears" (equalize the pressure between the air in your inner ear and the chamber air). This was done by pinching the nose, holding your mouth shut, and exhaling air into the middle ear thru the Eustachian tubes. The maneuver was called "valsalva."

They let us breathe the thin air in the chamber until our lips and fingernails were turning blue, and some were passing out. Then they allowed us to don our masks and suck pure oxygen to show how fast that could cure the problem. That low-oxygen condition is called hypoxia. They taught us how to recognize our own particular symptoms of the onset of hypoxia so we would go for the oxygen before we passed out in an airplane. My main symptom was a tingling in the legs. I could feel that long before I felt any fuzziness in the brain. This feeling may have saved my life many years later when I was flying at Flight Level 240 in a Merlin for the DEA. I felt that tingling and remembered. I checked my gauges and started an immediate, fast descent when I realized the pressurization in the plane had failed.

Part of our academic training was called "egress." We learned how to bail out of an airplane. They issued us a parachute with all kinds of cool gear like flares, lights, a radio, a signaling mirror, and condoms. They showed us how to use all that stuff, including how to use the condoms for water storage and for making floating devices. Captain Curry said the condoms were there in case you landed out on the prairie where there were friendly antelope, and you got lonely—whatever that meant. They also issued us a big orange pocket knife they called a "cut-four knife." The knife had a hooked blade (the cut-four blade). If you bailed out of your airplane and were floating down toward the earth, you were supposed to reach up and grab four of the parachute risers (the strings leading up to the canopy) and cut them with that hook. Yes, you read that correctly. This was supposed to help you guide yourself away from hazards on the ground (such as the burning airplane you had just jumped out of). But something in the back of my mind told me that if I was ever floating down serenely to earth under a good canopy, I would be satisfied not to attempt any improvements. The idea of cutting perfectly good risers seemed an insult to the guy who designed the chute.

The T-41 did not have an ejection seat; it didn't need one. It is far safer to land than to bail out of a light aircraft. You need altitude and speed to make a safe ejection, and those commodities were not readily available in the T-41. I liked the idea of gliding down to a farmer's field and landing peacefully among the scattering cattle much better than the idea of jumping out of an airplane with a parachute. There was a powerful explosive shell under that T-37 ejection seat. When you ignited the thing, it drove you out of the cockpit like a ball from a cannon. They showed us how to sit straight so you did not bust your spine when the shell went off. They showed us how to keep legs and arms in close to the body so they did not get ripped off. That kind of talk made me nervous. The whole idea of ejecting from a fast-moving craft was disturbing.

We did some parasailing to get used to hanging from a parachute, and then they dragged us behind a pickup truck to show what can happen if you make a parachute landing in a high wind. The wind can keep the parachute canopy open and can drag you along over cactus and barbed wire fences until you wish you had stayed with your burning plane. They hooked you to the pickup truck with a rope that ran from a clevis on the truck hitch to your parachute harness. You started out on your belly. They tromped on the gas until you were bouncing along behind like a rag doll and then, at a signal from the instructor, you had to flip yourself over on your back, reach up with both hands, and undo the two quick-release snaps at your shoulders. This had to be done while you were careening over rocks and bumps in a pasture, and it was easy to flip yourself too far and be back on your belly instead of your back. It was even easier to miss one or both of the quick-release snaps as you grabbed for them. The pickup kept right on going without mercy until you got free. That exercise did not improve my attitude about ejecting.

And then Captain Curry added more. He pointed out that in the T-37 the ejection seat and parachute were actually worthless at low altitudes and airspeeds. If you were below 1,000 feet and at less than 200 knots of airspeed, the chances your chute would open before you smashed into the ground were small. So if you caught fire on final approach, you might as well stay with the burning plane, because you're going to die anyway jumping out. I did not like that kind of talk. Curry piled on some more: If you're trying to bail out of the T-37 and your ejection system fails, you blow off the canopy, invert the airplane, trim full forward, and drop out. That is, if you still have control. If you are unable to invert, climb out onto the wing and dive off the trailing edge. I did not like that kind of talk, either.

But the lure of flying a jet was so intense that no matter how many different ways they revealed that the thing might kill me, I brushed it all off as nothing compared to the privilege of flying it. I forgot all about those things as I walked out to that sleek, shiny jet airplane with my instructor, flight helmet in one hand and parachute hooked nonchalantly over one shoulder, while overhead in the blue sky T-37s and T-38s pitched out and throttled back as they came in for their landings. The smell of the jet fuel, the roar of the engines, the *squeak, squeak* of tires on the runway—all a thrill. Now I was flying a machine that was not pulled by a corkscrew prop, but shoved through the air by exploding fire. It did not make that anemic *put, put* sound of a cylinder engine, but the commanding roar of jet propulsion.

The transition from T-41 to T-37 was by no means smooth for me. And it wasn't just that the speed was three times as fast. There were also all kinds of new buttons and switches and guages to get used to. In the T-41 I could adjust the seat forward and back to get the right distance from the rudder pedals. In the T-37 the seat was fixed. A crank brought the rudder pedals forward or back. When I first got in, I would, from habit, reach around for a seat lever. The only lever to be found down there was the ejection lever and, if you reached for that, the IP (instructor pilot) would explode and give you a most remarkable cussing, and he would vow that if you ever reached for that again, except to extract the safety pin, he would tear your arm off and beat you with it. And if your IP was Captain Simmons, he would embroider the thing so strong the cockpit would smell of brimstone and sulfur for a week.

As I first tried to taxi the T-37, I made a fool of myself. No, I should say they made a fool of me. They had just given us thirty hours in the T-41, which has no nose-wheel steering. When we had that figured out, they put us in an airplane that *has* nose-wheel steering. The T-37 nose-wheel steering was connected to the rudder pedals, engaged with a button on the stick. But when the wind tried to turn the T-37, I didn't remember that button. Suppose your nose wants to go left. You feed in right rudder as you were taught in the T-41. It keeps going left. You stomp on that right rudder with all your might. It keeps going left. Then you remember: ah, nose wheel steering! You press the button, and before you know it, you are running off the taxiway to the right, because you just called for a hard right turn when you engaged the button with full right rudder.

In flight the rudder played havoc again. Having trained us in the T-41 to stomp around on the rudder every time we made a little turn or added power in slow flight, they now put us into an airplane where never more than the slightest touch of rudder was needed. Captain Simmons shouted, "Quit horsing around with that rudder! Where the hell did you ever get that idea?"

Captain Simmons was my T-37 IP. He was a bit volatile, but I must say he never yelled at me without my deserving it. We did basically the same maneuvers as in the T-41, but it was like starting over. For one thing, we had two engines instead of one, which meant twice as many gauges to monitor. Any time there were two dials next to each other or two switches in the same area, I was bound to get them mixed up. Simmons took most of it calmly, but he got emotional whenever I dropped the speed brakes while trying to make a radio call. The slide switch for the speed brake and the button for the com radio were both on the right throttle. They in no way resembled each other in look or feel, but that did not stop me. The speed brake was a little door on the belly of the plane that hinged out and slowed you down fast. We used it mostly in landings. I used it mostly by mistake at first. I have to wonder what I would have been like trying to transition into a modern fighter, that has stick and throttle bristling with an infinite number of switches. A typical fighter pilot today has on his throttle a switch for radar, autopilot, radar antenna, weapons system, speed brakes, radio frequency, missile, chaff, flares and whatnot. On his stick he has switches for nose wheel steering, unlocking air-to-air missiles, machine gun, bombs, trim, sensor control, weapons selection, and . . . well, ask one of them. If I had been transitioning into a craft like that, I would have bombed every farm in west Oklahoma while searching for the radio button to ask for landing.

The higher speed was a definite problem at the beginning. The traffic pattern took seconds instead of minutes, and we flew them overhead like real pilots do. We came smoking down the runway to about the halfway point, wracked it into sixty degrees of bank while throttling back to sixty percent power on the tach, rolled out on downwind, dropped speed brakes, gear down at 150 knots, flaps at 135, turn, and before you know it, we were on final, and then on the runway in an exhilarating few seconds. The briefing room constantly echoed with instructors admonitions of "think fast, think ahead." And they would say, "You'll never fly this airplane if you don't stay ahead of it." Or as Simmons told me, "You can't park this airplane on downwind and think things over like you could in the T-41." (Simmons never flew the T-41. He didn't know any better.)

My biggest mistake in the T-37 was my refusal to add power on time. I could not get it through my thick skull that it took over ten seconds for those engines to spool up from idle to full power. Imagine those ten seconds: shove your imaginary throttles forward and count off one-thousand-one, one-thousand-two, up to ten. That's a long time! And if you are low on airspeed and altitude, it is an eternity. You had to start adding power way before you needed it. The J-69 engine of the T-37 was of the old centrifugal flow design, not the axial flow of later jets, and it took its sweet old time responding. As solo time approached Simmons yelled at me more and more about my power control. One day on final, when I was low on airspeed, adding dainty little increments of power and hoping that would do, he took the airplane from me, shoved in full power for a go-around and shouted, "Block, your name describes your fuckin' head." I wanted to tell him that yelling doesn't work for me. I wanted to tell him to be like Lieutenant Coady, but I didn't. You never criticized your IP.

But again luck was with me. Captain Tiggeman was a senior IP. He had only two students because he had a lot of administrative duties. One of those students, Lieutenant Ceffalo, required little of his time because he was the best stick in the class. He got an "excellent" on most of his flights. Simmons had four students and they were all of my caliber, so he had his hands full. They switched me over to Tiggeman for a while before solo, which helped me a lot.

The source of almost all my problems in flight training was that I was trying too hard. I wanted to do everything just right. I wanted more than anything to please my instructor, and if he yelled at me it only added to the pressure and the stress. I did worse instead of better. When I went out with Tiggeman the first time I was nervous, because he was a stranger to me. But Tiggeman was relaxed and easygoing—sleepy, compared to Simmons. Some instructors would "sabotage" the plane while students were busy with the checklist. They would pull circuit breakers and throw switches into unusual positions to see if you would catch them as you went through the checklist. Tiggeman never did that. He pretended not to pay attention as I went through the checklist in the chocks. He was looking around and humming to himself and drumming his fingers on the canopy rail. Sometimes he mumbled to himself. Once he yawned and said, "Ach, I shoulda got more sleep last night." And when I said, "Starting number one," and gave the crew chief the start signal, Tiggeman pointed up in the sky and said, "Hey, Bloch, look at that guy losing altitude in the pitch. See how sloppy that looks."

I said, "Yes, sir," and went on with starting the engine.

I knew Tiggeman was watching me closely, but just the fact that he cared enough to pretend he wasn't, made me feel good. I relaxed. I nailed my airspeed in the climb-out that morning. We were early so I got tower's permission to stay in the pattern and I rolled out on downwind exactly on altitude and 150 knots, right by the book. When I dropped the speed brakes and trimmed back, Tiggeman leaned forward in front of me, raised my sun visor and, knocking on top of my helmet, aid, "Is that Ceffalo in there?" He was telling me in a roundabout way that I was doing a good job, something I rarely got from Simmons (which was because I rarely did). When we went to the area to do our air work, Tiggeman kept up his lackadaisical humming. At one point he said, "Did you ever hear 'Soup and Onions' by Roy Meriwether?"

I said, "No, sir." And Tiggeman kept on humming.

If I asked him which maneuver I should do next, he would say, "I don't know. I'm just a passenger in here." He went on humming.

After Tiggeman had filled out my grade slip and gone over all the maneuvers, he said, "Bloch, you think slow, but you think right. Trust yourself and you won't have any trouble soloing."

I thought that over. It wasn't that my thinking was slow, but that I did not trust my decisions and vacillated back and forth before taking action. I needed to trust my judgment and act immediately. I think Simmons had tried to tell me that once, when he said, "You have to have a fuck-it-all attitude to be a good pilot."

A few days later I was scheduled with Tiggeman for my initial solo in the T-37. In the initial solo flight, you went up with the instructor and shot at least three good landings. He got out and you shot at least three more on your own while he watched and listened in the radio shack. On an initial solo you did not get many chances to redo bad landings, because if you ran through a lot of fuel in the dual part, there was not enough left in the tanks for solo. In that case you flunked. And if, while you were solo, you scared the hell out of your instructor at the radio shack, you also flunked.

I had over 1,700 pounds of fuel when Tiggeman got out. I could have done five or six landings on my own, but I got into trouble. I had made one touch and go and was on my second one. I slowed her on downwind with throttle and speed brakes like normal. I threw down the gear, checked the three green lights.

I radioed, "Caesar Six Four, gear check, initial solo," just like everything was normal. But it was not! I was holding an unusual amount of back pressure on the stick. I kept flicking forward on the trim button, but it only got worse as I wobbled around on final trying to figure out what was wrong. I thought maybe my trim was working in reverse, but I never heard of such a thing developing in flight. It could be wired backwards on the ground but we would have noticed that right away. I was feeling very uncomfortable so I shoved in full power and brought up the speed brakes. I cursed my luck. Everything had been going so smoothly! I brought up the gear and I heard tower asking me if there was a problem. I put up the flaps.

"Caesar Six . . . Ceasar Sixty . . . Six-Four, going around," I stuttered on the radio. That sounded foolish since obviously by now they could see I was going around. I knew they were already saying, "What the hell is that idiot up to?"

Well, the idiot now was holding a lot of forward pressure on the stick and unable to trim that off. On downwind I grabbed the stick with both hands and held the trim button full forward. No change. I ran it full aft, no change. And the green trim light, which is supposed to come on whenever the trim tab is in the neutral position, never came on. I had stuck trim. While I was in the middle of doing these checks, the controller called and asked if there was a problem.

I mashed my mike button and said, "One moment please," which is a radio call that caused great mirth for a month, since the proper call was, "stand by." After that, I was often told I should have been a phone secretary. But I had more immediate problems. I didn't bother going to the checklist because I knew what it said for stuck trim: land as soon as possible. I put down gear and flaps, and started my turn onto final.

I called, "Caesar Six-Four, gear check, full stop, stuck trim."

There was silence. Then Tiggeman came on and said, "Caesar Six-Four, confirm you have stuck trim."

I could tell from his voice that he was very skeptical. It made me have my own doubts, but I confirmed. I landed without a problem. When I pulled into the chocks, there stood Tiggeman waiting for me. As soon as I shut down the engines and raised the canopy, Tiggeman leaned into the cockpit, grabbed the stick, and ran the trim forward while he glared at the trim light. Then he ran it the other way, looking back to the tail at the trim tab.

He grinned widely and clapped me on the shoulder. "By golly, you do have stuck trim. That's a new one on me. I've never had stuck trim before."

Yes, I thought, *and why the hell did it have to happen to me, and on my initial solo?* It had never happened before, and during the thousands of hours of flying afterward, it never happened again. As I walked to the flight shack I saw my buddies waiting to throw me into the dunk tank, as was the custom when someone soloed. But Tiggeman, who had advanced ahead of me, waved them off and told them they would have to wait. They threw me in on the sixteenth of February of 1965, when the dunk tank had been standing during a frosty Oklahoma night and had a thin layer of ice on top. I did not mind the dunking. I *did* mind the ribbing I got about that radio call, and for days I blushed like a turkey waddle whenever anyone said with exaggerated inflection, "One moment, please."

The next day, when I returned from a morning flight, Lieutenant Uzzle sat at his desk. His flight suit was wet and he was taking apart his checklist and spreading it out on the table to dry. I was glad to see him wet: he had just soloed. I was glad, because he had been having a problem with his landings. And it again reminded me of what a nice guy Captain Tiggeman was. When I had returned from my initial solo, Tiggeman met me on the ramp to congratulate me.

He said, "Give me your checklist."

I reached down, unzipped the pocket on my suit leg, pulled out the checklist, and handed to him. I thought maybe he was going to autograph it for the occasion, although I had not heard of such a custom. I wasn't thinking of the dunk tank. After they threw me into the water and I staggered into the building, there was Tiggeman.

"I thought you might like to keep it dry," he said as he handed back my checklist.

I DID NOT HAVE a car. I had very few expenses and so money began piling up in the bank. When I had a few hundred dollars, I considered myself rich and began to contrive ways to spend it. Lieutenant Fernandez kept telling me I should buy a car. When I said I didn't have enough money he explained to me that was why banks were there—to lend you money. I went to the bank to see what kind of car I could buy on the salary of a second lieutenant. The banker said he would lend me money for anything. "You can buy yourself the biggest Cadillac in town with all the trimmings." I pointed out that I was only a second lieutenant. "Yes," he said, "But your income is steady and you can't quit your job. Best of all, the Air Force will make sure you live up to your financial obligations. So we know those payments will come rolling in."

My classmates drove sporty cars like Mustangs, Corvettes, Austin Healeys, and MGs. For a while I considered a Pontiac GTO, (I wanted as much horsepower as possible), but my brother said, "You'll kill yourself." Then I almost got a used Chevy 409, a four-speed with dual quads and a prositraction differential, just like in the Beach Boy song. Next I brooded over that 1965 Ford Mustang convertible. I looked and looked. To this day, I cannot believe what I finally bought. The Germans had just come out with the Volkswagen Golf, sold in the U.S. as the Rabbit and was known as the VW Fastback. It was cheap to drive, reliable, and a totally boring car. The Stearns County farmer frugality in me won out. I bought a little blue Fastback.

WE ENTERED THE AEROBATIC phase of training. I learned what it meant to "pull Gs." They had told us about this in physiology class, but you have to pull Gs to know what it means. If you haven't flown in a fast plane (modern jet pilots will laugh to hear me call the T-37 "fast," but I'm comparing it to the T-41, not the F-18), this is another of the things hard to explain, but here goes: When you sit on your couch watching TV, your butt pushes down on the cushion with a force—the force of gravity—one G. When you streak through the sky in a fast plane and make a tight turn, your body wants to continue straight ahead. You're pushed down into your seat by centrifugal force. The sharper the turn, the harder the centrifugal force pushes. That force is also measured in Gs. At sixty degrees of bank, you have to pull two Gs to keep level flight. Your body is twice as heavy as when sitting on the couch.

In class when they told us about how G forces act on one's body during aerobatics, I yawned. We pulled two Gs every day as we did the pitchout for landing. But I did not realize how savagely that force multiplies as we increase it by pulling back on the stick for an aerobatic maneuver. Captain Simmons very effectively enlightened me on that score. He had me do (I mean, attempt to do) a level turn at roughly eighty degrees of bank.

"Pull, pull!" he bellowed, as I increased the bank. "Pull, you're losing altitude! Pull." I got so busy trying to maintain altitude I forgot all about G forces. I forgot about tensing the muscles in my legs and abdomen. Soon something was wrong. I couldn't read the altimeter. I saw only a gray fog in front of my eyes. I groaned out, "I . . . I can't see!"

"I got it," Simmons said, rolling the plane back level. "How do you feel?"

My vision came back. I felt fine again after a couple of breaths, but the force that had driven me into my seat was traumatic and cruel. In hard training maneuvers we might pull above four or even five Gs, and combat pilots pull many more. That downward force causes the blood to drain out of the pilot's head. That's where the brain is (or should be), and the brain needs that blood for oxygen. The lack of oxygen in the brain causes "tunnel vision" so a person can see only in a little circle directly where the eyes are focused. Peripheral vision is gone. Load up some more Gs, and you black out. Fortunately, when you pass out, you automatically release the stick, the blood flow returns, and you're awake again. You can help keep the blood up in the brain by tensing the muscles in your legs, buttocks, and stomach. That way you can tolerate more Gs. In high performance airplanes you wear a G suit, which puts pressure on those muscles for you. I did not like pulling Gs at first. I made up my mind I'd rather watch someone else doing aerobatics while I sat on the ground to see the show.

The last time I flew with Tiggeman was on one of those aerobatic flights. Even pulling Gs, Tiggeman sounded as relaxed as if he sat in his lawn chair. As I pulled up into a loop, groaning under the 3G load, he said casually, "Hey, Bloch, have you seen the movie *Zorba the Greek*?"

As the G-load decreased near the top of the loop I gasped, "No, sir, I haven't."

"Good movie," he said. As I loaded up the Gs again in the dive on the backside, he started to hum the music. Tiggeman always pretended to be enjoying life immensely and paying no attention. But make no mistake: Tiggeman was a professional to the core. He saw every mistake, noted every flaw, and resented every slipshod performance. And when he filled out your grade slip, he remembered every detail. He could flunk you as easily as he could hum "Dixie." He did all that whistling and humming to give you a relaxed atmosphere in the cockpit, but that atmosphere dissipated when he critiqued your flight. I admired that man.

We were never allowed to turn the T-41 upside down, but we did it all the time in the T-37. We did barrel rolls, aileron rolls, loops, Cuban 8s, split Ss, Immelmanns, and spins. We did not have to be proficient in inverted spins, but to pass, we had to show proficiency in the regular spin (the right-side-up kind), so we practiced those almost every time we went to the area. It was hard to make that airplane spin. You had to go to idle and hold the stick all the way back and give it full rudder. The aircraft was so stable it would buck and shudder and wobble for a while before it would finally give up and drop off, twirling around and around and falling like a hunk of lead. The recovery was always the same. There was no feel involved, it was totally mechanical: *throttles idle, controls neutral, stick abruptly move full aft; determine direction of spin, full opposite rudder; one turn later, stick abruptly full forward; recover from the ensuing dive*—I can still do it in my sleep. It worked every time.

I was lucky. I never got sick. I could eat or drink anything before climbing into the airplane to do aerobatics. Full stomach, empty stomach—it made no difference. This was a big advantage. Some guys threw up. Some were washed out because they got sick every time. Others just somehow adjusted to it. They ate handfuls of Tums before they went up. Some secretly took pills for motion sickness. Some starved themselves for hours beforehand. One of my buddies (he graduated high in our class) told me just putting on his oxygen mask made him queasy.

I often wondered what it was like to live among the sand dunes of west Oklahoma and look up every day to see airplanes spinning around in the sky, doing aerobatics, flying in formation, diving and climbing and rolling among the clouds. It must have seemed like the jolliest thing to be a pilot. They would never have imagined men were up there graying out, redding out, and throwing up. They could never suspect the hard work, the stress, and the sweat in those maneuvers.

We had to take a checkride to make sure we were proficient in aerobatics, stall recoveries, and in the different traffic patterns, including doing patterns and landings on one engine. When we passed that ride, we started on instruments. There I found my niche. I felt great relief when I could fly the plane without constantly having to survey the big sky for other planes. My IP was responsible for that. I was tired of hearing: "Keep you nose out of the cockpit, head on a swivel, head on a swivel, goddamnit." All I had to do was take care of those few little instruments in front of my face. If the sky was clear, they made us strap a hood on our helmets so it blocked out all but the instrument panel.

In the T-41 we had to have a ceiling at several thousand feet and five miles visibility to fly. Now we needed only 200 feet and a mile. Now we flew "in the weather"—rain, fog, clouds, snow. When I first flew in fog or in a cloud (it's really the same thing) I was struck by the insanity of it all. Here I was bolting through the sky at hundreds of miles an hour, and I couldn't see two feet in front of my airplane. It was scary to think I might be closing on a radio tower, a mountain, or an Air Force Tanker. But in a short time I realized the grown-ups had this all figured out with navigation aids and flight plans, so there was no danger. Then it was fun.

We got a few hours of formation in the T-37, but we did not have to pass a checkride. It was mostly orientation for the real thing in the T-38. It was quite a shock. After spending months yelling at me about staying away from other airplanes and almost eliminating me for getting too close to a DC-3, now suddenly they yelled at me for not getting close enough. Captain Simmons demonstrated the wing position. The closer he got to lead's right wing, the farther I leaned away. Suddenly Simmons punched me in the shoulder and said, "Relax, damn it. Quit trying to climb into the seat with me."

In May, I had my final checkride in the T-37. The check pilot went over the maneuvers with me, pointing out all the things I'd screwed up. Then he pushed the filled-out grade slip in front of me. He had given me an Excellent! I was proud as a ruffed grouse on a drumming log. I was prouder of that Excellent than all the A's I ever got in college. (Well, okay, there weren't all that many. I'll include the B's.) I didn't tell anyone. When someone asked how I did on the check ride, I said, "I passed." That answer was interpreted as getting a Good or a Fair. But the next morning Simmons made it public. He came to his table, returned the salute of his students, and then said, "Yesterday, the third of May, was a lucky day. It was my birthday, and Bloch aced his checkride."

The real payoff came the next Friday night at the officers club. I was sitting at a table with the other bachelors of our flight. We had just ordered a round of beer and were settling in for some a serious Friday night drinking. I noticed Lieutenant Coady at one of the tables with a group of people. I longed to tell him about my checkride, but didn't have the guts to walk over there and disturb his company. And I certainly didn't want to act like a braggart and say, "Hey, I aced my checkride." But I wanted him to know that passing me on that T-41 elimination ride was justified. After a while Coady went to the bar. I saw my chance. I elbowed in next to him and ordered a round of beer and then pretended to see him for the first time.

I said, "You probably don't remember me. I'm Lieutenant Bloch."

"Why, sure I remember you," he said. "How do you like flying the T-37?"

I told him I had just passed my final check, and I got an Excellent. Well, he grabbed my hand and shook it until I thought it might come off. And later that night, as I sat drinking and trading flying lies with my buddies, the bartender set a beer in front of me.

He said, "It's from Lieutenant Coady."

Chapter Twenty-Five

THERE IT STOOD on the Vance AFB ramp—as cool a piece of flying machinery as had ever been invented. It looked like Mach One just sitting in the chocks. The lines of that plane were a streaking, screaming work of supersonic art. It looked like a fighter, a rocket, a guided missile. The Northrop T-38 Talon. Just to give an idea what a step up it was from the T-37: it had two J-85 engines, each muscling your ass through the air with 3,850 pounds of thrust (the T-37's J-69s gave an anemic nudge at barely over one thousand pounds). This was a hot plane. It set speed and climb records when it first flew.

There was no finer sight in Oklahoma than a T-38 take-off: She rolls into position at the head of the runway, nav lights flashing, heat waves shimmering from her twin pipes. She sits there a moment shivering under the strain of full military power as the pilot goes through the run-up check—her whole frame trembling with eagerness for the sky. With a sudden jerk as the pilot jumps off the brakes, she is rolling. Slowly at first, then rapidly accelerating before the blue flame of the afterburner, and soon melting into a blur of speed down the runway. Now she is airborne and she sits on her tail reaching for the sky. In seconds she's beyond the range of the ordinary eye, flying in the serene, supersonic sight of the Almighty.

Excuse that gaudy bit of syrupy coloring, but no pilot can approach this plane without slobbering. It was certainly a giant step up from the T-37. You needed a ladder to climb in. Now, that was more like it! Real fighter pilots don't step into a plane like we did into the T-37, where you felt you were sitting in a hole, and the crew chief looked down on you as he helped you strap in. Here we hooked a ladder to the side, climbed up several steps, and lowered ourselves into a narrow cockpit entirely surrounded by levers, switches, dials, handles, toggles, and buttons. And some of those were controls for air conditioning. God be praised! (We did not have that in the T-37.) And also for pressurization, alleluia! (Also not in the T-37.) This was luxury at its finest. The instructor sat behind you in a completely separate cockpit. He could not pound his fist on your knee to emphasize a point, or bang you upside the helmet to get your attention.

Supersonic! Just the word gave me chills. The nose of this slick beauty was narrow and sleek and had little resistance as it moved through the air. We could go faster than the speed of sound. And it had burner! Yes, twin afterburning engines to kick your ass out of any trouble you could fly yourself into. It had TACAN for navigation instead of VOR. It had a genuine ILS (instrument-landing system) with a guide bar, even! The ejection seat had a rocket tied to it so we could bail out at "zero, zero" (zero airspeed, zero altitude). You had to have an APU (auxiliary power unit) to start the thing, just like a real fighter plane. And we got to wear that badge of the fighter pilot: the G suit. Since it had the same airframe as USAF's F-5 Freedom Fighter, we could claim we were flying a fighter. T-38 students in the bars with the girls at midnight often humbly acknowledged that yes, indeed, they were true fighter pilots. (Girls didn't notice the Air Force wings missing from the uniform.) We took great pride in flying the T-38 and often thought it unfair we would get paid for this kind of "work." *If I crash,* I thought, *I'll die happy.*

And we could look down our noses at T-37 students. Their machines were "lumber wagons." Now we noticed the irritating, high, ear-piercing whine of the J-69 compressors. We called it "the six thousand-pound dog whistle," "the tweety bird," a "kerosene-burning siren," or "The Converter" (fuel into noise). Any derogatory name would do. We noticed for the first time the sound radiating from a T-37 on the taxiway was about the same as having all your little sisters screaming in your ears. Inside the T-38, all was quiet.

Only one thing could make a stubby-winged dart like this fly: speed. That's what made it thrilling—and dangerous. When approaching a stall in most airplanes, you had plenty of warning. They shuddered, buffeted and blew a stall warning horn. But the T-38's warning was subtle enough a greenhorn could miss it. When my IP, Lieutenant Raynes, first took me up in the T-38, he had me climb her high in the sky. He said, "Reduce the power to idle, but hold your altitude. Keep that nose up. Wings level. Hold her, hold her, hold her."

I could feel a little shaking, the controls got sloppy, and I was struggling to hold the wings level. I was waiting for a sign of a full stall.

Then Raynes said, "Okay, look at your vertical velocity."

God almighty! It showed a hell-dive—pegged on the downside. We were falling like a brick. The altimeter needle unwound like a windmill. We had completely stopped flying, were free falling, yet I could hardly tell. I'll remember that forever. If we had been anywhere near the earth we would have died in a ball of fire. This was no plane for amateurs. We were now in the big leagues.

The T-38 had some minor drawbacks. Icing conditions grounded it. Winter in Oklahoma had plenty foggy, drizzly days near freezing when ice formed on the leading edges of planes as they moved through the air. That kind of ice, breaking off and getting sucked into the engines, could wipe out compressor blades. You couldn't fly in icing or anywhere near forecast icing; or, as Lieutenant Huff used to say, "Don't even whisper 'icing' anywhere near the intakes."

After spending months merrily spinning around in the T-37, and having memorized half a page of the checklist as the spin recovery procedure, it was distressing to read the checklist spin procedure for the T-38. It simply said EJECT. That was it! If you somehow ham-handed your way into a spin, your only option was to bail out. You made no attempt to recover. The same was true if we lost both engines and couldn't get a restart. No "establish best glide speed" or "look for a suitable field." You just bailed out. In the T-37, we could glide for a mile and a half with a thousand feet of altitude. We had no best glide speed in the T-38 either. I think it was 260 KIAS, which basically meant: point the nose down and glide like a rock. If you spend time establishing anything or looking for a place to land—*bam!*—you've already landed.

MY INSTRUCTOR WAS First Lieutenant Raynes (later Captain Raynes), but I flew many missions with First Lieutenant Huff. Lucky again. It was fun to fly with Huff. Like Tiggeman, he had a talent for keeping a relaxed atmosphere in the cockpit. He too sang, though he liked a different kind of music. While Tiggeman was likely to hum Beethoven's "Ode to Joy," Huff was likely to beller out Porter Wagner's "Dooley" song about making moonshine. Huff was a joker. The first time I flew with him, as I was checking over my parachute, he said, "By the way, Bloch, if you ever hear me scream 'Bail out!' Don't ask why. You'll be talking to yourself."

There was a strict protocol for the establishment of communication between the cockpits. When we first plugged in our radio cord and threw on the master switch, we adjusted our mouthpiece, and said, "How do you read, sir?" The IP answered, "Loud and clear." If we didn't get that answer, we checked the switches and connections, and tried again. But when Huff was in the cockpit behind me, and I said, "How do you read, sir?" I was likely to hear a "burrrrrup" as he belched loudly into the mike. That was all. On occasion he might add, "Did ch'ya get that, Bloch?" When I said, "Yes, sir, loud and clear," he would say, "Well then, I reckon we have us a connection."

There was a definite backwoods twang about him, and he expressed himself in peculiar ways. "You see that little fuzzy bar that comes out there when you throw that there guide-bar switch?" (Talking about the guide bar on the ILS).

"Yes, sir."

"Now, that bar just hypnotizes some students. They think it's the greatest thing since sliced bread. They sit there and stare at it, while altitude and airspeed go to shit. You're not going to do that. You're going to watch your attitude indicator along with altimeter and airspeed, and only keep that bar in a corner of your eye. Do you think you can do that, Bloch?"

"Yes, sir."

"You promise you'll do it?"

"Yes, sir."

"You swear on the Dash-1?"

There was no such thing as an aircraft operator's manual; the book was called the Dash-1. It was our bible while in training. No book was as important as the Dash-1. When the weather kept us from flying, the IPs (both T-37 and T-38) entertained themselves by asking questions to see how well we had it memorized. That included plenty of questions of no value to a pilot, like the rotation rate of the T-37's J-69 engine (21,730 RPM—I remember it to this day). You had to know exactly how many quarts of oil your airplane held, even though it was not anticipated you might ever in your life have to change the oil. I didn't even know how many quarts of oil my car held, and I did change its oil.

When flying with Huff, if I pulled a little too hard on the entry into a loop or barrel roll, Huff would make a loud farting noise in his mike. Then he would say, "Hey, watch those Gs, I had beans for breakfast!"

Sometimes as we came smoking in on initial, shortly before the pitch, Huff would say, "Pretty darned good flight there, Bloch buddy. Now, if you don't fuck up the landing, we'll get along just fine in the post-flight briefing."

And Huff had courage. He never "rode the stick." That is, he didn't override my throttle and stick inputs with his own when I wasn't doing something just right. Huff would let me screw it up. I had to figure out for myself how to fly out of trouble. This was a great advantage for me. Some of my buddies complained their instructor was always riding the stick. It was hard to get the feel of an airplane that way. This was an especially valid complaint in the T-38, because it had hydraulic controls, and it was harder to get the feel of that thing to start with.

SOMETIMES WE HAD to pull RSU (radio supervisory unit) duty. The RSU was also called the "radio shack" or "mobile unit," a moveable glass shack that stood by the head of the active runway and was manned by two instructors and two students. It was equipped with radios, flare guns, and signal lights. You had to have permission from that unit to do anything on their runway.

Instructors ran the radios. They were the bosses of the runway. They "rogered" calls, approved takeoffs, approved or denied requests for closed patterns, gave landing instructions, cleared aircraft for landing, and occasionally sent someone around when they thought his pattern looked dangerous. One student recorded tail numbers and take-off and landing times, while the other did a gear check with binoculars. The Air Force was very worried about someone setting down with landing gear up. When the pilot lowered his gear, he had to check for three green gear-down lights on his panel (one for each wheel), and report "gear check" in his landing call: "Lightning Two-Zero, gear check, touch-and-go." They didn't trust Lightning Two-Zero. When he rolled out on final, a student put glasses on him and reported "all three wheels down, sir," to make sure.

It required a higher level of skill to solo a T-38 than the other planes. The instructor couldn't risk getting out if you were a little sloppy about airspeed, because you could kill yourself in a second. The afterburners would fly you out of trouble, but only if you recognized the trouble. Some trouble came up suddenly. I was at the RSU doing the gear checks one morning. Lieutenant Shaffer was in the pattern on his initial solo. Shaffer was a top stick. It was an unusually quiet day—not a breath of wind—ideal for an initial solo. But on still days, the jet wash sometimes lingered over the runway. Normally the wind quickly blew it away. Flying into someone's jet wash, was like flying into a horizontal tornado. Shaffer called "gear check." I confirmed with the glasses. I followed him with the glasses down final, smooth as silk all the way. As he flared for his landing, suddenly his plane rolled sharply to one side as he hit the jet wash of the plane before him.

"Sir!" I yelled, pointing. The controller was ahead of me, already yelling into the mike, "In the flare, hit the burners!" Off went Shaffer for another try. It wasn't a proper radio call, but no one mentioned that. Shaffer got the message.

I had no trouble on my initial solo except I came in high on my first pattern. As I lined up with the runway, the controller said, "On final go-around." I knew I was high, and he said it so gently I couldn't take offense. They didn't care as long as we didn't screw up the go-around. I felt bad for anyone having trouble soloing. I knew the gut-wrenching fear of failure from my T-41 troubles. Lieutenant Carpenter had problems landing. I liked him, loved his pretty little wife, Linda. When I saw him walking behind the IP to his plane, looking like a beaten dog, I felt like putting an arm on his shoulder and saying everything would be all right. But I never talked to him during that time. It was worthless. All the "you can do it" and the "we're all with you" did nothing to obscure the hideous face of failure. It was a lonely time and we had to fight the battle ourselves. I watched Carpenter silently in his misery and rejoiced when he finally made it.

On Friday night the week after I soloed, I was at the O Club. My instructor that day had been Captain Raynes. We were having a drink at the bar. Normally I wouldn't have assumed the honor of drinking with my instructor, but I owed Raynes a drink. He had bet me I couldn't park the plane's nosewheel perfectly centered on the little round parking spot marked on the ramp for each plane. (That was how the military kept them lined up so perfectly.) When we got out and examined the spot, I tried to argue the nose wheel was centered. Raynes appealed to the crew chief (a friend of his). He sided with Raynes. So I had to buy. Since Raynes was with two other captains, I had to include them. We had just started our drinks when someone squeezed in next to me and yelled at the bartender for two whiskies. I looked. It was none other than old Major Frogface with another major standing behind him. When I looked at Frogface, he looked at me, and I saw recognition flash in his face. I had to say something. I was sure he recognized me in spite of his thick glasses and the low lights in the bar.

I stuttered, "Oh, ah, h-hi, Major. You still, ah, flying T-41s?" It was all I could think of. I said it in a very pleasant tone; I was on top of the world that night. I'd just soloed and was having a drink with my instructor and his buddies, who were like gods to me. The major's jaw muscles got tight, veins stuck out in his neck, and he looked like the day he busted me on my checkride. Without a word he turned and left with his drinks. I looked after him astonished. He couldn't still be mad about my checkride, could he? I was somewhat embarrassed as I turned back to Raynes. I said, "I guess he didn't hear me."

But Raynes said, "Oh, he heard you, all right!" Raynes leaned back and looked at me like he was seeing me for the first time. "Lieutenant Bloch! I didn't know you were such a cold-blooded son-of-a-bitch."

I said, "What? What'd I do?" I said it innocently—no faking. I had no idea. But all three captains were in agreement and they piled on their comments.

"Nice going, Lieutenant."

"You just ruined that major's day."

"Hit him again, Bloch. Kick him in the nuts while he's down."

Finally Raynes, seeing my confusion, cleared it up for me. "Don't you see? With one glance at your shoulder patch he knew you're flying T-38s. He's still in that damn box kite. He'd give his liver to be in your boots. And you go and rub his nose in it—and in front of his friend."

The others agreed. They had a jolly time making fun of the T-41.

"It takes so long to fly downwind, you have to pack a lunch so you don't starve before you turn base."

"I'd rather fly a milk wagon with a plow horse for power."

"I hear the major likes to go down and race with farmers on their tractors."

"You can use that one, Lieutenant, to shoot the major down next time he comes for a drink."

Between each entry, they roared with laughter, sipped, and tried to top the last offering.

"On Sundays the major gets an early flight so he can swoop down and race the old ladies on their way to church."

"I hear that lately he's skipped the ladies and is racing the church."

I was a bit uneasy about all this frivolity, since I supposedly started it. I didn't want anyone to hear how they were abusing the major with me being part of the group. I did not want another run-in with that volcano. I glanced back at the major's table. No one seemed to be paying us any attention.

After that night I never again desired to murder the major. Those captains had done a fine job of it for me.

THE SWEETEST LINE in the T-38 Syllabus of Instruction was this: "No student will be graduated with less than twenty-five hours solo time in the T-38." Twenty-five hours! Alone in the sky in this airplane! Major Alexander had his misgivings about this. He gave us a stern sermon about hot-dogging, screwing off, and taking chances. He was the T-38 flight commander. His phone rang if anyone complained, and it was his butt in a sling if anyone crashed. He trusted that most of us would be out there practicing maneuvers, because we really couldn't afford to goof off. We had checkrides coming. He also knew every once in a while a student got carried away with the exhilaration of solo flight in a supersonic bird. He told us not to go over any towns at low level. He said, "All those housewives are watching their quiz shows and soap operas, and I don't want you guys messing up their TV reception."

In sunlight and starlight I flew that rocket alone. How to describe the thrill, pleasure, and satisfaction? If solitude brings one closer to God, then who's closer than the solo pilot? Monks are never that alone. What is solitude in the shadowy monastic catacombs compared to the lone pilot in the infinite sanctity of space among blessed clouds, and especially at night, riding the rushing wind in the vast solemnity of the stars? There is the absolute, boundless solitude—supreme, peaceful aloneness with God. What are the chantings and hymns compared to the unfaltering hum of the engines, and the ceaseless whisper of air moving over the canopy? Another thing: the glow of gold and green cockpit lights is a darned good imitation of the votive lights that flicker before the Virgin.

But I digress. We couldn't afford to screw off flying solo. Checkrides in the T-38 were harder to pass, and we had more of them. They included checkrides in navigation and formation. The most memorable flight I had was a navigation ride with Raynes. We went cross-country to Salt Lake City and Las Vegas, but the destinations were not the memorable parts. We took off after sunset on a Friday night for a short hop to Albuquerque. We had to climb up above a line of thunderstorms to avoid the turbulence and icing. It was dark by then, and you'd never believe the fireworks taking place below. The air above it was dazzlingly clear and smooth, with stars bright above, and below the long line of mountainous clouds piling up in the darkness. All up and down the line, thunderheads flashed and popped sprays of lightning. An entire mountain would softly flicker, then suddenly light up from top to bottom in a bright glow so we were flying in broad daylight for a second, our nav lights totally eclipsed—and then, just as suddenly, we were back in darkness with the *blink, blink* of our lights strobing along the white surface of the wings. Over and over huge thunderstorms, some with anvil heads, would leap into blinding brightness, then subside into a soft flickering glow. We could see them for hundreds of miles from north of Abilene on the left to way up into Colorado on the right.

The next day on the way to Salt Lake we flew a low-level leg through Monument Valley on the Arizona/Utah border. We dropped down and scooted over barren, rusty sand and did tight turns among the red buttes and mesas, among the cliffs and peaks. We went low over the highway where tourists were parked and pointing cameras at that mystic world, and up at us.

Raynes said, "That's the Three Sisters at nine o'clock. I got it." He took the plane and wracked her around, pointing her right at the three peaks. We closed so quickly, before I knew it he had zoomed between two of the peaks and, pulling up sharply, he did an aileron roll, yelling "Eeeeh haah!" as we climbed. It made me laugh. I still smile when I think about it. Monument Valley was not as beautiful as the thunderstorms, but it was an exciting ride.

EVERY SO OFTEN we received a stark reminder that all was not fun and games. We were preparing for war. Men were getting killed. One day they called us out for a funeral ceremony. We all stood in ranks on the ramp by the runways. Flying had stopped, and the place was deathly quiet. The chaplain gave a short talk by a coffin flown in on a C-130. I heard one of the instructors mumble, "Charlie was a damned good pilot." He had been killed in Vietnam. We were called to attention and given "eyes right," and watched as a four-ship of T-38s in fingertip formation came roaring over. As they approached the coffin, number two lit his burners, stood on his tailpipes and went streaking up into the clouds. The other three held missing-man formation as they passed to the west out of sight. All the women cried; the men squinted as if the sun was too bright. Some of us went with the coffin to the cemetery for the burial. They folded the flag that covered the coffin into a little triangle. An officer gave it to Charlie's mom. When he came to attention and saluted, she didn't see; she was bent over her flag, her shoulders shaking. She made choking noises in her throat.

We didn't dwell on those things. Soon we could hear the whine of compressors as engines were cranking again. By the time we got back to base the usual beehive activity of flying was in full progress. The war must go on.

ANY PILOT WHO has flown in a formation with a group of professional, disciplined pilots will say that nothing—and I mean nothing—compares to the fun of flying a tight formation in a fast airplane—far beyond any car race, parasailing, bungie jumping, or carnival ride. But it is work. On Lead's part, it requires intelligence and foresight, and, above all, smoothness. On Wing's part it requires discipline. IPs took great pride in flying formation correctly. "You're conducting a symphony," Tiggeman once told me about leading a formation. "If you're good, you produce a work of art. If you're not, you produce trash."

I liked flying Wing best. Lead has to do all the planning and clearing. He takes you around the sky in barrel rolls and Cuban eights, dives and zooms, and loops, and switches the formation from fingertip to echelon and to diamond (where you get to blacken your tail in the slot). At the end, when you're coming down initial and Lead calls, "Vance Air Force Base, Blue Flight initial, with four," and then those four pitch out—one, two, three, four in a row—there's nothing like it in the world. You feel an incomparable comradery with your fellow pilots.

Bachelors in our class were automatically with close comrades. The married guys got to live off-base, but we bachelors lived in the battered old BOQ. Actually, I never considered my room anything but luxury until we had a dust storm. The wind came up so fiercely one afternoon they cancelled all flights for the day. Acres of west Oklahoma dust and sand elevated into the sky and hurled against the windows. As Lieutenant Cunningham (who hated Oklahoma even in good weather) and I walked to the BOQ, leaning almost horizontally into the wind and holding one hand up to shield our eyes from the peppering sand, he shouted, "Well, Bloch, how do you like Okla-fucking-homa now?" I'd told him several times I liked it here, but I had to admit this was a bit much. Even shut up in my room at the BOQ, the dust was suffocating. It leaked through every crevice and cranny, every fracture and fissure. By suppertime I could draw pictures in the dust on the table. Wind gusts made the old wooden building creak and groan. Sleep was uneasy that night. Toward morning, the wind stopped. All was quiet. The sun rose, fuzzy red in the murky east. When we got to the flightline, the aircraft parking lot was wet, the aircraft standing in puddles of water like it had just rained. The crew chiefs had been up early, running the fire trucks down the lines to blast the dust from the airplanes.

Any time, you could find a bachelor to study with. I studied a lot with Lieutenant Doubrava. He was a big help. He made the same mistakes I did, but he didn't let it bother him. I'd worry about screw-ups for days. He wasn't bothered by such details. He shrugged off mistakes. "That's why we're here—to learn from our mistakes." Doubrava and I didn't routinely go to the O Club on Friday and Saturday nights. We questioned each other on emergency procedures, ate Swanson's TV dinners, and watched Patrick McGoohan in *Secret Agent* on TV.

Doubrava wasn't the typical student bachelor. He never got drunk, and he went to bed early Sunday nights to be ready for a week of flying. The typical bachelor got up on Monday with a hangover—got into a wrinkled flight suit and stumbled around looking for boots and checklist among dirty laundry on the floor and among empty beer cans, sardine-can ash trays, and stale bags of potato chips left over from Sunday's football games. For breakfast he ate cold pizza off the grimy coffee table or finished a half-eaten can of chili from the fridge. He found his boots (which he forgot to polish), then found he had left the polish can open, and it was dried out, so he spit on the boots and wiped them with a T-shirt from the floor, slipped them on, and headed for the flightline.

If you wanted to find company for dissipation, you could gather a squadron of bachelors in five minutes. When we weren't flying or in the classroom, a group of bachelors most always sat at the club. You didn't need an invite to sit down at a table or at the bar among your buddies. In the evenings some brought girls to the club, friendly girls, groupie girls from Enid, who loved the company of pilots and knew how to have fun. Single secretaries, most were divorced with a kid or two. The girls liked pilots because they were full of swagger, spent money freely and drove fast cars. Pilots didn't have to cruise Enid's Van Buren Street for girls. Girls found them. The girls liked the loud, bragging type the best, and those could always be found at the O Club on a Friday night.

Groupie girls were content to be passed from class to class. The pilots invited them to functions at the O Club. They knew how to treat a pilot, knew how to smile and whisper in your ear. My buddies, having been through this with dozens of girls before, in dozens of backseats, laughed it off. But when a girl got intimate with me, I fell in love, and they laughed at me. I didn't know holding hands, kissing, and whispering "I love you" in cars and parks on moonlit nights was just a game. Tomorrow night she'd be with another.

I complained about this to Ceffalo one day. A few days later Ceffalo's wife set me up with a girl from Phillips University. I'd planned to go snake hunting that Saturday afternoon and was impressed when the girl consented to go along. Groupie girls would have turned me down flat; they wanted to sit at the O Club and drink. We spent the afternoon talking. We admired the long feathers of a scissortail perched on a fencepost and watched him catch grasshoppers among the cactus. We talked of religion and philosophy. By sunset I was in love. She was the smartest girl I'd ever met. I knew she was smarter than I was. That made her extremely attractive. On top of that, she was very pretty and built like an athlete. I dated her regularly at Vance and was proud to bring her to the club. She could talk with anyone about any subject, and was not the least bit in awe of the pilots like the groupies were (or pretended to be). She often made fun of us for wearing our flight suits all the time. She called us "tin soldiers" and at times would make an exaggerated show of coming to attention and making an extravagant, flourishing salute. I thought she was funny. Some of my buddies thought she was a smart aleck.

But I was never distracted from my training. One evening the mission I was to fly was listed in the syllabus as, "Day-Night Out-and-Back (solo)." I drew up my flight plans and went over them with Captain Raynes.

He signed off on them, saying, "Are you sure you can find your way back?"

Find my way back?! I could do it blindfolded! I didn't tell him that, but that's what I was thinking. I had to fly the "out" part in daylight, and the "back" part in darkness. That night I ate dinner in Burns Flat, Oklahoma, with some B-52 pilots from the Clinton-Sherman Air Force Base. I had chosen Clinton-Sherman because it had the longest runway in the world (over 13,000 feet). I figured I couldn't screw that up. When it was dark I launched out of Clinton-Sherman for my return to Vance via Oklahoma City. I turned north over OKC at Flight Level 185 to a cluster of lights I was sure was Enid, Oklahoma. I had OKC set in the TACAN, but paid it little mind. I knew my way around the sky. I was looking at the stars and checking my gauges and imagining myself quite a pilot. I figured when I got over Enid, I'd get a TACAN penetration and ask for a GCA pickup. If I couldn't get that, I'd shoot the ILS approach. If they didn't approve either of those, I'd just enter on initial and make a normal landing. I checked the clock, checked the fuel. The engines purred like kittens.

When I arrived over Enid I rolled over on one wing to confirm where Vance was and to see how it looked at night from on high. It wasn't there! I looked on the other side. Oh, no! I had the wrong place! The coldest, ugliest stab of fear shot through me like 220 volts. I was paralyzed with dread. My brain froze into total inactivity. I could barely move my hands. But I had enough brain left to tell me the worst thing I could do was panic. I reminded myself of my navigation skills—although that seemed a mockery at the moment. I knew if worst came to worst, I could call for a DF steer (the ultimate humiliation). A "DF steer" was where the tower told you which way to turn based on the signal they received from your radio transmissions. It was a bitter pill to swallow and unheard of for a T-38 student approaching graduation. I throttled back and made a slow turn as I rechecked the TACAN. It said I should be over Vance. I looked down again. Then I saw very tiny rows of lights west of Enid. That must be Vance. Of course! I had never seen it from high altitude at night before, and had not recognized it. After I swallowed my heart and my liver (and I think my kidneys might have been up there too), I was back to normal.

AS GRADUATION APPROACHED, we began to get our assignments. Everyone, except a few married guys, wanted to fly fighters. Almost all the instructors would gladly have given up their job to fly a fighter. Bombers and tankers were referred to as BUFs (Big Ugly Fuckers). In stag bars across the country fighter pilots regularly heaped scorn upon BUF drivers. They said instead of spending Friday nights in the stag bars knocking back shots of Kentucky bourbon, BUF drivers went up town to take ballet lessons. Driving a bomber or tanker was the equivalent of driving a city bus. Bomber pilots had to have a whole team to guide their airplane through the sky. They had to have a co-pilot and an engineer along, and a bombardier to drop their ordinance—all things a fighter pilot did himself. A BUF driver couldn't find his way to the grocery store without a navigator. A United States Air Force fighter pilot was part of an elite fraternity. He considered his profession the finest on earth. If made the King of Siam, he'd consider that a demotion, an embarrassing degradation. During assignment time, a note appeared on the bulletin board in the flight room:

> Dear Abby:
> My cousin's a B-52 pilot. I'm engaged to be married next month. My question is: must I tell my future wife about my cousin, or would it be best to hide this from her and hope she never finds out? Sincerely, Captain R. Smith, USAF

I wanted to be a fighter pilot. For me this vocation was now the holiest calling—though it seemed the polar opposite of a priest. Most fighter pilots were not religious. Their idea of a deep religious discussion was an argument about whether it was proper to read the Bible while sitting on the shitter, or whether a baptism was valid if done with whiskey instead of water. These men were not holy, humble monks. They were irreverent, proud, and vain. They swore freely and were wanton in their pursuit of women. But they were also dedicated, loyal, zealously patriotic, and honest as the day is long. Duty, honor, and country were not just buzz words for them. They lived this mantra and were willing to die for their country, prepared to accept martyrdom for their cause.

Who is the saint here? The priest or the pilot? The priest says he's willing to die for what he believes, but deep in his heart knows he'll probably never have to face that deadly choice. In time of war, the fighter pilot must face every day the reality that this might be his last flight. Who has the loftier motive: the soldier who gives up his life for his countrymen, or the monk who gives up his life to save his own soul?

If you were a top stick in our class, like Lieutenant Krueger, you got to choose your assignment. He chose F-4 Phantoms to Europe. Almost everyone who had a choice chose an F-4. I wanted to fly the F-105 Thunderchief, but since there was no chance of my getting that, I didn't care. I loved everything about that Thunderchief: the shape, the roar of its afterburner, the fact it could do Mach Two, and the nickname. My love affair with that plane started when I saw one sitting on the ramp with the inscription, "Though I should fly through the valley of the shadow of death, I will fear no evil, for I am the meanest mother in the valley." And when the cocky pilot took off, sending the thunder of his engine to the far borders of Texas and down across the Rio Grande into Mexico, he turned his airplane upside down and climbed out inverted.

The Air Force seemed to have trouble deciding what to do with me. At first, I was told I was to go to Brazil and fly Caribous. It was some kind of secret assignment, and nobody seemed to know what it was all about. Captain Raynes said it must be a Special Forces assignment, and I'd be practicing short-field takeoffs and landings in jungle clearings with Special Forces troops on board.

Then we'd go to Vietnam for the real thing. This wasn't as romantic as a fighter assignment, but my adventure blood was up, and, with the help of Captains Tiggeman and Raynes, I convinced myself it was a better appointment than the F-4 Phantom. Neither of them liked the F-4. Tiggeman said, "The weird angles of its wings and tail are offensive to the eye. Look at the lines of the T-38—a fine work of art. The Phantom looks like a pile of welded pig-iron."

Raynes asked, "Why would you want to fly an F-4? You can't fly it solo, and you don't even have a gun! You don't need two pilots to fly one damn fighter."

And then one of the instructors who had flown F-100s out of Nellis told me, "Don't put in for the F-4. It's a piece of junk designed by the Navy. A fighter should have only one engine. You can't use two engines unless you have a tanker following you around."

Raynes was right. The F-4 Phantom had no gun back then. It had missiles, and not very good ones. The cannon was not added until later. So I didn't care. My assignment was fine. But in a short time they changed my assignment to C-130s, and then, just before graduation, the Air Force did a strange thing—and then I did care—they made me a flight instructor. The war in Vietnam was heating up, and they projected a need for lots of pilots, and that meant they needed lots of instructors. My next job was to go to PIT (Pilot Instructor Training) School at Randolph Air Force Base in San Antonio, and from there to one of the Air Training Command Bases to instruct students in flying.

I was floored! I was barely able to keep an airplane in the air myself, and now I was supposed to teach others? I didn't want the responsibility. I asked my flight commander to get me any other assignment. But the assignments came down from on high. There was no way to change them locally. There was one silver lining: it was this last change of assignment that allowed me to fly a final T-38 mission solo. The syllabus called for 120 hours in the T-38, but if a student was doing well, he could graduate with less (I had 119 hours). But the syllabus also said: "Students receiving fighter or PIT assignments will be graduated with not less than 120 flying hours." So they were forced to give me another hour in the T-38.

I was done with the whole UPT program. I had just passed my final check-ride and was on top of the world. Nothing could have increased my happiness. But then along came Captain Wood, the flight commander, who did just that. He came to my table and said, "Bloch, you're going to have to go back up."

At first I thought he meant some kind of checkride. But that wasn't it. It was because I was that one hour short.

Wood said, "I hope you don't mind going up there solo. We're kind of busy."

Don't mind? Don't *mind*? There was nothing I, or anyone else on that base, would rather have done than to take that airplane out solo with nothing to do but fly it around the sky—solo!—without any worry about checkrides or grade slips.

I went to the scheduler, got an airplane and an area slot, and I was off into the wild blue yonder. I was smoking along in the sweetest little supersonic jet ever invented, the mustang of the sky. I wrung her out. I pulled negative Gs into steep dives and as I approached Mach One, I would pull up sharply red-lining the G-meter and, standing her on her tail, plug in the burners, and do aileron rolls until I was dizzy. I dived and looped her up along the side of a big thunderstorm. It was the best ride I had—then or ever. And I was young.

Fool that I was, I scared myself. The thunderstorm was at the western edge of my area. I noticed it was building fast, so fast it was beating me in a climb. I thought, *we'll see about this.* I went close to the side of the storm. It was well-defined and boiling upward. I went into a dive, pulled up, lit the burners, and climbed, climbed, climbed. The storm boiled faster and faster. I kept trying to reach the top, but always it boiled a little higher. Suddenly I noticed that the stick was feeling mushy. I was running out of airspeed. Fear shot through me like a lightning strike. In a second I'd be falling like a rock. Stalls, spins, and ejections flashed into my mind. I pulled sharply to roll her to the nearest horizon, but she didn't respond; she just shuddered and fell off to one side like a sledge hammer—the side where the thunderstorm was. Into the storm I went and my whole world got dark in heavy clouds and tremendous rain. I was completely disoriented and scared stiff. I bent the throttles forward, but I was already in burner. I couldn't tell if I was upside down or right side up. But I could hear Simmons shouting, "Fly the gauges, god damnit. Get your head out of your ass." I finally found the attitude indicator and rolled wings level. The thunderstorm, having given me a head-rattling shake, spit me out several thousand feet below where had I entered. I was suddenly, miraculously flying right side up out in the bright sunshine. All was well again.

But I didn't feel so well. I had just risked my life and my airplane on silly, self-indulgent tomfoolery. And I wanted to call myself a pilot? To compound my horror, when I checked the fuel gauge I realized I had been using fuel at such a prodigal rate I barely had enough left to fill out a full hour without going into "min fuel." Minimum fuel was a required radio call, and if a solo called minimum fuel, there was an investigation. I stayed high in my area for a while and ran the airplane at glide speed using as little fuel as possible. I just kind of hovered around until I judged that a normal pattern and landing would give me the full hour. After I landed, I checked the fuel gauge. It was at min fuel, but I was taxiing by now and no call was required.

I DID NOT WRITE HOME about my graduation from pilot training. I knew Dad would think it was no big deal. He'd never waste his time driving all the way to Oklahoma for such a trivial matter. He had not come to my college graduation, and that took place ten miles from home. However, the Air Force—always efficient—sent a notice to the local papers in every student's hometown, and a letter to the parents. My sister, Beats, and her husband saw the letter. They came down. They brought along a pleased Mom and dragged along a reluctant Dad.

The North American F-100 Super Sabre was the first fighter the Air Force put into active service capable of flying supersonic in level flight. That was the plane the Air Force Thunderbirds flew for our graduation at Enid. They put a lot of emphasis on speed. They did a lot of low, screaming flyovers near the speed of sound, and the thunder of the engines (which followed behind and reached our ears only when they had already passed) made the tarmac tremble under our feet. In diamond formation they did the normal maneuvers like loops and slow rolls. The solos did the flashy crowd pleasers like the inverted passes. The final was the bomb burst, where they came from four directions and met going straight up with a solo flying up the contrail chimney and doing aileron rolls.

It was a perfectly sunny Oklahoma day, the Thunderbirds filled the sky with their smoky trails, and I was proud to be in the same Air Force as those men. The squadron commander pinned wings on our chests and saluted us as members of the greatest brotherhood on the earth. It would have impressed any parent. But my father, a true Stearns County farmer, took this all in with the stoic demeanor of a Plains Indian. That evening before he left, he showed how little he was impressed. He asked me if I wouldn't rather buy a farm in Stearns County and make an honest living. I tried to explain to him this was many a boy's lifetime dream. He answered by offering to lend me the money should I ever want to buy that farm. The irony of this conversation (which made me smile often afterwards) was that the phrase "buy the farm" to a pilot meant "getting killed in a crash."

Early the following morning I set off for my new assignment in San Antonio. I thought about those mornings at Vance just before sunup, when I could see the ghostly shadows of men with parachute and helmet moving among the silhouettes of the airplanes, and of the crescendo whine of engines spooling up, and the roar from the runway as a Lightning One Zero or a Mojack Three kicked in his afterburners, and then that sudden vision of flashing bright as a climbing jet bursts into the glory of morning sunlight while the earth below is still in shadow. *I might not miss Oklahoma,* I thought, *but I will not forget where my buddies and I got our wings.*

Chapter Twenty-Six

I HAD ALWAYS THOUGHT of the military as a Spartan organization—much as monasteries pretend to be—and as Vance Air Force Base actually was. So I was not ready for the luxury on display at Randolph Air Force Base in San Antonio. It must have been at that time the most beautiful air base in the world. The buildings were of that old California Spanish architecture like the missions on the West Coast. I mean everything, even the hangars, had those thick, white walls and arches, and red tile roofs, so that I thought I must be going into a church. My BOQ was of the same style, and it had a fireplace and a bar! I thought surely this was better than the Ritz in Paris or London. Outside, all the buildings were surrounded by lush, clipped lawns, and shaded by tall palm trees. It was January when I came to the instructor school, but the weather was Minnesota in July.

The class was small, and I was the junior. The others were mostly captains and majors with considerable flying time. I was outranked and outclassed. Again I felt the pressure to study hard just to catch up. Upon completion of the school, I was to be assigned to Laredo Air Force Base, Laredo, Texas, as a T-37 instructor pilot. I viewed this as a lucky assignment: I had never been to Laredo, and it was right next to Mexico. But I soon found I was alone in considering that a good assignment. I made friends with two other students going to instruct at Laredo, Major Halbach and Captain Wertz. When I expressed delight in the assignment, Captain Wertz painted a different picture for me.

"If you wanted to give the world an enema," he said, "you would insert the nozzle at Laredo, Texas."

Major Halbach, who everyone called "Smokey," was of the same opinion, but I didn't let that change my rosy glasses. I thought of Laredo as a land of cattle and cowboys, and of black-eyed señoritas with long hair, and of plates of good, greasy tacos with bowls of pinto beans like Carmen and I used to eat when we toured San Antonio at night.

Since I was assigned to instruct in the T-37, I was now sitting in the right seat as instructor with a "student" in the left. Though I was thoroughly familiar with all the switches and dials in the airplane, I had a very different view of everything from my new perch. I used my left hand instead of my right to tune the radios and set the arrows and numbers on the gauges. But that was a minor problem compared to the big one: I now had to talk as I flew. I had to gush like a geyser while I flew the blamed airplane. I had to give details of exactly what I was doing, and why, and even what I was thinking in the process. I had to babble constantly like a tape recorder. Before, when I made a sixty-degree bank turn in the pitchout, I said nothing, except maybe "Oh, shit, there goes my altitude," but now that same maneuver required constant chatter:

"Clear in the direction of the turn. Smoothly roll into the bank, trimming back as you roll. Establish the picture in the windscreen that you think puts you at sixty degrees to the horizon and level flight—a quick cross-check of the VVI to see if you're trending up or down, adjust the nose accordingly. Trim, trim. Cross-check the attitude indicator to make sure you have exactly sixty degrees of bank. Check altitude and make a correction looking outside. Begin your rollout well before your desired heading so you don't overshoot, rolling out smoothly and trimming forward as you roll. By the time you are wings level, you should be on a heading corrected for wind drift. Check your altitude, trim, trim, drop the speed brakes."

That chatter was just to make a simple pitchout! You can imagine the litany required for doing a more complicated maneuver like holding over a VOR station. Worst of all was trying to fit your explanations and techniques in between the radio chatter of approach control during a GCA approach. You had to fly the airplane, listen to the radio, read the approach plate, set in the courses, and change the radio frequencies—all the time blabbering like a used-car salesman. I was barely able to perform these maneuvers correctly *without* the talking. Now a check pilot could grade me down not only for the way I performed a maneuver, but also for what I said about it. I spent my evenings not thinking about how to fly the airplane, but how to talk about it.

PIT school took almost three months. I passed my final checkride and headed down to Laredo. There they put me back into another rickety old BOQ. Married officers had a choice of either living in base housing for free, or getting a housing allowance and living wherever they wanted. This was a screw job for the bachelors. The BOQ was a old wooden structure with outdated plumbing and electricity. Most of base housing was new, and the rental rates in Laredo were so low, that on a housing allowance one could afford a modern mansion with a maid.

There was no peace in the BOQ. Pilots in heavy flight boots constantly thundered on the wooden floors of the halls above me, below me, and right by my door. Pilots flying the morning shift were stomping around as early as four o'clock. Pilots doing night flying might come in as late as midnight—drunks from the O Club even later. Every bachelor IP had a powerful new stereo connected to two monstrous speakers with strident tweeters and rumbling woofers that shivered the building.

I did not live there long. Another stroke of luck for me, and this time a big one. At Vance I had a wise old master sergeant for a buddy. The Vance housing officer had told me bachelors would have to live in the BOQ, but the master sergeant said, "Don't listen to him. Here's what you do. Buy yourself a house trailer. The Air Force will ship it for you to your assigned base. When they put you in the BOQ, you go to the housing officer down there and tell him you already have a home off-base. After a bit of paper shuffling, they not only will allow you to live off-base, but will give you a housing allowance to boot."

This sounded like a scam—too good to be true. But I took a chance on the master sergeant. I bought a little silver house trailer with faded red trim for eight hundred dollars and filled out the paper work to get it shipped. It was the best investment I ever made. The system worked like magic—exactly as advertised. I was out of the Laredo Air Force BOQ in two weeks. I felt sorry for anyone living there, but most of them didn't seem to mind. They liked the comradery. It was like living in their old frat house back in college. They could have it.

They assigned me to "A Flight" of the 3640th pilot training squadron. I had a table with four students, all men about the same age. All had the same goal: they wanted to learn to fly jets. There was no variety among them in that. But there was wonderful variety in where they came from. Of those first four students, one was from Centralia, Missouri, one from Chicago, Illinois, one from Kensington, Maryland, and one from Covington, Kentucky.

If you want to learn to fly an airplane, become a flight instructor. The students will make all the mistakes you made when you were learning, and that reminds you again not to do that stupid stuff. They'll make new mistakes you never thought of, but that you might have made some time in the future. It's always easier to correct a mistake if you're calmly sitting on the side and not nervous about performing. And so, in a little while, I had seen and corrected almost every mistake a person could make in an airplane. There was no better way to learn. I didn't know this when I got my IP assignment or I would have looked at it as luck instead of misfortune.

And if you want to know a young man deeply and thoroughly, become his flight instructor. You get to know his strengths and weaknesses, to know his character to the core; to find out what the man is really like, not what others say about him or what he says about himself. All the flaws, all the virtues show like neon signs. An instructor gets to know him better than his wife or girlfriend knows him. The flight instructor shares his hopes and his dreams, his joy when he does well, his sorrow when he doesn't.

There were ten instructors in A Flight. Since I was the rookie, and of the lowest possible rank, I got to fly missions the others didn't want. We usually flew two flights a day, but if a student was in need of a flight, an instructor might have to fly a third mission. The scheduling officer would automatically put the lowest ranking man in that third mission. When we were on the morning schedule and it was A Flight's turn to put up the "weather ship," the scheduler put "Lt. Bloch" in that slot. Because I was a bachelor, I was often asked to take cross-country flights on weekends, when a married man had a conflict: wedding anniversaries, daughter's birthday party, PTA meeting, unhappy wife. Scheduling assumed I had no personal life, so I took the place of those who did.

But I didn't mind in the least. I liked to fly more than anything. I liked flying weather ship, even though it meant getting up at four in the morning. The weather ship went up to check the weather conditions out in the training areas before the start of the day. An instructor took a student along and checked the area, reported the weather to Laredo Base, then flew a regular training mission. I liked the weather mission because I was the first one airborne that morning. I walked out in semi-darkness on the parking ramp that, for once, was totally silent—a silence not broken until I started my engines. And as I rolled down the runway with the position lights glowing and the anti-collision lights flashing, every pilot and every maintenance man knew: "there goes the weather ship," and they knew the day's flying was underway.

And I certainly didn't mind cross-country flights. I got to fly anywhere I wanted in the country and they paid all my expenses. I was on my own then, and did not have to worry about the flight commander, the squadron commander, or the base commander looking over my shoulder. The most popular destination was Nellis AFB in Nevada, because that was near Las Vegas. Mostly I went wherever the student wanted to go (usually home to see Mom and Dad), so I got to see a lot of the country, and was treated like royalty in many people's homes. But I often went to Tinker AFB in Oklahoma and to Webb AFB near Big Spring, Texas, because I had girlfriends there. For several years I flew more hours than any other pilot in Air Training Command.

WHEN I CAME to A Flight, the students had already soloed and passed their mid-phase checks. They were just starting instrument flying. Great! That was the area in which I considered myself the most qualified. The students were all second lieutenants. When I was in pilot training at Vance AFB, all instructors outranked the students. Here, I was the same rank as my students.

Instructing can be a very frustrating business. At times I just couldn't get my point across no matter how many different ways I presented it. But I was less frustrated than some of those instructors who had breezed through their pilot training without any problems. Those men couldn't understand how their students could be so stupid. Those instructors had never had to spend much time thinking about how a maneuver was done, because they could do it right the first time they tried. When a student was having trouble, it was confusing to them. But I knew exactly what the poor bastard was going through. Whenever a student asked me if I had any trouble when I was in pilot training, I said, "Why, hell yes, and plenty!"

I knew how to fly now, and I knew how to talk, but there were still lessons I had to learn before I was a good instructor. Most of all I had to learn patience. I kept trying to be like Tiggeman and Huff to make students relax, but I was still so unsure of my own flying abilities I was afraid I might let a student go too far. However, as I gained confidence, I found I could let the student screw up without breaking into a sweat.

I found it especially hard to flunk someone. One day I was up with a student on an instrument ride. I conducted it as a rehearsal for the instrument checkride, which he was to take the next day. He did not do well, but I hated to flunk him. His wife had just had a baby and was still in the hospital. I thought he must be preoccupied. Maybe he was just having a bad day. I passed him, and sent him up for his checkride. I thought, *what the heck, maybe he'll have a good day.*

He didn't. The check pilot not only flunked him, but came and read me the riot act for sending up a student I should have known was marginal. He said, "You're new, but if this repeats, you'll quickly develop yourself a reputation as a lousy instructor." Lesson number one from Check Section.

I had another student, Lieutenant Roman, who was a good stick, but he was lazy and didn't hit the books. I sent him up for a mid-phase check. I was confident the check pilot would pass him for his good flying and overlook his weakness on procedure. Wrong. The check pilot never saw his good flying. He flunked Lieutenant Roman before they got airborne—flunked him for "lack of knowledge of the Dash-1." Lieutenant Roman did not know what the load meter should read after engine start, and when the check pilot asked him what he'd do if he lost both engines at 700 feet and 170 knots, he said he would establish best glide speed and look around for a suitable place to land. I guess he thought he was still in the T-41. After that I always asked my students what questions the check pilots asked them on the checkride, and I made a book of the questions. I used that to brief students before sending them for a check. Another lesson from Check Section.

One day I was flying an aerobatic mission. The student said he was feeling sick. He pulled out his barf bag. In college this guy had been a big, tough football player. He had played in the Sugar Bowl. I didn't think he was likely to throw up. I thought that, as long as he had his barf bag out, he'd keep thinking about barfing, so I took it away from him. He did a split S—a good one—but as he came out at the bottom, he suddenly released the stick, unhooked his oxygen mask, and threw up: on his checklist, on the map, on part of the instrument panel, and on of the floor. Horseshit! A lesson for me in physiology.

One day we almost lost a T-37, when Lieutenant Hilleman (not one of my students) was out on his second solo mission and got lost. He flipped over to the guard channel and got a DF steer from the tower. He landed with nothing but air in his tanks. Everyone knew about it because everyone monitored the guard channel (the emergency channel). From that day forward I made sure any solo student of mine knew his area, knew how to find his way home, and knew how to get a DF steer, just in case. Another lesson.

And so it went. I don't think I was a really good instructor until well into my second year. Even then I was learning. The most important lesson, and the most tragic, came from what happened to Captain Boyd one night. Captain Boyd was assigned to another instructor in our flight, but he flew with me a lot because his instructor was a senior captain with lots of other duties. Boyd outranked me. He was a captain, while I was still a lieutenant. This fact never interfered with our lessons. When we were in the cockpit he deferred to my rank as an instructor; when we met in the commissary or the O Club, I deferred to his rank as captain. Captain Boyd was an excellent student—easy to teach. He was a fast learner and always came to the flightline prepared for the day's lesson.

Boyd had easily passed all his T-37 checkrides that fall, and had gone on to fly the T-38. It was now the last day of January of that dreadful year 1968 (which I will get to later). That night the T-38s were flying night missions. I was getting ready to retire early, because I had weather ship in the morning. The phone rang. It was my neighbor Sergeant Jenson, a T-38 maintenance chief, calling from the flightline shack.

"Did you know we have a plane missing?"

"Who is it?"

"Don't know. I thought you might know," he said.

I called Base Operations. The major said, "Not sure, but right now it looks like we may have lost Captain Boyd. Keep this under your hat until we have confirmation."

In a short time we had confirmation.

The note on the bulletin board next day said: "30 Jan 68. At 2000 hours Captain Boyd took off on a T-38 C-10 mission. At 2020 hours the Control Ship reported seeing a shaft of fire shooting up from the ground out in the desert near the Mexican border. Base asked everyone to check in. Captain Boyd did not respond on the area channel, or on guard. The rescue helicopter was sent out immediately. LRD WX 8M SCT, high overcast."

What that bulletin says (in Air Force talk) is that Captain Boyd was on his first night solo flight. He took off at eight o'clock. The control ship saw the flash twenty minutes later. Boyd did not answer his radio. The weather at Laredo was 8,000-foot scattered, high overcast.

In February, on Valentine's Day, having completed a two-week investigation, the accident board briefed us. Captain Boyd's assigned area had been down along the Rio Grande south of Laredo. The high overcast that night would have made it harder to keep oriented, since there were no stars to use as a guide and fog along the lower river, but the lights of the town of Laredo would have been in the clear. Captain Boyd may have been flying along using the lights of Laredo as a horizon. When he got to the river, the western boundary of his area, he turned back. During this turn he would have lost the Laredo lights and may have become disoriented and lost altitude in the turn. He may have inadvertently entered some clouds below him and failed to go to his attitude indicator. When he saw the altimeter unwinding, he pulled back hard on the stick to raise the nose. He may have been inverted by that time, so pulling on the stick would have increased his dive angle. Recognizing he was in trouble, he went to burner. Then he hit the ground. His configuration: clean. (That means gear up, flaps up, speed brake up.)

I think the speculation by the investigating board was reasonable. The fact that Boyd had his speed brakes retracted showed he was not aware he was in a hell dive. I also think that what was being called eight-thousand scattered was actually an overcast layer down along the river, where fog forms at night. So when Captain Boyd was in his turn he may have seen no stars above and no lights on the earth below. He should have switched to instruments immediately when there was a question. However, those conditions should not have existed when students were on night VFR solo.

The board considered other possibilities. A Mexican national witnessed the crash, and said the plane was on fire before it hit the ground. The board found no indication of this among the pieces they reassembled. So they waited for a night with similar conditions and they placed the witness in the location he had been that night, and then they flew a T-38 out of the clouds over the crash site. The Mexican shook his head no, when they made the pass at cruise power. But when they made the pass in burner, he said, "*Asi, asi,*" to indicate that's the way it was. The plane was not on fire but the bright flame of the afterburners made him think it was.

The board eliminated electrical failure because both generators were running on impact. They considered failure of the ejection seat, but the gold key was still in the safety belt, so Boyd had not tried to eject. They considered, and rejected, pilot blackout, slab failure, and instrument failures. They rounded off the report: "Primary Cause: undetermined." And they added the most probable cause (which was standard and also stupendously obvious): "The Pilot allowed the aircraft to enter an attitude from which he was unable to recover."

I considered for a long time how this could happen to Captain Boyd. That man was no slouch of a pilot. I had flown with many worse, who later breezed through the T-38 program. But as I studied the contributing-factors section of the accident report, the mystery began to clear. This man should not have been up there that night. The board interviewed the captain's wife to find out what he had been doing and what he had been eating the last few days, and they looked in his medicine cabinet (routine). On the nineteenth of January, Captain Boyd had gone NFDS (None Flying Duty Status) because of a head cold. He was given Neosynephrine. He also had Actifed tablets in his medicine cabinet and may have been taking some of them. On the weekend of the twenty-seventh and twenty-eighth, the Boyd family (they had two little children) went down to Monterrey with Mrs. Boyd's parents. The captain got diarrhea and complained of nausea. The next day, Monday the twenty-ninth, he flew two flights, one solo and one formation. For supper he ate chicken and potatoes. He said he felt feverish and went to bed early. On the morning of the thirtieth, he had a little cereal for breakfast and lay around the house all morning with no energy. He took only a piece of bread along to the fightline. Other students at his table said he ate part of a candy bar. He flew two flights that afternoon, then, when it got dark, he went up on that final flight.

Captain Boyd should have been at home in bed that night. He was not feeling well—that is obvious. This stage of the T-38 program was stressful enough when a person was healthy. Captain Boyd had flown two flights already that day, which, in his condition, would have been very tiring. Ultimately it was up to the captain to ground himself that night, but there was much pressure on a student to perform. A student never wanted to look like a baby and would push himself to the limit and beyond.

This was another big lesson for me. After that no student of mine went up for a third flight in a day unless he was a very strong student, was on a late-phase flight, and unless I had closely cross-examined him about his preparation, his health, and his state of mind.

Chapter Twenty-Seven

I N THOSE DAYS radar did not cover the entire training area. There was only the radar for approach control, so it was easy (especially if assigned one of the outlying areas) to slip out and go goofing off somewhere. I seldom did such a thing, because I felt a great responsibility to prepare the student for his next checkride. Once in a while, if I had a really strong student, we would zip over to Padre Island and buzz the shrimp boats in the Gulf. Dogfighting, which some instructors did routinely, was a silly waste of time. The fight was always a draw when flown by the two instructors, and if we let our students have the airplane they got shot down in seconds. No student could win against an instructor. Whenever we heard over the radio a rapid: *"Kitch, chit, chit, chit, chit,"* we knew some instructors were dogfighting out there, and one of them was claiming a kill.

The one bit of screwing off I did routinely was on night flights. We had no T-37 night-checkride, so I did this goofing off whenever the conditions were right. It didn't rob the student of stick time. I let him fly the whole time. The best conditions for this were when we had an assigned area above a cumulus cloud deck on a night when the moon was full. The moon then lit up the mountainous clouds in fantastic silvery brightness, and sent the dark canyons between into dismal, deep blackness. Then we would race low among the clouds and zigzag and wind our way between them, sometimes racing right up to a mountain, then popping up at the last second and rolling over its top inverted so the plane's vertical stabilizer just shaved the top, or we would Split S down into the dark of a canyon and pull up and burst back into bright moonlight doing aileron rolls, or rolling out in a sort of Immelmann. Or we continued in the loop and plunged back into the dark. It was as exhilarating as low-level navigation and as wonderful as flying between the rock forma-tions in Monument Valley—but without the risks. If we misjudged and ran into a mountain in this magic valley—*zip*—you simply passed through un-harmed. And if we dived too deeply, we didn't crash on the canyon floor, but came out below the clouds. Then we looked for a shaft of moonlight coming through a hole and zoomed back up, riding a moonbeam into the wonder-land above.

Enough of this. I've inflicted sufficient sappy poetry of sky and airplane on the reader. South Texas was hell-fire in the summer. Temperatures climbed to afternoon highs of over 100 degrees with a blowtorch of a wind roaring out of

Mexico. On the shimmering tarmac, the ambient temperature could easily make 120. By the time we pulled into position for takeoff, with the canopy down and locked, the cockpit of the un-air-conditioned T-37 was like a bake oven ready for the bread. We could feel the sweat trickling down our foreheads and running down our backs. As we bent over to look at the checklist, sweat dripped onto our helmet visors, clouding our vision. At the end of the flying day, as pilots walked to their cars, patterns of salt stains on the backs of their flight suits marked where sweat had dried in the post-flight briefings. We could tell which pilots were flying the air-conditioned T-38s: no salt. We used to eat salt pills like candy. There were salt pill dispensers all over the squad rooms to make sure no pilot was without a free supply. We often took two or three just before leaving the building and washed them down with a bucket of water. That was before Gatorade—and before modern medicine.

Ah, but it was good to be young then and to be flying for the greatest Air Force in the world. There was no end to the dreams one could dream—and no, the sky was not the limit. In those days an ambitious young pilot could apply with NASA to be an astronaut and bring the universe into play. However, any desire I might have had to enter that profession vanished like smoke in the early days of 1967. The TV showed how NASA fried three of their best astronauts in a flash fire that engulfed the space capsule during a launch simulation at Cape Canaveral. That put an end to my desire for a career as an astronaut. I determined that, if I was going to fry in an aircraft, I'd do so all on my own, without any help from NASA.

Really, most of us did not have a snowball's chance in hell of being an astronaut. A person had to have connections and brains for that, and moreover had to have a willingness to work hard. Hard work was not something for which everyone readily volunteered. It was common to hear at the O Club sour-grape remarks about being an astronaut:

"You're not flying, you're just riding."

"You're at the mercy of those fat-assed desk jockeys at mission control."

"I'd rather lower myself to flying B-52's."

"It's all flown by computer. There's no pilot input. A monkey can do it. In fact, a monkey *has* done it!"

THE PILOTS OF the 3640th knew things the U.S. news media did not know, or at least did not report. We knew we were taking heavy airplane losses in Vietnam. Our F-105s were going up north and hitting targets not far from Hanoi in an area heavily defended with triple-A, with SAMs, and with Russian MiGs. The Air Force was losing dozens of F-105s; they rained out of the sky like mallards in Minnesota duck season. A ridge near Hanoi was called "Thud Ridge," from the frequently heard "*thud*" of F-105s hitting the ground there. (Thud was also a nickname for the F-105.) I read an Air Force report that said that during the previous year (1966) we had lost three hundred F-105s! I thanked God I did not get that Thunderchief assignment I'd wanted out of pilot training.

The Air Force often sent that F-105 "fighter-bomber" out there alone, without cover like normal bombers had. The desk jockeys saw no reason to cover a fighter with a fighter. But a heavily loaded F-105 was nothing but a bomber—a sitting duck for maneuverable enemy fighters. It could only be competitive as a fighter after it dropped its ordinance. Only later did F-100 Super Sabers and F-4 Phantoms fly cover for F-105 bombing missions. Meantime our downed pilots were going to Hanoi's Hoa Lo POW camp ("the Hanoi Hilton") or the camp at Son Tay, and they were enduring the most brutal living conditions and torture there—all of this unreported in the American press. Many POWs died there. President Johnson did not want these things made public. He had an election coming up.

Pilots returning from a tour in Vietnam did not give glowing reports about the F-4 Phantom. When it was finally used to fly cover for the Thud, it had no guns and its missiles were shit. The pilots called their Sidewinder missile "Sandwinder," because it mostly missed its target and spiraled down into the sand. The Phantom was faster than the MiG-17, but the MiG could out-turn it. It made me wonder about the starry-eyed Phantom pilot who had declared one night at the O Club: "It's so fucking maneuverable you can fly up your own asshole with it." Even I, who knew little about fighters, could see a major flaw when I watched F-4s coming into Laredo AFB on Friday nights for R&R. I saw they certainly did not deserve the name Phantom, for they trailed black smoke behind like a sign reading "here I am." An enemy pilot could easily spot that tell-tale smoke streaming across the sky.

CAPTAIN FREDERICK BRADSTREET was A Flight's scheduling officer—and a strange one he was. He had somehow combined in his head the morals of a strict, sober Quaker and of a dissolute, unruly dog. He was a peculiar mixture of preacher and muleskinner, of altar boy and alley cat. I had never met anyone nearly like him, nor have I since. I might never have had more than a passing acquaintance with Bradstreet had he not been our scheduling officer. He happily volunteered my services when one of the other flights needed help.

One day Bradstreet said to me, "You're Catholic."

"Does it show?" I asked.

"I saw you in church on Sunday."

I said, "I didn't see you there."

"That's because I was up in the choir loft. Did you ever sing in a choir?"

I said I had. He said I should join their choir, as they needed men. I told him that, having spent a good deal of my youth in the seminary, I had my fill of singing in church. In the following weeks Bradstreet continued to assign me the extra missions; their frequency, in fact, increased. I did not mind. But one afternoon, as I was getting ready to leave the flight room I got called back.

"You're scheduled here for an acrobatic training mission with B Flight. Guess you didn't notice," Bradstreet said, pointing at his board.

This time I had a conflict. I had a date that afternoon with a real live girl. I had met her in Nuevo Laredo the night before. She was a stunning Mexican and her father owned a big ranch on the Mexican side of the river, down by Falcon Lake. I had visions of hunting and fishing there.

"I can't make that flight," I said. "I have a meeting to go to. It's real important."

"Your meeting will have to wait. Your job comes first," said Bradstreet, and it came out as short and cold as it's written here.

"This is really gonna put me in a bind. Look, I'll take a night flight or weather ship in the morning. Just let me out of this one."

"Are you coming to choir practice on Wednesday night?" Bradstreet looked straight at me and raised his hand with the eraser, to indicate that I had to but say the word.

I was flabbergasted. "You mean to tell me that, if I promise to come to choir practice, you'll take my name off the board?"

"That's right."

"Done," I said, and the word had barely cleared my teeth when Bradstreet made a quick swipe with the eraser, scribbled another officer's name in the slot, and turned to advise the guy he had another flight that day.

I never could figure that man. Based on his talent for cursing on the flight-line, and for drinking VO at the O Club, I had not judged him a religious man. But there he was at every choir practice. There he was on Sunday mornings singing with the ladies like a devoted little altar boy. With the Sunday morning sunlight lighting the window behind him, it wasn't hard to imagine a halo shining around his head.

The first Sunday morning, after we sang the nine o'clock High Mass, Bradstreet invited me to breakfast. We went across the river to Papa Gallo's. Papa Gallo's was—probably still is—a whorehouse. It was not just any whorehouse, but the biggest and best in Boystown, Nuevo Laredo. It was getting near noon, but since it was Sunday, there were few customers in the place. The girls sat around filing their nails and fixing their makeup. When we walked in, Bradstreet was the immediate center of attention.

"Sam, Sam!" came from all corners of the room. The girls came over smiling and laughing, and some of them hugged "Sam." Bradstreet said, "This is my friend, Don," and in a second I was surrounded by girls rubbing themselves up against me and purring like kittens. Bradstreet waved them aside.

"He doesn't wanna fuck," he said. "We're here to eat breakfast."

We ate in the dining room with the whores. We were the only two at the table who were not working girls of the house. It was a grand breakfast of *huevos rancheros* (ranch-type fried eggs) served family style. In the middle of the table were platters of bacon, sausage, and corn tortillas; a big plate of raw onions surrounded with lemon wedges for relish; and a bowl of fiery salsa for sauce. There was a bowl of pico de gallo, which the cook refreshed several times while we ate. It was good, hot food, all full of Mexican fire. Many of the girls spoke no English except words related to their profession, so the conversation was somewhat limited, but still there was a lot of laughing and a lot of talking about "Sam."

I learned the background behind this mysterious happening later. Bradstreet occasionally patronized Papa Gallos, but that was not what made him so popular. There were steady customers who showed up every few days and left big tips and who were far less popular. What made "Sam" so well-liked was this: About a year ago one of the girls had found herself pregnant. She wanted the baby, but could not afford it. She was about to get an abortion. Bradstreet heard about it, and gave the girl a hundred dollars for a promise not to abort the baby. He promised to give her what she needed to take care of the child. He made good on his promise. He gave her money and brought her baby clothes and toys he scrounged from the Air Force wives. The Papa Gallo hookers were so touched by this that they made "Sam" into a saint. And the Air Force wives liked Captain Bradstreet, because he was such a good uncle to his little "nephew."

On the flightline Bradstreet made fun of the regulations and procedures, delighting the students with his readiness to label it all as "chickenshit" or "horse manure." But when that man got into the cockpit, he was a polished professional. One morning the instructors were all scrambled to the flightline for a hurricane evacuation. Hurricane Beulah had been boiling in the Gulf for days. It had passed over the Yucatan and took a direct aim at South Texas. The scheduling board designated Lead and Wing for two-ship formations to ferry all the airplanes to Big Spring. The flight leaders were all veterans. Some of the young instructors whined about flying wingman the whole trip, but I liked it. Lead had all the responsibilities. I was scheduled to fly Wing in a two-ship with Bradstreet as Lead. He had to do the planning, get the clearances, make the radio calls. All I had to do was stay in position until we got to Webb AFB up by Big Spring, Texas.

After the main briefing, the flight leaders were supposed to brief with their wingmen. This was Bradstreet's briefing: "You know how to fly formation, what's there to brief?"

As we walked out to our airplanes he asked, "You know your hand signals?" I said, "What am I, a student?"

He smiled. "Sorry. Anyway, we'll do all hand signals. It's going to be a gaggle up there with all those airplanes in the sky and everyone talking on the radio at once."

Our airplanes were parked side by side. I hurried through my prestart checklist to be ahead of Bradstreet. I looked over at him, waiting for the start signal. His head was down, still doing his checks. Then he glanced at me, and when he saw I was looking at him, he gave his crew chief the start signal and I signaled mine. Our compressors wound up together. After start I heard him call for taxi, and when we had instructions, he looked at me. I gave him a thumb up to indicate I was on and had the instructions. Bradstreet returned the thumb up. I raised my hands to give chocks-out. I watched Bradstreet, and when he raised his hands we both gave the signal. We moved out of the chocks together. I swung into trail, and we taxied between the rows of airplanes. When we reached the taxiway and Bradstreet took the left side of the yellow line, I moved into position on his right wing. When we got clearance for takeoff from tower, Bradstreet looked at me. I signaled thumb up, he answered. We swung onto the runway and did our runup checks. Bradstreet looked back. I gave a thumb up. He tapped his helmet, nodded, and we both released brakes on the nod. After we got airborne he gave the gear up signal, tapped and nodded, and up went our gear. Same with flaps. My airplane never moved out of position.

So went the whole flight. Bradstreet was a great lead. He was smooth. He was considerate. He never did anything I had not anticipated. Anytime we approached a turn, he made sure I was on the high wing. If I was on the wrong side approaching a turn, he gave his wing a jerk, the signal to move to the other side. I would slide over, and he would glance back to make sure I was there. When he wanted a fuel check, he would look at me and make a drinking motion with his fist and extended thumb. I would loosen formation, check the fuel, and slide back in. When he glanced back, I gave thumb up to show my fuel was normal. We said nothing on the radios. The center frequency was all cluttered as the other formations checked in. It was full of "How do you read?" and "Green Two, are you on?" or "Go to 234.5," or "Move out for fuel check," and so on.

I have to admit that by the time we got to Webb, I felt pretty insignificant to the flight. I was no more important than an ornament on Bradstreet's airplane. But Bradstreet dispelled that feeling as we walked in to close our flight plan at Base Ops.

He said, "You did a hell of a job. If I'm ever in the air over Hanoi, I hope you're on my wing."

I said, "What the hell did I do? I just flew Wing."

"Exactly. You weren't out there horsing around. You followed my lead, you didn't make extraneous radio calls, you were always where you were supposed to be. Discipline. That's the mark of a good wingman."

I knew what he meant. A good wingman was hard to find. Many of the instructors thought it was smart to goof off out there on the wing. Some bragged about how they did barrel rolls around Lead, or moved into the slot where Lead had a hard time finding them. Or they would drop way back and then do a rejoin. When they got bored with flying Wing, they did anything to break up the monotony. They thought this was funny, but if you were Lead it was not. You were responsible for the damn fool out there. It was like being responsible for an unruly child in a mine field.

CAPTAIN LYON WAS our flight safety officer. One weekend he asked me to go with him on a cross-country. He was going to visit relatives in Kentucky. We were allowed to take these cross-countries almost any time, because the squadron wanted to make sure their pilots kept current on instruments and navigation. I jumped at the chance to fly with a veteran instructor. I thought I might learn something new—which I did. I saw St. Elmo's fire for the first time.

It was in the springtime when the atmosphere was very unstable, and it was a great time to practice instruments. On that one trip we flew in rain, hail, thunder, lightning, icing, fog, and sleet. We were flying late at night on an IFR clearance high over Bowling Green in a rollicking thunderstorm. We were shuddering along in the turbulence when I noticed a kind of shimmering glow on the windscreen—like a whitish neon light. At first I thought I was seeing things, but it spread rapidly. The pallid fire ran rampant all over the canopy and sometimes along the leading edges of the wings. It shimmered and flowed like liquid, yet stayed on the canopy in the rushing airstream. It flowed back and forth and organized itself in a kind of "H" pattern with the sides sizzling along the vertical parts of the canopy rail, and a horizontal bar across the middle right at eye level. It became a quivering, shivering, greenish glow—a fluttering fluorescence, flickering like wisps of colored flame. This was hard to believe, because one must think that such a thing would be immediately washed off by the blast of the airstream and the rain, but there it stayed the whole time, until we ripped free of the storm.

Lyon called it St. Elmo's fire. He said he had seen it before, though never so thick or so brilliant. I said I'd never heard of such a thing except that once back home a farmer had told me a piece of rotten wood I had found, which glowed green in the dark, glowed so because it was "a coal from the fire of St. Elmo." I saw St. Elmo's fire again a few more times on other flights, but never anything like that night in the thunderstorm over Kentucky.

I WENT TO THE BASE post office one day looking for a letter. The Mexican girl I dated for a while was so desperate to get away from me she converted to the Mormon religion and moved to Salt Lake City. She promised to be true, to write me faithfully, and she did—twice: once to tell me she was happy in her new home, and once to tell me she was getting married (not to me). But that day there was a letter for me. When I opened it, lo and behold, it was from Frank Ward out of Santa Barbara, California.

I had written Frank back when I started pilot training at Vance. I got no answer. I guessed he must be back in prison, so I wrote him, in care of San Quentin. I was right. I got a big envelope from the California State Prison, San Quentin, with a note stating that Frank Ward was there all right, but there were restrictions. There was a folder of several pages called "Rules and Regulations Governing Correspondence and Visiting Privileges." The rules said that all mail was subject to censoring, that I must be on a mailing list, and that I could not send stamps. (I assumed they confiscated the four-cent stamps I had sent.) Another rule stated in bold print that the register number of the inmate had to be written on the lower left hand corner of the envelope. I didn't know Frank's register number. It was one of those beautiful catch-22s that occur so often in organizations run by the government. I could not write to Frank unless I had his number, but I could not get his number unless I could write to Frank to ask for it.

Months later I got a letter from a Stephen Bristol, who turned out to be Frank's parole agent. He included an address for Frank, so I was finally able to write to him. Now here was a letter from the old bandit.

Frank started his letter like this: "Hey, Kid, I hear those trains blow, and I see them go by, and I get itchy feet. But I won't go. Last month I went, and almost froze to death riding on a piggyback all the way to San Luis Obispo. Besides, I have to be here in case my parole officer shows up."

I thought, *I bet he went up to San Luis Obispo to make that easy score on the washeteria by the railroad tracks.* He went on to explain he had not served his time at San Quentin because he was old and sick. They had sent him to the California Men's Colony at San Luis Obispo, where they had put him on the west side with the milder offenders. But Frank screwed up (as usual) and hit another inmate in the mouth, so they sent him to live with the rougher boys in CMC east side, which was right by the tracks of the Southern Pacific. He could listen to the trains rumble by in the night like at the hobo jungle. Now he was out on parole again and back in Santa Barbara.

Frank had moved to the Southern Hotel. The old wooden hotel where he had been staying when I was in Santa Barbara had burned down, along with

Frank's clothes, pictures, papers, and "all my money!" (He should have said "all *the* money!" because any money lying around Frank's room was likely not his.) He complained about having to stay sober because the parole officer would send him back to prison if he caught him drunk. The "phony son-of-a-bitch comes around every week without warning." He closed his letter by saying "they aren't going to get me again." (He did not say he would not plunder again.)

During that year I got several more letters from Frank. Sometimes I needed a dictionary to get his meaning. For example—and I apologize to the reader ahead of time for the translations in parenthesis, which assumes that he is as ignorant as I was. For example, Frank called the prison guards "gunsils" (sodomites), and said the parole officer was always threatening him with "durance vile" (a long stretch in the pen). His last letter to me was postmarked at Santa Barbara on Christmas Eve. He finished that letter with:

> The miners came in '49
> The whores in '51
> They stewed it all together here
> And made the native son.

He signed off: "I am one of those native sons-of-bitches, maybe one of the worst. So long, Kid. Frank.

That was the last I ever heard of him.

ALL PILOTS AT the 3640th expected to serve at least one tour in Vietnam. As the fighting became more intense, we watched the TV news every day. I had no TV at home, but in the break room at the 3640th a TV was always going. Pilots were always discussing the news. It was a bad time to be in the U.S. Army. Thousands of our soldiers died every month in Vietnam, and ten times as many were wounded. It was a good time to be in a U.S. college. The students were having a merry time demonstrating against the war. While dozens of American soldiers bled out every day on muddy Vietnam battlefields, their "peers" back home danced and sang, and wore flowers in their hair.

Students were running the asylum. Professors were reduced to spectators as demonstrations erupted all over the country—not just in the colleges. High schools, and even some grade schools, joined the fun. They had food fights. They set off fire alarms. They chewed gum in class! They wanted better food, more dances, and less homework—oh, yes, and also less of that war thing. The littlest student in the smallest school in Podunk, USA, could get his picture in the paper by carrying an anti-war sign. Attendance at college classes was dismal. The students had more important things to do. Their attendance was mainly at "demonstrations." They let their hair grow long and dressed like Silver and Reesey and the rest of the gang at Sausalito. The jocks who wore their football jackets and sweatshirts and still went to the barbershop were laughed at and taunted as comic and irrelevant leftovers from dreary days gone by. You will still often hear the summer of 1967 referred to as "the summer of love." It was actually a summer full of hate, and of destruction of property by war protestors. While some young men were fighting their war for them, these guys sat at home and complained about how unjust the war was. They never admitted (even today) that they were afraid to go, and they resented the men who did go because the contrast made them look like cowards. It was the draft that made the war "unjust." When the draft ended, the protests ended.

I paid little attention to the war protesters. I was busy flying. Often demonstrations amounted to nothing more than students sitting on steps singing "We Shall Overcome." That song became the mantra of college kids all over the world. Sometimes on the evening news you could hear demonstrating students in Japan or Germany or France sing that song in English, and I don't think they knew what it meant—or cared. They called them "sit-ins," because they consisted of rebellious students planting their asses any place they were not wanted. They held "sit-ins" and "be-ins" and "smoke-ins" and "love-ins." This inspired the goofballs at NBC to open a new and insipid TV show called *Laugh-In*. To compound their foolishness, they moved that show into the Monday-night eight o'clock slot where it replaced *The Man from U.N.C.L.E.*, which was the only TV show I watched. There was no Monday night football back then.

That year of 1967 was like a slow fuse burning toward the 1968 explosion. I was slowly losing faith in our leaders to effectively conduct a war. Lyndon Johnson would not allow American pilots to attack the MiGs on the ground at the airport in Hanoi, nor to bomb the harbor at Haiphong, where the supply shipments for the Viet Cong came from. When Christmas came that year, we of the 3640th sat at the club and talked about what torture it must be for an American POW to hear how the war was going, and to hear what was going on back home. Congressmen, college professors, and CBS News anchors were speaking out against the war, while they suffered in prison for trying to serve them in that very war. Few Americans knew anything about the American POWs in Hanoi. We cursed President Johnson for the cover-up and the press for helping him.

Chapter Twenty-Eight

1968

PERHAPS YOU ARE TOO YOUNG to remember 1968—or too old and have forgotten. I have not forgotten. The fuse had burned down to the dynamite. It was a watershed year in my life, and in the life of the nation. I remember. It was a year crammed with one dreadful thing after another, the devil's own year. There will not be a year to eclipse 1968 until Judgment Day. During that year the nation lost its will to fight the war in Vietnam. During that year I made up my mind to quit the Air Force.

It was the kind of year that makes men ask themselves what they had done to deserve all this. Preachers rained fire and brimstone from the pulpits and said they had warned the people all along that, if they did not mend their evil ways, the wrath of God would be upon them, and now the time of retribution had come. Never mind that those preachers and other preachers in other countries in other times had been making that same prophesy since the time of Moses, with that same declaration that the time was now come.

Early in the year, our protesting students found themselves a martyr to rally around. On January second of every year in Havana, Castro held a big government-funded rally. Attendance was mandatory. The people had to show their appreciation for the Great Revolution. That year Castro put up an enormous picture of Che Guevara. He was now the hero of their revolution, and their great martyr—for Che was now dead. American protesters, even those who never heard of Che before, called themselves "revolutionaries" and "disciples of Che." Che had been killed in Bolivia the previous October, where he had been trying to raise an army of jungle Indians. Che miscalculated the situation in Bolivia. He thought he could raise an army of peasants in a few months and overthrow the government, as had been done in Cuba. But Bolivia was doing fairly well for the first time in history, and the people were not (just then) of that unhappy kind that would shed their blood in a revolution, especially one led by a foreigner. His "army of peasants" did not catch fire. Che found himself more and more isolated, until he surrendered to the Bolivian Army, which promptly killed him.

The Bolivian Army did Che a great favor. Instead of leaving this world a failure, he was the canonized saint of all revolutions. He would be the "pure revolutionary." His deeds and even the clothing he wore were now sacred. For decades, any good revolutionary wore green military fatigues, a beard, and a black beret, and chanted anti-government slogans—no matter the government. Young protesters on the streets of America in 1968 chanted "*Como Che, como Che.*"

Captain Boyd was killed in January of that year on his night solo. That cast a gloomy pall over the base for a while. It was also an election year. The pilots of the 3640th followed the daily news closely. The outcome of the election would make a huge difference in the lives of many of us. All over the country, citizens of the U.S. were glued to their TVs every evening for news of the war. By February of 1968, CBS with Cronkite and NBC with Huntley and Brinkley were getting the highest ratings ever. Reporters could get "same day" pictures from the battlefield with satellite relays from Japan to New York.

The people were stunned by the pictures of war on TV. The price of a color TV had gone way down during 1967 and now, on their new color sets, for the first time, people could see blood that was red—much more upsetting than the black blood they saw on their old black-and-white sets. Every day they saw pictures of blood-soaked bandages on young men lying on stretchers. There were lots of pictures of body bags being carried onto transport planes. And all this came on the heels of 1967, when Johnson had been assuring the nation that we were winning the war. Red blood caused a big change in public opinion.

The print media stepped up coverage, too. They used the most graphic pictures they could get their hands on. Those pictures were fresh, sent from Vietnam by electronic scanner. The most famous picture was one that no one living then will forget: a South Vietnamese general executing, with his pistol, a skinny little guy with his hands tied behind his back. It was taken on a street in Saigon.

Everybody talked about the war over beer mugs and around water coolers. People were eager to express their opinion and to hear that of others. Politicians began to appear on shows like Johnny Carson's *Tonight Show* to give their views on the war. They got on Rowan and Martin's *Laugh-in* and told jokes about the opinions of other politicians. Hollywood movie stars suddenly turned into political commentators, hogging the mike on prime time shows and at demonstrations against the war. Every day that war and the protests were right in everyone's face, right on everyone's color TV.

That year the Selective Service announced it was going to draft over 300,000 boys (they said men). That was a big increase over 1967, and that made young people see the war as even more unjust. President Johnson's State of the Union speech in January sounded to us at the 3640th like one thing: more war. He and his vice-president (Hubert Humphrey from Minnesota) and his secretary of defense, Robert McNamara (from Mars, I think), were going to continue sending more troops. There was no plan, no strategy—just send more cannon fodder. All three networks carried the speech. That was new, too. For the first time the State of the Union speech generated enough interest to preempt other shows. CBS even canceled *Green Acres*, for God's sake.

The pilots of the 3640th complained there was no substance to the Johnson's speech. Nothing new. Nothing about how to fight the war, or why. The pilots in Vietnam had long complained that the administration constantly sent orders that limited their ability to win the war. "You can't bomb this, you can't bomb that. You can't go north of this line, you can't go west of that one." Pilots were risking their lives to hit insignificant targets chosen by political desk jockeys who studied maps in the safety of their offices in Washington. General Westmoreland, supposedly in charge of the war, was constantly overruled by Johnson and McNamara, especially in his efforts to bomb the Ho Chi Minh Trail in Laos and Cambodia. Generals who had spent their lives studying the art of war were being overruled by clueless bureaucrats in Washington, D.C.; they said the generals were unable "to think outside of the box." That was McNamara. The administration was micromanaging the war and making a total hash of it.

Johnson and McNamara both combed their hair straight back like they were facing a furious headwind. And they were—one of their own making. They got us into the war and now they had no idea how to win, and worse yet, how to get out of it. So they just quit. By springtime they had both bowed out. McNamara resigned his position, and Johnson announced he would not run for a second term. General Westmoreland also resigned that spring. What the hell—let the soldiers on the battlefield figure it out for themselves.

In the unhappy background of all this, during that whole year the Pueblo Incident ran like static on a bad radio. The Pueblo Incident (or Affair, or Fiasco—whatever you want to call it) started shortly after Johnson gave his more-war State of the Union speech. North Korea seized one of our Navy's boats, with eighty-three men on board. Johnson and McNamara did nothing about it except "hold talks." So there was this little turd of a country thumbing its nose at us all during 1968. Johnson and McNamara could not make up their minds what to do about the Pueblo Incident any more than they could about the war.

Early in that year the Viet Cong launched the notorious Tet Offensive. Tet is the Vietnamese New Year Celebration, and our politicians had made a nice, little cease-fire agreement for those Tet festivities—you know, to show the Viet Cong how nice we could be. On the very morning of the first day of the agreement, the Viet Cong attacked all over South Vietnam in a balls-to-wall campaign that lasted for months. The North Vietnamese Army had already attacked our base at Khe Sahn, just south of the DMZ. Khe Sahn was one of the most remote U.S. outposts. Bloody fighting went on there through February and even into part of March. It was grim. Dozens of U.S. Marines were killed every few days; bloody bandages on the TV every day. Finally, after the Khe Sahn ground was red with blood, McNamara allowed our Air Force B-52s to break up the Viet Cong positions on the hills around Khe Sanh.

THE ACADEMY AWARDS, which were handed out in April, were delayed a couple days that year because some idiot shot Martin Luther King, Jr. Everyone in the country knew who King was by then. He had been in the news for years. He had appeared on the cover of *Time* as their Man of the Year for 1963, and he had won the Nobel Peace Prize in 1964. He had been on TV over and over giving speeches about civil rights (and he was a real orator, not a bore like President Johnson). But he was by no means universally liked. He did not have the hero status of today—not among whites, nor among blacks. Many white people saw him as a "rabble-rouser." Many blacks labeled him an "Uncle Tom" because he did not call for blood in the civil rights revolution. The popularity of Martin Luther King has grown tremendously since he was shot that day in April of 1968.

They buried Martin Luther King in Atlanta during Holy Week. President Johnson did not go to the funeral. He was worried about anti-war demonstrations. Besides, he was now a lame duck. He had announced at the end of March that he would not be running for a second term. He saw the writing on the wall when rumors surfaced that Bobby Kennedy was going to run, and when a lightweight candidate like Eugene McCarthy (from Watkins, Minnesota) began to score points. McCarthy had made a strong showing in the New Hampshire primary and was polling well in Wisconsin. McCarthy was especially popular with young men of draft age, because he ran a completely anti-war campaign. Students dropped out of their universities in order to campaign for him. They slept on floors and skipped meals just to spread the word. And why not? If the war was over, the threat of the draft was over. The McCarthy fans went wild in celebration when Johnson backed out of the race. They thought he was quitting because he was afraid of them. But he was quitting because he was afraid of Vietnam.

McCarthy kids would have been far more effective and would have had a better public image if many of them had not sported the long hair and beards of the drug culture. This tied peaceniks and beatniks and McCarthyniks together. The general population was pro-peace but still not pro-drugs. McCarthy ads always showed the senator surrounded by adoring youngsters, but they were always the scrubbed-up kind. The ads would say, "Our children have come home." I paused and listened when I saw McCarthy appear on TV, because he was a St. John's graduate, and was "the Honorable Eugene McCarthy, United States Senator from Minnesota." He had given the commencement address when I graduated at St. John's. At first I liked the senator, but that wore off fast. He never really said anything except that obvious mantra: peace is better than war. There was no power in his speech, no drama, no pounding, no drive. He was as boring as a Benedictine monk teaching cosmology on a morning in late May. Bobby Kennedy was much more interesting.

The baby boomers were hitting their teens and were flooding the schools. They were used to getting what they wanted. They didn't want soldiering; they wanted drugs. Marijuana and LSD were cool in college. Timothy Leary told them LSD was the key to human happiness, so the boomers "tuned in, turned on, and dropped out." They chanted, "Hell no, we won't go." They sang (ad nauseum) "We Shall Overcome," "We Shall Not Be Moved," and "Kumbaya."

They directed their anger against boys in uniform. They sometimes spit on soldiers returning from Vietnam. Reporters loved to cover the protesters, so people got to see it all on TV. All over the country students from Oregon to Florida, from Berkeley to Radcliffe, were on TV wearing "Fuck the draft" signs. Girls wore T-shirts labeled "Pull Out!" French students in Paris were waving North Vietnamese flags, chanting "U.S. go home."

NOW IT WAS D-DAY, the sixth of June. I was flying with Major Holt that morning. I think it was on a routine IP checkride, because I was in the right seat. When I plugged in my communications cord, before I could ask, "How do you read?" Holt asked me, "Did you hear about Kennedy?"

"I heard he was doing fine," I said, going through the prestart checklist.

Holt said, "Ah, no. Not so fine. He's dead."

Bang! Another victim of 1968. Bobby Kennedy, the brother of John Kennedy, would surely have been elected president of the United States that fall. He had already easily won the South Dakota primary and had beaten McCarthy in California where Johnson's vice president, Hubert Humphrey (who was now in the race, too), had received a dismal twelve percent of the vote. But along came another crazy idiot with a gun, and now Bobby was gone. Immediately there were still more riots. The rioters who appeared after the Martin Luther King assassination came back again. Now almost everybody had an excuse to throw bombs, burn cars, and break windows. All summer long, smoke from riots hung over major cities. Smoke from the war hung over Vietnam.

Since the beginning of the year, there had been news coming out of Czechoslovakia. The tight communist controls were being loosened. The people were trying to run their own country for a change. In August things were still going well, until the Soviets had enough of all that freedom stuff. Like the North Koreans, the Russians knew we were too busy in Vietnam to bother about other countries. They sent in troops and tanks, and rolled over Czechoslovakia like a steam roller over a bug. We did nothing.

In August, the Democratic convention in Chicago became the biggest news on TV. It trumped even the war. It made stars of news reporters. By the time it was over, Walter Cronkite, Chet Huntley, and David Brinkley were better known than the candidates themselves, better known than rock stars or movie stars. The convention was held at the end of August, the week of President Johnson's birthday. He had insisted on holding the convention that week, back when he figured it would be nothing more than his own coronation, but a lot of fetid water had gone over the damn dam since then.

Hippies and yippies flooded the streets of the city. Yippies were members of the Youth International Party which, as far as I could tell, was a group of hippies a little madder than the regular ones. They called themselves an international party because they had gotten some young people from France to join. (That was not hard to do; a Frenchman would join anything.) Hippies thought to change the world by rioting in the streets and getting stoned. Yippies thought to change the world by acting like clowns and getting stoned. Protesters were excluded from the convention hall, but they ran a candidate anyway—a pig. They said they were running a pig because they wanted a candidate that looked like Hubert Humphrey and Mayor Daley. Those two, they said, were both fat, red-faced, double-chinned, and had little squinty eyes. They hated Humphrey because he was running against their dreamboat, McCarthy, and they hated Daley because he sent the police after them when they broke stuff. All day long they chanted, "Fuck you, Daley." The protesters held a circus in Chicago, and the press covered everything they did or talked about. The press ran big headlines about things they threatened to do, even if they had no intention of actually carrying out the threat. So every day we heard new threats: they were going to put LSD into the water system, they were going to kidnap the candidates and take them to Siberia, they were going to launch mortar rounds at the convention center, and were going to stick Molotov cocktails up Daley's exhaust pipe.

Mayor Daley estimated there were ten thousand protesters in the city. They romped around the streets of Chicago with their candidate pig and with their transistor radios pressed to one ear to hear what was going on inside the convention hall. They staggered in disbelief when they heard the convention was adopting a pro-war stance, basically continuing Johnson's policies. I have to say, this was a real surprise for me, too. After McNamara left, after the Tet offensive, after Johnson's resignation, and the success of the McCarthy and the Kennedy campaigns, I thought the Democrats would surely have an anti-war plank to counter the Republicans. The Republicans had held a convention in Miami Beach a few weeks before. It was dull as dishwater by comparison. Nobody paid attention. They nominated Richard Nixon, who was clever enough to capitalize on all the 1968 rioting by putting himself forward as the "law and order" candidate. He also capitalized on the anti-war sentiment by hinting he had a plan for stopping the war.

The rules were different in those days. The Democratic machine at the convention could ignore the vote of the primaries and nominate anybody they wanted. The protesters did not understand this and went crazy when Hubert Humphrey got the nomination. Their hero, McCarthy, was being tossed aside like garbage, and the establishment dummy, Humphrey, was getting the nomination. No. It could not be. Not after all their hard work. Not after the death of Bobby Kennedy. Emotions boiled over. Fighting all over Chicago.

The protesters did not realize what they were doing. Though they hated Hubert Humphry, they hated Nixon even more, yet they were practically campaigning for Nixon by making the Democrats look like a party of nuts. These were children having a tantrum. In fall, Richard Nixon easily won the election.

IN SEPTEMBER THERE came some comic relief. The annual Miss America pageant was held in Atlantic City. It was like a small, comic version of Chicago. It was the only time the TV in the break room of the 3640th was tuned to a Miss America pageant. A group of lady nuts from New York held Chicago-copycat demonstrations in the streets of Atlanta. Like the Chicago protesters, they tried to crash the party at the convention center. They marched and fought in the streets, carried signs and broke windows. They ran an animal candidate for Miss America (a sheep instead of a pig). They wanted to show how all women were hurt by beauty competitions. They said the contest made young ladies think the most important thing about a woman was her looks, and so felt inferior because they could not measure up to the beauty standards of Miss America. They brought out a bewildered, live ewe and crowned her Miss America. They sang: "Ain't she sweet, making profits off her meat."

They brought out a trash can, "The Freedom Trash Can," into which they threw their high-heeled shoes, girdles, bras, false eyelashes, and curlers (all symbols of their great oppression). Several screaming ladies got on TV and predicted that in ten years no woman would ever use such items. They were going to set the whole pile on fire, but the police stopped them. The police thought the wooden boardwalk might catch fire. Then the protestors auctioned off a big Miss America puppet and hung Bert Parks, the host of the pageant, in effigy. During this convention I could hear laughing and clapping and cheers from the break room of the 3640th. Of all the Miss America shows, it was the best ever. They have not done another one like it since.

Even this gaggle in Atlanta became an anti-war protest. The ladies said they were there to expose "the male chauvinism, the commercialization of beauty, the racism, and the oppression of women." But they were able to drag in the war issue, and that became primary. The protesters came on TV saying that by sending Miss America candidates to entertain troops in Vietnam, the women served as "death mascots" in an immoral war.

IT WAS THE YEAR the Olympics were held in Mexico City. The games started in mid-October, but first the city had to clean up the blood in the streets. Mexico City was one of the fastest growing cities in the world. Poor people from all over the country streamed in, hoping to improve their lives. Instead, they created heart-breaking slums. The Mexican government had no more clue of how to solve the slum problem than Johnson and McNamara had about solving Vietnam. All summer the students from the university had been protesting against their government. They had a simple, childlike request of their government: "We demand a solution to the problems of Mexico."

Encouraged by all the groovy rioting in the United States, the protests became more violent. They, too, started breaking things and setting fires. They, too, shouted anti-war slogans. They, too, were admirers of Che, and admirers of revolutions—both the old Mexican kind where poor farmers died using pitchforks to fight soldiers with rifles, and the new kind where spoiled, angry students shook their fists and threw rocks at soldiers with rifles. But the Institutional Revolutionary Party, which now ruled Mexico, did not like revolutions anymore. Their love of revolutions went out the window right after the one Great Revolution put them in power.

The Mexican students were determined to exploit the attention focused on Mexico City by those Olympic Games. Mexican President Gustavo Díaz Ordaz was equally determined to stop that exploitation. In September, he ordered one of his army generals to occupy the campus of the National Autonomous University. Student protesters were attracted to that university like moths to a flame. The cauldron boiled over on the second of October, ten days before the start of the Olympics.

No one will ever know how many were killed when the soldiers hosed down the students with their rifles. The government said a few, the students said hundreds. Our press went along with the students and the general impression was that hundreds were massacred there in Mexico City that day. It was a drastic measure, but President Ordaz got what he wanted. The student movement in Mexico vanished. The students licked their wounds in silence. To add salt to those wounds, Luis Echeveria, the minister of the interior at the time, who worked closely with President Ordaz in stomping on the students, later became the president of Mexico. The students completely gave up.

Some in our military thought the "Mexican method" was the way to handle protesters: "exterminate the cowards." I did not have the total contempt for the counter-culture people my fellow officers did. I knew Reesey and Silver and the Sausalito gang were among them. They were screwed up, but they did not deserve to die for that. I was plenty screwed up myself.

American news reporters were no longer just reporting the news about the war. They were giving their opinions, and they were always anti-war. Even fence-riders like Walter Cronkite came out and stated flatly that the war was "unwinnable." This fueled the protests. Spitting on soldiers in public was common. Pilots returning from Vietnam were called "baby killers." Because of the bad reporting of our news media, I had the impression that the protesters, the rioters, the spitters were the majority opinion. That was not true. The media did not cover the feelings of the everyday American worker— plumber, electrician, truck driver, farmer. I thought most of the country was against the war, against the military, against fighting communism. By the end of 1968, I was no longer a career soldier. Johnson, McNamara, and Westmoreland had quit. What the hell was I doing in this war? I knew this: if I went to Vietnam, I would be going with reservations. That is no way to go to war. That was how Johnson and McNamara went to war. If you are not ready to give it your all, stay at home.

I was not afraid to die. I was still young and didn't know the meaning of the word. The thought that I might die in Vietnam didn't bother me nearly as much as the thought of what it would do to my mother. The only time in my life I ever wept at a gravesite was when I saw the tiny headstones on the graves of my brothers Richard and Ralph. They had died when still babies. I didn't know them. They had died before I was born. I didn't cry for them, I cried for my mother. God, how she must have suffered! I didn't want her to suffer over me. I couldn't bear the thought of mom crying over that folded flag while the bugle wailed taps at the cemetery of Seven Dolors in Albany. I didn't want my mother to read a telegram (like other mothers of soldiers did), a telegram that would say: "The Secretary of the Air Force regrets to inform you that your son has been killed in action in defense of freedom in Vietnam. His many friends and the president join me in expressing our sorrow at your profound loss . . . etc., etc." I wasn't willing to put her through even a tiny bit of that in order to defend a country that forced its young men to go to war and then spit on them when they returned.

IN DECEMBER, TWO of my heroes died: Thomas Merton and John Steinbeck, both favorite authors of mine. And then finally for contrast to this ridiculous year of turmoil, we watched on TV a scene of profound peace. It was Christmas Eve. Three of our astronauts, flying on Apollo 8, entered lunar orbit that night. They sent live pictures from a quarter-million miles away as they orbited the moon. They showed pictures of the Earth and the Moon floating in the vast silent space. All over the world, people watched. It was the largest TV audience in history until that time. To close their broadcast, the three men on the spaceship took turns reading from Genesis, chapter one, about the creation of the world. The last man ended with, "And from the crew of Apollo 8, we close with good night, good luck, a Merry Christmas, and God bless all of you—all of you on the good Earth." They had mentioned God more than a dozen times in two minutes. Those pictures of the lonely, little planet Earth in that infinite space gave me a deep sense of stillness, of solitude, and of peace. How little we meant to the universe! How trivial that little country of Vietnam. How meaningless that war.

You had to be living in those days to understand the splendor of Apollo 8. Those three men were the first crew launched by a Saturn V rocket. They were the first to blast out from the John F. Kennedy Space Center down by Cape Canaveral in Florida. It was the first manned mission ever to completely leave the gravitational pull of the earth (to actually leave an earth orbit). It showed the world we had moved ahead of the Soviets in the space race. We were the first humans to fly into the gravitational field of another celestial body. Our men were the first to fly far enough away from Earth to be able to look back and see it as a whole planet. We were the first humans to look directly at the far side of the Moon. By this one flight, we were able to show the world that (though we may seem screwed up with riots and war) we knew what we were doing in the field of technology. Apollo 8 took three days to travel to the Moon. It orbited the moon ten times and came home, a triumph to end that year of tragedy.

Chapter Twenty-Nine

LIKE MANY MOTOR SKILLS, flying performance is best when one is relaxed. Students who didn't give a damn often did better than those who tried too hard. I knew it well, because I was in that latter group at the beginning of my training at Vance. I tried for perfection and suffered over anything less. And now it was frustrating to watch a student making the same mistake: caring too much, trying too hard. Those boys wanted Air Force wings more than anything on earth. I remembered that, once I soloed, I was much better in the aircraft. Soloing gave one confidence, and that allows a person to relax. Therefore, no matter how bad he was, I always tried my best to solo a student.

For a while they moved me from A Flight to C Flight, where I flew for Major Holt. He had a student, a "Lieutenant Goober," who was about to flunk out. Holt asked me to fly with him. He had already failed several times and had only one more try before he went up for elimination. His instructor said he was too dangerous for solo and would kill himself if left to his own devices.

He said, "He can't maintain an altitude. He either comes in high on final, or he drags it in. He often rounds out hot, then balloons in the flare, and fails to see that he must go around."

I hated this kind of flight. It put a lot pressure on the instructor. I could just flunk the guy and be safe—and also be a coward—or I could send up a dangerous student and risk the man's life. To add to the pressure, it was Wives Day at C Flight that day. All the wives would be there to join their husbands for a noon lunch in the flight room. Everyone would be watching Lieutenant Goober come in from his flight and would all know immediately if he flunked or passed. The lieutenant was very well-liked by his fellow students, and his pretty little wife was equally popular among the wives. He was an awkward, gawky southern boy, complete with drawl and accent. They affectionately called him "Goober" after that character, a lovable screw-up, on the *Andy Griffith Show*.

Lieutenant Goober and I left out of Laredo Air Force Base shortly before noon, headed for Barfly. Barfly was the Laredo auxiliary field where we practiced touch-and-goes and flameout landings. It was also where we went for initial solos. I had arranged a noontime slot because there was little traffic at Barfly over the noon hour. If this student was as dangerous as his instructor said, I wanted the sky as empty as possible, should I decide to send him up by himself. I had also talked to the captain in charge of the mobile control unit at Barfly and told him I was planning to solo a very weak student.

The captain said, "I don't give a shit who you solo out here. In fact, I could use a little excitement. Just tell him not to crash into my mobile unit. There's plenty of room out there among the cactus and the yucca."

Lieutenant Goober did okay on the takeoff. He rotated at sixty-five knots (got the nose a little high, but not bad), gear up at 100, flaps up at 110 (or thereabout) and I had no complaints on the flight to Barfly except for some altitude deviations, which I let pass. I could tell he was very nervous—and who can blame him? He was flying with a strange instructor, and his performance in the next hour might be the determination of his entire life's work. I tried to help relax him by humming to myself and looking out to the side as though I was not paying any attention to what he was doing. I tried to be like Captain Tiggeman.

Goober called Barfly for landing and set the altimeter. When he rolled out on initial, he was right on airspeed and not real bad on altitude. He called initial. Things were looking up. In the back of my mind I started to think he might be passable. But when he rolled into the pitch, oh, God, he allowed the nose to drop drastically and went into a screaming dive. I noticed he was not trimming at all. I blamed that on his instructor, and it angered me. It was a simple technique that could be performed mechanically with no feel for the airplane, and yet it was a tremendous help in maintaining altitude in the pitchout. I always told my students to trim in time with the low-power warning horn that sounded in the pitch as soon as the power was reduced to sixty percent. I wanted to see the *click, click, click* of the trim button in time with the *beep, beep, beep* of the warning horn. I was thinking some of Lieutenant Goober's problems might have been from poor instructing.

I hoped with all my might to solo this guy. I thought maybe if I flew five or six patterns with him I could teach him enough to solo. This was another pressure call. If you flew too many patterns with the student, you were too low on gas to solo him. He had to do at least three solo landings, and then we had to have enough gas left to get back to Laredo.

About three-quarters of the way around the pitchout, Lieutenant Goober noticed his altitude and raised the nose. He raised it too high and zoomed up past his altitude. I said nothing. He dropped speed brakes, gear, flaps, and called "gear check, touch and go." Again his nose dropped too far in the turn, so he rolled out low on final. But he did add power as his airspeed bled down, though he added too much, so he was hot in the flare. He ballooned, lowered the nose again, and glory be! This man knew exactly where the runway was! His depth perception (often faulty in students who had landing problems), was perfect. He rounded out a second time only inches above the runway and chopped the power, floated a little, touched down. As the tires squeaked onto the tar, I said to myself, *I'm going to solo this guy. I don't care if he stinks up the sky with his patterns, I know he's safe when he gets near the ground.*

I said, "Go," for we were eating up the runway fast with that long landing. He made his call "on the go," and we climbed for another pattern. Same results. Diving and zooming through the altitudes, little or no trimming, another ballooned landing. After he had cleaned up the airplane in the climb, I said, "I got it."

I said, "Lieutenant, I'm going to do this pattern until final. I want you to watch my thumb on the trim button. No, don't look outside, just look at my thumb."

He watched my thumb as I trimmed forward in the climb and as I trimmed back on downwind. I said, "Drop speed brakes, trim, trim, trim; gear, trim, trim, trim. Keep the pressure off the stick. That way, when you're distracted for a moment, the nose does not go wandering all over the horizon."

I ran the trim back to get the airplane out of trim and gave him the airplane, saying, "There, that's a hundred knots on final, out of trim, you keep the nose steady and trim it."

He took the stick, up came the nose, but he pushed it down and trimmed. He added a little power, reacting to the lower airspeed (he should have just lowered the nose, but I liked the fact that he reacted quickly to the low airspeed), and now he was coming in a little high. He lowered the nose just before the flare, so we came in hot once more. Another ballooning landing—but not nearly as radical, and he was so good at recovering I loved him for it. When he added power to go around and called "on the go" I made a sudden decision. I chopped the power and called to mobile, "On the runway will be full stop."

That was an unusual call, because mobile was expecting a touch-and-go, but since there was little traffic it wouldn't be a problem.

The captain at the mobile unit said, "That's approved."

I took the airplane on a high-speed taxi up the ramp and told Lieutenant Goober to do his after-landing checks. I was in a hurry. I wanted Goober to have no time to think—he was nervous enough. I reminded him to add "initial solo" to his radio calls, and to be sure to do his checklist. I shut down the engine on my side of the airplane as I taxied. I parked near the head of the runway, turning the nose into the wind. I checked the fuel and told Goober to do four touch-and-goes and then a fifth one for full stop. I unlocked the canopy and climbed out. I leaned in and secured my shoulder harness and seat belt. I stepped back from the intake of the right engine and gave Goober the signal to start. He signaled back and bowed his head into the checklist.

There was a long pause. *Damn it. What the hell is he doing? Praying?* Finally he reached for the starter switches, and I could hear the engine beginning to whine. After a little while he gave me thumbs up to show he was ready. I came to attention and snapped him my smartest salute as Captain Tiggeman had done to me when I first soloed in the T-37 years ago. He shyly reached up to answer the salute, and I saw he had tears in his eyes. I signaled for him to put down the visor on his helmet. Then I turned and walked toward the runway. Mobile gave me a green light and I crossed. Behind me I could hear the J-69s spooling up as Second Lieutenant Goober took the active.

"God I hope you know what you're doing!" said the captain as I entered the mobile unit.

I said, "He'll do better when he's by himself."

"Well, he can't do much worse, and he already forgot to say 'initial solo' when he called ready for takeoff."

I said, "If that's the only thing he screws up, I'll kiss that boy in front of everybody in the flight room."

Lieutenant Goober looked good on takeoff, but I could see he was fighting the airplane on downwind. I felt like grabbing the mike and yelling, "trim, trim, trim," but I left it alone. He dived again in the final turn and this time came in low on final. I had expected him to come in hot and high, balloon and recover. That kind of landing he could do. But he was dragging this one in. I held my breath. *God, I hope he keeps his airspeed up!*

"There's gonna be cactus in the gear well," said the captain dryly.

Real funny. But Goober made a good landing—a little hard, but right on the numbers. Good. He had recovered well from a dragged-in approach and I knew he could recover from high and hot. I relaxed. I even began to joke with the captain. When he said, "You want me to tell him to full stop?" I said, "Hell no, I might give him an Excellent. You should see my other students!"

Actually, I had never soloed anyone this bad, but I had seen an intelligence in Goober that made me let him go. He had judgment; he was a bit slow to correct, and I gambled he wasn't too slow. And I was right. He improved with every pattern, so that by the time he called "full stop," even the captain was a believer.

"That guy learns best by himself," he said. "You should let him fly home alone and you should walk."

When we got back to Laredo, I debriefed the lieutenant in the instructor's room, because the student room was full of wives and noise. The clanking of dishes and chatter of women could be heard up and down the halls. It took me only seconds to fill out the grade slip. I knew I had to give Goober a Fair no matter what. I was not about to flunk him, and I could not give him a Good or Excellent, because that would reflect on the judgment of his instructor. I pushed the grade slip across the table and said, "Your last landing at Barfly was excellent, but I still have to give you a Fair overall."

"Thank you, sir, I know you do,"and I noticed his voice was broken.

I didn't look at him, thinking he might be embarrassed if he had tears in his eyes. I said, "Go eat."

Later, when the party was over, Lieutenant Goober found me in the hall and introduced me to his wife. The look of gratitude she gave me put a lump in my throat. They were both grateful for giving him a chance to solo, but the lieutenant would never know how grateful I was to him for proving me right. And he proved it again and again in the rest of his training in the T-37. I instructed him in the instrument phase and he got the highest grade of anyone at his table. Not only that, even his fellow students were grateful. During the rest of the time Goober's class was in the T-37 phase, I often got a beer set in front of me at the O Club with the bartender saying, "It's from C Flight." When I looked around, there would be a table full of Goober's buddies saluting with beer steins. Goober was never there at the O Club. He was at home studying.

I LIKED FLYING for Major Holt. Sometimes I had to fly for Major Walker in B Flight. I didn't care so much for Major Walker. A good leader has confidence in himself and that translates into confidence in his men. A poor leader, having little confidence in himself, will micro-manage everything and everyone under his command. Walker was one of those micro-managers, and had the additional weakness of wanting to be liked. With that desire he would be too easy and amiable for days, and then when he saw discipline slipping, he would panic and suddenly turn into a martinet. He was extremely fond of flattery, always giving the brown nosers in his command special treatment.

His favorite way of showing familiarity with his men was by telling sexual and scatological jokes that were graphic, coarse, and disgusting without the redeeming quality of being funny. He was a handsome man with a dark complexion and full head of hair, and he liked to make jokes about Major Holt's bald head. Major Holt was confident and dignified. He was the same day after day. He wanted respect for the rules and regulations, but was reasonable about applying them to individual situations. I never had any doubt about what he expected of me. Best of all, he was repulsed by brown nosing.

Walker's B Flight was right across the hall from Holt's C Flight. Walker had the irritating habit of dropping into Holt's flight room any time uninvited. One day Major Holt was having a flight instructor's meeting. Holt sat at the head of the table, the flight instructors all around the table. I sat at the far end. In the middle of the meeting, Walker walked in behind Holt. Walker put a finger to his lips. He sneaked up quietly behind Holt, grinning like a naughty little boy. Walker lightly stroked the top of Holt's bald head. Holt stopped talking. He rolled his eyes upward, one corner of his mouth drawn back in irritation. He didn't look around. He knew it was Walker.

Walker, still stroking, announced to the room, "It feels just like my wife's ass."

Everyone laughed, and Walker was delighted with his joke.

But not for long.

Holt, still looking upward, reached up with his right hand, and with great concentration he stroked his head in a similar manner. Then he said slowly and with great deliberation: "You know, you're right. It does feel like your wife's ass."

The men roared. Walker tried to say something, but the laughter and the shouts of the men downed him out. Walker retreated in total defeat.

ON CROSS-COUNTRY FLIGHTS, the T-37 syllabus called for one low-level navigation leg. The point of low-level flying was to show a student how to navigate at levels where only a small part of the terrain was visible. Finding a checkpoint like a bridge on the Colorado was one thing at five thousand feet, finding it at one hundred feet was another matter. If off even a little, one could miss it. Low-level flying was common in combat, both to avoid radar and limit exposure to anti-aircraft artillery. Low-level flying was a thrill beyond anything one could do on motorcycle or dune buggy. Zipping across tree tops, over hills and down rivers at high speed was excitement and a pleasure that had no equal. The danger involved added spice to the ride.

I enjoyed giving the plane to the student and saying, "Take her down low and let her go."

And they would say, "How low can I go, sir?"

"As low as you want."

And the student would drop down to what he thought was really low (just as I did in training when I flew with Captain Simmons) and would cruise along for a while, thinking he was barely missing the trees. The ground went by so fast all was a blur and altitude was hard to judge. After a while I would say, "I got it," and roll it off on one wing and zoomed down until we actually were just skimming the tree tops. I would hear the student take a deep breath over the intercom. Then I would say, "This is more like low-level. Okay, you got it." And as soon as the student took the airplane, it would begin to creep up away from the blurring terrain. It was scary for them, but also fun, and often a student after graduating from the T-37 would tell me it was the best flight of the whole program.

One Monday morning Colonel Martin, our squadron commander, called me into his office. This was a rare happening, and it always meant trouble. I had been called on his carpet once before, when a major with the temperament of Frogface wrote a letter of reprimand on me. I had filed a flight plan to New Orleans that weekend, a route that would carry me over Houston. The weatherman said there were water spouts in the Houston area, but I filed anyway, with San Antonio as an alternate. I thought I would take a look at the water spouts, and if they looked dangerous I would go to my alternate. This major, who happened to be supervising that day, was one of those panicky fellows who found the responsibilities of leadership too heavy to carry, and he demanded I be reprimanded for my reckless attitude. (I suspected what actually happened was that the thought of a mere lieutenant flying in rough weather had scared the major so badly he had to retreat to the latrine and resort to a bottle which he had resolved not to employ anymore during duty hours.) But Colonel Martin, on that occasion, simply tore up the letter and told me to be more cautious about where I planned to fly. "You're a good instrument pilot," he said, "but don't let that go to your head."

But this Monday morning was different. No letter was pending. I even allowed myself the luxury of speculating the colonel might be calling me in to tell me what a good job I was doing—a thought which the colonel rapidly dispelled. The colonel gave me "at ease," and asked if I had been cross-country that weekend. I said yes. He asked if I had done a low-level mission from Del Rio to Laredo on Sunday afternoon. I said yes, I did, and told him I often used that leg for low level because it was a short flight and low-level sucks up a lot of fuel. The colonel said he could well believe the fuel part, especially at the level I was doing it. I began to feel uneasy about where this was going.

He said, "I have a friend who likes to fish the Rio Grand near Piedras Negras. He was doing just that yesterday afternoon standing on the bank of the river, when suddenly a jet went screaming by. He says that jet was flying lower than the tip of his fishing rod and the cliff on which he was standing was not very high. He says it was impossible to get a tail number because the thing passed in a flash. We checked all the flight plans. That jet could only have been you."

"Yes, sir," I said mildly, "that sounds about right."

The colonel gaped, wide-eyed. "No, that does not sound about right! It sounds about way wrong. You're going to have to explain why you are flying at ten feet above the terrain when the manual says you have to have at least five hundred. Have you done this before?"

"Yes, sir, on every cross-country," and then I added (by way of showing how careful I was about these things), "weather permitting."

The colonel allowed his body to collapse back in his chair with his head drooped to one side, staring at the floor. He slowly shook his head. "How did you get the idea that you could ignore the five-hundred-foot rule?"

This was a darned good question. The Air Force always went by the manual and yet I tossed it out the window on every low-level mission. And I was not normally a rule-breaker.

"Sir," I said. "I'm not making excuses. I just want to answer your question. It came from my training."

The colonel sat up and leaned forward, one ear pointed toward me, eyebrows raised as if to say, "I've got to hear this!" I told him that on my low-level navigation ride in the T-37, the instructor took the plane down low, and I remember seeing the fans of Oklahoma windmills turning above my head. I told him that on my low-level navigation ride in the T-38, we went down through Monument Valley at an altitude that allowed me to see the cameras of the tourists along the roadside as they snapped our picture. I told him that during IP school at Randolph in San Antonio, my instructor and I skimmed over Calavaras Lake as low as the tops of the masts on the sailboats.

The colonel looked as though he had been struck by lightning. He said, "So, I am to believe that just by pure coincidence, all the instructors of Lieutenant Bloch were the kind that disregard Air Force regulations." He picked up his pen. "Who were those instructors?"

I cleared my throat, hesitated, and looked around the room. "Colonel, I am explaining why I thought we could violate the regs in this case. I thought five hundred feet was not really low-level, and that it was put in the manual only because the brass want to cover their . . . want to make it look good for the public. I didn't tell you this to snitch on my instructors."

The colonel relaxed a bit. He dropped his pen, and nodded. "They're likely gone by now, anyway—on new assignments or dead from crashing into windmills and monuments." He pulled back one side of his mouth in a wry half-smile and said with raised eyebrows, "Bloch, I want you to come to attention and listen good."

I snapped to.

"You are not allowed to break regulations under any circumstances, ever! I don't care what you learned or what you hear from others. Is that clear?"

"Yes, sir."

"Completely clear!"

"Yes, sir."

"Get out of here." He waved a half-salute as though I didn't deserve a whole one. Then he said, "Wait a minute. What I don't understand is why I haven't heard of this before when you've been flying like this all this time. Surely your students talked about this at the club and other instructors heard about it. Are other instructors doing this with their students, too? Are they?"

I said, "Well, sir. I don't know what the others are doing. I think they're following the regs and probably think my students are exaggerating when they talk about how low we were flying. All students think they're barely missing the tree tops even at five hundred feet. But no matter what others are doing, sir, I assure you I'll stay at five hundred feet."

"On behalf of the United State Air Force and the taxpayers of this country I thank you," said the colonel with stinging sarcasm. "Beat it."

I left much relieved, though I still expected to get hell from my flight commander and to hear jokes at the O Club about my fishing the Rio Grande. But let me say what a stand-up guy Colonel Martin was: he never told anyone about this, and it all blew over without a ripple on the water (no pun intended). I loved the old man and it hurt me deeply when, a few years later, I had to give testimony to an accident board—testimony that in no way helped his case.

It happened like this. I came out of the BX one day and saw several instructors looking off to the south. A column of black smoke rose from the desert below our practice area. That always got our attention. One of the men said it was a brush fire, but I learned the truth when I got home. My neighbor waved me over to where he was sitting at his patio table getting drunk with a young sergeant friend from maintenance. He said, "Shake hands with the sergeant, he just bailed out of a spinning T-37 and got a ride back to base with the rescue chopper."

I immediately sat down. I was all ears. I had often wondered what it would be like to bail out of a T-37, especially one in a spin. The sergeant had been up with Colonel Martin and they had been doing spins. On one spin the colonel remarked that the plane was not recovering. He was slamming the controls around, and he suddenly told the sergeant to eject.

The T-37 Dash-1 said that if spin recovery had not happened by ten thousand feet AGL, you had to eject. I asked the sergeant, "What was your altitude?"

He said, "I have no idea, but I saw the needle on the altimeter was going around like a windmill, and I knew that wasn't good."

I asked, "Did he yell, 'bail out, bail out, bail out'?" (That was the recommended call for ejection.)

The sergeant said, "I don't know if he said it three times, because I was gone after the first one."

The accident report stated simply that while in a spin the colonel ejected when he saw the altimeter passing ten thousand. The accident investigating team interviewed a lot of us T-37 instructors. They tried to determine how many spins I had done in my life. They asked me if I had ever had any trouble. I felt I was betraying Colonel Martin but I had to admit that the only time I had any trouble recovering from a spin was when I failed to follow the Dash-1 procedures. In the end the accident was chalked up to pilot error. That was not a good thing to have on your record.

Chapter Thirty

CONSIDERING ALL THE FLYING we did, there were few fatal accidents, just enough to keep us on our toes. One sunny afternoon as I walked back to the flight shack with my student, we saw black smoke boiling up not far from the head of the active T-38 runway. A check pilot and student were killed while making their turn onto final for landing. I felt bad. I knew the pilot was probably taking a big chance with a weak student and letting the student get too low on airspeed. On a checkride the check pilot had to flunk the student if he had to take over the plane. This sometimes caused check pilots to allow students too much leeway. Too much concern for the student killed them both.

On another clear day near sunset, I was doing aerobatics with a student when we saw smoke down by the highway to Zapata. We heard a call on the radio: a T-37 was down with "two Copenhagens." Back in Laredo, I asked Captain Wertz what a Copenhagen was. He said, "Code for dead body." The two Copenhagens were fellow T-37 instructors. They had been out flying together on a practice mission. It was one of those awful things that happened when two macho instructors got together. They were probably showing off, trying to see who had the most guts. It was an easy trap to fall into. The accident board said a wing broke off. That only happened in excessive G maneuvers. They were both excellent pilots. It was tragic they would allow themselves to goof off to the extent of putting themselves in that kind of danger. It wouldn't have happened if they had been with a student.

Those accidents didn't scare me. I was confident I wouldn't put myself in those situations. But some accidents did not depend on pilot judgment. One such killed an instructor, though his student got back alive. In the late fall buzzards come down from up north on their way to Mexico for the winter. A bird the size of a buzzard can kill you. It was easy to spot a big kettle of buzzards when dozens were circling one spot, but there were many loners out there. Those were almost impossible to see until you were right upon them. This day the instructor and student took off on runway one-seven, headed for the areas. They'd turned southwest, climbing at 200 knots, when a buzzard shattered the windscreen in front of the instructor. The flight surgeon said he died instantly, buzzard bones driven through his visor into his skull. The student was not hurt, but shaken. He'd soloed not long before. I saw the cockpit when the plane was parked in the chocks. Blood, feathers, guts, and bits of canopy were all over.

That accident actually increased my confidence in the T-37. Even with all that damage, an inexperienced pilot was able to bring the airplane home. I felt safer flying the airplane than driving my car.

HOWEVER, THE RANDOM nature of the deaths from accidents and from the war in Vietnam shook my confidence in God. What my religion told me and what reality told me didn't match. God was a loving, omniscient, all-merciful being who took a personal interest in each one of us—and He provided us with a guardian angel to protect us from harm? That seemed a bit askew in light of what I saw around me. I thought monks might find it easy to remain constant in their beliefs isolated behind monastery walls—isolated from war, from airplane crashes, and human suffering. I determined I'd try not believing in God awhile. I'd be an atheist—not a bitchy one like Madalyn Murray O'Hair, who couldn't mind her own business—but just a quiet, peaceable one. I'd see if life made more sense that way. If other people wanted to believe, fine. If their religion brought them peace, I could only look upon that with envy. If believing in God didn't make sense, maybe not believing would.

Right away I realized some practical advantages. Instead of going to Mass Sunday morning, I could ride my motorcycle. No more worry about saying certain prayers at certain times, about committing sins and then having the additional worry of how to present them in the confessional. It was very liberating.

But after several months of freedom, I found that, as a non-believer, I had no way to explain the order of things. The whole beautiful universe, even if meaningless, couldn't be accidental, couldn't happen at random with no intelligence behind it. The harmony in nature became just as big a problem for me as haphazard accidents had been before. Non-belief was challenged by too much order, belief by too much chance. Either way was a puzzle. It was just as tough not to believe as to believe.

When something lucky happened to an atheist, he had no god to thank. I, too, hit a buzzard one day. I was flying solo on a test flight for Major McDougal, but I was lucky. The buzzard hit out on the right wing, caving in a good part of the leading edge, but didn't puncture a fuel tank or damage any control cables. On the way back to base, every time I looked out at my smashed wing, I rejoiced the buzzard hadn't hit a few feet more to the left. He would certainly have joined me in the cockpit. I found myself thanking God for my luck—just out of old habit. This atheism business wasn't that easy. It seemed more comforting to believe in God than to reject God. So I believed again—until another tragedy came along and blew my faith to pieces. I wavered back and forth between theism and atheism for months, even years, finding little peace either way. That eluded me until I was much older—and wiser.

Major MacDougal (Major Mac) was the head of Test Section at Laredo. He offered me the job of T-37 test pilot. The Air Force had sent me to school to be an academic instructor, and now I was teaching T-37 flight engineering and general aerodynamics. This might sound impressive. Basically all I did was teach student pilots how to pass multiple-choice tests required by the Air Force in those subjects. Major Mac thought it qualified me to be a test pilot.

"You're perfect for the job," he said. "If you crash an airplane and kill yourself, the brass won't question why I sent up a man with your credentials. If I send up some greenhorn and he screws up, it'll be my fault. If you screw up, it's all your fault."

I thanked him for this warm analysis of my qualifications and immediately took the job with no reservations. I could go up solo any time I wanted. I'd still be flying with students at times, still be teaching academics, but now I'd also be testing airplanes—solo. Planes coming out of maintenance had to be tested before they could be released to the flightline for training missions.

Major Mac was a wiry, banty rooster. He had more time in propeller planes than General Billy Mitchell. He didn't like jets. He'd say, "When you take off, you're already on fire and low on fuel." He always had a rum-soaked cigar blamped between his teeth, one he seldom lit. He chewed them all day with great relish, discarding them when they ran low on flavor. By four in the afternoon, his trash basket was half full of obscene, soggy, smelly brown lumps.

He was the best boss I ever had—intelligent, fair, funny, and easygoing. I never heard him swear, though his language was colorful. He used substitute words. He would say, "John Brown! I was mad!" or "Get that blasted, Johnny Walker airplane up in the sky and see what the dickens is wrong with it."

He heavily sprinkled his language with similes that involved "Hogan's goat": mad as Hogan's goat, stupid as Hogan's Goat, sick as Hogan's goat. Within minutes he could use contradictory Hogan's-goat similes. One minute he might say, "That lieutenant moves slower than Hogan's goat," and a minute later, "That plane came zipping through here faster than Hogan's goat."

He never said anything I considered offensive, and certainly would never blaspheme. He was a religious man, but not obtrusively so. When he found out I was not regularly seen in church on Sundays, he said, "Captain Bloch," (I had made captain by then—not for of anything I did, but because I had put in the required time without killing myself), "Captain Bloch, I know you think you're indestructible. All young men think that. But while you're flying test, you should follow the straight and narrow. That includes going to church on Sundays. Just for insurance."

Test flying was no more dangerous than normal flying and safer than flying with students. The crew chief was still responsible for the condition of the plane, and he wouldn't pronounce it ready unless confident it would fly. "Test Pilot" was really a misnomer in this case, mostly just a formality—nothing like what real test pilots did. This was kindergarten stuff compared to what Chuck Yeager or Bob Hoover did pushing a new aircraft to its limits. Often my test flight was just testing radios or navigation equipment that some pilot had written up because he had employed the wrong switches. Sometimes I could tell from the write-up that the real problem was the instructor had a hangover that morning and didn't feel like flying. The crew chief, finding nothing wrong, did little more than wipe off hydraulic fluid, shrug and put the thing up for a test flight.

I now had the greatest job on earth. I had to show up for my academic classes, but I could fly all I wanted, and I could choose the kind of flight I wanted. If I wanted to fly instruments I volunteered with the flight in the instrument phase. If aerobatics, I chose the flight in that phase. If I wanted to fly alone, I flew for Major Mac. If I could have kept things that way, I certainly would have made a career of the Air Force, but you can't be a twenty-year captain. An officer must be "upwardly mobile" in the Air Force—keep bucking for rank. Besides, rumors circulated that Laredo AFB would be closed when the war ended.

This isn't to say I never had any problems on test flights. Even for a write-up as minor as "hydraulic pressure sometimes fluctuates out of normal range in flight," we'd put the airplane through an entire battery of tests, sometimes coming up with new problems. I flew my first test flight with Major Mac; after that, I used the same procedures alone. After takeoff I'd clean up the airplane, then recycle the gear and flaps, watching the hydraulic pressure gauge. I'd make sure the gear warning lights flashed red and the flap gauge worked properly. I'd make sure all three green gear-safe lights came on. Then, as I reached five thousand feet and still climbing at 200 KIAS, I'd roll inverted and fly upside down half a minute while picking cockpit debris off the canopy. This was Major Mac's idea. Nothing bugged him more than finding foreign objects in the cockpit. The crew chief was supposed to thoroughly inspect and vacuum the cockpit before sending it up.

We usually put the plane through most normal maneuvers including some aerobatics and spins while watching for EGT, oil pressure, or RPM fluctuations. We checked all the navigation equipment and the radios, including a check on guard. Done, I often had enough gas to goof off awhile. Sometimes I'd get a plane I'd just flown that day with a student and had the com radio replaced. Since I knew the plane, I'd spend a whole hour horsing around just for the fun of it, then sign off on it.

The T-37 had a "pendulous hose" (the source of many bawdy jokes) in the oil tank. Inverted, the hose would flop to the upper part of the tank to continue siphoning oil to the engine. As the hose aged, it lost elasticity and could get jammed against the wall of the tank above the oil. An engine could burn up in a few seconds with no oil pouring over the bearings. An oil warning light let you know whenever this happened. The checklist said to shut down the engine when that light came on. Since I flew inverted every test flight and since those hoses at Laredo were aging, this happened often. I'd come back with only one engine. That wasn't a problem. The T-37 did just fine on one engine. It was a great irritation for maintenance though, and they'd begin cussing as soon as they saw me taxiing back with only one engine going.

But I got along fine with crew chiefs. I wasn't a stickler and never raised a stink in front of the major. Major Mac wanted any debris found in the cockpit stuffed into a barf bag and delivered to his desk. He'd use that to indict the negligent chief. I usually just handed the bag to an embarrassed crewman, who'd swear it wouldn't happen again. I often picked up washers, nuts, bits of safety wire, and crumbs from a sandwich. Sometimes I found larger objects, and that really embarrassed the chief. I found a student's checklist (which I delivered to the grateful student), a sergeant's house key (which he had been missing for days), and a United States Air Force safety-wire pliers that nobody would claim. I still have it in my toolbox, and I use it often.

IN 1969, THE GOVERNMENT went to the lottery system to determine the draft, a big change from "draft the oldest man first," which had forced me into the military. Now they drew capsules from a big glass jar. They had a capsule for each day of the year, the order they were drawn determining the order you would be drafted in 1970. If June 14th was drawn first, all men with that birthdate (ages eighteen to twenty-six) were in the first group drafted. The second capsule determined the second group, and so on. Drawings were to be held every year. Student deferment for graduate studies was abolished. That draft dodge ended. My old seminary buddies were still safe. Ministers, priests, and seminarians were still automatically exempt as they had been since the draft was established. I never envied them. I didn't look back with fondness on my seminary days. My former seminary brethren still rose and ate and slept month after month in a narrow, stagnant existence. I wasn't crazy about the military life, but I wouldn't have traded with them.

ALL THIS TIME my love life was a shambles. I never seemed to establish a permanent connection with a woman. I now had what I considered essential for marriage: money, car, and a place to live. I now lived in a fancy apartment with Captain Cook, who instructed in B Flight. I got dates easily, but after a while I didn't like them, or (more often) they didn't like me. They had a habit of running off and getting married to some bum, leaving me deeply betrayed and humiliated. Had they left me for a U.S. senator or the Duke of Windsor, it wouldn't have been so bad. But they married shiftless out-of-work men, drifters who left them, or alcoholics who beat them.

Captain Cook didn't have this problem. All the girls he dated seemed to like him. One Saturday morning, collapsed in his chair only in his underwear, trying to smoke off his usual Saturday-morning hangover and wondering whether a beer would make it worse or better, he saw me getting dressed.

"Where the hell you going at this ungodly hour?" he asked. (It was 9:45.)

I said, "I have a date. I have to pick her up in a few minutes."

He shook his head sadly. "Now, right there you can see it. That's what's wrong with you. You don't know women. (He was always telling me this.) You never make a date for a Saturday morning. Any girl available on Saturday morning can't be any fun. If she was, she'd have had a date Friday night and would be sleeping off a hangover on Saturday. You're barking up the wrong tree."

After a while I decided I had to go back home and marry a farm girl from Stearns County. I thought I could communicate better with someone raised the way I was. That is exactly what I did. The next time I took leave, I went home. I found a girl who fit exactly what I was looking for. She was Bea Buerman of Farming, Minnesota. She was tall, pretty, blonde, blue-eyed, raised on a small dairy farm, of a large German-speaking family, and Catholic. Who could ask for more?

I dated her while on leave, then courted her by mail. She went to teach school that fall in Las Vegas. I often took my cross-country flights to Nellis AFB to meet with her. After a while I said, "You know, Bea, we should get married."

She said, "Okay, when?"

North of Nuevo Laredo was dusty, sleepy little Santa Cruz. It had mud buildings, a little mud church with a rusty bell, burros and mangy dogs on the street. Captain Cook and I used to ride our motorcycles up there on Saturday afternoons and scare the burros and dogs, and drink beer in a little house owned by a dark Mexican lady. I wanted to go to Santa Cruz, grab the padre and two witnesses, and get married in their little church. Bea said, "No. If I'm going to do this, I'm having a proper, old-time Stearns County wedding back home. I want Mom, Dad, my whole family, your family, friends and neighbors to come to Dad's farm and celebrate with us. That's a real wedding."

We got married the summer of 1970. I made a good choice. Bea's still with me after all these years. I'm pretty sure any of the girls I dated before, any of those flashy girls I met in the Air Force, wouldn't have put up with what Bea did. She married me at a bad time. I was just leaving the Air Force and had no job prospects. I instructed in T-41s awhile at Laredo Municipal Airport, then we began an odyssey of moving. During the first two years of marriage, we moved more than six times, dragging our stuff around the country like nomads. Actually, we didn't have much "stuff." All we had for furniture was a card table and two folding chairs. We had a mattress and a lamp for the bedroom, a little black-and-white TV with a ten-inch screen, and Bea's sewing machine.

I left the Air Force with great reluctance. I would have stayed had it not been for the protestors, and for our fickle leaders in Washington. They vacillated between wanting to fight and wanting to back out. I was not willing to risk my life under bewildered leaders. I was fed up with the whole system. When the Air Force offered me a regular commission, I turned it down. My flight commander called me in, saying I was a fool to do that. He talked about the honorable history of the Air Force, the benefits of being a career officer, the need for men willing to fight for freedom. Still I turned it down. I did not like the military structure, the saluting and marching, and I bitterly resented the fact I had to show respect for officers who outranked me, even when those men did not deserve respect.

In subsequent years, in spite of trouble finding a job and all the moving, I didn't regret my choice. Every time I thought I might have made a mistake, a news event would put that thought to rest. The silly Paris "peace talks," began with months of arguing about the shape of the conference table (while men were dying on battlefields), and did not improve when a compromise for the table shape was found. Cease-fires, broken treaties, resumptions of bombing, more cease-fires, full-scale war, and so on. I knew how distressing it must be for an Air Force pilot to see this on the nightly news, knowing his career and maybe even his life depended on the outcome of these insane, fickle, juvenile talks.

Jane Fonda, often on the news preaching the wonders of communism and the evils of capitalism, openly professed her love for North Vietnam and hatred of the United States. She showed her support by going to Hanoi and being photographed schmoosing with the North Vietnamese Triple A gunners, soldiers, and politicians. She claimed the "rumors" about torture of our POWs were lies. Instead of being challenged, she was praised in the American press and by American politicians. She was the news media's darling; they never mentioned that giving aid and comfort to the enemy was treason. They were more likely to challenge returning POWs. Some of our politicians (Ted Kennedy, former attorney general Ramsey Clark) went to Hanoi to show their support! Catholic priest Daniel Berrigan went. Their messages, passed on by the media, were generally the same: Vietnamese soldiers are good, Americans soldiers are bad.

Any anti-war dupes were welcomed in Hanoi with open arms; impartial groups such as the international Red Cross were never permitted. I knew I'd made the right decision to get out of the Air Force when a schmuck like John Kerry took the stage. In spring of 1971, John Kerry, a naval reserve officer, was invited to speak in front of the Senate's foreign relations committee. He accused fellow soldiers of being war criminals. He talked of rape and torture and murder in Vietnam by American soldiers. He said they cut off ears, burned people alive in their villages, and raped women. He offered no proof, but became the face of the antiwar movement and another darling of the media.

Nothing changed until after President Nixon took office. The most shameful thing about the Johnson administration was the insistence on hiding the fact that we had hundreds of men rotting in POW prisons in North Vietnam. Johnson knew about the prisoners, knew they were being tortured and living under conditions prohibited by the Geneva Convention, yet said nothing. No real pressure was brought on the North Vietnamese over this until Nixon came along. The daring raid on the Son Tay prison to rescue POWs would never have taken place under Johnson or under McGovern. The raid on Son Tay, done by Army Special Forces volunteers and Air Force helicopter crews, was promoted as a failure in the U.S. press (the prisoners had been moved) but was actually a roaring success. It showed North Vietnam for the first time that the U.S. had not forgotten their fighting men. It finally brought the POW issue to the table and caused dramatic improvement in the treatment of our POWs. But to get those facts, you'd have to talk to a POW, not to a "news reporter."

In the third week of January of 1973, the *Minneapolis Tribune* had two big news headlines. The first: LYNDON B. JOHNSON DIES. The second: PEACE ACCORD REACHED; SATURDAY CEASE-FIRE SET. Johnson never saw the end of the war. He missed it by a few days. In announcing the cease-fire, President Nixon declared all prisoners of war in Indo-China would be released within sixty days, and all U.S. troops would be removed from Vietnam during that period. I was still glad I was out of that war. When peace came in early 1973, it was a hollow peace, a pyrrhic victory. The heartbreaking scene of U.S. forces executing a humiliating exit while our Vietnamese allies of more than a decade were left to face an uncertain future was disgusting to any American soldier. The warriors coming home got no parades, no "thank you" in the street. The POWs were released, the brutal treatment and torture confirmed, but Jane Fonda called the POWs—in spite of their scars, broken bones, and limping walks—"hypocrites and liars." (The wounds evidently self-inflicted.)

During the first few years after leaving the Air Force, I sometimes missed the camaraderie of my Air Force buddies. When I served with them, I was so idealistic I often thought them men of low morals. They blasphemed, got drunk on Friday nights, swore in front of their women. Several years later I realized men of all professions are that way, many much worse. Now I'm older and have worked with many different professions, I can say this: taken as a group (and in spite of all their foibles and failings) U.S. Air Force pilots were the most honorable men I've worked with in my life—the most professional, reliable, and by far the most honest. They came out best, not because they were so perfect, but because the other professions were not. And in that comparison I include the clergy of the Catholic Church of the United States.

One more thing: those pilots had the most fun.

I DETERMINED NOW that I would settle down to a steady job with normal hours. I'd punch a clock at the same time every morning, put in my eight hours, and go home and forget about the job until the next day. I thought I'd get a nice quiet job with no worries, no stress. I'd lead a peaceful life, taking on nothing more exciting than a game of cards in the evening. That was my plan.

That isn't what happened. The job I finally accepted, that of special agent with the Drug Enforcement Administration, was in many ways the direct opposite. The part of my life ahead of me was by far the most *irregular*. That job was hectic, bewildering, comical, astonishing, stupefying, tiring, laughable, irritating, scary, and fun.

It was another big adventure, and this one would last for twenty years.

The adventure continues with *Flying Uncle's Junk,* to be released in the spring of 2016. The book tells of the author's life as a special agent/pilot with the Drug Enforcement Administration.